THE UPSTART
Small Business Legal Guide

Second Edition

Robert Friedman

Upstart
Publishing Company
Specializing in Small Business Publishing
a division of Dearborn Publishing Group, Inc.

Acquisitions Editor: Danielle Egan-Miller
Managing Editor: Jack Kiburz
Interior Design: Lucy Jenkins
Cover Design: The Publishing Services Group
Typesetting: Elizabeth Pitts

Published by Upstart Publishing Company, a division of Dearborn Publishing Group, Inc.

Printed in the United States of America

99 00 10 9 8 7 6 5 4 3 2

Library of Congress Cataloging-in-Publication Data

Friedman, Robert, 1953–
    The Upstart small business legal guide : how to understand legal issues and protect your small business, complete with forms / Robert Friedman.—2nd ed.
        p. cm.
    Includes index.
    ISBN 1-57410-092-0
    1. Business law—United States. 2. Small business—Law and legislation—United States—Popular works. I. Title.
KF390.B84F75 1998
346.7307—dc21   93-35161
                                         CIP

Upstart books are available at special quantity discounts to use as premiums and sales promotions, or for use in corporate training programs. For more information, please call the Special Sales Manager at 800-621-9621, ext. 4384, or write to Dearborn Financial Publishing, Inc., 155 North Wacker Drive, Chicago, IL 60606-1719.

Contents

List of Forms

Chapter 18

Chapter 19

Chapter 20

Introduction

The *Upstart Small Business Legal Guide,* unlike any other book for small business owners, features the following:

- *Ready-to-use forms* with explanations of how and when to use them
- *Checklists* for getting started in business, purchasing a business, paying taxes, buying real estate, negotiating leases, and maintaining employee benefit plans
- *Worksheets* for computing start-up expenses
- *Tips* on how to save legal costs and taxes
- *Tips* on how to avoid lawsuits and legal hassles
- *Recent decisions* by federal and state courts throughout the United States explained in laypersons' terms
- *Tips* on how to make the most economical use of an attorney's services
- *Definitions* of legal terminology in plain language
- *Money-saving and money-making ideas* on a broad range of topics of concern to small business owners
- *Cross-references* to other relevant sections of the book, because every area of the law is affected by at least one other area of the law. This cross-referencing technique will enable you to analyze problems and think them through like a lawyer does!
- *Resource lists* to help you find additional information

- *Warnings* about extremely dangerous legal pitfalls
- *Hot Sites* link you to useful Web sites.

To make the most effective use of your new legal guide, be certain that you follow these guidelines:

- Review the "Checklist for Getting Started in Business" in Chapter 2 to determine what you must do to establish your business on a sound footing.
- Read the chapters cross-referenced in the checklist.
- Determine which situations require the advice of an attorney.
- Estimate your monthly expenses and the cost of furniture, fixtures, and equipment by using the worksheets.
- The "How and When to Use the Forms in This Chapter" section at the beginning of each set of forms will alert you to which forms are necessary for the procedure you have in mind.
- Make sure that you fill in the blanks on any form you use. Delete material that does not apply to your situation, and make certain that you have all necessary parties sign the form.
- Keep copies of all contracts, tax returns, and forms.
- File the forms with the appropriate agency.

1

You and Your Attorney

Although you do not have to seek the advice and services of an attorney for each and every step of starting and running a business, this guide will alert you to situations when you do need an attorney's expertise. Even when you should seek the services of an attorney, this guide will save you time and money by showing you how to select an attorney, how fees are determined, what questions to ask your attorney, and what information to have ready when you meet with your attorney. (See "Preventive Legal Audits" on page 3.)

CLIENT'S RIGHTS

You have a right to expect that your business attorney will

- promptly return your phone calls;
- be available on short notice to provide straightforward and prompt answers to your questions;
- solve your problems;
- have experience representing businesses;
- never surprise you with an *unexpected bill;*
- recommend ways for you to save legal costs, cut taxes, and prevent lawsuits; and
- be *up-to-date* on the most recent changes in the law.

WHEN TO SEE AN ATTORNEY

Many business owners avoid consulting an attorney in order to save money. In many cases, the savings can be substantial. However, when the situation becomes complex and less cut-and-dried, an attorney should be consulted. The following is a list of some situations where complications are more than likely to arise. Keep these in mind as you use this book to save legal costs.

1. Business start-up. An attorney can assist you when you start up a business by clarifying your business objectives and analyzing your business proposal. Your attorney can evaluate the soundness of your business plan, research, and risk analysis. He or she should be able to recommend bankers, accountants, insurance professionals, government officials, and financial planners.

2. Incorporation. An experienced business lawyer can speed up the incorporation process and have your business incorporated in one day in the case of an emergency. The services he or she can provide include the following: reserving the corporate name you have selected; preparing the Certificate of Incorporation, minutes, and bylaws; filing the Certificate of Incorporation and other necessary forms; arranging for shareholders', directors', and officers' meetings; and updating the corporate minute book.

If the corporation has more than one shareholder, the start-up stage is the appropriate time to establish a shareholders' agreement, employment contracts, covenants not to compete nor to disclose, and buy-out arrangements. You should consult with your lawyer before you sign any of these agreements.

3. Partnerships. A well-drafted partnership agreement will provide for such things as capital contributions; profit and loss distributions; limitations on partners' powers; retirement; and transfer of interest. Your lawyer's assistance can be invaluable in preparing an ironclad agreement. (See the forms in Chapter 3 entitled "Partnership Agreement" and "Business Certificate.")

It is always wiser to settle certain matters at the very beginning of the relationship. Employment agreements, covenants not to compete nor to disclose, and buy-out arrangements are more likely to be agreed on when the enterprise is in a fledgling status, and the parties are more willing to accommodate one another, than later when personal differences may arise. The attorney for the business can provide the objective sounding board the parties need to reach an agreement on these issues.

4. Limited liability companies (LLCs). An attorney can explain the advantages of LLCs over corporations, partnerships, and sole proprietorships; prepare and file the Articles of Organization; publish the necessary legal notices; and draft the Operating Agreement.

5. Leases. Landlords as well as tenants should contact attorneys regarding the drafting of real estate and equipment leases (see Chapter 15).

6. Real estate. An attorney should be consulted before a purchase contract is signed. Consult an attorney regarding local codes; environmental concerns; zoning regulations; assessments against the property; liens that may have been placed on the real estate; the existence, validity, and terms of any leases; the purchaser's right to assume existing mortgages; and services that must be provided by the landlord. (See "Buying Real Estate" and "Are You Violating Zoning Laws?" in Chapter 14.)

7. Contracts. Consult an attorney before you sign a contract, not after. Contracts should be drafted to avoid possible misunderstandings.

Your lawyer's advice should be sought before you sign any of the following: employment contracts (see Chapter 11), contracts with customers providing for interest and attorneys' fees in the event of default (see Chapter 18), agreements granting the seller a security interest, computer contracts, franchise contracts (see Chapter 6), contracts for the purchase of a business (see Chapter 3), stock buy-sell agreements (see "How to Restrict the Transfer of Stock" in Chapter 13), and contracts with vendors (see Chapter 9).

8. Debt collection. The earlier an attorney is contacted for debt collection, the better your chances of recovery (see Chapter 18).

9. Litigation. An attorney can help you avoid lawsuits and legal hassles. If your business is incorporated, you must engage an attorney to represent it whenever it sues or is sued.

10. Patents, inventions, trademarks, trade secrets, copyrights. See Chapter 10.

11. Labor/Management relations. Disciplinary proceedings, contract negotiations, labor arbitration, pension claims, employee manuals, and the defense and prevention of discrimination charges.

12. Unemployment hearings.

13. Bankruptcy and reorganization. See Chapter 18.

14. Buying/Selling/Merging a business. See Chapter 5.

15. Estate planning. Attorneys can provide guidance concerning wills; trusts; estate, gift, and income taxes (see Chapter 13); S corporations (see Chapter 4); powers of attorney; family partnerships (see Chapter 3); health care proxies; living wills; and guardianships (see Chapter 13).

16. Reducing property taxes. See Chapter 14.

17. Tax return preparation/planning.

18. Divorce. See Chapter 16.

19. Criminal problems. Speeding and drunk-driving tickets.

20. Compliance with environmental laws. See Chapter 14.

21. Compliance with employment discrimination laws. See Chapters 11 and 17.

22. Licensing. See Chapter 2.

23. Formal written opinions. When a business is sold or borrows money, opinions are often requested relating to specific regulatory problems, the priority of liens, absence of defaults, and other matters. A bank or purchaser of the business may request a formal written opinion from the corporation's lawyer stating that

1. the corporation is duly incorporated and validly existing in good standing in a specific state;

2. the corporation has power to own its properties and conduct its business as now being conducted and to perform its obligations under a certain agreement;

3. the corporation has corporate power to execute, deliver, and perform a contract;

4. an agreement or other document was duly authorized, executed, and delivered by the corporation;

5. certain shares of stock have been duly authorized, validly issued, and are fully paid and nonassessable;

6. upon closing the transaction, the purchaser will have acquired valid title to certain property free and clear of security interests, liens, claims, and encumbrances;

7. to the attorney's best knowledge, the transaction does not conflict with or constitute a breach or violation of any of the terms of other specified documents, such as the certificate of incorporation, bylaws, outstanding indentures, or all outstanding judgments or decrees;

8. registration of a securities issue is unnecessary; and

9. the lawyer knows of nothing that would render inaccurate any material statements made by the client in any of the relevant documents.

24. Electronic media policy. A policy should be drafted that restricts the use of computers, e-mail, telephones, voice mail, fax machines, external electronic bulletin boards, wire services, online services, and the Internet (see Chapter 20).

PREVENTIVE LEGAL AUDITS

Preventive legal audits are a comprehensive appraisal of a company's legal affairs whereby the attorney can make constructive recommendations for changes in a company's procedures. Annual preventive legal audits can help you

- avoid court,
- avoid jail and fines,
- reduce legal costs,
- improve your reputation and public relations,
- take advantage of future trends,
- educate your employees, and
- improve your work environment.

> "About half the practice of a decent lawyer consists in telling would-be clients that they are damned fools and should stop."
>
> —Elihu Root

The future of medicine is to examine and define problems before they occur. The future of the legal profession is the same: Protect your company's legal health before a disaster such as a lawsuit, criminal prosecution, or disrupted work environment occurs.

Businesses need help spotting potential legal problems before they occur. They often neglect legal matters such as partnership agreements or fail to comply with employment regulations such as documenting reasons for firing an employee. They do not realize they have a problem until they end up in court.

Preventive legal audits preempt trouble before it occurs. For a flat fee, attorneys with extensive backgrounds in business visit a company, analyze legal vulnerability, and draft a remedial plan for the client explaining potential legal exposure; recommend compliance guidelines, legal forms, and employee training; and provide written reminders regarding leases, loans, and other agreements. Satisfaction with the plan should be guaranteed by the law firm.

The legal issues reviewed include: OSHA compliance; ADA compliance; accounts receivable; credit and collections; human resources (benefits; employee manual); pension/retirement plans; antitrust violations; insurance (malpractice; workers' compensation; general liability; disability); buy-sell shareholder agreements;

fraud; corporate structure (bylaws/minutes); limited liability company Articles of Organization and Operating Agreement; workplace violence prevention; real estate (leases, entity, income, expenses, and zoning); record retention/storage; loans, payroll, accounts payable (phony invoices, kickbacks); environmental compliance (lead paint, asbestos, hazardous materials, sick buildings); consumer laws; product liability; employee theft; licensing agreements; Securities and Exchange Commission requirements; tax planning (S corporation status and alternative minimum tax); contract forms (purchase orders, warranties, brochures); recent legal developments affecting the company; tax return filings; and electronic media.

You can save a considerable amount on your legal fees if you have the following information and questions ready for the attorney's review:

1. Exact name in Certificate of Incorporation or Articles of Organization
   - Does the name reflect a trade name or trademark?
   - Is the name misleading in view of the present business operations?
   - Does the name need to be protected in other states in which the company plans to do business?
2. Date of incorporation
   - Should the state of filing be changed because of advantageous tax laws in other states?
3. Transaction of business in foreign states
   - Which states is the company qualified to do business in?
   - Does the company conduct business out of the state (e.g., distributors, leases, warehouses, sales personnel, contracting, offices, franchising, manufacturing, or joint ventures)?
4. Articles of Organization or Certificate of Incorporation
   - Have the articles or certificate been amended?
5. Purposes authorized by the Certificate of Incorporation or Articles of Organization
   - Actual business operations
6. Capital structure
   - Capital stock (authorized and issued)
   - Treasury stock
   - Long-term indebtedness
   - A provision in the bylaws or Operating Agreement for the addition or continua-

tion of shareholders'/members' preemptive rights, restrictions on the transfer of stock, and S corporation status requirements
7. Bylaws and Operating Agreement
   - Shareholders' and directors' meetings
   - Fiscal year
   - Names and titles of those authorized to sign checks and documents
   - Indemnification of directors and officers (members/managers) against liabilities arising from board actions taken in good faith
8. The name and address of the resident agent
9. The location of books and records
   - Minute books
   - Books of account
   - Stock transfer records
10. Property information
    - Real property owned or leased or with options
    - Personal property description
    - Accounts receivable
    - Income from rents and franchises
    - Partnership or joint venture contracts
    - Patents, copyrights, and trademarks
    - Uniform Commercial Code (UCC) filings
11. Employee and labor relations
    - Labor union contracts
    - Employee information
    - Pension/profit-sharing plans
    - Workers' compensation
    - Hospitalization and other medical benefits
    - Group insurance
12. Name and address of all banks
    - Long-term and short-term credit obligations
    - Company's credit rating
13. Name and address of insurance carriers and brokers
    - Insurance coverage in effect
14. Governmental regulation
    - Special business licenses or permits
    - State and federal motor-vehicle permits
    - Alcohol or drug permits
    - Trade name registrations
    - Zoning permits
    - Environmental permits
15. Pending litigation
16. Names and addresses of legal counsel and other advisers

HOW TO FIND AN ATTORNEY

With over 900,000 attorneys to choose from in the United States, it is often difficult for the average business owner to find the right attorney. People usually pick an attorney based on his or her reputation; references from friends, relatives, local bar associations, or other organizations; from the Yellow Pages or newspaper or television advertisements; or from prepaid legal plans.

In selecting an attorney, ask him or her the following questions:

- What is your experience with the type of legal matter that I have?

- What are your initial consultation fee and hourly rates?

- Have you lectured at seminars held for the general public or other attorneys or written books or articles?

- How many attorneys are in your firm? Is it a full-service firm?

- What days and hours is the office open?

- Does the firm have specialists? In what areas? Although in some states attorneys cannot hold themselves out as specialists, they may still state that their practice is "limited" to a certain area of the law, such as divorce, corporate, or criminal.

- What percentage of your practice is devoted to my type of legal problem? For example, if you have a real estate problem, you may want an attorney who devotes the majority of his or her time to real estate matters.

- Does the firm provide tax return preparation and tax planning?

- Does the firm publish a client newsletter in which it explains new developments in the law? Are informational pamphlets on the law available?

- Is the attorney familiar with the following areas of federal and state law: income and estate taxation, corporation, agency, partnership, securities, antitrust, contracts, products liability, and the UCC?

- Does the attorney have knowledge and experience with such nonlegal concepts as corporate finance, financial accounting, management techniques, and how to work with bankers, brokers, insurers, and industrial development agencies?

PREPAID LEGAL PLANS

Individuals, employers, unions, or associations belong to a plan. When they need legal services for specified matters such as wills or real estate closings, they are referred to a panel attorney. Clients either pay no fee for the legal services or a reduced fee.

Over 85 million Americans belong to prepaid legal plans, and most of them are middle-class people who would otherwise not seek the services of an attorney. Legal service plans help members prevent legal problems before they occur. A lawyer can review a document or contract before you sign it. Or you can consult with an attorney before suing a merchant or landlord.

> "Because legal services are increasingly necessary in a complex society, prepaid legal service plans analogous to health insurance have become an important means of assuring basic rights to millions of citizens."
>
> —Ralph Nader

The four basic types of prepaid legal plans are:

1. Group legal service plans. Employers, unions, or associations pay for membership in the plan. Union plans are usually negotiated between labor and management as part of a collective bargaining agreement. Union members are often automatically enrolled.

2. Employee-paid plans. Employees pay a small amount through payroll deductions.

3. Personal legal service plans. Individuals join for a minimal monthly or annual fee, usually through a credit card company.

4. Business plans. Small businesses pay a monthly or an annual fee for basic business-related legal services.

Payment to the panel attorneys varies by the plan. Lawyers may be paid directly by the clients (who may or may not be reimbursed by the plan), may collect from the plan after submitting a claim form, or may collect a fixed monthly amount per participant covered.

Most of the plans provide the following benefits:

- Free consultation by telephone or in the office. Members may call or meet with a panel attorney regarding almost any personal legal matter for up to 30 minutes at no charge. They may consult an attorney as often as they need to, as long as each consultation is about a different matter. Most members' legal problems are solved through consultation alone.

- Free follow-up services. Some problems can be solved by merely having the panel attorney write a letter or make a phone call on the member's behalf at no charge.

- Free document review. A panel attorney will review personal documents such as leases, insurance policies, or sales contracts at no charge and will also explain the terms of the documents and answer specific questions.

- Wills at no charge or for a small fee

- 20 to 30 percent discount off of regular hourly rates or flat fees on most additional services, such as real estate closings, traffic tickets, and divorces

- Written fee agreements specifying which services the attorney will perform, how much it will cost, and how it will be billed

- Quality control. Members complete a form to evaluate the lawyer and the services performed.

- Grievance procedure. If there is a disagreement with the panel attorney over fees or other matters, the plan will attempt to resolve the dispute through an informal grievance process or mediation.

- Confidentiality. All matters are handled between the member and the panel attorney on a strictly confidential basis.

HOW MUCH ARE ATTORNEYS' FEES?

Hiring an attorney may not be as expensive as you may think. Attorneys charge for their services using one or a combination of these four methods: (1) flat fee, (2) contingent fee, (3) hourly charge, or (4) monthly retainer.

Flat fees are usually charged for traffic cases, incorporation of a small business, uncontested divorces, basic wills, and bankruptcy. Contingent fees are generally charged for personal injury cases and bill collections. In the contingent fee arrangement, you pay the attorney a certain percentage of your recovery if, and only if, you win. But the attorney cannot guarantee the results. If you sue for $1 million and you recover only $99 after trial or settlement, the attorney's fee will be $33 if there is a one-third contingency fee arrangement.

Hourly fees are generally charged for all other types of cases, including defense of lawsuits and estate planning. Some companies retain an attorney on a monthly retainer basis whereby the attorney is paid a specified monthly fee regardless of the amount of time he or she spends on the client's matters.

Regardless of the type of fee, the client must pay for all disbursements, such as process service fees, investigations, court costs, travel expenses, long-distance calls, expert testimony, medical reports, appraisals, and all other out-of-pocket expenses. Ask for a written fee agreement that sets forth the services to be performed by the attorney, the amount of the legal fee (hourly rate, contingent, or flat), and the amount of disbursements.

ETHICAL CONSIDERATIONS

According to the American Bar Association Code of Professional Responsibility, where a lawyer is justified in representing two or more clients having differing interests, it is nevertheless essential that each client be given the opportunity to evaluate the need for representation free of any potential conflict and to obtain other counsel if he or she so desires. Thus, before a lawyer may represent multiple clients, he or she should explain fully to each client the implications of the common representation and should accept or continue employment only if the client consents. If other circumstances are present that might cause any of the multiple clients to question the undivided loyalty of the lawyer, the lawyer should also advise all of the clients of those circumstances.

A lawyer employed or retained by a corporation or similar entity owes allegiance to the entity and not to a shareholder, director, officer, employee, representative, or other person connected with the entity. Occasionally a lawyer for an entity is requested to represent a shareholder, director, officer, employee, representative, or other person connected with the entity in an individual capacity; in such cases, the lawyer may serve the individual only if the lawyer is convinced that differing interests are not present.

2

How to Get Started in Business

To ensure the success of your business, you should anticipate and provide for its financial needs and ensure that it will satisfy all legal requirements. The following checklist sets out a series of guidelines that will prevent yours from becoming one of the hundreds of businesses that fail each and every week. You can determine which steps are applicable to your business by reading the chapters cited in the checklist.

HOT SITE

Small Business Legal Survival

(http://www.friran.com/small_business.html)

CHECKLIST FOR GETTING STARTED IN BUSINESS

❑ Decide whether to buy an existing business (Chapter 5, "Checklist for the Purchase of a Corporation or Its Assets"), start a new business, or buy a franchise (Chapter 6).

❑ Decide on the form of business: general partnership, limited liability company, corporation, limited partnership, or sole proprietorship (Chapter 3).

❑ Prepare a business plan. (See "The Business Plan Outline" in this chapter.)

❑ Estimate how much cash you will need to start your business—advertising, fixtures, decorating, inventory, fees, working capital, etc.—and estimate your monthly expenses. (See worksheets at the end of this chapter.)

❑ If the business will be incorporated, select the state of incorporation. (Compare the features of corporation laws, organization fees, and taxes of other states.) (Chapter 3)

❑ If you will form a partnership, draft the partnership agreement (Chapter 3).

❑ Check local ordinances regarding zoning (Chapter 14), permits, and licenses your business may require.

❑ File a business certificate (d/b/a) (Chapter 3).

❑ Determine whether to file for S Corporation status (Chapter 4).

❑ Schedule incorporation to obtain maximum state tax savings.

❑ Check federal securities requirements.

❑ Check "blue sky" law requirements.

❑ Check costs of qualification in foreign states.

❑ Obtain a minute book, corporate seal, and stock certificates.

❑ Conduct a market analysis to determine the viability of your enterprise.

❑ Select and reserve a corporate name (first and second choices).

❑ Select officers and directors (names, addresses, and Social Security numbers).

❑ Develop marketing, advertising, and public relations plans.

❑ Develop a capitalization/borrowing/credit/ debt service plan and cash flow plan.

- ❏ Develop income projections.
- ❏ Adopt corporate bylaws or an LLC Operating Agreement.
- ❏ Develop a reimbursement plan for expenses and time worked by officers and consultants prior to incorporation.
- ❏ Select a date and place for the annual meeting of shareholders/directors.
- ❏ Open a separate business checking account. The bank will require a certified copy of your business certificate or a copy of your incorporation or LLC filing receipt. Establish banking procedures and check-signing authority. Maintain a reserve for three to six months of expenses.
- ❏ Install a business phone line. Use an answering machine or answering service. Order telephone directory advertising.
- ❏ Mail and e-mail announcements of your business start-up to the media, potential customers, and friends.
- ❏ Obtain free counseling services from SCORE (SBA Service Corps of Retired Executives) or Small Business Development Centers (SBDCs).
- ❏ To prevent workplace violence, implement procedures for employee screening, physical security, incident response teams, and a reporting system (see Chapter 19).
- ❏ Obtain and design a Web site for marketing, order taking, and communications (see Chapter 20).
- ❏ Identify all patents, trademarks, service marks, or copyrights your business will have to register or purchase (Chapter 10).
- ❏ Retain an attorney (Chapter 1).
- ❏ If you have to borrow money, review potential sources of collateral and prepare a loan package and business plan.
- ❏ Shop around for the best interest rate and terms on a loan.
- ❏ Find an accountant, preferably a certified public accountant (CPA) familiar with tax requirements, and have him or her set up recordkeeping, payroll, and tax-withholding accounts (Chapter 7). Your CPA should help you prepare cash flow and financial statements for your business plan and recommend tax strategies.
- ❏ Obtain all necessary government forms, such as workers' compensation and Immigration and Naturalization Service forms (Chapter 11) and forms for unemployment insurance.

- ❏ Identify product suppliers, the mechanics of delivery of supplies to your business, delivery time, and risk of loss (Chapter 9).
- ❏ Lease (see "How to Negotiate Commercial Leases" in Chapter 15) or buy real estate (see "Need Help in Purchasing Real Estate?" in Chapter 14) to house your business.
- ❏ If walk-in trade is important, check vehicular or pedestrian traffic patterns at the site you have selected.
- ❏ Draft necessary employment contracts (Chapter 11, "Employment Agreement").
- ❏ Prepare covenants forbidding employees and/or consultants from revealing your trade secrets, trade lists, or other confidential information and from competing with you after they leave your employ (Chapter 11).
- ❏ Prepare an employment application and job descriptions (Chapter 11, "Is Your Employment Application a Danger Spot?" and "Employment Application" form).
- ❏ Set up a recordkeeping system including payroll records (Chapter 7).
- ❏ Ensure that your will and/or living trust provides for the equity in your business (Chapter 13).
- ❏ Draw up a buy-sell agreement for stock (Chapter 13).
- ❏ Apply for an employer identification number (Chapter 7) and state sales tax identification number.
- ❏ Establish credit procedures (Chapter 18, "Are Debtors Getting Away with Murder?" and "Application for Credit" form).
- ❏ Establish check-cashing procedures and safeguards (Chapter 18).
- ❏ Lease or buy equipment (Chapter 15, "Lease It and Save!").
- ❏ Establish an employee compensation and benefits package (Chapter 8, "Fringe Benefits").
- ❏ Prepare an employee manual (Chapter 11, "Beware of Your Employee Manual," and "Employee Manual" form).
- ❏ Decide whether to hire or lease employees, independent contractors, and/or utilize a special service firm for various bookkeeping and payroll functions (Chapter 11).
- ❏ If you are buying used equipment, check with your state department of taxation to determine whether there are any liens for unpaid sales tax against the equipment; check with the county and state to deter-

mine whether there are any Uniform Commercial Code (UCC) filings or chattel mortgages; and obtain a bill of sale from the seller containing an affidavit that he or she has full right to sell and transfer the equipment and that it is free and clear of any and all liens, mortgages, debts, and other encumbrances or claims of any kind (Chapter 5).

❏ Have an independent appraiser calculate the replacement value of your property to determine how much insurance you need.

❏ Find a competent insurance broker and obtain the following insurance (Chapter 16): workers' compensation; disability; liability; fire; business interruption; life; automobile; crime; group health; delayed profits; rental value; and flood. Compare premium prices among agents.

HOT SITE

The Consumer Information Center (www.pueblo.gsa.gov) has pamphlets on the "Americans with Disabilities Act: Guide for Small Businesses," "General Information Concerning Patents," "Guide to Business Credit for Women, Minorities and Small Businesses," "Resource Directory for Small Business Management," "Running a Small Business," "Selling a Business," and "Starting a Business."

WHY BUSINESSES FAIL

Most businesses are unsuccessful because they fail to

- plan properly,
- monitor financial statements,
- understand pricing,
- monitor cash flow,
- manage growth,
- borrow properly, and/or
- plan for transition periods.

A sound, well-thought-out business plan will anticipate and help your business avoid these problems.

CREATING BUSINESS PLANS

A good business plan accomplishes the following:

- It allows the new business owner to determine the feasibility of the proposed business and identifies its start-up requirements.

- It provides a basis for outside investors and banks to determine whether to invest in or lend money to the business.

- It provides the groundwork for more detailed operational plans and serves as a valuable management tool for monitoring and planning future growth.

The Business Plan Outline

Summary.

1. Name of the business
2. Business location and floor plan descriptions
3. Description of the product or service, marketing techniques, and existing competition
4. Expertise of management
5. Summary of financial projections
6. Amount of financial assistance requested (if applicable)
7. Form of, and purpose for, the financial assistance (if applicable)
8. Purpose for undertaking the project (if financial assistance is sought)
9. Business goals

The company's background.

1. Name, date, and place of formation
2. Legal structure (sole proprietorship, partnership, limited liability company, limited partnership, or corporation)
3. Significant changes (including dates) in ownership, structure, new products or product lines, and any acquisitions
4. Principals and the roles they played in forming the company

The product or service.

1. Relative importance of each product or service, including sales projections
2. Product evaluation (use, quality, performance)

3. Comparison with competitors' products or services and competitive advantages over other producers

4. Demand for product or service and factors affecting demand other than price

The project. If financing is sought for a specific project, describe the project; the purpose for which it is undertaken; its cost; and the amount, form, and use of the financial assistance.

Management.

1. Organizational chart

2. Key individuals (include supervisory personnel with special talents or abilities)
   - Responsibilities
   - Personal résumés (describing skills and experience as they relate to activities of the business)
   - Present salaries and other compensation
   - Planned staff additions

3. Other employees
   - Number of employees at year-end and total payroll expenses for each of the previous five years broken down by wages and benefits
   - Method of compensation
   - Planned staff additions

Ownership.

1. Names, addresses, and business affiliations of principal holders of common stock and other types of equity securities

2. Degree to which principal shareholders are involved in management

3. Principal nonmanagement shareholders

4. Names of directors, areas of expertise, and the role of the board when business becomes operational

5. Amount of stock currently authorized and issued

Marketing strategy/Market analysis.

1. Description of the industry
   - Industry outlook
   - Principal markets (commercial/industrial, consumer, government, international)
   - Industry size—current as well as anticipated in the next few years
   - Major characteristics of the industry; effects of major social, economic, techno-

logical, or regulatory trends on the industry

2. Description of major customers
   - Names, locations, products, or services sold to each
   - Percentage of annual sales volume contributed by each major customer over previous years (if applicable)
   - Duration and condition of contracts

3. Description of market and its major segments

4. Description of competition: companies with which your business competes and how your business compares with these companies

5. Description of prospective customers

6. Description of firm's marketing activities
   - Overall marketing strategy
   - Pricing policy
   - Method of selling, distributing, and servicing the product
   - Geographic penetration, field/product support, advertising, public relations and promotions, and priorities among these activities

7. Description of selling activities—the methods for identifying prospective customers and how and in what order you will contact the relevant decision makers, your sales effort, number of salespersons, number of sales contacts, initial order size, and estimated sales and market share

Technology.

1. Technical status of your product (idea stage, development stage, prototype) and the relevant activities and other steps necessary to bring the product into production

2. Current patent or copyright position (if applicable)

3. New technologies that may become practical during the next five years if they will affect the product

4. New products (derived from first-generation products) the firm plans to develop to meet changing needs

5. Regulatory or approval requirements and status; any other technical and legal considerations that may be relevant to the technological development of the product

6. Research and development efforts and future plans for research and development

Production/Operating plan.

1. How the firm will perform production or delivery of service in terms of:
   - *Physical facilities*—owned or leased, size and location, expansion capabilities, types and quantities of equipment needed
   - Include a facilities plan and description of planned capital improvements (if any) and a timetable for those improvements.
   - *Suppliers*—names and locations, length of lead time required, usual terms of purchase, contracts (amounts, duration, and condition) and subcontractors
   - *Labor supply (current and planned)*—number of employees, unionization, stability (seasonal or cyclical), and fringe benefits
   - *Technologies/skills* required to develop and manufacture the products
   - *Cost breakdown* for materials, labor, and manufacturing overhead for each product. Include cost versus volume curves for each product or service.
   - *Manufacturing process*
2. Discuss whether production or operating advantages enjoyed by your firm will continue.
3. Specify standard product costs at different volume levels.
4. Review the schedule of work for the next one to two years.

Financial.

1. Auditor's name and address
2. Legal counsel's name and address
3. Banker's name, location, contact officer
4. Controls: cost system and budgets your firm uses
5. Cash requirements, currently and over the next five years, and how these funds will be used
6. Amount to be raised in debt and/or equity
7. Financial statements and projections for the next five years:
   - Profit and loss or income statements by month until break-even point and then by quarter
   - Balance sheets as of the end of each year
   - Cash budgets and cash flow projections
   - Capital budgets for equipment and other capital acquisitions
   - Manufacturing/shipping plan

8. Financial materials for lenders and venture capitalists who will require:
   - A funding request indicating the desired financing, capitalization, use of funds, and future financing
   - Financial statements for the past three years
   - Current financial statements
   - Monthly cash-flow financial projection, including the proposed financing, for two years
   - Projected balance sheets, income statement and statement of changes in financial position for two years, including the proposed financing

PERMITS AND LICENSES

Your business may be required to have one or more of the following licenses or permits:

1. **Business licenses.** Check with the city and county governments to determine which business licenses are required.

2. **Health, fire, and other special permits.** Any business that processes or sells food to the public must have a health department permit. Businesses that handle flammable materials or have large numbers of people on their premises may also be required to have a fire department permit. If you expect to discharge any substance into the air, sewer system, or the local waterways, you may have to obtain a special permit from agencies controlling pollution and environmental health.

3. **Occupational permits.** Most states require special licensing, which may require a written or oral examination, for businesses in certain categories such as the following:
   - Occupations that involve direct physical contact with customers, such as hairdressing, massage, or medical treatment
   - Occupations that call for special technical expertise that may be related to consumer safety or health, such as plumbing, electrical work, auto repairs, pest control, engineering, or dry cleaning
   - Real estate agencies, insurance agencies, and collection agencies

4. **Sales tax permits.**
   - Those who sell products directly to the public usually must collect a sales tax. (Food products are exempt from a sales tax in some states.)
   - If you sell products only to wholesalers, retailers, or other middlemen, you usually do not have to collect a sales tax, but you must maintain tax exemption forms.
   - Some states require those who sell services to collect a sales tax.
   - Many states require that you pay a bond or an advance deposit against sales taxes to be collected when you first apply for a permit.

5. **Federal licensing.** Required for gun dealers, security and investment brokers and advisers, radio and television stations, and drug manufacturers.

HOW AND WHEN TO USE THE FORMS IN THIS CHAPTER

Worksheets. These forms should be used to determine your monthly expenses and the cash necessary to start your business.

Worksheet—Estimated Monthly Expenses.

Worksheet—List of Furniture, Fixtures, and Equipment.

Worksheet

Estimated Monthly Expenses

Item	Your estimate of monthly expenses based on sales of $ _____ per year	Your estimate of how much cash you need to start your business (See column 3.)	What to put in column 2 (These figures are typical for one kind of business. You will have to decide how many months to allow for in your business.)
	Column 1	Column 2	Column 3
Salary of owner-manager	$	$	2 times column 1
All other salaries and wages			3 times column 1
Rent			3 times column 1
Advertising			3 times column 1
Delivery expense			3 times column 1
Supplies			3 times column 1
Telephone and telegraph			3 times column 1
Other utilities			3 times column 1
Insurance			Payment required by insurance company
Taxes, including Social Security			4 times column 1
Interest			3 times column 1
Maintenance			3 times column 1
Legal and other professional fees			3 times column 1
Miscellaneous			3 times column 1
Starting Costs You Have to Pay Only Once			Leave column 2 blank
Fixtures and equipment			Fill in worksheet on page 16 and put the total here
Decorating and remodeling			Talk to supliers from whom you buy these
Starting inventory			Suppliers will probably help you estimate this
Deposits with public utilities			Find out from utilities companies
Legal and other professional fees			Lawyer, accountant, and so on
Licenses and permits			Find out from city offices what you have to have
Advertising and promotion for opening			Estimate what you'll use
Accounts receivable			Cash required to buy more stock until credit customers pay
Cash			For unexpected expenses or losses, special purchases, etc.
Other			Make a separate list and enter total
Total Estimated Cash You Need to Start			Add up all the numbers in column 2

15

Worksheet

List of Furniture, Fixtures, and Equipment

Leave out or add items to suit your business. Use separate sheets to list exactly what you need for each of the items below.	If you plan to pay cash in full, enter the full amount below and in the last column.	If you are going to pay by installments, fill out the columns below. Enter in the last column your down payment plus at least one installation.			Estimate of the cash you need for furniture, fixtures, and equipment
		Price	Down payment	Amount of each installment	
Counters	$	$	$	$	$
Storage shelves, cabinets					
Display stands, shelves, tables					
Cash register					
Safe					
Window display fixtures					
Outside sign					
Delivery equipment if needed					
Total Furniture, Fixtures, and Equipment (Enter this figure also in worksheet on page 15 under "Starting Costs You Have to Pay Only Once.")					$

3

How to Select the
Best Business Form

What is the best form of business for you: partnership, limited partnership, limited liability company, corporation, or sole proprietorship? You should consider the management, liability, transfer to future generations, complexity, availability and taxability of employee benefits, and tax aspects of each of these forms of business.

Business owners need creditor protection from tort liability claims arising out of the operation of the business, environmental liability claims, professional malpractice exposure, and protection of assets from a retaliatory spouse during a divorce (see Chapter 18).

SOLE PROPRIETORSHIPS

A sole proprietorship is the simplest business organization form. It is the easiest to organize and discontinue. The business has no separate existence apart from the owner. For that reason there are virtually no requirements that you register your business at a state office. The one exception to this rule will require you to file a business certificate (see form at the end of this chapter) with the appropriate city or county official if you will be doing business under a name other than your own.

The liabilities of a sole proprietorship will be your personal liabilities. This means that if the business cannot pay its debts, all of your personal assets are subject to the claims of the business's creditors. Furthermore, your ownership (proprietary) interest ends when you die.

Each asset in a sole proprietorship is treated separately for tax purposes, rather than as part of one overall ownership interest. Therefore, a sole proprietor who sells his or her entire business as a going concern must calculate gain or loss separately on each asset.

Sole proprietors are liable for self-employment tax. They cannot defer income tax by having the business retain its profits. Business losses can be used to offset other income of the sole proprietor.

PARTNERSHIPS

A partnership exists when two or more persons carry on a business for profit as co-owners. Each partner has unlimited personal liability for all the partnership's debts and implied authority to legally bind the partnership.

Although no formal partnership agreement is required by law, it is highly advisable to adopt a written agreement. Unless there is an agreement to the contrary, partners share profits equally, share losses in the same portion as profits, and are personally liable for partnership debts.

The partnership agreement (see form at the end of this chapter) should include provisions setting out the following:

- The partnership name, business purpose, and business location

- The amount of the contribution each partner will make

- The accounting year and method
- Each partner's responsibilities
- The length of the agreement
- Allocation of profits and losses (they do not have to be shared in the same percentages)
- How expenses will be disbursed
- The partners' authority to obtain loans, buy goods and supplies, sign contracts, hire and discharge employees, and sign checks
- How and when the partnership can go into debt
- Which partners will receive guaranteed payment for services rendered or for use of capital
- When partners will be entitled to draws
- What happens in the event of a partner's death
- The right to terminate the business
- How major disagreements will be resolved
- Contributions that may be required for a retirement fund

Partners must file a business certificate with the appropriate city or county clerk (see "Business Certificate" at the end of this chapter) and should apply for a federal identification number (see IRS Form SS-4 in Chapter 7).

Partners' Property Rights

Each partner has the following three property rights:

1. *Rights in specific partnership property.* Unless there is something in writing to the contrary, all property acquired with partnership funds is considered to be partnership property. Each partner has the right to possess and use partnership property for partnership purposes only.

2. *The partner's interest in the partnership.* This refers to the partner's right to share in profits and surplus funds (or losses).

3. *The partner's right to participate in management of the partnership*

Is It Really a Partnership?

You may be doing business as a partnership without realizing it. If you are engaged in a business that pays a portion of its profits to a second person, you should determine whether

the Internal Revenue Code views the business as a partnership. The IRS can treat a business as a partnership even in the absence of a written partnership contract. If the IRS determines that a partnership exists, it may disallow the way certain transactions are reported. For example, expenses paid by a partner on behalf of the partnership are not deductible by the partner unless there is a written partnership contract stating that the partner is to pay for those expenses.

The partnership itself is not taxed. It is a conduit through which income and other items pass directly to the partners, who report their distributive shares on their personal income tax returns. But a partnership must report its profit or loss on IRS Form 1065.

For federal income tax purposes, a partnership exists when two or more people join together to carry on a business jointly. It also includes a syndicate, group, pool, joint venture, or other unincorporated organization that carries on any business, financial operation, or venture that is not a trust, estate, or corporation.

Under both state laws and the Internal Revenue Code, a partnership relationship will be found where two or more persons agree to share profits and losses. The sharing of an office and expenses, however, does not necessarily mean a partnership exists if there is no intent to share profits. Factors used to determine whether a partnership exists include the following:

- The partner's conduct in carrying out the partnership agreement
- The relationship of the parties
- The abilities and contributions of each
- The control each partner has over the partnership income and the purpose for which the income is used
- The perceptions of disinterested parties

Sharing in Gains and Losses

A partner's share of income, gain, loss, deductions, or credit usually is fixed by the partnership agreement. The agreement may provide that all items will be shared in the same percentage or that various items be split in different percentages. So, for example, the partners may agree to share profits equally and to share losses on a 70–30 basis if it will be to the advantage (usually for tax reasons) of one partner to absorb a greater segment of paper losses. The agreement may allocate depreciation or gain or loss on property contributed by a partner, but it may not have tax avoidance as its principal purpose. (See the "Partnership Agreement" form at the end of this chapter.)

All tax elections such as accounting methods, depreciation methods, involuntary conversions, amortizing organization fees, and installment sales are made at the partnership level and apply to all partners.

LIMITED PARTNERSHIPS

A limited partnership consists of (1) one or more general partners who manage the business and have unlimited liability for all obligations incurred by the partnership, and (2) one or more limited partners whose liability is limited to the extent of their capital contributions and who do not participate in management. Unlike the general partnership, which may arise solely by the partners' conduct, a limited partnership can be formed only by the filing and publishing of a certificate.

The limited partnership offers the principal advantages of a general partnership plus the advantages of limited liability for the limited partners. The limited partners have two types of asset protection: (1) liability for the partnership's debts is limited to the extent of their partnership interest; and (2) partnership assets are protected from their own creditors. A limited partner retains limited liability as long as he or she does not take an active part in managing the business and does not allow his or her surname to appear in the partnership name. The only other exception to limited liability arises when a limited partner knows a statement in the partnership certificate is false and a third person relies on those false statements to his or her detriment.

The status of a limited partner is similar to that of a shareholder in a corporation. Both enjoy limited liability—their risk is limited to the investment they made in the enterprise. Both have only a passive role in management: limited partners elect general partners; shareholders elect directors; both may vote on major corporate or partnership structural matters. Both are entitled to inspect the books and records of their business. Finally, a limited partner's interest, like a corporate shareholder's stock interest, is a security and must

be registered under, and comply with, the federal securities laws if it will be offered for sale to the public.

A limited partnership certificate must be filed with the appropriate state's secretary of state. A copy of the certificate must be published in a local newspaper. The certificate must contain (1) the names and addresses of all partners, (2) their respective contributions and profit shares, and (3) the duration of the partnership.

Continuity is more easily maintained in a limited partnership than in a general partnership, although it is not perpetual as in a corporation. The partnership is dissolved upon the death of the sole general partner or all general partners or at the expiration of the term stated in the certificate. Death or withdrawal of a (general or limited) partner may not automatically dissolve the partnership if the certificate so provides or if unanimous consent of the remaining partners is obtained to continue the business.

FAMILY PARTNERSHIPS

Family partnerships (FPs) reduce estate taxes and protect assets from creditors' claims. They allow a person to retain control over assets without having them eroded by estate taxes. FPs are structured as either limited partnerships (Georgia being the most favorable state) or limited liability companies (Virginia being the most favorable state).

Parents can establish an FP by transferring assets such as real estate, marketable securities, or an interest in a family business without adverse tax consequences. The parents retain exclusive control over the partnership, such as the power to make management decisions, to sell assets, and to determine the time and amount of distribution to the partners. The FP has the following features:

- The parents may receive compensation for the reasonable value of their services.

- The parents can give interests to their children, either outright or in trust, over a period of time at discounted values of 20 to 40 percent.

- The children are taxed on their proportionate share of the income, which provides an effective income-tax-shifting device.

- The assets owned by the FP are not subject to an individual partner's creditors' claims.

- After the interests are transferred to the children, any appreciation in the FP's assets attributable to those interests will escape taxation in the parents' estates, and the parents retained interest are entitled to valuation discounts.
- The business can be passed to the younger generation without losing it to a forced tax sale or liquidity crisis.

LIMITED LIABILITY COMPANIES

The limited liability company (LLC) is a hybrid business entity that combines the best features of partnerships and corporations. It eliminates certain disadvantages of limited partnerships and corporations. The first LLC statute was adopted in Wyoming in 1977. In 1988, the IRS classified an LLC as a partnership for federal income tax purposes.

LLCs are ideal for corporate joint ventures, entrepreneurial businesses, family businesses (see previous section), start-up businesses, high technology and research businesses, oil and gas investments, investments in theatrical productions, real estate investments, venture capital projects, professionals (accountants, lawyers, doctors, etc.), transactions involving international investors, management leveraged buyouts, structured finance transactions (receivable financing), and commodity pools.

Articles of Organization

The LLC is formed by filing Articles of Organization (see the form at the end of this chapter) with the appropriate secretary of state and publishing a notice of organization.

The Articles of Organization usually must contain the following:

- The name of the LLC. The name must include an indication that it is a limited liability company such as "Limited Liability Company"; an abbreviation such as "Limited Liability Co." or "Ltd. Liability Co."; or the initials "L.L.C." or "LLC."
- The county in which the office is to be located
- The date of dissolution (if the LLC is to have a specific date of dissolution in addition to the events of dissolution set forth in the statute)

- A designation of the secretary of state as agent for service of process
- (Optional) The designation of a registered agent (in addition to the secretary of state)
- (Optional) A statement indicating whether the LLC is to be managed by one or more members or a class or classes of members or by one or more managers or by a class or classes of managers. If no statement is made in the Articles of Organization to the contrary, management is vested in the members.
- (Optional) If all or specified members are to be liable in their capacity as members for all or specified liabilities of the LLC, it must be stated in the Articles of Organization. Otherwise, liability of members is limited.
- (Optional) The members may elect to include other provisions, not inconsistent with the statute, such as: (1) the business purpose of the LLC, (2) a statement indicating any limitations on the authority of members or managers, and (3) any provisions required or permitted to be included in the Operating Agreement.
- A statement that the company terminates on the occurrence of certain events such as the death, resignation, expulsion, bankruptcy, or other withdrawal of a member within a certain number of years after creation, typically 30 years. The right of the members to reform after a termination event must be stated in the Articles.

Operating Agreement

The Operating Agreement, which is similar to the bylaws of a corporation, contains members' rights and obligations, and required procedures for the LLC's operation. It can set forth the basis for distributions and allocations of cash flow, profits, and losses; the rights, obligations, and responsibilities of the members; and the procedures for operation. A member may withdraw from an LLC at the time of an event specified in the Operating Agreement or with the consent of two-thirds of the members. If the Operating Agreement does not provide for withdrawal, and if consent is not given by a two-thirds vote, a member may still withdraw by giving a statutory six months' written notice. The Operating Agreement may bar a member from withdrawing.

Members vote in proportion to their respective share of the profits unless otherwise provided in the Operating Agreement. A majority vote of the members is required to adopt a proposal, with certain exceptions.

An LLC can indemnify its managers, employees, and agents for acts that are not undertaken in bad faith or for personal profit.

The Operating Agreement can provide for the elimination or limiting of the personal liability of managers to the LLC or its members for damages for any breach of duty, subject to certain exceptions. The Operating Agreement should contain the time and place for meetings of members; quorum requirements; the manner in which membership meetings should be conducted and decisions reached; restrictions on transferability of membership interests; voting rights; the distribution of profits, losses, and cash flow; the selection of management; and the rights of the members to remove managers.

Members and managers. The members of an LLC are its owners. Most LLC statutes (except for Texas and New York) require that it have at least two members. Members of an LLC may include an individual corporation, a partnership, other LLC trusts, or a foreign entity. There is no limit on the maximum number of members that an LLC may have. Many LLC statutes permit the Articles of Organization to provide for classes or groups of members having such relative rights and powers as provided in the Operating Agreement. A properly formed LLC is taxed as a partnership, but its members enjoy limited liability like corporate shareholders. Members are not personally liable for the debts, obligations, and liabilities of the LLC.

A person may become a member of an LLC on the effective date of the initial Articles of Organization in accordance with the Operating Agreement or, if the Operating Agreement makes no provision for admitting new members, on the vote or the written consent of a majority of the members. An Operating Agreement may prohibit assignment of a member's interest. If the Articles of Organization make no provision for the vesting of management in one or more managers, management is vested by default in all of the members. Managers are required to perform their management duties in good faith, exercising a "prudent man" standard of care.

In most states, except as provided in an Operating Agreement, the assignment of a membership interest entitles the assignee to receive the assignor's distributions and allocations of profits and losses. In New York, in order for the assignee to exercise any rights or powers of a member, including the right to participate in the LLC's management to vote except as otherwise provided in the Operating Agreement, at least a majority of the remaining members must consent to the assignee's admission as a member.

Taxation. LLCs, like partnerships, are not subject to income taxation. Gains, losses, income, deductions, and credits that flow through the company are tax-free and deducted by the members. LLCs have a number of tax advantages over corporations: For example, an LLC can designate "special allocations" among the members, and tax treatment is favorable when disposing of an LLC, similar to a partnership or an S corporation.

Taxation in the state or city where the LLC will be doing business should be considered. Florida and Texas, for example, impose income or franchise taxes; and both New York State and New York City have special taxes and fees.

Advantages of LLCs. LLCs have the following advantages over other types of entities, especially for the acquisition and holding of real estate:

- Greater informality and flexibility of management. Members can participate in management and/or structure control of decision making as desired. The Operating Agreement allows flexibility to be designed into management and decision making. Controls over certain decisions may be given to some members and for only certain periods of time or upon the occurrence of specified events. Formal board approval for many transactions is not necessary as it is in corporations.

- No stock structure and shareholder limitations as in S corporations. The flexibility in the allocation of income, gain, and loss is very advantageous. Whereas an S corporation can have only one class of stock, more than one class of ownership interest can be created in an LLC. In addition, distinctions can be made between the equity interest of employees, investor-nonmanagers, or investor-managers based on the future success of the business, a part of the business, or realization of proper loss on the sale of the business.

- Inability of creditors of members, who are treated as assignees of economic interest, to force a sale or dissolution of the LLC

- Ability to hold real estate in the LLC name, which allows transfers of interest within the LLC without recording requirements
- LLC's ability to own 100 percent of the stock of a corporation
- No management restrictions as in a limited partnership
- Partnership "pass-through" tax treatment
- Special allocations and distributions. LLC members may divide income and tax liability among themselves. For example, a 10 percent member could obtain 10 percent of cash flow but 40 percent of depreciation deductions for a particular property.
- Ability of investors to participate in management without losing their liability protection as in a limited partnership
- Favorable treatment of nonrecourse debt. Losses may be in excess of capital contributions subject to substantial economic affect.
- Avoids corporate-level income tax gain when appreciated property is sold
- Attractive to foreign investors familiar with the *limitada* (Central and South America), the SARL (France), and the GmbH (Germany). The foreign investor who acts as a manager or executive may qualify for a green card as an immigrant transferee. S corporations do not permit foreign investors.

Disadvantages of LLCs. The disadvantage of LLCs are as follows:

- No body of law governing LLCs has been developed and uniformity among state laws is lacking. The laws covering the nature and characteristics of LLCs vary greatly from state to state. There are variations, for example, in filing and periodic reporting requirements; and some states make provisions or impose limitations not found in LLC statutes of other states.
- A member usually may not transfer his or her interest without the vote or written consent of a significant percentage of the remaining members, thus limiting the use of LLCs that have a large number of members or are publicly traded entities.

Professional limited liability companies and limited liability partnerships. Each member of a medical or dental service, engineering, land surveying, architectural and/ or landscaping service LLC must be licensed to practice the profession.

Professionals practicing in a general partnership form may register to be a limited liability partnership (LLP). A partner of an LLP is liable only for his or her professional negligence or wrongful act or misconduct or that of any person acting under his or her direct supervision and control. New York and Minnesota also limit the liability of partners of an LLP for contractual and other debts and obligations.

Limited life. Unlike a corporation, an LLC usually does not have a perpetual existence. An LLC is usually dissolved upon the first of the following to occur:

- The latest date for dissolution set forth in the Articles of Organization
- The occurrence of events specified in the Operating Agreement
- The written consent of two-thirds (or such other percentage designated in the Operating Agreement) of the members or for the entry of a decree of judicial dissolution

In addition, an LLC is dissolved upon the bankruptcy, death, dissolution, expulsion, incapacity, or withdrawal of any member unless the LLC has at least two members and is continued with the consent of the majority of all the remaining members or such lesser percentage set forth in the Operating Agreement.

Mortgage financing. When LLCs obtain mortgage financing, title insurance companies require the following:

- Certificate of Good Standing or status letter from the secretary of state
- Articles of Organization indicating that there is no limitation of the LLC's authority regarding real estate or financing
- Operating Agreement indicating who has authority to execute real estate documents
- Resolution by the members or managers authorizing the real estate transaction
- Deed in the name of the LLC and not in the names of the managers and members
- Guarantees by members or managers in their individual capacities

For further information on LLCs, refer to *How to Profit by Forming Your Own Limited Liability Company!* (Upstart Publishing Company) by Scott E. Friedman.

CORPORATIONS

A corporation comes into existence when a certificate of incorporation, signed by at least one incorporator over 18 years of age, is filed with the secretary of state. Although they are the owners of the corporation, shareholders usually exercise direct authority only by electing a board of directors and by voting to approve certain board proposals—for example, amendments of the certificate of incorporation, the sale of the business, or voluntary dissolution.

The board of directors in turn establishes corporate business policies and elects officers—for example, a president, vice-presidents, and a treasurer—to effectuate those policies. Officers are directly accountable to the board of directors, not to the shareholders.

In smaller corporations, the lines separating the duties of shareholders, directors, and officers tend to become blurred because the same individual(s) may serve in all three capacities. A properly run corporation, however, will observe the niceties of those distinctions. (For a thorough guide to the proper operation of your corporation, see *The Corporate Forms Kit,* published by Upstart Publishing Company.)

Because the authority of a corporation, its directors, and officers is limited by statute, this business form does not require as complex a business agreement as does a partnership. However, it is sound business planning (for even a small number of shareholders who are close friends or relatives) to enter into (1) a shareholders' agreement governing buy-outs in the event of death, disability, or retirement; (2) employment contracts; and (3) the identity of those shareholders who will serve on the board of directors.

Qualification in Other States

If a corporation or LLC that is formed in one state transacts local business in another state, it is required to file and qualify as a "foreign" corporation or LLC to do business in the second state. This subjects it to the local state's regulations and enables it to sue and be sued in the local state.

If a corporation or LLC intends to transact a substantial part of its business activities in a foreign jurisdiction, it should apply for qualification in that state. However, the following activities usually do not require qualification: (1) holding directors' or shareholders' meetings, (2) maintaining bank accounts, (3) using inde-pendent contractors for sales, (4) soliciting orders to be accepted outside the state, and (5) conducting isolated business transactions.

The qualification procedure begins with a name check. Prompt selection and reservation of a name in the foreign jurisdiction will avoid the possibility of later denial of authorization to do business on the basis of an unacceptable name.

A state may subject foreign corporations or LLCs doing business within its borders to various provisions of its laws, such as those regarding director or officer misconduct. The businesses may be exempted from certain of those provisions if they are listed on a national securities exchange or if less than one-half of their total business income is allocable to the local state.

Therefore, a company doing business in one state only ordinarily should be formed in that state. Otherwise, it may be subjected to regulation and taxation not only in its own state of incorporation but also in the state in which it is doing business. Formation in another jurisdiction may be advantageous despite the additional expense if (1) a company anticipates doing substantial local business within that state, (2) it wishes to avoid a particularly onerous law, or (3) it wishes to obtain the benefit of a particular provision of another state's company law.

Delaware

The best alternative state usually is Delaware. It is the state most accommodating to corporations and management. Incorporation in Delaware is especially desirable if a corporation plans to operate with little or no surplus or has a large number of inaccessible shareholders, which makes it difficult to obtain their consent when needed. See your attorney to determine how your state's corporation laws compare with those of Delaware.

Delaware's special close corporation provisions permit shareholders to directly manage the business of the corporation without a board of directors. Shareholders are deemed to be directors and assume the liabilities of directors. The shareholders have no liability to employees as in New York and some other states. Delaware permits loans to directors if they are also officers or if the loan is approved by the board of directors. No shareholder approval is necessary as in other states such as New York. Shareholder approval for stock options to officers, directors, or employees is not required as in such other states as New York.

Delaware permits fewer than unanimous written consents of shareholders without a meeting. Dividends out of surplus or net profits in the current or preceding fiscal year are permitted. Other states, such as New York, allow dividends only out of surplus.

For further information, read *How to Form Your Own Corporation without a Lawyer for under $75* by Ted Nicholas, published by Upstart Publishing Company.

PARTNERSHIP VERSUS CORPORATION: NONTAX ASPECTS

Partnerships and corporations differ in several respects: the potential liability of investors, the duration of the business, and the ease with which new investors can be brought into the business.

For many people, the potential threat of unlimited liability for the debts of the business is the greatest negative feature of the partnership form of business. Each partner is individually liable for all of the debts of the partnership. A corporation's shareholders, directors, and officers do not run that risk. Shareholders are obliged only to pay for the shares they have agreed to buy and to honor any guarantees they may have made for the corporation. The only other risk shareholders run is that some states may hold them liable for unpaid wages or salaries owed to employees. Corporate officers are at risk if they fail to collect and/or pay withholding taxes, wages, and state franchise taxes. Corporate directors are at risk only if they make illegal dividend or other distribution payments to shareholders.

If the members of a partnership wish to admit a new partner, every existing partner must agree to admit the new person. In effect, any one partner can veto the wishes of the majority in any major partnership decision.

A corporation has a perpetual life. A partnership continues only so long as specified in the partnership agreement or until the death, bankruptcy, withdrawal, or expulsion of a partner.

Shareholders can agree to similar restrictions on the transfer of shares (the ownership interest in a corporation). In the absence of such a restriction, share ownership can be changed easily, merely by the transfer or sale of the shares.

Corporations can raise capital by simply selling new stock, bonds, or other securities. Partnerships, on the other hand, must obtain a loan, new partners, contributions by current partners, or restriction of the partnership.

Tax Aspects

One of the chief drawbacks of the corporation form is that its profits are taxed twice. Because a corporation is viewed as a "person," federal and state governments impose an income tax on any profits it earns. Then, when those profits are distributed to shareholders as dividends, they are taxed as income in the shareholders' hands.

This undesirable result can be avoided if a corporation elects to be an S corporation. If the election is made, the corporation will not be treated as a taxable entity. Its gains "pass through" to the shareholders without being taxed as corporate profits. Each shareholder, of course, will pay a tax on his or her share of the business's profits; but the corporation's profits will be taxed only once, not twice.

If your corporation has less than 75 shareholders (none of whom are nonresident aliens) and only one class of stock, it may qualify to be free from income taxes under the S rules. For further details, see Chapter 4, "How to Make Your Corporation Tax-Free."

If the decision is made to form an S corporation, then other advantages and disadvantages come into play. On the plus side, profits are taxed at the rate imposed on individuals (capped at 31 percent), which is lower than the top corporate rate of 39 percent. Further, the pass-through of profits is not subject to the self-employment tax as in a partnership.

The partnership itself is not taxed. The partnership tax return is merely an information return. In a partnership, the partners pay individual taxes on their proportionate shares of the partnership. Unlike a corporation, income tax cannot be deferred by retaining profits.

Small businesses that are not incorporated (sole proprietorships, partnerships, limited liability companies, and limited liability partnerships) may choose whether to be taxed as a corporation or partnership simply by checking a box on a form. The only companies that are not able to check a box are publicly traded companies, companies that are formed under a state incorporation law, and certain foreign-owned companies.

HOW AND WHEN TO USE THE FORMS IN THIS CHAPTER

Partnership Agreement. This form should be adopted for all partnerships because it spells out each partner's rights and responsibilities. The agreement provides for the division of profits and losses and anticipates the retirement, death, or disability of a partner.

Business Certificate. This form should be filed by partnerships and sole proprietorships in order to register the business name or assumed name. If the business is sold, an amended certificate should be filed. Filing is generally made at the county seat.

Limited Liability Company Articles of Organization. This form is filed with the secretary of state.

PARTNERSHIP AGREEMENT

This Contract, made and entered into on the   day of   , 19   by and between   and   of

and   respectively.

1. *NATURE OF BUSINESS:* That the said parties have this day formed a partnership for the purpose of engaging and conducting a   and such other businesses of a similar or related nature as may be agreed upon from time to time by the partners.

2. *NAME:* The partnership is to be conducted under the name of   (hereinafter referred to as   ) and maintain offices at

3. *CAPITAL:* The partners shall contribute capital in the following amounts and proportions:

Partner	Amount	Proportion
_____	_____	_____ %
_____	_____	_____ %

The partnership shall maintain a capital account record for each partner; should any partner's capital account fall below the agreed to amount, then that partner shall (1) have his share of partnership profits then due and payable applied instead to his capital account; and (2) shall pay any deficiency to the partnership if his share of partnership profits is not yet due and payable or, if it is, his share is insufficient to cancel the deficiency.

4. *DUTIES.* The partners shall provide their full-time services and best efforts on behalf of the partnership. No partner shall receive a salary for services rendered to the partnership. Each partnership shall have equal rights to manage the partnership business.

5. *ALLOCATION OF DEPRECIATION OR GAIN OR LOSS ON CONTRIBUTED PROPERTY:* The partners understand and agree that the general allocation rule set forth in Section 704 (c)(1) of the Internal Revenue Code of 1954 shall apply, and that the depreciation or gain or loss arising with respect to contributed property shall be allocated equally between the partners, in determining the taxable income or loss of the partnership and the distributive share of each partner, in the same manner as if such property had been purchased by the partnership at a cost equal to such adjusted tax basis.

6. *DRAWING ACCOUNTS.* Partners shall be entitled to make   draws upon the assets of the partnership, but only if (1) working capital after payment of the draws shall be sufficient to satisfy debts, and (2) the capital accounts of the partnership will not be impaired.

7. *PROFIT AND LOSS:* At the end of each fiscal period, the net profit or loss shall be shared in the following proportions:

Partner	Proportion
_____	_____
_____	_____

8. *ACCOUNTING:* The investment and all transactions completed in the operation of the business are to be recorded in books of account in accordance with accepted accounting procedures. These books are to be open for the inspection of each partner at all times.

   a) In _____ of each year, the partnership shall make a complete account of its assets and liabilities. In the event the accounting discloses that one partner has withdrawn more money than he has agreed to draw, the excess shall be paid to the partnership. If, after allowances are made for debts, current liabilities and working capital needs, there are profits remaining, those profits shall be considered "net profits" for the purpose of distribution as described in paragraph 7 above, and shall be distributed in accordance with the schedule in that paragraph.

   In the event debts, current liabilities, and working capital needs exceed available assets, the partners will make capital contributions sufficient to eliminate the deficiency. If capital contributions are required they shall be made in the proportions set out in paragraph 3 above.

9. *ELECTION TO CONTINUE BUSINESS:* In the event of the retirement, death, or disability of a partner, the remaining partner shall have the right to continue the business of the partnership under its present name, either by himself or in conjunction with any other person or persons he may select, but he shall pay to the retiring partner, or to the legal representative of the deceased or disabled partner, as the case may be, the value of his interest in the partnership, as provided in the following paragraph.

10. *VALUATION OF PARTNER'S INTEREST:* The value of the interest of a retiring, deceased, or disabled partner shall be the sum of: (a) his capital account, (b) any unpaid loans due him, (c) his proportionate share of accrued net profits remaining undistributed in his drawing account, and (d) his interest in any prior agreed appreciation in the value of the partnership property over its book value. No value for good will shall be included in determining the value of the partner's interest.

11. *DURATION:* The said partnership is to continue for a period of years from _____ , 199____ unless the partners mutually agree in writing to a shorter period.

12. *TERMINATION:* At the conclusion of this contract, unless it is mutually agreed to continue the operation of the business under a new contract, the assets of the partnership, after all liabilities are paid, are to be divided in the same proportion that profits are shared.

13. *LIMITATIONS ON PARTNERS' POWERS:* No partner shall, without the consent of the other partners:

   a) Borrow money in the firm name for firm purposes, utilize collateral owned by the partnership as security for such loans, nor enter into any contract in amounts greater than _____ Dollars ($ _____) on behalf of the partnership;

   b) Assign, transfer, pledge, compromise or release any of the claims of or debts due the partnership except upon payment in full, or arbitrate or consent to the arbitration of any of the disputes or controversies of the partnership;

   c) Make, execute or deliver any assignment for the benefit of creditors or any bond, confession of judgment, chattel mortgage, deed, guarantee, indemnity bond, surety bond, or contract to sell or contract of sale of all or substantially all the property of the partnership;

d) Lease or mortgage any partnership real estate or any interest therein or enter into any contract for any such purpose;

e) Pledge or hypothecate or in any manner transfer his interest in the partnership, except to the other party of this agreement;

f) Become a surety, guarantor, or accommodation party to any obligation.

14. *RETIREMENT:* Any partner may retire from the partnership upon 60 days prior notice to the other partner.

15. *NON-COMPETE AGREEMENT:* A partner who retires or withdraws from the partnership shall not directly or indirectly engage in a business which is or which would be competitive with the existing or then anticipated business of the partnership for a period of   , in those   of this State where the partnership is currently doing or planning to do business.

16. *ARBITRATION:* Any controversy or claim arising out of or relating to this contract or breach thereof shall be settled by arbitration in accordance with the rules of the American Arbitration Association and judgment upon the award rendered may be entered in any court having jurisdiction thereof.

In Witness Whereof, the partners have executed this agreement on the date above written.

_____

_____

Business Certificate

I HEREBY CERTIFY that I am conducting, or transacting, business under the name, or designation, of

_____
(Name of business)

at _____
(No. and Street address of business

_____
(City, Town or Village)   (County)   (State)   (ZIP)

My full name is* _____
(No initials)

and I reside at _____
(No. and Street address of Individual)

_____
(City, Town or Village)   (County)   (State)   (ZIP)

I FURTHER CERTIFY that I am successor in interest to _____
(Name of person or persons previously conducting this business)

_____

the person, or persons, previously using this name, or names, to carry on, conduct, or transact this business.

IN WITNESS WHEREOF, I have this _____ day of _____ made and signed this Certificate.

_____
(Signature of person conducting business.)

STATE OF
COUNTY OF   ss.:

On this _____ day of _____ , before me personally appeared

_____, to me known and known to me to be the individual in and who
(name of person conducting business)

executed the foregoing certificate, and he (she) thereupon duly acknowledge to me that he (she) executed the same.

Subscribed and sworn to before me, this _____ _day_

_of_ _____ .

*Print or Type name.
*If under 18 years of age, state "I am _____ years of age."

_____
Notary Public,
Commissioner of Deeds,

Business Certificate
© 1975 Sanders Legal Publishers, Buffalo, NY

Source: Sanders Legal Publishers, Inc. Used with permission.

Index No.

CERTIFICATE
of

(Name of person conducting business - No initials)

(No. and Street address of person conducting business)

(City, Town or Village - State - ZIP)

**CONDUCTING BUSINESS
UNDER THE NAME OF**

(Name of business)

(No. and Street address of business)

(City, Town or Village - State - ZIP)

LIMITED LIABILITY COMPANY
ARTICLES OF ORGANIZATION
OF

_____

FIRST: The name of the limited liability company is:

SECOND: The county within this state in which the office of the limited liability company is to be located is:

THIRD: (optional) The latest date on which the limited liability company is to dissolve is:

FOURTH: The secretary of state is designated as agent of the limited liability company upon whom process against it may be served. The post office address within or without this state to which the secretary of state shall mail a copy of any process against the limited liability company served upon him or her is:

FIFTH: (optional) The name and street address within this state of the registered agent of the limited liability company upon whom and at which process against the limited liability company can be served is:

SIXTH: The future effective date of the Articles of Organization, if not effective upon filing, is:

SEVENTH: The limited liability company is to be managed by (check appropriate box):

❏ 1 or more members

❏ A class or classes of members

❏ 1 or more managers

❏ A class or classes of managers

EIGHTH: If all or specified members are to be liable in their capacity as members for all or specified debts, obligations, or liabilities of the limited liability company as authorized pursuant to Section 609 of the Limited Liability Company Law, a statement that all or specified members are so liable.

IN WITNESS WHEREOF, this certificate has been subscribed this   day of   , 199   , by the undersigned who affirms that the statements made herein are true under the penalties of perjury.

_____   _____
(Signature)   (Name and capacity of signer)

If the limited liability company shall maintain more than one office in this state, set forth the county in which the principal office is to be located.

1. The future effective date may not exceed 60 days from the date of filing and must be a date certain.

2. The articles may include any other provisions not inconsistent with law.

4

How to Make Your Corporation Tax-Free

Would you and your corporation like to receive the following benefits?

- Avoid the double taxation problem of C corporations by paying no corporate federal income tax or state corporate franchise tax

- As a shareholder, be able to benefit from the corporation's deductions and credits on your own individual income tax return

- Aid your family financial planning by reducing your income tax through shifting income to family members in lower tax brackets

- Invest earnings inside or outside the corporation without the accumulated earnings penalty tax

- Reduce the likelihood of an IRS "excessive compensation" challenge

You and your corporation can enjoy these benefits if it qualifies as an S corporation. You can incorporate and still reap the tax advantages of a partnership by electing to be an S corporation for state and federal tax purposes.

A qualifying domestic corporation may "elect" to be generally exempt from federal income taxes and will continue to be exempt as long as the election is in effect. Corporations that have made a valid election are known as S corporations or "electing small business corporations." Corporations that have not made an S election are known as regular C corporations.

The corporation's taxable income or loss (with certain adjustments or limitations) for the current tax year is taken into account pro rata by the shareholders on their individual returns. Jobs, investment and research, and develop-

ment credits and losses are passed through to the shareholders on a pro-rata basis.

The amount of deductible loss is limited to the shareholder's basis for stock plus any loans made by him or her to the corporation. But the losses may be carried forward to future tax years.

THE PROS AND CONS OF S CORPORATIONS

S Corporation Advantages

Ease of reorganization. Changing from a regular C corporation to an S corporation is accomplished simply by filing election IRS Form 2553. It does not require a reorganization of the business and does not alter the shareholders' insulation from legal liability as would be the case in changing over to a partnership. You should distribute any accumulated earnings and profits of the corporation before making the election to avoid double taxation on some future distribution.

Tax shelters for children. The tax rate of the parents is applied to the income of children under age 14. With a profitable S corporation, parents can give their children tax shelters that produce passive losses and make them shareholders in the S corporation. The corporate earnings will be passive income for the children who are not active in the business, and this income will be offset by passive losses

33

from other tax shelters. This technique can be used in commercial enterprises but not in personal service corporations. (See "Alternative Minimum Tax," which follows.)

Lower tax rate. The maximum corporate tax rate is higher than the maximum personal income tax rate. Even if individual rates are increased by new legislation in future years, the S election can be easily revoked.

Cash method of accounting. Regular C corporations (other than personal service corporations) are required to use the accrual (rather than cash) method of accounting if their average annual gross receipts exceed $5 million for a three-year base period.

Alternative minimum tax. A regular C corporation is subject to an alternative minimum tax (AMT) of 20 percent instead of its normally computed tax if the taxes exceed those calculated under the regular rates.

The corporate AMT of 20 percent is applied to taxable income as modified for certain preference addbacks, including an adjustment equal to one-half of the excess "book" income over minimum taxable income. This penalizes the corporation that reports higher earnings to shareholders and creditors than it does on its tax return. The AMT ensures that all profitable corporations, especially those benefiting from certain preferences such as depreciation, pay some federal income tax on their true economic income. S corporations are not subject to the AMT.

Double taxation. The double tax on a regular C corporation's earnings is practically unavoidable. The tax costs of dissolving the corporate form to establish a partnership, for example, will significantly outweigh any lower tax rate benefits for corporations with taxable income under $100,000.

S Corporation Disadvantages

State income tax. Some states do not recognize S corporation status, and the corporation could be subject to state tax. S corporation dividends may be taxed at the minimum state personal rate. Certain state credits, such as job incentive credits, are not available to S corporations.

Calendar year. An S corporation cannot defer taxes by adopting a fiscal year. S corporations and personal service corporations must change their taxable year to conform to the taxable year of the majority of their principal owners unless an acceptable business purpose exists for nonconformity. A noncalendar tax year currently used by a regular corporation will likely be lost upon its conversion.

Passive losses. A closely held C corporation (where more than 50 percent of the shares are held by fewer than six individuals during the last half of the tax year) may offset passive losses against net active income—that is, taxable income computed without regard to portfolio income, loss, gain or expense, or income or loss from passive activities. Tax-sheltered losses and credits as well as investment losses will be offset against the corporation's "net active income" if the investment that produces them belongs to the corporation.

S CORPORATIONS DISTINGUISHED FROM PARTNERSHIPS

The S corporation is not taxable at the corporate level (with the exception of certain capital gains), thereby avoiding the double-taxation problem. The S corporation effectively elects to be treated like a partnership; and its shareholders are treated almost as if they are partners.

The S corporation, however, is not subject to the same income tax rules as a partnership. Although there are some similarities in the tax rules that apply to S corporations and partnerships, there are two main differences.

First, cash distributions from a partnership to a partner usually are not taxable to the partner. Cash distributions from an S corporation to its shareholders can be nontaxable in some circumstances but frequently will be treated as ordinary taxable dividends.

Second, for a partnership, income gain, loss, credit, and deduction items keep their same character when passed through to the partners. These same items do not usually keep their same character when passed from the S corporation to its shareholders. For example, charitable contributions are still charitable contributions when passed through from a partnership but not when passed through from an S corporation. Examples of items that keep the same character when passed through an S corporation include net long-term capital gains, net operating losses, and investments in property qualifying for the investment credit.

Third, pass-through profits are not subject to the self-employment tax as they are in a partnership.

QUALIFICATIONS

To qualify for the S election, the corporation must meet the following requirements:

- It must be a *domestic corporation.* This means it must be created or organized in the United States or under the laws of the United States or any state or territory.

- It may have only *one class of stock,* although separate stock classes are permitted if they differ in voting rights as opposed to economic rights.

- It *must not have more than 75 shareholders.* A husband, a wife, and their estates are treated as one shareholder.

- It must have *only individuals, estates, or certain trusts as shareholders* (including the qualified S trust).

- It *must not have a nonresident alien as a shareholder.*

Ineligible corporations are those that are members of affiliated groups, certain financial institutions, insurance companies, possessions' corporations, and domestic international sales corporations (DISCs).

S corporation stock may be held by an electing small business trust. All beneficiaries of the trust must be individuals except that charitable organizations may hold contingent remainder interests. No interest in the trust may be acquired by purchase. Interest in qualifying trusts must be acquired by gift, bequest, or other nonpurchase acquisition. The trust pays tax at the highest individual rate on its S corporation income without any deduction for its distributions to trust beneficiaries. Thus, nonresidents can enjoy the benefits of S corporation status. A grantor trust may remain an S corporation shareholder for two years after the date of the grantor's death.

HOW TO MAKE THE ELECTION

The S corporation election is made on IRS Form 2553 (see the form at the end of this chapter) and filed with the IRS.

An election remains in effect for succeeding tax years until terminated or revoked. All original stockholders must consent to the election by signing Form 2553 or an attached statement. If an attached statement is used, it must show the names and addresses of the corporation and shareholders, the number of shares owned, and the dates acquired. Consent of a new stockholder is not required. However, the election will be terminated if the new shareholder affirmatively refuses to consent.

If the election is made after the start of the first year for which the election is to be effective, consents must be filed by all shareholders who held interests before the date of election even if they have sold their interest.

An election may be filed during the entire taxable year before the year in which the election is to be effective and before the 16th day of the third month of the current taxable year. An election that is ineffective because of late filing is automatically effective in the following year.

Even if the election is filed on time, it will not take effect until the following year unless all those with shareholder interest before the filing date consent to the election. No extensions for making the election will be granted. A late election may be treated as filed on time if there is reasonable cause.

Ownership of Other Corporations

An S corporation may own 80 percent or more of the stock of a C corporation. However, it may not file a consolidated return with its affiliated C corporation and there are special rules concerning dividend distributions.

An S corporation may also own a qualified subchapter S subsidiary (QSSS), which includes any domestic corporation that qualifies as an S corporation and is 100 percent owned by an S corporation parent that elects to be treated as such. For income tax purposes, it is not treated as a separate corporation, and all of its assets, liabilities, income, expenses, and credit items are treated as belonging to the parent corporation.

Newly Organized Corporations

The first tax year of a newly organized corporation will usually be for a period less than 12 months. An election may be made for this short tax year as long as it is made before the 16th day of the third month of the corporation's first taxable year. If the first taxable year of a new corporation is for a period of less than two and one-half months, the election may be made for that year within two and one-half months from the beginning of the taxable year.

The first taxable year begins when the corporation has shareholders, acquires assets, or begins doing business, whichever occurs first. A valid election may not be filed before a corporation is formally incorporated. However, if under state law corporate existence begins with filing the Articles of Incorporation, the first day of the tax year begins on the date of the filing even though the corporation has no assets and does not begin doing business until a later date.

Ask your tax adviser about electing S corporation status for state income tax purposes. Washington, D.C., and the following states do not recognize S corporations for state income tax purposes: California, Connecticut, Louisiana, Michigan, New Hampshire, New Jersey, North Carolina, Tennessee, Utah, and Vermont.

WHEN SHOULD THE S CORPORATION BE USED?

The S corporation should be used if the corporation has losses and the shareholders have a sufficient basis in their stock or loans to permit deduction of those losses and sufficient taxable income to benefit from the losses. It should also be used if the corporation is profitable and there is no need for accumulating additional working capital or if a potential accumulated-earnings problem exists and the shareholders wish to have the corporation's earnings distributed to them at only one level of taxation.

TERMINATING THE ELECTION

The S corporation election may be terminated by filing a formal corporate statement of revocation. All stockholders must sign consents to revoke. If the revocation is filed during the first month of the corporation's tax year, it is effective for that year and following years. If filed later, it becomes effective for the next year.

An election may also be terminated because the corporation becomes disqualified. This can happen, for example, if a new stockholder is added to the corporation and either affirmatively refuses to consent to the election or brings the number of stockholders above the permissible limit. The termination is effective for the year the event occurs, regardless of how late in the year.

HOW AND WHEN TO USE THE FORM IN THIS CHAPTER

Election by a Small Business Corporation (IRS Form 2553). This form must be filed before the 16th day of the third month of the election year. Check with your state tax commission to see whether there is an S election available for state taxes and if there are minimum franchise or corporate taxes.

Department of the Treasury
Internal Revenue Service

Instructions for Form 2553
(Revised September 1996)

Election by a Small Business Corporation

Section references are to the Internal Revenue Code unless otherwise noted.

Paperwork Reduction Act Notice.—We ask for the information on this form to carry out the Internal Revenue laws of the United States. You are required to give us the information. We need it to ensure that you are complying with these laws and to allow us to figure and collect the right amount of tax.

You are not required to provide the information requested on a form that is subject to the Paperwork Reduction Act unless the form displays a valid OMB control number. Books or records relating to a form or its instructions must be retained as long as their contents may become material in the administration of any Internal Revenue law. Generally, tax returns and return information are confidential, as required by section 6103.

The time needed to complete and file this form will vary depending on individual circumstances. The estimated average time is:

Recordkeeping	6 hr., 28 min.
Learning about the law or the form	3 hr., 41 min.
Preparing, copying, assembling, and sending the form to the IRS	3 hr., 56 min.

If you have comments concerning the accuracy of these time estimates or suggestions for making this form simpler, we would be happy to hear from you. You can write to the Tax Forms Committee, Western Area Distribution Center, Rancho Cordova, CA 95743-0001. **DO NOT** send the form to this address. Instead, see **Where To File** below.

General Instructions

Caution: *The instructions below reflect the rules in effect for tax years beginning after December 31, 1996. For the rules in effect for tax years beginning before January 1, 1997, see the September 1993 revision of the instructions.*

Purpose.—To elect to be an S corporation, a corporation must file Form 2553. The election permits the income of the S corporation to be taxed to the shareholders of the corporation rather than to the corporation itself, except as noted below under **Taxes an S Corporation May Owe.**

Who May Elect.—A corporation may elect to be an S corporation only if it meets **all** of the following tests:

1. It is a domestic corporation.

2. It has no more than 75 shareholders. A husband and wife (and their estates) are treated as one shareholder for this requirement. All other persons are treated as separate shareholders.

3. Its only shareholders are individuals, estates, certain trusts described in section 1361(c)(2)(A), or, for tax years beginning after 1997, exempt organizations described in section 401(a) or 501(c)(3). An election can be made by a parent S corporation to treat the assets, liabilities, and items of income, deduction, and

credit of an eligible wholly-owned subsidiary as those of the parent corporation. See section 1361(b)(3) for details.

Note: *See the instructions for Part III regarding qualified subchapter S trusts.*

4. It has no nonresident alien shareholders.

5. It has only one class of stock (disregarding differences in voting rights). Generally, a corporation is treated as having only one class of stock if all outstanding shares of the corporation's stock confer identical rights to distribution and liquidation proceeds. See Regulations section 1.1361-1(l) for more details.

6. It is not one of the following ineligible corporations:

a. A bank or thrift institution that uses the reserve method of accounting for bad debts under section 585;

b. An insurance company subject to tax under the rules of subchapter L of the Code;

c. A corporation that has elected to be treated as a possessions corporation under section 936; or

d. A domestic international sales corporation (DISC) or former DISC.

7. It has a permitted tax year as required by section 1378 or makes a section 444 election to have a tax year other than a permitted tax year. Section 1378 defines a permitted tax year as a tax year ending December 31, or any other tax year for which the corporation establishes a business purpose to the satisfaction of the IRS. See Part II for details on requesting a fiscal tax year based on a business purpose or on making a section 444 election.

8. Each shareholder consents as explained in the instructions for column K.

See sections 1361, 1362, and 1378 for additional information on the above tests.

Taxes an S Corporation May Owe.—An S corporation may owe income tax in the following instances:

1. If, at the end of any tax year, the corporation had accumulated earnings and profits, and its passive investment income under section 1362(d)(3) is more than 25% of its gross receipts, the corporation may owe tax on its excess net passive income.

2. A corporation with net recognized built-in gain (as defined in section 1374(d)(2)) may owe tax on its built-in gains.

3. A corporation that claimed investment credit before its first year as an S corporation will be liable for any investment credit recapture tax.

4. A corporation that used the LIFO inventory pricing method for the year immediately preceding its first year as an S corporation may owe an additional tax due to LIFO recapture.

For more details on these taxes, see the Instructions for Form 1120S.

Where To File.—File this election with the Internal Revenue Service Center listed below.

If the corporation's principal business, office, or agency is located in ▼	Use the following Internal Revenue Service Center address ▼
New Jersey, New York (New York City and counties of Nassau. Rockland, Suffolk, and Westchester)	Holtsville. NY 00501
New York (all other counties), Connecticut, Maine, Massachusetts, New Hampshire, Rhode Island, Vermont	Andover, MA 05501
Illinois. Iowa, Minnesota, Missouri, Wisconsin	Kansas City, MO 64999
Delaware. District of Columbia, Maryland, Pennsylvania, Virginia	Philadelphia, PA 19255
Florida, Georgia, South Carolina	Atlanta, GA 39901
Indiana, Kentucky, Michigan, Ohio, West Virginia	Cincinnati, OH 45999
Kansas. New Mexico, Oklahoma, Texas	Austin. TX 73301
Alaska, Arizona, California (counties of Alpine, Amador, Butte, Calaveras, Colusa, Contra Costa, Del Norte, El Dorado. Glenn, Humboldt, Lake, Lassen, Marin, Mendocino, Modoc, Napa, Nevada. Placer, Plumas, Sacramento, San Joaquin, Shasta, Sierra, Siskiyou, Solano. Sonoma, Sutter, Tehama. Trinity, Yolo, and Yuba), Colorado. Idaho, Montana, Nebraska, Nevada, North Dakota, Oregon, South Dakota, Utah, Washington, Wyoming	Ogden, UT 84201
California (all other counties), Hawaii	Fresno, CA 93888
Alabama. Arkansas, Louisiana, Mississippi, North Carolina, Tennessee	Memphis, TN 37501

When To Make the Election.—Complete and file Form 2553 **(a)** at any time before the 16th day of the 3rd month of the tax year, if filed during the tax year the election is to take effect, or **(b)** at any time during the preceding tax year. An election made no later than 2 months and 15 days after the beginning of a tax year that is less than 2½ months long is treated as timely made for that tax year. An election made after the 15th day of the 3rd month but before the end of the tax year is effective for the next year. For example, if a calendar tax year corporation makes the election in April 1997, it is effective for the corporation's 1998 calendar tax year. However, an election made after the due date will be accepted as timely filed if the corporation can show that the failure to file on time was due to reasonable cause. If the failure is due to reasonable cause, attach an explanation to Form 2553. See section 1362(b) for more information.

Acceptance or Nonacceptance of Election.—The service center will notify the corporation if its election is accepted and when it will take effect. The corporation will also be notified if its election is not accepted. The corporation should generally receive a determination on its election within 60 days after it has filed Form 2553. If box Q1 in Part II is checked on page 2, the corporation will receive a ruling letter from the IRS in Washington, DC, that either approves or denies the selected tax year. When box Q1 is checked, it will generally take an additional 90 days for the Form 2553 to be accepted.

Cat. No. 49978N

Do not file Form 1120S for any tax year before the year the election takes effect. If the corporation is now required to file **Form 1120**, U.S. Corporation Income Tax Return, or any other applicable tax return, continue filing it until the election takes effect.

Care should be exercised to ensure that the IRS receives the election. If the corporation is not notified of acceptance or nonacceptance of its election within 3 months of date of filing (date mailed), or within 6 months if box Q1 is checked, take follow-up action by corresponding with the service center where the corporation filed the election. If the IRS questions whether Form 2553 was filed, an acceptable proof of filing is **(a)** certified or registered mail receipt (timely filed); **(b)** Form 2553 with accepted stamp; **(c)** Form 2553 with stamped IRS received date; or **(d)** IRS letter stating that Form 2553 has been accepted.

End of Election.—Once the election is made, it stays in effect until it is terminated. If the election is terminated in a tax year beginning after 1996, the corporation (or a successor corporation) can make another election on Form 2553 only with IRS consent for any tax year before the 5th tax year after the first tax year in which the termination took effect. See Regulations section 1.1362-5 for more details.

Specific Instructions

Part I

Note: *Part I must be completed by all corporations.*

Name and Address of Corporation.—Enter the true corporate name as stated in the corporate charter or other legal document creating it. If the corporation's mailing address is the same as someone else's, such as a shareholder's, enter "c/o" and this person's name following the name of the corporation. Include the suite, room, or other unit number after the street address. If the Post Office does not deliver to the street address and the corporation has a P.O. box, show the box number instead of the street address. If the corporation changed its name or address after applying for its employer identification number, be sure to check the box in item G of Part I.

Item A. Employer Identification Number (EIN).—If the corporation has applied for an EIN but has not received it, enter "applied for." If the corporation does not have an EIN, it should apply for one on **Form SS-4**, Application for Employer Identification Number. You can order Form SS-4 by calling 1-800-TAX-FORM (1-800-829-3676).

Item D. Effective Date of Election.—Enter the beginning effective date (month, day, year) of the tax year requested for the S corporation. Generally, this will be the beginning effective date of the tax year for which the ending effective date is required to be shown in item I, Part I. For a new corporation (first year the corporation exists) it will generally be the date required to be shown in item H, Part I. The tax year of a new corporation starts on the date that it has shareholders, acquires assets, or begins doing business, whichever happens first. If the effective date for item D for a newly formed corporation is later than the date in item H, the corporation should file Form 1120 or Form 1120-A for the tax period between these dates.

Column K. Shareholders' Consent Statement.—Each shareholder who owns (or is

deemed to own) stock at the time the election is made must consent to the election. If the election is made during the corporation's tax year for which it first takes effect. any person who held stock at any time during the part of that year that occurs before the election is made, must consent to the election, even though the person may have sold or transferred his or her stock before the election is made. Each shareholder consents by signing and dating in column K or signing and dating a separate consent statement described below.

An election made during the first 2½ months of the tax year is effective for the following tax year if any person who held stock in the corporation during the part of the tax year before the election was made, and who did not hold stock at the time the election was made, did not consent to the election.

If a husband and wife have a community interest in the stock or in the income from it, both must consent. Each tenant in common, joint tenant, and tenant by the entirety also must consent.

A minor's consent is made by the minor or the legal representative of the minor, or by a natural or adoptive parent of the minor if no legal representative has been appointed.

The consent of an estate is made by an executor or administrator.

If stock is owned by a trust that is a qualified shareholder, the deemed owner of the trust must consent. See section 1361(c)(2) for details regarding qualified trusts that may be shareholders and rules on determining who is the deemed owner of the trust.

Continuation sheet or separate consent statement.—If you need a continuation sheet or use a separate consent statement, attach it to Form 2553. The separate consent statement must contain the name, address, and EIN of the corporation and the shareholder information requested in columns J through N of Part I.

If you want, you may combine all the shareholders' consents in one statement.

Column L.—Enter the number of shares of stock each shareholder owns and the dates the stock was acquired. If the election is made during the corporation's tax year for which it first takes effect, do not list the shares of stock for those shareholders who sold or transferred all of their stock before the election was made. However, these shareholders must still consent to the election for it to be effective for the tax year.

Column M.—Enter the social security number of each shareholder who is an individual. Enter the EIN of each shareholder that is an estate, a qualified trust, or an exempt organization.

Column N.—Enter the month and day that each shareholder's tax year ends. If a shareholder is changing his or her tax year, enter the tax year the shareholder is changing to, and attach an explanation indicating the present tax year and the basis for the change (e.g., automatic revenue procedure or letter ruling request).

If the election is made during the corporation's tax year for which it first takes effect, you do not have to enter the tax year of any shareholder who sold or transferred all of his or her stock before the election was made.

Signature.—Form 2553 must be signed by president, treasurer, assistant treasurer, chief

accounting officer, or other corporate officer (such as tax officer) authorized to sign.

Part II

Complete Part II if you selected a tax year ending on any date other than December 31 (other than a 52-53-week tax year ending with reference to the month of December).

Box P1.—Attach a statement showing separately for each month the amount of gross receipts for the most recent 47 months as required by section 4.03(3) of Rev. Proc. 87-32, 1987-2 C.B. 396. A corporation that does not have a 47-month period of gross receipts cannot establish a natural business year under section 4.01(1).

Box Q1.—For examples of an acceptable business purpose for requesting a fiscal tax year, see Rev. Rul. 87-57, 1987-2 C.B. 117.

In addition to a statement showing the business purpose for the requested fiscal year, you must attach the other information necessary to meet the ruling request requirements of Rev. Proc. 96-1, 1996-1 I.R.B. 8 (updated annually). Also attach a statement that shows separately the amount of gross receipts from sales or services (and inventory costs, if applicable) for each of the 36 months preceding the effective date of the election to be an S corporation. If the corporation has been in existence for fewer than 36 months, submit figures for the period of existence.

If you check box Q1, you will be charged a $200 user fee (subject to change). Do not pay the fee when filing Form 2553. The service center will send Form 2553 to the IRS in Washington, DC, who, in turn, will notify the corporation that the fee is due.

Box Q2.—If the corporation makes a back-up section 444 election for which it is qualified, then the election will take effect in the event the business purpose request is not approved. In some cases, the tax year requested under the back-up section 444 election may be different than the tax year requested under business purpose. See **Form 8716**, Election To Have a Tax Year Other Than a Required Tax Year, for details on making a back-up section 444 election.

Boxes Q2 and R2.—If the corporation is not qualified to make the section 444 election after making the item Q2 back-up section 444 election or indicating its intention to make the election in item R1, and therefore it later files a calendar year return, it should write "Section 444 Election Not Made" in the top left corner of the first calendar year Form 1120S it files.

Part III

Certain qualified subchapter S trusts (QSSTs) may make the QSST election required by section 1361(d)(2) in Part III. Part III may be used to make the QSST election only if corporate stock has been transferred to the trust on or before the date on which the corporation makes its election to be an S corporation. However, a statement can be used instead of Part III to make the election.

Note: *Use Part III only if you make the election in Part I (i.e., Form 2553 cannot be filed with only Part III completed).*

The deemed owner of the QSST must also consent to the S corporation election in column K, page 1, of Form 2553. See section 1361(c)(2).

 Printed on recycled paper

*U.S. Government Printing Office: 1996 — 405-493/40153

Form **2553**

(Rev. September 1996)

Department of the Treasury
Internal Revenue Service

Election by a Small Business Corporation

(Under section 1362 of the Internal Revenue Code)

▶ **For Paperwork Reduction Act Notice, see page 1 of instructions.**

▶ **See separate instructions.**

OMB No. 1545-0146

Notes: 1. This election to be an S corporation can be accepted only if all the tests are met under **Who May Elect** on page 1 of the instructions; all signatures in Parts I and III are originals (no photocopies); and the exact name and address of the corporation and other required form information are provided.

2. Do not file **Form 1120S,** U.S. Income Tax Return for an S Corporation, for any tax year before the year the election takes effect.

3. If the corporation was in existence before the effective date of this election, see **Taxes an S Corporation May Owe** on page 1 of the instructions.

Part I   Election Information

Please Type or Print	Name of corporation (see instructions)	**A** Employer identification number
	Number, street, and room or suite no. (If a P.O. box, see instructions.)	**B** Date incorporated
	City or town, state, and ZIP code	**C** State of incorporation

D Election is to be effective for tax year beginning (month, day, year) . . . . ▶ ___/___/___

E Name and title of officer or legal representative who the IRS may call for more information

F Telephone number of officer or legal representative

( )

G If the corporation changed its name or address after applying for the EIN shown in **A** above, check this box . . . . ▶ ☐

H If this election takes effect for the first tax year the corporation exists, enter month, day, and year of the **earliest** of the following: (1) date the corporation first had shareholders, (2) date the corporation first had assets, or (3) date the corporation began doing business . . . . ▶ ___/___/___

I Selected tax year: Annual return will be filed for tax year ending (month and day) ▶ ....

If the tax year ends on any date other than December 31, except for an automatic 52-53-week tax year ending with reference to the month of December, you **must** complete Part II on the back. If the date you enter is the ending date of an automatic 52-53-week tax year, write "52-53-week year" to the right of the date. See Temporary Regulations section 1.441-2T(e)(3).

J Name and address of each shareholder; shareholder's spouse having a community property interest in the corporation's stock; and each tenant in common, joint tenant, and tenant by the entirety. (A husband and wife (and their estates) are counted as one shareholder in determining the number of shareholders without regard to the manner in which the stock is owned.)	**K** Shareholders' Consent Statement. Under penalties of perjury, we declare that we consent to the election of the above-named corporation to be an S corporation under section 1362(a) and that we have examined this consent statement, including accompanying schedules and statements, and to the best of our knowledge and belief, it is true, correct, and complete. We understand our consent is binding and may not be withdrawn after the corporation has made a valid election. (Shareholders sign and date below.)		**L** Stock owned		**M** Social security number or employer identification number (see instructions)	**N** Shareholder's tax year ends (month and day)
	Signature	Date	Number of shares	Dates acquired		

Under penalties of perjury, I declare that I have examined this election, including accompanying schedules and statements, and to the best of my knowledge and belief, it is true, correct, and complete.

Signature of officer ▶   Title ▶   Date ▶

See Parts II and III on back.   Cat. No. 18629R   Form **2553** (Rev. 9-96)

Part II Selection of Fiscal Tax Year (All corporations using this part must complete item O and item P, Q, or R.)

O Check the applicable box to indicate whether the corporation is:

1. ☐ A new corporation adopting the tax year entered in item I, Part I.

2. ☐ An existing corporation retaining the tax year entered in item I, Part I.

3. ☐ An existing corporation changing to the tax year entered in item I, Part I.

P Complete item P if the corporation is using the expeditious approval provisions of Rev. Proc. 87-32, 1987-2 C.B. 396, to request **(1)** a natural business year (as defined in section 4.01(1) of Rev. Proc. 87-32) or **(2)** a year that satisfies the ownership tax year test in section 4.01(2) of Rev. Proc. 87-32. Check the applicable box below to indicate the representation statement the corporation is making as required under section 4 of Rev. Proc. 87-32.

1. Natural Business Year ▶ ☐ I represent that the corporation is retaining or changing to a tax year that coincides with its natural business year as defined in section 4.01(1) of Rev. Proc. 87-32 and as verified by its satisfaction of the requirements of section 4.02(1) of Rev. Proc. 87-32. In addition, if the corporation is changing to a natural business year as defined in section 4.01(1), I further represent that such tax year results in less deferral of income to the owners than the corporation's present tax year. I also represent that the corporation is not described in section 3.01(2) of Rev. Proc. 87-32. (See instructions for additional information that must be attached.)

2. Ownership Tax Year ▶ ☐ I represent that shareholders holding more than half of the shares of the stock (as of the first day of the tax year to which the request relates) of the corporation have the same tax year or are concurrently changing to the tax year that the corporation adopts, retains, or changes to per item I, Part I. I also represent that the corporation is not described in section 3.01(2) of Rev. Proc. 87-32.

Note: *If you do not use item P and the corporation wants a fiscal tax year, complete either item Q or R below. Item Q is used to request a fiscal tax year based on a business purpose and to make a back-up section 444 election. Item R is used to make a regular section 444 election.*

Q Business Purpose—To request a fiscal tax year based on a business purpose, you must check box Q1 and pay a user fee. See instructions for details. You may also check box Q2 and/or box Q3.

1. Check here ▶ ☐ if the fiscal year entered in item I, Part I, is requested under the provisions of section 6.03 of Rev. Proc. 87-32. Attach to Form 2553 a statement showing the business purpose for the requested fiscal year. See instructions for additional information that must be attached.

2. Check here ▶ ☐ to show that the corporation intends to make a back-up section 444 election in the event the corporation's business purpose request is not approved by the IRS. (See instructions for more information.)

3. Check here ▶ ☐ to show that the corporation agrees to adopt or change to a tax year ending December 31 if necessary for the IRS to accept this election for S corporation status in the event (1) the corporation's business purpose request is not approved and the corporation makes a back-up section 444 election, but is ultimately not qualified to make a section 444 election, or (2) the corporation's business purpose request is not approved and the corporation did not make a back-up section 444 election.

R Section 444 Election—To make a section 444 election, you must check box R1 and you may also check box R2.

1. Check here ▶ ☐ to show the corporation will make, if qualified, a section 444 election to have the fiscal tax year shown in item I, Part I. To make the election, you must complete **Form 8716,** Election To Have a Tax Year Other Than a Required Tax Year, and either attach it to Form 2553 or file it separately.

2. Check here ▶ ☐ to show that the corporation agrees to adopt or change to a tax year ending December 31 if necessary for the IRS to accept this election for S corporation status in the event the corporation is ultimately not qualified to make a section 444 election.

Part III Qualified Subchapter S Trust (QSST) Election Under Section 1361(d)(2)*

Income beneficiary's name and address	Social security number
Trust's name and address	Employer identification number

Date on which stock of the corporation was transferred to the trust (month, day, year) . . . . ▶   /   /

In order for the trust named above to be a QSST and thus a qualifying shareholder of the S corporation for which this Form 2553 is filed, I hereby make the election under section 1361(d)(2). Under penalties of perjury, I certify that the trust meets the definitional requirements of section 1361(d)(3) and that all other information provided in Part III is true, correct, and complete.

_____   _____
Signature of income beneficiary or signature and title of legal representative or other qualified person making the election   Date

*Use Part III to make the QSST election only if stock of the corporation has been transferred to the trust on or before the date on which the corporation makes its election to be an S corporation. The QSST election must be made and filed separately if stock of the corporation is transferred to the trust after the date on which the corporation makes the S election.

♺ *Printed on recycled paper* *U.S. Government Printing Office: 1996 — 405-493/40152

5

Buying or Selling a Business

Whether you are buying or selling a business, you should fully understand the key components of the transaction—that is, the price, method of payment, contingencies, and tax consequences. This discussion of buying and selling a business will be presented primarily from the seller's point of view.

CONSIDERATIONS

If you decide to sell your business, it is important that you ensure a maximum return on your time, money, and energy invested. Carefully review the following considerations:

- Is now the best time to sell? It may not be a good time to sell if your business is doing poorly, if your business is involved in a lawsuit, if the economy is too sluggish, or if credit is too tight.

- What will the legal, moral, and financial impact be on your employees, suppliers, and family?

- What will the impact be on your personal financial situation?

- What is your real reason for selling? Is it health, boredom, workload, business problems, or money?

- Have you considered all of the alternatives, such as franchising, developing a partnership, merging with a similar company, going public, partial retirement, or absentee ownership?

PREPARATION

Once you have decided to sell, you must do the following:

- Evaluate and rate your business.
- Update your financial records.
- Select advisers who can objectively weigh your business and any offers you will receive. Your advisers may be a mergers and acquisition firm, investment banker, business broker, CPA, attorney, and/or appraiser.
- Price your firm.
- Market your business.

You can make your business as attractive as possible by emphasizing the following:

- The company's history, including the number of years it has been successful and the amount of goodwill it has built up

- The human factor. Focus on your staff—its competence, morale, and whether key people will remain with the company after the sale.

- Products and services. Stress the quality, price, reputation, delivery, and competitiveness of your company's goods or services.

- Your company's financial performance and the orderly condition of its books and records

- The condition and functionality of your company's facilities and equipment

- Long-term contracts your company has with customers and vendors

- Good relationships your company enjoys with lenders

- Good location with parking, accessibility, well-maintained surroundings, and/or close transportation

- Any competitive advantage your company derives from price, products, and/or services

To set a price, you must clarify exactly what it is you are selling—assets, stock, real estate, leases, franchises, a part of your business, training, or consulting. The value of your business consists of the following five items:

1. Tangible net worth (assets less liabilities)

2. Net income (gross earnings less expenses, including costs of goods and services, wages, and operating costs)

3. Value of your business as an investment (The return on item #1 above the dollar amount of your company's tangible net worth is invested in something else of comparable risk at prevailing interest rates.)

4. Excess earning power (net income less earning power, which is the value of item #3 plus your salary as the owner)

5. Intangible assets, including location; technological resources and special skills; trademarks, patents, and copyrights; new products and services; earnings trends within your industry; growth potential; personnel; competition in the marketplace; and customer goodwill

THE CONTRACT

Before an offer is made, the prospective buyer should propose the financial structure of the contract, including the amount of payments, when they are to be paid, and the form in which they are to be made. Methods of payment may include cash; stock; notes payable, in which the seller agrees to carry back a note for part of the purchase price with interest; earn-out payments (an *earned-out* situation is one in which the buyer agrees to pay additional money if the company earns a certain amount of predetermined profits); and consulting and employment contracts. The contract may also include a *noncompete clause,* in which the seller agrees not to compete within certain appropriate geographic limits for a reasonable period of time.

The sales contract should contain a description of what the buyer intends to purchase; the date, expiration date, and closing date of the offer; price; terms; repayment schedule; down payment and any contingencies; and the allocation of the purchase price (see "Price Allocation," later in this chapter). The contract must also require the purchaser to comply with the bulk-sale law requirements (see "Bulk Transfer and Sales Tax Regulations" below) and to obtain a sales tax certificate. It will affirm the buyer's right to the due diligence process. Under the contract, the seller will provide the purchaser with corporate minutes authorizing the sale (see form at the end of this chapter). Under the due diligence process, the buyer has an opportunity to review all of the company's records, books, facilities, contracts, and, if the offer contains such contingencies, to talk with the employees, customers, and suppliers.

A bill of sale will be used to transfer personal property (see form at the end of this chapter). A real estate contract will provide for the transfer of the real estate.

BULK TRANSFER AND SALES TAX REGULATIONS

Bulk transfer laws protect creditors of a going business from being cut off by the sale of the business or its assets. A *bulk transfer* is a sale of a major part of the materials, supplies, merchandise, or other inventory of the business or the major part of the goods, wares, and merchandise or a restaurant not in the ordinary course of the seller's business.

The buyer must obtain from the seller a signed and sworn list of the seller's creditors, their addresses, and the amount due them. Any bulk sale (except one made by auction sale) will be ineffective against the seller's creditors unless the buyer provides notice to the creditors at least ten days before the buyer either takes possession of the goods or pays for them (whichever happens first). The notice must be personally delivered or sent by either registered or certified mail to all of the creditors. The notice must state that a bulk sale is about to be made and include a property schedule, the names and business addresses of the seller and the buyer, all other business names and addresses used by the seller within the past three years, and the address to which creditors should send their bills.

Whenever a person who is required to collect sales tax sells, transfers, or assigns in bulk any part or the whole of a business's assets (tangible, intangible, or real property) otherwise than in the ordinary course of business, the purchaser, transferee, or assignee must notify the state commissioner of taxation and finance by registered mail of the proposed sale and of the price, terms, and conditions at least ten days before taking possession or paying.

The purchaser will be personally liable for all sales taxes owed by the seller unless, after notifying the tax department, the purchaser withholds all money or other consideration due the seller until the department has had the opportunity to notify the purchaser of any taxes owed by the seller. The liability of the purchaser is limited to the total purchase price or the fair market value of the business assets transferred, whichever is higher.

In addition, if the purchaser of a business or business assets is required to file a sales tax certificate of registration with the tax department, he or she must file the certificate at least 20 days before commencing business or opening a new place of business or taking possession of or paying for the business or business assets, whichever is earliest. A nonrefundable deposit should accompany the offer.

PRICE ALLOCATION

It is important for federal tax purposes to allocate the purchase price of a business among the various assets of that business. This information is needed when filing IRS Form 8594, "Asset Acquisition Statement." (See Form 8594 at the end of this chapter.) Allocation of the purchase price can affect income tax deductions for the new business owner.

Goodwill is the amount paid for a business in excess of all other assets. It is not deductible. Goodwill must be capitalized and recovered when the business is eventually sold again. If a goodwill amount is omitted from the sales contract, the IRS will reassign value from the covenant-not-to-compete amount.

The *covenant-not-to-compete* amount is deductible over the life of the agreement. Substantial value should be assigned to the covenant not to compete.

Tax Treatment of Various Business Assets

Buildings	Depreciable
Copyrights and patents	Amortizable
Covenant not to compete	Amortizable
Customer lists	Amortizable
Employee contracts	Amortizable
Equipment	Depreciable
Goodwill	Nondeductible—must be capitalized
Inventory	Deductible as cost of sales
Land	Nondeductible—must be capitalized
Trademark	Nondeductible—must be capitalized

CHECKLIST FOR THE PURCHASE OF A CORPORATION OR ITS ASSETS

Two methods for buying a business owned by a corporation are available. The buyer may purchase (1) all of the assets of the seller, or (2) all of, or a controlling number of, shares of stock in the seller's business from its shareholders, thereby becoming the new sole or controlling shareholder of the selling corporation.

Whichever method you select, you will want to ensure that the seller lives up to his or her claims and promises. You can achieve this by having the seller's representations and warranties included in the contract of sale and having the seller back up his or her representations and warranties by (1) escrowing a portion of the purchase price, (2) deferring a portion of the purchase price with nonnegotiable notes, and (3) having the seller's available net worth verified by an independent expert.

Purchasing Assets

The following provisions regarding representations and warranties by the seller should be included in the contract of sale. (Note that *S* refers to the seller corporation and its parent.)

- *Organization and standing.* S is duly organized, validly existing, and in good standing under state laws.
- *Authority.* S has full corporate authority to operate the business.
- *Conflicting agreements; no liens.* The contract does not constitute a breach by S of its certificates of incorporation or bylaws; or constitute a default; or result in violation of any agreement, contract, instrument, order,

judgment, or decree to which S is a party; or result in a violation by S of any existing law or of any order, decree, writ, or injunction of any court or governmental department.

- *Consents.* No consent from, or other approval of, any governmental entity or other person is necessary in connection with the contract.

- *Real property; leaseholds.* No real estate is owned or held under a lease by S or is used in connection with or, to the knowledge of S, is necessary for the business except for business space. (Or if other real estate is necessary, the right to use that property is transferable.)

- *Title to purchased property.* S owns all the right, title, and interest in all of the purchased property and will own that property on the closing date free and clear of all mortgages, liens, charges, encumbrances, or title defects.

- *Inventory.* The inventory is merchantable and fit for intended use and is free of any material defects in workmanship.

- *Compensation due employees.* Attach a complete list showing the names and job descriptions of all persons employed by S. In addition, show that S does not have any outstanding liabilities other than amounts listed for payment of wages, vacation pay, salaries, bonuses, reimbursable employee business expenses, pensions, contributions under any employment benefit plans, or any other compensation.

- *Union agreements and employment agreements.* Show whether S is a party to any union, collective bargaining, or similar agreement covering any employees employed in the conduct of S's business and whether S has any employment agreements with any employees that are not terminable at will on 30 days' notice.

- *Contracts and agreements.* S has performed all of its obligations under the contracts to be assumed by the buyer, and no contract is in default or in threat of default.

- *Insurance.* Attach a list and description of all insurance that S will continue in full force and effect through the closing date.

- *Licenses, permits, and consents.* There are no licenses and permits currently required by S for the operation of S's business. (Or if there are, they are transferable.)

- *Litigation.* There are no actions, suits, proceedings, or investigations pending or, to the knowledge of the seller, threatened against or involving S or brought by S or affecting any of the purchased property.

- *Pension plans.* There are no profit-sharing, pension, or other plans of compensation or employee benefit plans for any of S's employees other than those specified in the contract.

- *Subsidiaries.* There are no wholly or partly owned subsidiaries of S or other entities in which S has a proprietary interest.

- *Bank accounts.* Attach a list showing each and every bank account, banking arrangement, and safe-deposit box owned or operated in connection with the business. Specify the bank or type of account or other arrangement and the balance or amount of funds in each account or deposit box or subject to such arrangement.

- *Purchase order and commitments of seller.* Attach a list of all unfilled purchase orders and purchase commitments S may have outstanding if they relate to goods or services used in the ordinary course of business. State also whether the suppliers described in these orders and commitments are in default.

- *Customer orders and commitments.* List unfilled customer orders and commitments that have not been canceled. On the closing date, the buyer receives all advances or prepayments received by S from such customers.

- *Medical, hospitalization, life, and other insurance.* List all medical, health, hospitalization, and life insurance plans, programs, and policies in effect pertaining to any of S's employees.

- *Necessary property.* S is selling all machinery and equipment and other assets required by the buyer to manufacture its product lines and continue its business.

- *Patents and trademarks.* Ascertain whether S owns any patents, trademarks, inventions, patent rights, trade secrets, formulae, trade names, or copyrights and whether S has applied for any patents or trademark registrations except for those listed in the contract.

- *Contracts, agreements, and commitments.* There are no material contracts, agreements, or other commitments, written or oral, not listed in the contract to which S is a party, or by which it is bound, or which pertain to any of S's business.

- *Liabilities.* S shall have no liabilities of any kind except liabilities under the assumed contracts disclosed on the balance sheet.

Sale of Shares

When selling shares of a corporation, the following provisions and warranties should be included in addition to those listed earlier under "Purchasing Assets" (again S refers to the seller corporation and its parent):

- *Shares.* A list of the class or classes of shares of stock that will be transferred and the number of shares within each class that will be transferred is included.
- *Extent of control.* On closing, the shares to be transferred will equal the agreed-to percentage of ownership in the corporation.
- *Title to shares.* S owns good title to the shares being transferred and shall deliver them on the closing date, free and clear of any liens, charges, or encumbrances.
- *Fully paid shares.* The shares being transferred by S are fully paid, nonassessable shares.
- *Full voting rights.* S has not given any proxies or any other assignment of the right to vote the shares being transferred to another person. (If so, the proxy or assignment will be revoked before the closing.)
- *No restrictions.* Neither the Certificate of Incorporation nor the bylaws of the corporation contain any restrictions on the transfer of the shares being sold. (If such restrictions do exist, S will supply at closing a waiver of the restrictions.)
- *Taxes.* The corporation has filed all federal, state, and local tax returns and has paid all taxes. S warrants that there are neither audits nor notice of audits pending.
- *Financial statements.* S warrants that the financial statements appended to the agreement accurately and fairly represent the corporation as of the date they were prepared and that there have been no material changes since that date.

Successor Liability

The mere sale of corporate property from one company to another does not make the purchaser liable for the seller's unassumed tort liabilities. Rather, such liability has been imposed upon the purchaser only when (1) the purchaser expressly or impliedly assumes the seller's obligations, (2) the transaction is a de facto merger, or (3) the purchasing corporation is engaged in a fraudulent scheme to avoid the selling of the corporation's liabilities.

FRAUDULENT SALE OF A BUSINESS

Instead of starting a business from scratch, you may find it advantageous to buy an existing business with a proven track record. Although most sellers of businesses are trustworthy, occasionally purchasers of a business are victimized by fraud.

If you are the victim of fraud in the purchase of a business, you may have three types of claims against the seller, each of which has different damages that you may recover and elements that must be proven.

Common Law Fraud

A fraud that consists of an untrue representation, knowingly made, regarding information that is material to the value of the business or a knowing or misleading concealment of this kind of information is *common law fraud,* also known as *deceit.* The proof of the fraud must be that the seller knew of the undisclosed condition or possibly that the seller was reckless or grossly negligent in not knowing about the condition. Depending on the jurisdiction, the damages recoverable may be either the benefit-of-the-bargain standard (the majority of jurisdictions) or the out-of-pocket standard (New York and California). The out-of-pocket standard is the difference between the price paid by the buyer and the actual value of the business as of the date of sale. Under the benefit-of-the-bargain standard, the measure is the difference between the value of the business as it was represented to be and the value of the business as it actually existed on the date of sale.

Some jurisdictions (e.g., Oregon and New Jersey) allow the defrauded party—under certain circumstances—to make a choice between the two measures. As long as the victim paid less than the value of what the victim thought he or she was buying, the benefit-of-the-bargain measure is preferable. Most jurisdictions also allow punitive damages for fraud.

Breach of Warranty

If the fraud consists of a factual misrepresentation in the contract of sale—for example, the seller overstates actual earnings—there may be a cause of action for *breach of warranty*. The only proof required for breach of warranty is that the condition as represented in the agreement does not exist. If the seller knew that a contractually represented condition did not exist, fraud and breach of warranty are available. The damages for breach of warranty are the benefit-of-the-bargain standard.

Both of the standards provide for consequential damages directly traceable to the fraud or breach. However, lost profits are only awarded under the benefit-of-the-bargain standard.

Security Laws

If the sale was structured as the sale of the common stock of the business being sold, both state and federal security law claims may exist. You may allege breach of warranty in addition to security claims. Out-of-pocket damages usually are awarded and, in certain situations, benefit-of-the-bargain damages.

If a federal securities law claim may result in a lesser award than a state law claim, the buyer may be entitled to recover under the more favorable of the two laws. Therefore, both federal and state claims should be alleged. Federal security laws usually do not provide for punitive damages. See your attorney immediately if you are victimized by fraud.

HOW AND WHEN TO USE THE FORMS IN THIS CHAPTER

Sole Proprietorship Sales Agreement. This form provides for bank and seller financing, representations by the seller, covenants not to compete, and the seller to act as a consultant.

Corporate Stock Sales Agreement. This form provides that a corporation's shares will be sold on the installment basis, with both life insurance and various other forms of security to protect the seller until the buyer completes all payments to the seller.

Asset Purchase Agreement. This form provides for the sale of the assets of a corporation, including inventory, equipment, fixtures, and the real estate. The agreement includes provisions for bulk transfer laws, sales tax, and environmental conditions.

Minutes of the Special Meeting of Shareholders and Directors. This provides evidence that the sale of corporate assets has been properly approved.

Bill of Sale. This form is executed at closing. It contains a covenant not to compete, warranty of title, and the seller's representations.

IRS Form 8594—Asset Acquisition Statement. This allocates the purchase price of a business among the various assets of the business.

IRS Form 4797—Sales of Business Property. This is used to report sales or exchanges of property used in trade or business.

SOLE PROPRIETORSHIP SALES AGREEMENT

AGREEMENT made on this   day of   , 19   , between   d/b/a   , hereinafter referred to as "seller," and   , residing at   , hereinafter referred to as "purchaser."

1. **TERMS OF SALE.** Seller agrees to sell, and purchaser to purchase, the business operated by seller at   , including the equipment, goodwill, customer client list, covenant not to compete and the name "   " as more particularly set forth in Exhibit "A" attached hereto and made a part hereof. The purchase price to be paid by the buyer is $, payable as follows: when the seller signs this contract, a deposit of $ in certified funds to be held in escrow by seller's attorney in his trust account; the balance of $ shall be payable at closing. The allocation of the purchase price shall be determined by purchaser's accountant and set forth in writing as a rider to this agreement. In the event this transaction does not close, or if the purchasers are unable to obtain financing as set forth in paragraph 2 herein, the seller shall retain $ as long as such failure to close is not attributable to material act, admission, breach of representation or warranty by the seller. The books of the business shall be closed as of   .

2. **BANK FINANCING.** Purchaser shall apply for an SBA loan from   Bank in an amount not to exceed $. The mortgage interest rate will not exceed   percent per annum, except that if purchaser accepts a mortgage commitment permitting the rate to be changed prior to closing, or if purchaser's mortgage commitment expires before closing and will be renewed only at a changed interest rate, purchaser will be bound by such change provided such change is to a rate of not more than   percent per annum. If a mortgage commitment for this loan is not received by the purchaser by the   day of   , 19   , either purchaser or seller may cancel this contract by written notice to the other. The same shall apply if the commitment is granted but later canceled without fault of the purchaser.

3. **SELLER FINANCING.** Purchaser shall give seller a promissory note in the amount $, secured by accounts receivable, the equipment listed in Schedule "A," and a collateral mortgage on   , payable as follows: $ monthly, including principal and interest at   percent for   years. There shall be no penalty for prepayment.

4. **CLOSING.** The closing shall take place at the office of the seller's attorney,   , at   , on the   day of   , 19   at   . Upon payment of the portion of the purchase price due to seller, seller shall deliver to purchaser such instruments of transfer as are necessary to transfer to purchaser the business and property referred to in Paragraph 1. Such instruments of transfer shall effectively transfer to purchaser full title to the business and property referred to in Paragraph 1, free of all liens and encumbrances.

5. **REPRESENTATIONS OF SELLER.** Seller represents and warrants that:
   a) All debts and liabilities are the responsibility of the seller until the   of   , 19   .
   b) He is the owner of and has good and marketable title to the property referred to in Paragraph 1, free of all restrictions on transfer or assignment and of all encumbrances.

c) He has to his knowledge operated the business in accordance with all laws, ordinances, and rules relating to the business.

d) No proceedings, judgments, or liens are now pending or threatened against him or against the business.

e) He will, up to the date of closing, operate his business in the usual and ordinary manner and will not enter into any contract except as may be required in the regular course of business.

f) He will duly comply with the provisions of Article 6 of the state Uniform Commercial Code dealing with bulk transfers.

g) The income and expenses for all locations for the years _____, which were provided by seller's attorney to purchaser's attorney, are true, complete, and correct in all material respects.

6. **BOOKS AND RECORDS.** Seller will allow the purchaser, commencing on the date of the execution of this agreement and upon the payment of the deposit as provided in Paragraph 1 hereof, on reasonable notice and without unreasonable interruption to the normal operation of the seller's business, to have access, during normal business hours, to the books and records of _____, all as the purchaser, from time to time, may reasonably request. The seller will make every attempt available to answer all questions of the purchaser as to the conduct of the business of _____ .

7. **NONDISCLOSURE.** During the pendency of this agreement prior to the closing, seller and purchaser agree not to disclose the terms and conditions of this agreement to any other party who does not have a right to know the terms of this agreement. The purchaser further agrees that disclosures to those who have a right to know, such as purchaser's attorneys or accountants, shall be made to them only on a confidential basis and only upon their agreement not to disclose the same to any other party.

8. **COVENANT NOT TO COMPETE.** Seller shall not engage in a business similar to that involved in this transaction in any capacity, directly or indirectly, within the counties of _____ and _____, located in the state of _____, for a period of _____ years from the date of closing.

9. **ASSIGNABILITY.** This agreement is not assignable by the purchaser without the written consent of the seller, except assignment to a corporation to be formed by the purchaser.

10. **RISK OF LOSS.** Seller assumes all risk of destruction, loss, or damage by fire prior to the closing of this transaction. In the event of any such destruction, loss, or damage, purchaser may terminate this agreement.

11. **CONDITIONS PRECEDENT TO PURCHASER'S OBLIGATIONS.** The obligations of purchaser under this agreement are subject to fulfillment of each of the following conditions prior to or at the closing:

a) All proceedings, instruments, and documents required of seller under this agreement shall be reasonably satisfactory in form and in substance to purchaser's counsel.

b) The instruments and conveyances of transfer executed and delivered by seller at the closing shall be valid in accordance with their terms and shall effectively vest in purchaser good and marketable title to the assets and business as contemplated by this agreement, free and clear of any liabilities, obligations, or encumbrances, except those liabilities and obligations expressly assumed by buyer as provided herein.

c) There shall not have been any material breach of the representations or warranties of seller contained in this agreement, and such representations and warranties shall be substantially correct on the closing date, except as affected by transactions contemplated herein and changes occurring in the ordinary course of business.

d) Between the date of execution of this agreement and the closing date, there shall not have been any material adverse change in the business or business prospects of seller.

e) The manner in which seller is conducting his business shall not be in violation of any applicable law or regulation materially affecting the properties, assets, and rights to be sold pursuant to this agreement, and seller shall not be a party to, or be threatened with, any litigation or proceeding relating to any transaction contemplated by this agreement.

f) Income tax returns that are satisfactory to purchaser.

g) Real estate lease satisfactory to purchaser.

h) Franchise agreement satisfactory to purchaser.

i) Assignment of real estate lease and franchise agreement to purchaser.

j) Financial statement—audited by a certified public accountant at seller's expense—satisfactory to purchaser.

k) A list of assets including equipment and inventory satisfactory to purchaser.

l) Seller shall supply to purchaser at seller's expense all permits and certificates required by local, state, and federal regulations, codes, laws, statutes, and ordinances.

12. **SELLER TO ACT AS CONSULTANT.** The seller hereby agrees,   months after the closing date of the sale of   , to act as consultant for a fee of   dollars ($) per month in helping the purchaser to maintain the business relationship with the customers and to give help in any way he can for the continued operation and success of the business. This consultation work can be done in person, by letter, or by telephone. It is not required by the purchaser that the seller be at the location of the business to be acting as said consultant to the business.

13. **ENTIRE AGREEMENT.** This contract of sale with   riders contains the entire agreement between the seller and the buyer, and nothing is binding on either of them that is not contained in this contract. This contract is intended to bind the seller and the purchaser and those who succeed to their interests. This contract supersedes all prior agreements.

14. **SIGNATURES.** Unless all of the persons whose names appear at the beginning of the contract sign it on or before the   day of   , 19   , this contract shall not become effective.

15. **LAW.** This agreement shall be construed in accordance with the laws of the state of   .

_____
(Purchaser)

_____
(Seller)

CORPORATE STOCK SALES AGREEMENT

THIS AGREEMENT, made on   , 19   , between   of   (hereinafter referred to as "W") and   of   (hereinafter referred to as "K").

W agrees to sell to K and K agrees to purchase from W,   shares of   , INC., a corporation incorporated in the State of   (hereinafter referred to as "C") as follows:

1. **PURCHASE PRICE.** The purchase price to be paid by K to W for said   shares shall be   dollars ($) per share for a total purchase price of   dollars ($). K hereby deposits the sum of $.

2. **CLOSING DATE.** The delivery to K of certificates for the shares of C sold hereunder by W and the payment of the initial installment of the purchase price thereof by K to W will be at 10:00 a.m. on   19   (hereinafter referred to as the "closing date") at the offices of   ,   St.,   .

3. **DELIVERY OF CERTIFICATES.** On the closing date, W shall deliver to K the certificates evidencing   shares of C agreed to be sold hereunder duly endorsed for transfer, and K shall pay W the sum of   dollars ($) representing the initial installment of the purchase price to be paid for said shares by K The balance of the purchase price of   dollars ($) will be paid by K to W in the amounts and on or before the dates indicated in Schedule A at which time W shall deliver to K the certificates of shares stated therein.

4. **WARRANTIES.** W warrants, represents, and agrees as follows:

   a) W has full, complete, and absolute title to the   shares of C to be sold pursuant to this agreement.

   b) W's Title to said shares is free and clear of any lien, charge, or encumbrance, and said shares aggregating   shares, constitute all of the outstanding shares of C, and by sale of said shares hereunder, K will receive good and absolute title thereto, free from any liens, charges, or encumbrances.

   c) C is a corporation duly organized and existing under and by virtue of the laws of the State of   and is in good standing under the laws of this state.

   d) Said outstanding shares of said corporation have heretofore duly been issued.

   e) All of the said issued and outstanding shares are valid, fully paid, and no assessment is outstanding against the same or any part thereof.

   f) W is presently the sole officer and director of C.

   g) On   , 19   , C shall have the amount of inventory necessary for the normal operation of a   in accordance with the inventory to be taken on   , 19   . W makes no representations as to the exact dollar amount of inventory to be in existence on   , 19   . The corporation owns no automobiles.

5. Between the signing of the contract and   C will not:

   a) transfer, sell, or otherwise dispose of any corporate property or assets material to the operation of its business other than in the ordinary and usual course of its business as heretofore conducted, except such items as shall have become no longer useful, obsolete, worn out, or rendered of no further use and, if theretofore useful in the conduct of its business and operation, as may have been replaced with other items of substantially the same value and utility as the items transferred, sold, exchanged, or otherwise disposed of;

   b) create, participate in, or agree to the creation of any liens or encumbrances on its corporate property, except liens for current taxes or liens created in the ordinary and usual course of its business as heretofore conducted in connection with normal purchases of food store supplies and food;

   c) enter into any leases, contracts, or agreements of any kind or character or incur any liabilities except those to which it is presently committed and which are disclosed herein or in the exhibits hereto and purchase orders placed for raw materials and supplies and agreements to sell products to customers arising in the ordinary and usual course of business as heretofore conducted;

   d) make any payments or distributions to any of its officers, shareholders, or employees, except dividends, wages, and salaries made to employees in the ordinary and usual course of the business as heretofore conducted including therein contributions pursuant to health, insurance, and pension plans presently in effect;

   e) amend or repeal its articles of incorporation or by-laws nor issue any shares in addition to, and other than, the shares heretofore issued, or reissue any treasury shares; nor

   f) elect any officers or directors without the consent of W.

6. **SUCCESSORS AND ASSIGNS.** The provisions of this agreement shall inure to the benefit of and bind the successors and assigns of K and W and their executors, administrators, heirs, successors, and assigns.

7. **NOTICES.** All notices required or permitted to be given hereunder shall be in writing and shall be sent by first-class mail postage prepaid, deposited in the United States mail, and if intended for W shall be addressed to   Dr.,   , and if intended for K shall be addressed to   Rd.,   . Either party may, by written notice to the other, change the address for notices to be sent to it.

8. **BOOKS AND RECORDS.** During the period from the date of this agreement to the closing date, W shall afford K and her attorneys free access to C's records, files, books of account, and tax returns, provided that K's investigation and use of the same shall not unreasonably interfere with C's normal operation. K agrees not to disclose nor use, at any time, any information concerning C disclosed to or acquired by K in connection with this agreement. K shall take all reasonable precautions to prevent any other persons from acquiring confidential information obtained from C.

9. **LIFE INSURANCE.** K shall pay life insurance premiums on   dollars ($)

   policy on the life of K with proceeds payable in the event of K's death during the term of this agreement

   to W, only to the extent of unpaid purchases of stock with the remainder payable to a person designated

   by K.

10. **LICENSES.** K shall obtain the necessary approvals from the state agency or authority regarding the

    corporate change. K will bear all necessary excuses to obtain same. W shall cooperate in signing any

    necessary papers incident thereto.

    _____

SCHEDULE A

1. The dollar   ($) balance referred to in paragraph #3 of the attached Stock Sales Agreement for the purchase of the shares of stock shall be secured as follows:

   a) A security agreement, promissory note, and UCC filings in the amount of $ to be signed by K personally and prepared by K's attorney granting W a first lien on inventory and equipment of the corporation, and

   b) A nonassumable mortgage against K's residence at   Rd.,   , in the amount of   dollars ($).

2. The above-mentioned note shall:

   a) Be payable as follows: Approximately dollars   ($) monthly, including principal and interest, commencing   , 19   , with the final payment to be made on   , 19   .

   b) Interest shall be paid at the rate of   percent annually on   .

   c) Interest shall be calculated at the rate of   percent annually and a pro-rate proportion of the annual rate shall be paid monthly.

   d) Contain provisions (i) setting a two percent (2%) late penalty for payments made after the 15th day of any month; (ii) requiring the payment by K of W's attorneys' fees in the event of a default by K; (iii) denying the right to prepay the note, in whole or in part.

3. The shares   shall be delivered as follows:

DATE	NUMBER OF SHARES

ASSET PURCHASE AGREEMENT

This Agreement by and between   , a corporation organized and existing pursuant to the laws of the state of   , and   , sole shareholder of said corporation (hereinafter collectively referred to as the "Seller"), and   , as agent of a corporation to be formed, residing at   (hereinafter referred to as the "Buyer");

WITNESSETH

Whereas Seller owns and operates a restaurant business located at   , city/village of   , county of   and state of   , and desires to sell the assets of the business hereinafter listed to the Buyer; and

Whereas the Buyer desires to purchase the assets of said Corporation upon the terms and conditions hereinafter stated; and

Whereas this purchase and sale is limited to the assets hereinafter specifically set forth, and it is the intention of the parties that Buyer shall not assume any liabilities of the Corporation or the individual shareholders.

NOW, THEREFORE, the parties hereto in consideration of the mutual covenants, agreements, and undertakings hereinafter set forth, do hereby agree as follows:

1. Sale of Inventory, Equipment, and Fixtures:

Corporation agrees to sell and Buyer agrees to purchase all of the rights, title, interest, and goodwill of the Corporation in and to the following of its assets of a restaurant business located at   , as follows: (a) $ of inventory. Additional inventory of $ will be paid to Seller at closing at market value. Ordered inventory of $ shall be accepted, modified, or canceled at Buyer's option. (b) The right to use the Seller's name during the year 19   . After 19   , Buyer may use the name   . Seller shall transfer or change names to effect use of name by Buyer. (c) Fixtures and equipment, including the telephone system and fax machine. (d) Goodwill.

2. Leasehold

This Contract is contingent upon Buyer obtaining the landlord's consent for assignment of the lease.

3. Covenant Not to Compete

Seller covenants that after the closing date of this Agreement, he shall not solely or jointly with any other person, firm, or corporation, either directly or indirectly, carry on, engage in, or be interested in any manner in a   business within   County or adjacent counties for a period of   years.

4. Representations by Seller

Seller jointly and severally covenants and represents:

a) That Corporation is the owner of, and has good and marketable title to, all of the assets specifically enumerated in Appendices A and B of this Agreement, free and clear of all debts and encumbrances, and said assets shall be enjoyed by Buyer free and clear of all encumbrances.

b) That Corporation has entered into no contracts related to its business, such as union agreements, other than the utility bills accruing in the ordinary course of business.

c) That there are presently and will be at the time of closing, no liens or security interests against the property and assets being transferred herein.

d) That all of the inventory, equipment, and fixtures to be transferred are now and at the closing date will be located at _____ and will not be removed therefrom without the written consent of the Buyer.

e) Consents. No consent from or other approval of a governmental entity or other person is necessary in connection with the execution of the Agreement or the consummation by Seller of the business of Seller by Buyer in the manner previously conducted by Seller.

f) Inventory. The Inventory is merchantable and fit for intended use and is free of any material defects in workmanship. The finished goods Inventory is of a type, quantity, and quality usable and salable in the ordinary course of business of the Seller.

g) Insurance. Exhibit "C" annexed hereto lists and describes all insurance policies and invoices now in force with respect to the purchased property and the business of the Seller. Buyer has the option to assume the insurance policy subject to insurance company approval.

h) Licenses. Permits and Consents. There are no licenses or permits currently required by the Seller for the operation of the business of the Seller.

i) Litigation. There are no actions, suits, proceedings, or investigations pending or, to the knowledge of the Seller, threatened against or involving Seller or brought by Seller or affecting any of the purchased property at law or in equity or admiralty or before or by any federal, state, municipal, or other governmental department, commission, board, agency, or instrumentality, domestic or foreign, nor has any such action, suit, proceeding, or investigation been pending during the 24-month period preceding the date hereof; and Seller is not operating its business under or subject to, or in default with respect to, any order, writ, injunction, or decree of any court of federal, state, municipal, or governmental department, commission, board, agency, or instrumentality, domestic or foreign.

j) Compliance with Laws. To the best of its knowledge, Seller has complied with and is operating its business in compliance with all laws, regulations, and orders applicable to the business conducted by it, and the present uses by the Seller of the purchased property do not violate any such laws, regulations, and orders. Seller has no knowledge of any material present or future expenditures that will be required with respect to any of Seller's facilities to achieve compliance with any present statute, law, or regulation, including those relating to the environment or occupational health and safety.

k) Disclosure. No representation or warranty by the Seller contained in this Agreement, and no statement contained in any certificate or other instrument furnished or to be furnished to Buyer pursuant hereto, or in connection with the transactions contemplated hereby, contains or will contain any untrue statement of a material fact or omits or will omit to state any material fact that is necessary in order to make the statements contained therein not misleading.

l) Liabilities. Seller has as of the purchase date and shall have on the closing date no liabilities of any kind whatsoever, contingent or otherwise.

m) Environmental Affidavit. Seller will provide an affidavit certifying that there presently is not nor ever has been any dumping or storage of toxic, Superfund, or hazardous wastes on the premises.

5. Sales Tax

Seller shall be responsible for and shall pay all presently due and owing state sales tax due for any inventory or supplies as described herein that were purchased by Seller prior to the closing date hereof. Corporation, prior to the closing date, shall fill out and file all required forms notifying the state taxing authorities of the transfer of assets. Buyer shall pay the Seller the sales tax applicable to the transfer under this Agreement of the fixtures and equipment, inventory, and supplies described herein at closing.

6. Bulk Transfer

The parties have agreed to waive the requirements of the Bulk Transfer provisions of the Uniform Commercial Code (UCC). Seller shall jointly and severally indemnify Buyer against any and all claims made by the creditors of the Corporation. Seller's indemnification, representation, and warranty shall survive the closing of this agreement.

7. Seller Support

Seller shall assist, advise, and instruct Buyer or his agents as to all aspects necessary to properly conduct and manage the property and business for at least _____ weeks, _____ days per week, in person for _____ hours per day and _____ years by telephone.

8. Bills

Seller will provide Buyer with copies of bills for electric, telephone, real estate taxes, garbage removal, and all rental charges for the years _____ .

9. Indemnification Provisions

It is agreed by and between the parties that the Seller shall jointly and severally indemnify and hold Buyer and its assigns harmless from any and all claims of any nature whatsoever, including without limitation:

a. Tort claims;

b. Any creditor claims; and

c. Any claims that may be made hereinafter on account of federal and state franchise taxes, Social Security taxes, sales taxes, unemployment taxes, and all other taxes of whatever nature or form on account of the operation of Corporation ending on and accruing up to the closing date.

d. Any claims for wages, vacation, sick pay, or fringe benefits claimed by Corporation's employees for periods prior to the closing date. Corporation shall furnish Buyer with a list of all Corporation's employees, full- and part-time, their current rate of compensation, and fringe benefits.

10. Allocation of Purchase Price

Inventory	$_____
Equipment	$_____
Land	$_____
Building and Fixtures	$_____
Covenant not to compete	$_____
TOTAL	$_____

11. Covenants of Seller

The Seller covenants with the Buyer as follows:

a. The Bill of Sale to be delivered at the closing date will transfer all the assets enumerated in the attached appendices free and clear of all encumbrances and will contain the usual warranties;

b. The business will be conducted up to the closing date in substantially the same manner as it has been conducted in the past and in accordance with all applicable laws and regulations;

c. The Seller assumes all risk of destruction, loss, or damage due to fire, storm, flood, or other casualty up to the closing date.

12. Conditions Precedent of Buyer

The obligations of the Buyer hereunder are subject to the conditions that on or prior to the closing date:

(a) Representations and Warranties True at Closing. The representations and warranties of the Seller contained in the Agreement or any certificate or document delivered pursuant to the provisions hereof or in connection with the transactions contemplated hereby shall be true on and as of the closing date as though such representations and warranties were made at and as of such date, except if such representations and warranties were made as of a specified date and such representations and warranties shall be true as of such date.

(b) Seller's Compliance with Agreement. The Seller shall have performed and complied with all agreements and conditions required by this Agreement to be performed or complied with by it prior to or at the closing of the Agreement.

(c) Resolutions and Seller's Certificate. The Seller shall have delivered to the Buyer copies of the resolutions of the board of directors of the Seller authorizing the transactions contemplated herein, with such resolutions to be certified to be true and correct by its secretary or assistant secretary, together with a certificate of an officer of the Seller, dated the closing date, certifying in such detail as the Buyer may request to the fulfillment of the conditions specified in subparagraphs (a) and (b) above.

(d) Injunction. On the closing date, there shall be no effective injunction, writ, preliminary restraining order, or any order of any nature issued by a court of competent jurisdiction directing that the transactions provided for herein or any of them not be consummated as herein provided.

(e) Approval of Proceedings. All actions, proceedings, instruments, and documents required to carry out this Agreement, or incidental thereto, and all other related legal matters shall have been approved by counsel for the Buyer.

(f) Casualty. The purchased property or any substantial portion thereof shall not have been adversely affected in any material way as a result of any fire, accident, flood, or other casualty or act of God or the public enemy, nor shall any substantial portion of the purchased property have been stolen, taken by eminent domain, or subject to condemnation. If the closing occurs hereunder despite such casualty as a result of the waiver of this condition by Buyer, the Seller shall assign or pay over to the Buyer the proceeds of any insurance or any condemnation proceeds with respect to any casualty involving the purchased property that occurs after the date hereof.

(g) Adverse Change. There shall have been between the purchase date and the closing date no material adverse change in the assets or liabilities or in the condition, financial or otherwise, or in the business, properties, earnings, or net worth of Seller.

(h) Closing of the real estate Contract.

(i) Purchaser obtaining approval for a $ loan.

(j) Seller's tax returns showing net income of at least

$ for the years   .

13. Closing Date

This Agreement shall be closed and the necessary documents delivered at the office of the clerk of the county of   on   , 19   , or at such other time and place as may be mutually agreed upon, and payment shall be then made. At the closing, the Seller shall deliver to Buyer an appropriate long-form Bill of Sale of the assets specified to be sold and the keys to the premises in return for payment as called for herein. If this transaction shall not close due to any action by Seller, Buyer's deposit shall be returned to Buyer in full, without offset.

14. Miscellaneous

a. This Agreement supersedes all prior agreements between the parties and may not be changed orally.

b. The terms and conditions of the Agreement shall be binding upon the distributees, representatives, successors, and assigns of the respective parties.

c. This Agreement shall be construed pursuant to the laws of the state of   .

d. This Agreement may be executed in two (2) or more counterparts, each of which shall be deemed to be an original and all of which shall constitute a single instrument, and the signature of any party of any counterpart shall be deemed a signature to any and may be appended to any other counterpart.

15. Entire Agreement/Modification

This Agreement contains the entire agreement between the parties hereto with respect to the transactions contemplated herein and no representation, promise, inducement, or statement of intention relating to the transactions contemplated by this Agreement has been made by any party that is not set forth in the Agreement. This Agreement shall not be modified or amended except by an instrument in writing signed by or on behalf of the parties hereto.

16. Financing

Buyer shall supply Seller with financial statements from 19   and 19   . Buyer will sign a personal guarantee of the wrap-around mortgage referred to in the real estate contract. Seller will file UCC liens for the personal property. The said liens will be subordinate to the extent of

to   Bank's UCC liens. Seller will supply Buyer with copies of cancelled checks on a quarterly basis. If Seller is more than 21 days late in providing said canceled checks, Buyer will thereafter have a right to make mortgage payments directly to the lender. Buyer will have the right of offset on Seller's failure to pay the first mortgage.

_____

_____

_____

MINUTES OF THE SPECIAL MEETING OF SHAREHOLDERS AND DIRECTORS

Upon motion duly made, seconded and carried, and upon the authorization of the shareholders of this corporation, the following resolutions were adopted by the affirmative vote of a majority of the directors present at the time of the vote:

RESOLVED, that the President be and (s)he is hereby authorized and empowered to execute, acknowledge, and deliver to   proper bills of sale, transferring to her/him all of the rights, assets, supplies, and property referred to in the asset purchase agreement dated   in consideration of   dollars payable in cash at the time of transfer of title. It is further

RESOLVED, that the signing of these minutes by all stockholders and directors shall constitute full ratification of and waiver of notice of meeting by the signatories.

Dated:

_____

_____

_____

Sanders Legal Publishers
Prudential Bldg.,Buffalo,N.Y. 14202

BILL OF SALE

Know all Men by these Presents, that

of the first part, for and in consideration of the sum of

lawful money of

the United States, to   in hand paid, at or before the ensealing and delivery of these presents, by

of the second part, the receipt whereof is hereby acknowledged, ha   bargained and sold, and by these presents do   grant and convey unto the said part   of the second part,
executors, administrators, successors and assigns,

To have and to hold, the same unto the said part   of the second part,   executors, administrators and assigns forever. And   do   , for   heirs, executors and administrators covenant and agree to and with the said part   of the second part, to **Warrant and Defend** the sale of the said

hereby sold unto the said part   of the second part,   executors, administrators, successors and assigns, against all and every person and persons whomsoever.

In Witness Whereof,   ha   hereunto set   hand   and seal   this   day of
Nineteen Hundred and

In Presence of

_____ LS

_____   _____ LS
Witness

_____   _____ LS
Witness

_____   _____ LS
Witness

Source: Sanders Legal Publishers, Inc. Used with permission.

65

the receipt whereof is hereby acknowledged, and in consideration of the within sale, hereby agree not to re-establish, re-open, be engaged, or in any manner become interested, directly or indirectly, in any business like or similar to the business hereby sold, and not to solicit any of the trade of same. within a radius of square blocks around the premises No.
for a term of years from the date hereof.

In Witness Whereof, have hereunto set hand and seal the day of Nineteen Hundred and

In Presence of

_____ LS

_____ LS

STATE OF NEW YORK
COUNTY OF
        OF   }ss.:

being duly sworn, depose(s) and say(s) that reside at

   That the same person(s) who executed the within bill of sale.
   That the sole and absolute owner(s) of the property described in said bill of sale, and each and every part thereof, and full right to sell and transfer the same.
   That the said property, and each and every part thereof, is free and clear of any and all liens, mortgages, debts and other encumbrances or claims of whatsoever kind or nature.

   That not indebted to anyone and no creditors.
   That there are no judgments existing against , in any Court, nor are there any replevins, attachments, or executions issued against now in force; nor has any petition in bankruptcy been filed by or against
   That this affidavit is made for the purpose and with the intent of inducing

to purchase the property described in said bill of sale, knowing that will rely thereon and pay a good and valuable consideration therefor.

Sworn to before me, this day of 19

Notary Public/Commissioner of Deeds   My Commission expires

STATE OF NEW YORK
COUNTY OF
        OF   }ss.:
  On this day of Nineteen Hundred and
before me, the subscriber, personally appeared

to me personally known and known to me to be the same person(s) described in and who executed the within Instrument, and he executed the same.

Notary Public/Commissioner of Deeds   My Commission expires

BILL OF SALE
WITH AFFIDAVIT

19

19

DATED

FILED

66

(Rev. Jan. 1996)

Department of the Treasury
Internal Revenue Service

Asset Acquisition Statement
Under Section 1060

▶ **Attach to your Federal income tax return.**

OMB No. 1545-1021

Attachment
Sequence No. **61**

Name as shown on return	Identification number as shown on return

Check the box that identifies you: ☐ Buyer   ☐ Seller

Part I   **General Information**—To be completed by all filers.

1 Name of other party to the transaction	Other party's identification number

Address (number, street, and room or suite no.)

City or town, state, and ZIP code

2 Date of sale	3 Total sales price

Part II   **Assets Transferred**—To be completed by all filers of an original statement.

4 Assets	Aggregate Fair Market Value (Actual Amount for Class I)	Allocation of Sales Price
Class I	$	$
Class II	$	$
Class III	$	$
Class IV	$	$
Total	$	$

5   Did the buyer and seller provide for an allocation of the sales price in the sales contract or in another written document signed by both parties? . . . . ☐ Yes ☐ No
If "Yes," are the aggregate fair market values listed for each of asset Classes I, II, III, and IV the amounts agreed upon in your sales contract or in a separate written document? . . . . ☐ Yes ☐ No

6   In connection with the purchase of the group of assets, did the buyer also purchase a license or a covenant not to compete, or enter into a lease agreement, employment contract, management contract, or similar arrangement with the seller (or managers, directors, owners, or employees of the seller)? . . . . ☐ Yes ☐ No
If "Yes," specify (a) the type of agreement, and (b) the maximum amount of consideration (not including interest) paid or to be paid under the agreement. See the instructions for line 6.

For Paperwork Reduction Act Notice, see instructions.

511

Cat. No. 63768Z

Form **8594** (Rev. 1-96)

Part III | **Supplemental Statement**—To be completed only if amending an original statement or previously filed supplemental statement because of an increase or decrease in consideration.

7 Assets	Allocation of Sales Price as Previously Reported	Increase or (Decrease)	Redetermined Allocation of Sales Price
Class I	$	$	$
Class II	$	$	$
Class III	$	$	$
Class IV	$	$	$
Total	$		$

8   Reason(s) for increase or decrease. Attach additional sheets if more space is needed.

_____

_____

_____

_____

_____

_____

_____

_____

_____

9   Tax year and tax return form number with which the original Form 8594 and any supplemental statements were filed.

_____

Paperwork Reduction Act Notice

We ask for the information on this form to carry out the Internal Revenue laws of the United States. You are required to give us the information. We need it to ensure that you are complying with these laws and to allow us to figure and collect the right amount of tax.

The time needed to complete and file this form will vary depending on individual circumstances. The estimated average time is:

Recordkeeping . . . .   8 hr., 5 min.

Learning about the law or the form . . . . 1 hr., 17 min.

Preparing and sending the form to the IRS. . . 1 hr., 29 min.

If you have comments concerning the accuracy of these time estimates or suggestions for making this form simpler, we would be happy to hear from you. You can write to the IRS at the address listed in the instructions for the tax return with which this form is filed.

General Instructions

Section references are to the Internal Revenue Code unless otherwise noted.

A Change To Note

The Revenue Reconciliation Act of 1993 changed the definition of Class IV assets from goodwill and going concern value to amortizable section 197 intangibles. See "Class IV assets" under **Definitions** below.

Purpose of Form

Both the seller and buyer of a group of assets that makes up a trade or business must use Form 8594 to report such a sale if goodwill or going concern value attaches, or could attach, to such assets and if the buyer's basis in the assets is determined only by the amount paid for the assets ("applicable asset acquisition," defined below). Form 8594 must also be filed if the buyer or seller is amending an original or a previously filed supplemental Form 8594 because of an increase or decrease in the buyer's cost of the assets or the amount realized by the seller.

Who Must File

Subject to the exceptions noted below, both the buyer and the seller of the assets must prepare and attach Form 8594 to their Federal income tax returns (Forms 1040, 1041, 1065, 1120, 1120S, etc.).

Exceptions. You are not required to file Form 8594 if any of the following apply:

1. The acquisition is not an applicable asset acquisition (defined below).

2. A group of assets that makes up a trade or business is exchanged for like-kind property in a transaction to which section 1031 applies. However, if section 1031 does not apply to all the assets transferred, Form 8594 is required for the part of the group of assets to which section 1031 does not apply. For information about such a transaction, see Regulations section 1.1060-1T(b)(4).

3. A partnership interest is transferred. See Regulations section 1.755-2T for special reporting requirements.

When To File

Generally, attach Form 8594 to your Federal income tax return for the year in which the sale date occurred. If the amount allocated to any asset is increased or decreased after Form 8594 is filed, the seller and/or buyer (whoever is affected) must complete Part I and the supplemental statement in Part III of a new Form 8594 and attach the form to the Federal tax return for the year in which the increase or decrease is taken into account.

Penalty

If you fail to file a correct Form 8594 by the due date of your return and you cannot show reasonable cause, you may be subject to a penalty. See sections 6721 through 6724.

Definitions

"Applicable asset acquisition" means a transfer of a group of assets that makes up a trade or business in which the buyer's basis in such assets is determined wholly by the amount paid for the assets. An applicable asset acquisition includes both a direct and indirect transfer of a group of assets, such as a sale of a business.

A group of assets makes up a "trade or business" if goodwill or going concern value could under any circumstances attach to such assets. A group of assets could qualify as a trade or business whether or not they qualify as an active trade or business under section 355 (relating to controlled corporations). Factors to consider in making this determination include (a) any excess of the total paid for the assets over the aggregate book value of the assets (other than goodwill or going concern value) as shown in the buyer's financial accounting books and records, or (b) a license, a lease agreement, a covenant not to compete, a management contract, an employment contract, or other similar agreements between buyer and seller (or managers, directors, owners, or employees of the seller).

The buyer's "consideration" is the cost of the assets. The seller's "consideration" is the amount realized.

"Fair market value" is the gross fair market value unreduced by mortgages, liens, pledges, or other liabilities. However, for determining the seller's gain or loss, generally, the fair market value of any property is not less than any nonrecourse debt to which the property is subject.

"Class I assets" are cash, demand deposits, and similar accounts in banks, savings and loan associations and other depository institutions, and other similar items that may be designated in the Internal Revenue Bulletin.

"Class II assets" are certificates of deposit, U.S. Government securities, readily marketable stock or securities, foreign currency, and other items that may be designated in the Internal Revenue Bulletin.

"Class III assets" are all tangible and intangible assets that are not Class I, II, or IV assets. Amortizable section 197 intangibles are Class IV assets. Examples of Class III assets are furniture and fixtures, land, buildings, equipment, and accounts receivable.

"Class IV assets" are amortizable section 197 intangibles, which generally include:

- Goodwill,
- Going concern value,
- Workforce in place,
- Business books and records, operating systems, or any other information base,
- Any patent, copyright, formula, process, design, pattern, know-how, format, or similar item,
- Any customer-based intangible,
- Any supplier-based intangible,
- Any license, permit, or other right granted by a governmental unit,
- Any covenant not to compete entered into in connection with the acquisition of an interest in a trade or a business, and
- Any franchise (other than a sports franchise), trademark, or trade name.

However, the term "section 197 intangible" **does not** include any of the following:

- An interest in a corporation, partnership, trust, or estate,
- Interests under certain financial contracts,
- Interests in land,
- Certain computer software,
- Certain separately acquired interests in films, sound recordings, video tapes, books, or other similar property,
- Certain separately acquired rights to receive tangible property or services,
- Certain separately acquired interests in patents or copyrights,
- Interests under leases of tangible property,

- Interests under indebtedness,
- Professional sports franchises,
- Certain transaction costs.

See section 197(e) for further information.

Allocation of Consideration

An allocation of the purchase price must be made to determine the buyer's basis in each acquired asset and the seller's gain or loss on the transfer of each asset. Use the residual method for the allocation of the sales price among the amortizable section 197 intangibles and other assets transferred. See Regulations section 1.1060-1T(d). The amount allocated to an asset, other than a Class IV asset, cannot exceed its fair market value on the purchase date. The amount you can allocate to an asset also is subject to any applicable limits under the Internal Revenue Code or general principles of tax law. For example, see section 1056 for the basis limitation for player contracts transferred in connection with the sale of a franchise.

Consideration should be allocated as follows: **(a)** reduce the consideration by the amount of Class I assets transferred, **(b)** allocate the remaining consideration to Class II assets in proportion to their fair market values on the purchase date, **(c)** allocate to Class III assets in proportion to their fair market values on the purchase date, and **(d)** allocate to Class IV assets.

Reallocation After an Increase or Decrease in Consideration

If an increase or decrease in consideration that must be taken into account to redetermine the seller's amount realized on the sale, or the buyer's cost basis in the assets, occurs after the purchase date, the seller and/or buyer must allocate the increase or decrease among the assets. If the increase or decrease occurs in the same tax year as the purchase date, consider the increase or decrease to have occurred on the purchase date. If the increase or decrease occurs after the tax year of the purchase date, consider it in the tax year in which it occurs.

For an increase or decrease related to a patent, copyright, etc., see **Specific Allocation** below.

Allocation of Increase

Allocate an increase in consideration as described under **Allocation of Consideration**. If an asset has been

disposed of, depreciated, amortized, or depleted by the buyer before the increase occurs, any amount allocated to such asset by the buyer must be properly taken into account under principles of tax law applicable when part of the cost of an asset (not previously reflected in its basis) is paid after the asset has been disposed of, depreciated, amortized, or depleted.

Allocation of Decrease

Allocate a decrease in consideration as follows: **(a)** reduce the amount previously allocated to Class IV assets, **(b)** reduce the amount previously allocated to Class III assets in proportion to their fair market values on the purchase date, and **(c)** reduce the amount previously allocated to Class II assets in proportion to their fair market values on the purchase date.

You cannot decrease the amount allocated to an asset below zero. If an asset has a basis of zero at the time the decrease is taken into account because it has been disposed of, depreciated, amortized, or depleted by the buyer, the decrease in consideration allocable to such asset must be properly taken into account under principles of tax law applicable when the cost of an asset (previously reflected in basis) is reduced after the asset has been disposed of, depreciated, amortized, or depleted. An asset is considered to have been disposed of to the extent the decrease allocated to it would reduce its basis below zero.

Patents, Copyrights, and Similar Property

You must make a specific allocation (defined below) if an increase or decrease in consideration is the result of a contingency that directly relates to income produced by a particular intangible asset, such as a patent, a secret process, or a copyright, and the increase or decrease is related only to such asset and not to other assets. If the specific allocation rule does not apply, make an allocation of any increase or decrease as you would for any other assets as described under **Allocation of Increase** and **Allocation of Decrease.**

Specific Allocation

Limited to the fair market value of the asset, any increase or decrease in consideration is allocated first specifically to the patent, copyright, or similar property to which the increase or decrease relates, and then to the other assets in the order described under

Allocation of Increase and **Allocation of Decrease.** For purposes of applying the fair market value limit to the patent, copyright, or similar property, the fair market value of such asset is redetermined when the increase or decrease is taken into account by considering only the reasons for the increase or decrease. The fair market values of the other assets are not redetermined.

Specific Instructions

For an original statement, complete Parts I and II. For a Supplemental Statement, complete Parts I and III.

Enter your name and taxpayer identification number (TIN) at the top of the form. Then check the box for buyer or seller.

Part I

Line 1—Enter the name, address, and TIN of the other party to the transaction (buyer or seller). You are required to enter the TIN of the other party. If the other party is an individual or sole proprietor, enter the social security number. If the other party is a corporation, partnership, or other entity, enter the employer identification number.

Line 2—Enter the date on which the sale of the assets occurred.

Line 3—Enter the total consideration transferred for the assets.

Part II

Line 4—For a particular class of assets, enter the total fair market value of all the assets in the class and the total allocation of the sales price.

Line 6—This line must be completed by the buyer and the seller. To determine the maximum consideration to be paid, assume that any contingencies specified in the agreement are met and that the consideration paid is the highest amount possible. If you cannot determine the maximum consideration, state how the consideration will be computed and the payment period.

Part III

Complete Part III and file a new Form 8594 for each year that an increase or decrease in consideration occurs. Give the reason(s) for the increase or decrease in allocation. Also, enter the tax year(s) and form number with which the original and any supplemental statements were filed. For example, enter "1994 Form 1040."

 Printed on recycled paper

1996

**Department of the Treasury
Internal Revenue Service**

Instructions for Form 4797

Sales of Business Property

(Also Involuntary Conversions and Recapture Amounts Under Sections 179 and 280F(b)(2))

Section references are to the Internal Revenue Code unless otherwise noted.

Paperwork Reduction Act Notice

We ask for the information on this form to carry out the Internal Revenue laws of the United States. You are required to give us the information. We need it to ensure that you are complying with these laws and to allow us to figure and collect the right amount of tax.

You are not required to provide the information requested on a form that is subject to the Paperwork Reduction Act unless the form displays a valid OMB control number. Books or records relating to a form or its instructions must be retained as long as their contents may become material in the administration of any Internal Revenue law. Generally, tax returns and return information are confidential, as required by section 6103.

The time needed to complete and file this form will vary depending on individual circumstances. The estimated average time is:

Recordkeeping . . . . . 30 hr., 8 min.

**Learning about the law
or the form** . . . . . . 13 hr., 10 min.

Preparing the form . . . 18 hr., 53 min.

**Copying, assembling, and
sending the form to the IRS** . 1 hr., 20 min.

If you have comments concerning the accuracy of these time estimates or suggestions for making this form simpler, we would be happy to hear from you. See the instructions for the tax return with which this form is filed.

General Instructions

Purpose of Form

Use Form 4797 to report:

● The sale or exchange of property used in your trade or business; depreciable and amortizable property; oil, gas, geothermal, or other mineral properties; and section 126 property.

● The involuntary conversion (from other than casualty or theft) of property used in your trade or business and capital assets held in connection with a trade or business or a transaction entered into for profit.

● The disposition of noncapital assets other than inventory or property held primarily for sale to customers in the ordinary course of your trade or business.

● The recapture of section 179 expense deductions for partners and S corporation shareholders from property dispositions by partnerships and S corporations.

● The computation of recapture amounts under sections 179 and 280F(b)(2), when the business use of section 179 or listed property drops to 50% or less.

Other Forms To Use

● Use **Form 4684,** Casualties and Thefts, to report involuntary conversions from casualties and thefts.

● Use **Form 8824,** Like-Kind Exchanges, for each exchange of qualifying business or investment property for property of a like kind. For exchanges of property used in a trade or business (and other noncapital assets), enter the gain or (loss) from Form 8824, if any, on line 5 or 17.

● If you sold property on which you claimed investment credit, get **Form 4255,** Recapture of Investment Credit, to see if you must recapture some or all of the credit.

Special Rules

Allocation of purchase price.—If you acquire or dispose of assets that constitute a trade or business, the buyer and seller must allocate the total purchase price using the residual method and must file **Form 8594,** Asset Acquisition Statement.

At-risk rules.—If you report a loss on an asset used in an activity for which you are not at risk, in whole or in part, see the instructions for **Form 6198,** At-Risk Limitations. Also, get **Pub. 925,** Passive Activity and At-Risk Rules. Losses from passive activities are first subject to the at-risk rules and then to the passive activity rules.

Installment sales.—If you sold property at a gain and you will receive a payment in a tax year after the year of sale, you generally must report the sale on the installment method unless you elect not to do so.

Use **Form 6252,** Installment Sale Income, to report the sale on the installment method. Also use Form 6252 to report any payment received in 1996 from a sale made in an earlier year that you reported on the installment method.

To elect out of the installment method, report the full amount of the gain on a timely filed return (including extensions).

Get **Pub. 537,** Installment Sales, for more details.

Involuntary conversion of property.—You may not have to pay tax on a gain from an involuntary or compulsory conversion of property. Get **Pub. 544,** Sales and Other Dispositions of Assets, for details.

One-time exclusion on the sale of a home used for business.—If you rented or used part of your home for business and meet the requirements to take the one-time exclusion for persons age 55 or older, you may be able to exclude part or all of the gain figured on line 26. For details on electing the one-time exclusion and allocating the sales price, expenses of sale,

(a) Type of property	(b) Held 1 year or less	(c) Held more than 1 year
1 Depreciable trade or business property:		
a Sold or exchanged at a gain	Part II	Part III (1245, 1250)
b Sold or exchanged at a loss	Part II	Part I
2 Depreciable residential rental property:		
a Sold or exchanged at a gain	Part II	Part III (1250)
b Sold or exchanged at a loss	Part II	Part I
3 Farmland held less than 10 years upon which soil, water, or land clearing expenses were deducted:		
a Sold at a gain	Part II	Part III (1252)
b Sold at a loss	Part II	Part I
4 Disposition of cost-sharing payment property described in section 126	Part II	Part III (1255)
5 Cattle and horses used in a trade or business for draft, breeding, dairy, or sporting purposes:	**Held less than 24 months**	**Held 24 months or more**
a Sold at a gain	Part II	Part III (1245)
b Sold at a loss	Part II	Part I
c Raised cattle and horses sold at a gain	Part II	Part I
6 Livestock other than cattle and horses used in a trade or business for draft, breeding, dairy, or sporting purposes:	**Held less than 12 months**	**Held 12 months or more**
a Sold at a gain	Part II	Part III (1245)
b Sold at a loss	Part II	Part I
c Raised livestock sold at a gain	Part II	Part I

Where To Make First Entry for Certain Items Reported on This Form

Cat. No. 13087T

and the adjusted basis of the home, see the instructions for **Form 2119**, Sale of Your Home.

To report the sale and the one-time exclusion on Form 4797, figure the gain on the part that was rented or used for business in Part III. Do not take the exclusion into account when figuring the gain on line 26, but do take it into account when figuring section 1250 recapture, if any, on line 28g. On line 2 of Part I, write "Section 121 exclusion" and enter the amount of the exclusion in column (g). Complete Part II of Form 2119 and attach it and Form 4797 to your return.

Passive loss limitations.—If you have an overall loss from passive activities, and you report a loss on an asset used in a passive activity, use **Form 8582**, Passive Activity Loss Limitations, to see how much loss is allowed before entering it on Form 4797.

You cannot claim unused passive activity credits when you dispose of your interest in an activity. However, if you dispose of your entire interest in an activity, you may elect to increase the basis of the credit property by the original basis reduction of the property to the extent that the credit has not been allowed because of the passive activity rules. Make the election on **Form 8582-CR**, Passive Activity Credit Limitations, or **Form 8810**, Corporate Passive Activity Loss and Credit Limitations. No basis adjustment may be elected on a partial disposition of your interest in an activity.

Recapture of preproductive expenses.—If you elected out of the uniform capitalization rules of section 263A, any plant that you produce is treated as section 1245 property. For dispositions of plants reportable on Form 4797, enter the recapture amount taxed as ordinary income on line 24 of Form 4797. Get **Pub. 225**, Farmer's Tax Guide, for more details.

Section 197(f)(9)(B)(ii) election.—If you elected under section 197(f)(9)(B)(ii) to recognize gain on the disposition of a section 197 intangible and to pay a tax on that gain at the highest tax rate, include the additional tax on Form 1040, line 38 (or the appropriate line of other income tax returns). On the dotted line next to that line, write "197." The additional tax is the amount that, when added to any other income tax on the gain, equals the gain multiplied by the highest tax rate.

Transfer of appreciated property to political organizations.—Treat a transfer of property to a political organization as a sale of property on the date of transfer if the property's fair market value when transferred is more than your adjusted basis. Apply the ordinary income or capital gains provisions as if a sale had actually occurred. See section 84.

Specific Instructions

To show losses, enclose figures in (parentheses).

Part I

Section 1231 transactions are:

- Sales or exchanges of real or depreciable property used in a trade or business and held for more than 1 year. To figure the holding period, begin counting on the day after you received the property and include the day you disposed of it.

- Cutting of timber that the taxpayer elects to treat as a sale or exchange under section 631(a).

- Disposal of timber with a retained economic interest that is treated as a sale under section 631(b).

- Disposal of coal (including lignite) or domestic iron ore with a retained economic interest that is treated as a sale under section 631(c).

- Sales or exchanges of cattle and horses, regardless of age, used in a trade or business by the taxpayer for draft, breeding, dairy, or sporting purposes and held for 24 months or more from acquisition date.

- Sales or exchanges of livestock other than cattle and horses, regardless of age, used by the taxpayer for draft, breeding, dairy, or sporting purposes and held for 12 months or more from acquisition date.

Note: *Livestock does not include poultry, chickens, turkeys, pigeons, geese, other birds, fish, frogs, reptiles, etc.*

- Sales or exchanges of unharvested crops. See section 1231(b)(4).

- Involuntary conversions of trade or business property or capital assets held more than 1 year in connection with a trade or business or a transaction entered into for profit.

These conversions may result from (a) part or total destruction, (b) theft or seizure, or (c) requisition or condemnation (whether threatened or carried out). If any recognized losses were from involuntary conversions from fire, storm, shipwreck, or other casualty, or from theft, and they exceed the recognized gains from the conversions, do not include them when figuring your net section 1231 losses.

Section 1231 transactions **do not** include sales or exchanges of:

- Inventory or property held primarily for sale to customers.

- Copyrights, literary, musical, or artistic compositions, letters or memoranda, or similar property (a) created by your personal efforts, (b) prepared or produced for you (in the case of letters, memoranda, or similar property), or (c) received from someone who created them or for whom they were created, as mentioned in (a) or (b), in a way that entitled you to the basis of the previous owner (such as by gift).

- U.S. Government publications, including the Congressional Record, that you received from the Government, other than by purchase at the normal sales price, or that you got from someone who had received it in a similar way, if your basis is determined by reference to the previous owner's basis.

Line 9—Nonrecaptured net section 1231 losses.—Part or all of your section 1231 gains on line 8 may be taxed as ordinary income instead of receiving long-term capital gain treatment. These net section 1231 gains are treated as ordinary income to the extent of the "nonrecaptured section 1231 losses." The nonrecaptured losses are net section 1231 losses deducted during the 5 preceding tax years that have not yet been applied against any net section 1231 gain for determining how much gain is ordinary income under these rules.

Example. If you had net section 1231 losses of $4,000 and $6,000 in 1991 and 1992 and net section 1231 gains of $3,000 and $2,000 in 1995 and 1996, line 8 would show the 1996 gain of $2,000, and line 9 would show nonrecaptured net section 1231 losses of $7,000 ($10,000 net section 1231 losses minus the $3,000 that was recaptured because of the 1995 gain). The $2,000 gain on line 8 is all ordinary income and would be entered on line 13 of Form 4797. For recordkeeping purposes, the $4,000 loss from 1991 is all recaptured ($3,000 in 1995 and $1,000 in 1996) and you have $5,000 left to recapture from 1992 ($6,000 minus the $1,000 recaptured this year).

Figuring the prior year losses.—You had a net section 1231 loss if section 1231 losses exceeded section 1231 gains. Gains are included only to the extent taken into account in figuring gross income. Losses are included only

to the extent taken into account in figuring taxable income except that the limitation on capital losses does not apply.

Line 10.—For recordkeeping purposes, if line 10 is zero, the amount on line 8 is the amount of net section 1231 loss recaptured in 1996. If line 10 is more than zero, you have recaptured in 1996 all your net section 1231 losses from prior years.

Part II

If a transaction is not reportable in Part I or Part III and the property is not a capital asset reportable on Schedule D, report the transaction in Part II.

If you receive ordinary income from a sale or other disposition of your interest in a partnership, get **Pub. 541**, Partnerships.

Line 11.—Report other ordinary gains and losses, including property held 1 year or less, on this line.

Section 1244 (small business) stock.—Individuals report ordinary losses from the sale or exchange (including worthlessness) of section 1244 (small business) stock on line 11.

To qualify as section 1244 stock, all of the following requirements must be met:

1. You acquired the stock after June 30, 1958, upon original issuance from a domestic corporation (or the stock was acquired by a partnership in which you were a partner continuously from the date the stock was issued until the time of the loss).

2. If the stock was issued before November 7, 1978, it was issued under a written plan that met the requirements of Regulations section 1.1244(c)-1(f), and when that plan was adopted, the corporation was treated as a small business corporation under Regulations section 1.1244(c)-2(c).

3. If the stock was issued after November 6, 1978, the corporation was treated as a small business corporation, at the time the stock was issued, under Regulations section 1.1244(c)-2(b). To be treated as a small business corporation, the total amount of money and other property received by the corporation for its stock as a contribution to capital and paid-in surplus generally may not exceed $1 million.

4. The stock was issued for money or other property (excluding stock or securities).

5. The corporation, for its 5 most recent tax years ending before the loss, derived more than 50% of its gross receipts from sources **other than** royalties, rents, dividends, interest, annuities, and gains from sales and exchanges of stocks or securities. (If the corporation was in existence for at least 1 tax year but fewer than 5 tax years ending before the loss, the 50% test applies for the tax years ending before the loss. If the corporation was not in existence for at least 1 tax year ending before the loss, the 50% test applies for the entire period ending before the loss.) However, the 50% test does not apply if the corporation's deductions (other than the net operating loss and dividends-received deductions) exceeded its gross income during that period.

6. If the stock was issued before July 19, 1984, it must have been common stock.

The maximum amount that may be treated as an ordinary loss is $50,000 ($100,000 if married filing jointly). Special rules may limit the amount of your ordinary loss if (a) you received section 1244 stock in exchange for property with a basis in excess of its fair market value or (b) your stock basis increased from contributions to capital or otherwise. See **Pub. 550**, Investment Income and Expenses, for more details. Report on Schedule D losses in excess of the maximum amount that may be treated as an ordinary loss (and gains from the sale or exchange of section 1244 stock).

Keep adequate records to distinguish section 1244 stock from any other stock owned in the same corporation.

Line 18.—Enter any recapture of section 179 expense deduction included on Schedule K-1 (Form 1065), line 25, and on Schedule K-1 (Form 1120S), line 23, but only if it is due to a disposition. Include it only to the extent that you took a deduction for it in an earlier year. See instructions for Part IV if you have section 179 recapture when the business use percentage of the property dropped to 50% or less.

Line 20b(1).—You must complete this line if there is a gain on Form 4797, line 3; a loss on Form 4797, line 12; **and** a loss on Form 4684, line 35, column (b)(ii). Enter on this line and on Schedule A (Form 1040), line 22, the **smaller** of the loss on Form 4797, line 12; or the loss on Form 4684, line 35, column (b)(ii). To figure which loss is smaller, treat both losses as positive numbers.

Part III

Generally, **do not** complete Part III for property held 1 year or less; use Part II instead. For exceptions, see the chart on page 1.

Part III is used to figure recapture of depreciation and certain other items that must be reported as ordinary income on the disposition of property. Fill out lines 21 through 26 to determine the gain on the disposition of the property. If you have more than four properties to report, use additional forms. For more details on depreciation recapture, see Pub. 544.

Note: If the property was sold on the installment sale basis, see the Instructions for Form 6252 before completing this part. Also, if you have both installment sales and noninstallment sales, you may want to use a separate Form 4797, Part III, for each installment sale and one Form 4797, Part III, for the noninstallment sales.

Line 22.—The gross sales price includes money, the fair market value of other property received, and any existing mortgage or other debt the buyer assumes or takes the property subject to. For casualty or theft gains, include insurance or other reimbursement you received or expect to receive for each item. Include on this line your insurance coverage, whether or not you are submitting a claim for reimbursement.

For section 1255 property disposed of in a sale, exchange, or involuntary conversion, enter the amount realized. For section 1255 property disposed of in any other way, enter the fair market value.

Line 23.—Reduce the cost or other basis of the property by the amount of any qualified electric vehicle credit, diesel-powered highway vehicle credit, enhanced oil recovery credit, or disabled access credit.

However, **do not** reduce the cost or other basis on this line by any of the following amounts:

1. Deductions allowed or allowable for depreciation, amortization, depletion, or preproductive expenses;

2. The section 179 expense deduction;

3. The downward basis adjustment under section 50(c) (or the corresponding provision of prior law);

4. The deduction for qualified clean-fuel vehicle property or refueling property; or

5. Deductions claimed under section 190, 193, or 1253(d)(2) or (3) (as in effect before the enactment of P.L. 103-66).

Instead, include these amounts on line 24. They will be used to determine the property's adjusted basis on line 25.

Increase the cost or other basis by any qualified electric vehicle credit recapture amount.

Line 24.—For a taxpayer other than a partnership or an S corporation, complete the following steps to figure the amount to enter on line 24:

Step 1.—**Add** the following amounts:

1. Deductions allowed or allowable for depreciation, amortization, depletion, or preproductive expenses;

2. The section 179 expense deduction;

3. The downward basis adjustment under section 50(c) (or the corresponding provision of prior law);

4. The deduction for qualified clean-fuel vehicle property or refueling property; and

5. Deductions claimed under section 190, 193, or 1253(d)(2) or (3) (as in effect before the enactment of P.L. 103-66).

Step 2.—From the step 1 total, **subtract** the following amounts:

1. Any investment credit recapture amount if the basis of the property was reduced for the tax year the property was placed in service under section 50(c)(1) (or the corresponding provision of prior law). See section 50(c)(2) (or the corresponding provision of prior law).

2. Any section 179 or 280F(b)(2) recapture amount included in gross income in a prior tax year because the business use of the property dropped to 50% or less.

3. Any qualified clean-fuel vehicle property or refueling property deduction you were required to recapture because the property ceased to be eligible for the deduction.

You may have to include depreciation allowed or allowable on another asset (and refigure the basis amount for line 23) if you use its adjusted basis in determining the adjusted basis of the property described on line 21. An example is property acquired by a trade-in. See Regulations section 1.1245-2(a)(4).

Partnerships should enter the deductions allowed or allowable for depreciation, amortization, or depletion on line 24. Enter the section 179 expense deduction on Form 1065, Schedule K, line 24. Partnerships should make the basis adjustment required under section 50(c) (or the corresponding provision of prior law). Partners adjust the basis of their interest in the partnership to take into account the basis adjustments made at the partnership level.

S corporations should enter the deductions allowed or allowable for depreciation, amortization, or depletion on line 24. Enter the section 179 expense deduction on Form 1120S, Schedule K, line 21, but only if the corporation disposed of property acquired in a tax year beginning after 1982. S corporations should make the basis adjustment required under section 50(c) (or the corresponding provision of prior law). Shareholders adjust the basis in their stock in the corporation to take into account the basis adjustments made at the S corporation level under section 50(c) (or the corresponding provision of prior law).

Line 25.—For section 1255 property, enter the adjusted basis of the section 126 property disposed of.

Line 27—Section 1245 property.—Section 1245 property is depreciable (or amortizable under

section 185 (repealed), 197, or 1253(d)(2) or (3) (as in effect before the enactment of P.L. 103-66)) and is one of the following:

● Personal property.

● Elevators and escalators placed in service before 1987.

● Real property (other than property described under tangible real property below) subject to amortization or deductions under section 169, 179, 185 (repealed), 188 (repealed), 190, 193, or 194.

● Tangible real property (except buildings and their structural components) if it is used in any of the following ways:

1. As an integral part of manufacturing, production, extraction, or furnishing transportation, communications, or certain public utility services.

2. As a research facility in these activities.

3. For the bulk storage of fungible commodities (including commodities in a liquid or gaseous state) used in these activities.

● A single purpose agricultural or horticultural structure (as defined in section 168(i)(13)).

● A storage facility (not including a building or its structural components) used in connection with the distribution of petroleum or any primary petroleum product.

● Any railroad grading or tunnel bore (as defined in section 168(e)(4)).

See section 1245(b) for exceptions and limits involving:

● Gifts.

● Transfers at death.

● Certain tax-free transactions.

● Certain like-kind exchanges, involuntary conversions, etc.

● Exchanges to comply with SEC orders.

● Property distributed by a partnership to a partner.

● Transfers to tax-exempt organizations where the property will be used in an unrelated business.

● Timber property.

See the following sections for special rules:

● Section 1245(a)(4) for player contracts and section 1056(c) for information required from the transferor of a franchise of any sports enterprise if the sale or exchange involves the transfer of player contracts.

● Section 1245(a)(5) (repealed) for property placed in service before 1987, when only a portion of a building is section 1245 recovery property.

● Section 1245(a)(6) (repealed) for qualified leased property placed in service before 1987.

Line 28—Section 1250 property.—Section 1250 property is depreciable real property (other than section 1245 property). Section 1250 recapture applies when an accelerated depreciation method was used.

Section 1250 recapture does not apply to dispositions of the following property placed in service after 1986 (or after July 31, 1986, if elected):

1. 27.5-year (or 40-year, if elected) residential rental property.

2. 22-, 31.5-, or 39-year (or 40-year, if elected) nonresidential real property.

● Real property depreciable under ACRS (pre-1987 rules) is subject to recapture under section 1245, except for the following, which are treated as section 1250 property:

- 15-, 18-, or 19-year real property and low-income housing that is residential rental property.

- 15-, 18-, or 19-year real property and low-income housing that is used mostly outside the United States.

- 15-, 18-, or 19-year real property and low-income housing for which a straight line election was made.

- Low-income rental housing described in clause (i), (ii), (iii), or (iv) of section 1250(a)(1)(B). See instructions for line 28b.

See section 1250(d) for exceptions and limits involving:

- Gifts.
- Transfers at death.
- Certain tax-free transactions.
- Certain like-kind exchanges, involuntary conversions, etc.
- Exchanges to comply with SEC orders.
- Property distributed by a partnership to a partner.
- Disposition of a main home.
- Disposition of qualified low-income housing.
- Transfers of property to tax-exempt organizations where the property will be used in an unrelated business.
- Dispositions of property as a result of foreclosure proceedings.

Special rules:

- For additional depreciation attributable to rehabilitation expenditures, see section 1250(b)(4).

- If substantial improvements have been made, see section 1250(f).

Line 28a.—Enter the additional depreciation for the period after 1975. **Additional depreciation** is the excess of actual depreciation over depreciation figured using the straight line method. For this purpose, do not reduce the basis under section 50(c)(1) (or the corresponding provision of prior law) in figuring straight line depreciation.

Line 28b.—Use 100% as the percentage for this line, except for low-income rental housing described in clause (i), (ii), (iii), or (iv) of section 1250(a)(1)(B). For this type of low-income rental housing, see section 1250(a)(1)(B) for the percentage to use.

Line 28d.—Enter the additional depreciation after 1969 and before 1976. If straight line depreciation exceeds the actual depreciation for the period after 1975, reduce line 28d by the excess. Do not enter less than zero on line 28d.

Line 28f—Corporations subject to section 291.—The amount treated as ordinary income under section 291 is 20% of the excess, if any, of the amount that would be treated as ordinary income if such property were section 1245 property, over the amount treated as ordinary income under section 1250. If you used the straight line method of depreciation, the ordinary income under section 291 is 20% of the amount figured under section 1245.

Line 29—Section 1252 property.— Partnerships should skip this section. Partners should enter on the applicable lines of Part III amounts subject to section 1252 according to instructions from the partnership.

You may have ordinary income on the disposition of certain farmland held more than 1 year but less than 10 years.

Refer to section 1252 to determine if there is ordinary income on the disposition of certain farmland for which deductions were allowed under sections 175 (soil and water conservation) and 182 (land clearing) (repealed). Skip line 29 if you dispose of such farmland during the 10th or later year after you acquired it.

Gain from disposition of certain farmland is subject to ordinary income rules under section 1252 before being considered under section 1231 (Part I).

When filling out line 29b, enter 100% of line 29a on line 29b, except as follows:

- 80% if the farmland was disposed of within the 6th year after it was acquired.
- 60% if disposed of within the 7th year.
- 40% if disposed of within the 8th year.
- 20% if disposed of within the 9th year.

Line 30—Section 1254 property.—If you had a gain on the disposition of oil, gas, or geothermal property placed in service before 1987, you must treat all or part of the gain as ordinary income. Include on line 24 of Form 4797 any depletion allowed (or allowable) in determining the adjusted basis of the property.

If you had a gain on the disposition of oil, gas, geothermal, or other mineral properties (section 1254 property) placed in service after 1986, you must recapture all expenses that were deducted as intangible drilling costs, depletion, mine exploration costs, and development costs, under sections 263, 616, and 617.

Exception. Property placed in service after 1986 and acquired under a written contract entered into before September 26, 1985, and binding at all times thereafter is treated as placed in service before 1987.

Note: *In the case of a corporation that is an integrated oil company, amounts amortized under section 291(b)(2) are treated as a deduction under section 263(c) when completing line 30a.*

Line 30a.—If the property was placed in service before 1987, enter the total expenses after 1975 that:

- Were deducted by the taxpayer or any other person as intangible drilling and development costs under section 263(c). (Previously expensed mining costs that have been included in income upon reaching the producing state are not taken into account in determining recapture.); and

- Would have been reflected in the adjusted basis of the property if they had not been deducted.

If the property was placed in service after 1986, enter the total expenses that:

- Were deducted under section 263, 616, or 617 by the taxpayer or any other person; and

- Which, but for such deduction, would have been included in the basis of the property; plus

- The deduction under section 611 that reduced the adjusted basis of such property.

If you disposed of a portion of section 1254 property or an undivided interest in it, see section 1254(a)(2).

Line 31.—Section 1255 property.—

Line 31a.—Use 100% if the property is disposed of less than 10 years after receipt of payments excluded from income. Use 100% minus 10% for each year, or part of a year, that the property was held over 10 years after receipt of the excluded payments. Use zero if 20 years or more.

Line 31b.—If any part of the gain shown on line 26 is treated as ordinary income under sections 1231 through 1254 (e.g., section 1252), enter the smaller of **(a)** line 26 reduced by the part of the gain treated as ordinary income under the other provision or **(b)** line 31a.

Part IV

Section 179 property—column (a).—If you took a section 179 expense deduction for property placed in service after 1986 (other than listed property, as defined in section 280F(d)(4)), and the business use of the property was reduced to 50% or less this year, complete column (a) of lines 35 through 37 to figure the recapture amount.

Listed property—column (b).—If you have listed property that you placed in service in a prior year and the business use dropped to 50% or less this year, figure the amount to be recaptured under section 280F(b)(2). Complete column (b), lines 35 through 37. Get **Pub. 463,** Travel, Entertainment, Gift, and Car Expenses, for more details on recapture of excess depreciation.

Note: *If you have more than one property subject to the recapture rules, use separate statements to figure the recapture amounts and attach the statements to your tax return.*

Line 35.—In column (a), enter the section 179 expense deduction claimed when the property was placed in service. In column (b), enter the depreciation allowable on the property in prior tax years. Include any section 179 expense deduction you took as depreciation.

Line 36.—In column (a), enter the depreciation that would have been allowable on the section 179 amount from the year it was placed in service through the current year. Get **Pub. 946,** How To Depreciate Property. In column (b), enter the depreciation that would have been allowable if the property had not been used more than 50% in a qualified business. Figure the depreciation from the year it was placed in service until the current year. See Pub. 463 and Pub. 946.

Line 37.—Subtract line 36 from line 35 and enter the recapture amount as "other income" on the same form or schedule on which you took the deduction. For example, if you took the deduction on Schedule C (Form 1040), report the recapture amount as other income on Schedule C (Form 1040).

Note: *If you filed Schedule C or F (Form 1040) and the property was used in both your trade or business and for the production of income, the portion attributable to your trade or business is subject to self-employment tax. Allocate the amount on line 37 before entering the recapture amount on the appropriate schedule.*

Be sure to increase the basis of the property by the recapture amount.

Printed on recycled paper

*U.S.GPO:1996-407-383

Form **4797**	**Sales of Business Property**	OMB No. 1545-0184
Department of the Treasury Internal Revenue Service	(Also Involuntary Conversions and Recapture Amounts Under Sections 179 and 280F(b)(2)) ▶ Attach to your tax return. ▶ See separate instructions.	19**96** Attachment Sequence No. **27**

Name(s) shown on return	Identifying number

1 Enter here the gross proceeds from the sale or exchange of real estate reported to you for 1996 on Form(s) 1099-S (or a substitute statement) that you will be including on line 2, 11, or 22 . . . . | **1** |

Part I — Sales or Exchanges of Property Used in a Trade or Business and Involuntary Conversions From Other Than Casualty or Theft—Property Held More Than 1 Year

(a) Description of property	**(b)** Date acquired (mo., day, yr.)	**(c)** Date sold (mo., day, yr.)	**(d)** Gross sales price	**(e)** Depreciation allowed or allowable since acquisition	**(f)** Cost or other basis, plus improvements and expense of sale	**(g)** LOSS If (f) is more than (d) plus (e), subtract the sum of (d) and (e) from (f)	**(h)** GAIN If (d) plus (e) is more than (f), subtract (f) from the sum of (d) and (e)
2							

3 Gain, if any, from Form 4684, line 39 . . . . | **3** | | |

4 Section 1231 gain from installment sales from Form 6252, line 26 or 37 . . . . | **4** | | |

5 Section 1231 gain or (loss) from like-kind exchanges from Form 8824 . . . . | **5** | | |

6 Gain, if any, from line 34, from other than casualty or theft . . . . | **6** | | |

7 Add lines 2 through 6 in columns (g) and (h) . . . . | **7** | ( ) | |

8 Combine columns (g) and (h) of line 7. Enter gain or (loss) here, and on the appropriate line as follows: . . . . | **8** | | |

Partnerships—Enter the gain or (loss) on Form 1065, Schedule K, line 6. Skip lines 9, 10, 12, and 13 below.

S corporations—Report the gain or (loss) following the instructions for Form 1120S, Schedule K, lines 5 and 6. Skip lines 9, 10, 12, and 13 below, unless line 8 is a gain and the S corporation is subject to the capital gains tax.

All others—If line 8 is zero or a loss, enter the amount on line 12 below and skip lines 9 and 10. If line 8 is a gain and you did not have any prior year section 1231 losses, or they were recaptured in an earlier year, enter the gain as a long-term capital gain on Schedule D and skip lines 9, 10, and 13 below.

9 Nonrecaptured net section 1231 losses from prior years (see instructions) . . . . | **9** | |

10 Subtract line 9 from line 8. If zero or less, enter -0-. Also enter on the appropriate line as follows (see instructions): | **10** | |

S corporations—Enter this amount on Schedule D (Form 1120S), line 13, and skip lines 12 and 13 below.

All others—If line 10 is zero, enter the amount from line 8 on line 13 below. If line 10 is more than zero, enter the amount from line 9 on line 13 below, and enter the amount from line 10 as a long-term capital gain on Schedule D.

Part II — Ordinary Gains and Losses

11 Ordinary gains and losses not included on lines 12 through 18 (include property held 1 year or less):

12 Loss, if any, from line 8 . . . . | **12** | | |

13 Gain, if any, from line 8, or amount from line 9 if applicable . . . . | **13** | | |

14 Gain, if any, from line 33 . . . . | **14** | | |

15 Net gain or (loss) from Form 4684, lines 31 and 38a . . . . | **15** | | |

16 Ordinary gain from installment sales from Form 6252, line 25 or 36 . . . . | **16** | | |

17 Ordinary gain or (loss) from like-kind exchanges from Form 8824 . . . . | **17** | | |

18 Recapture of section 179 expense deduction for partners and S corporation shareholders from property dispositions by partnerships and S corporations (see instructions) . . . . . | **18** | | |

19 Add lines 11 through 18 in columns (g) and (h) . . . . | **19** | ( ) | |

20 Combine columns (g) and (h) of line 19. Enter gain or (loss) here, and on the appropriate line as follows: . . . . | **20** | | |

a For all except individual returns: Enter the gain or (loss) from line 20 on the return being filed.

b For individual returns:

(1) If the loss on line 12 includes a loss from Form 4684, line 35, column (b)(ii), enter that part of the loss here and on line 22 of Schedule A (Form 1040). Identify as from "Form 4797, line 20b(1)." See instructions . . . . | **20b(1)** | |

(2) Redetermine the gain or (loss) on line 20, excluding the loss, if any, on line 20b(1). Enter here and on Form 1040, line 14 . | **20b(2)** | |

For Paperwork Reduction Act Notice, see page 1 of separate instructions.   Cat. No. 13086I   Form **4797** (1996)

Part III Gain From Disposition of Property Under Sections 1245, 1250, 1252, 1254, and 1255

21	(a) Description of section 1245, 1250, 1252, 1254, or 1255 property:		**(b) Date acquired** (mo., day, yr.)	**(c) Date sold** (mo., day, yr.)
A				
B				
C				
D				

	Relate lines 21A through 21D to these columns ▶		Property A	Property B	Property C	Property D
22	Gross sales price (**Note:** *See line 1 before completing.*)	**22**				
23	Cost or other basis plus expense of sale	**23**				
24	Depreciation (or depletion) allowed or allowable	**24**				
25	Adjusted basis. Subtract line 24 from line 23	**25**				
26	Total gain. Subtract line 25 from line 22	**26**				
27	**If section 1245 property:**					
a	Depreciation allowed or allowable from line 24	**27a**				
b	Enter the **smaller** of line 26 or 27a	**27b**				
28	**If section 1250 property:** If straight line depreciation was used, enter -0- on line 28g, except for a corporation subject to section 291.					
a	Additional depreciation after 1975 (see instructions)	**28a**				
b	Applicable percentage multiplied by the **smaller** of line 26 or line 28a (see instructions)	**28b**				
c	Subtract line 28a from line 26. If residential rental property or line 26 is not more than line 28a, skip lines 28d and 28e	**28c**				
d	Additional depreciation after 1969 and before 1976	**28d**				
e	Enter the **smaller** of line 28c or 28d	**28e**				
f	Section 291 amount (corporations only)	**28f**				
g	Add lines 28b, 28e, and 28f	**28g**				
29	**If section 1252 property:** Skip this section if you did not dispose of farmland or if this form is being completed for a partnership.					
a	Soil, water, and land clearing expenses	**29a**				
b	Line 29a multiplied by applicable percentage (see instructions)	**29b**				
c	Enter the **smaller** of line 26 or 29b	**29c**				
30	**If section 1254 property:**					
a	Intangible drilling and development costs, expenditures for development of mines and other natural deposits, and mining exploration costs (see instructions)	**30a**				
b	Enter the **smaller** of line 26 or 30a	**30b**				
31	**If section 1255 property:**					
a	Applicable percentage of payments excluded from income under section 126 (see instructions)	**31a**				
b	Enter the **smaller** of line 26 or 31a (see instructions)	**31b**				

Summary of Part III Gains. Complete property columns A through D through line 31b before going to line 32.

32	Total gains for all properties. Add property columns A through D, line 26	**32**	
33	Add property columns A through D, lines 27b, 28g, 29c, 30b, and 31b. Enter here and on line 14	**33**	
34	Subtract line 33 from line 32. Enter the portion from casualty or theft on Form 4684, line 33. Enter the portion from other than casualty or theft on Form 4797, line 6	**34**	

Part IV Recapture Amounts Under Sections 179 and 280F(b)(2) When Business Use Drops to 50% or Less
See instructions.

			(a) Section 179	**(b) Section 280F(b)(2)**
35	Section 179 expense deduction or depreciation allowable in prior years	**35**		
36	Recomputed depreciation. See instructions	**36**		
37	Recapture amount. Subtract line 36 from line 35. See the instructions for where to report	**37**		

★ U.S. GOVERNMENT PRINTING OFFICE: 1996-407-382

♲ *Printed on recycled paper*

6

Franchises

With the proper guidance of the franchisor, a franchise can be very lucrative. However, you should exercise extreme caution. Do not rely on federal and state regulation alone. Never accept the terms of the franchise contract as being written in stone.

THE PERILS AND PITFALLS OF FRANCHISES

"High income and independence," "success," "huge profits" are the promises made in many franchise advertisements in the business opportunities sections of newspapers and magazines. These promises are the usual starting point of the sometimes risky and financially devastating relationship of the franchisor and franchisee.

Franchises are undergoing rapid growth. Nearly one-third of all retail sales in the United States are conducted from franchise locations.

Franchising is neither an industry nor a business but a method of doing business and marketing a product and/or service. The greatest attractions of franchising are the promised assistance that the franchisor will provide in getting a new business organized—and the franchisor's goodwill and advice.

The rights and obligations of the franchisor and franchisee are spelled out in the franchise agreement. The franchisor grants the franchisee the right and the license, known as a *franchise,* which is a contractually limited use of its trademark, logo, goodwill, and marketing know-how, including the use of trade secrets and copyrights, access to systemwide promotion, standardized marketing and operating procedures, product and service research, and group purchasing power. This is known as the *entire business format franchise.* Typically, it is used in fast-food restaurants and car rentals.

The other type of franchise is a *product distribution arrangement,* in which there is a distribution system for a specific product, such as bicycles, appliances, or cosmetics, under the manufacturer's name and trademark.

Keep in mind that no matter how hard you work at your franchise, your right to operate the business is fixed for the time period specified in the franchise agreement. You may have no right to share in the goodwill that has been created by your efforts.

The franchisor's potential for profit and exploitation is enormous. The payment of a substantial franchise fee and the uncertainties, delays, and expense of litigation provide the franchisor with tremendous leverage in dealing with the franchisee. To adequately protect yourself as a potential franchisee, you should obtain the aid of a professional to investigate the nature and characteristics of a particular franchise operation; all of the costs of the franchise; the availability of financing; the prospective returns; the training, experience, and work involved; and you should compare these factors with competitive operations.

	Franchise Business	*Independent Business*
Initial investment	Franchise fee plus costs of furnishing, equipping, staffing, and stocking. (Economies of scale may ease start-up costs.)	No franchise fee. All other costs the same.
Form of business organization	Franchise agreement may restrict the form of business to sole proprietorship, give the franchisor veto over partners in a partnership, or restrict stock ownership in a corporation.	Free to choose any form of organization and select any partner or shareholder.
Trademark and trade names	Licensed to use the franchisor's trademark, which may have wide consumer acceptance.	Develop and register own names and trademarks and build consumer acceptance through own efforts.
Knowledge and experience necessary	Usually none. Franchisor provides training and advice regarding location, operating procedures, and bookkeeping forms.	Entrepreneur must be competent to make sound business decisions regarding location, operations, and bookkeeping.
Inventory	Must be purchased from a franchisor or approved sources.	May determine own source of supply.
Equipment and supplies	May be required to purchase from franchisor or approved sources.	Determines own source of supply.
Goods or services offered	Merchandise is restricted.	Free to choose.
Location of business	Restricted to a particular area. Franchisor's permission is necessary to move or open second location.	Free to choose; may expand at will.
Risk	Profit reduced by royalties and other payments to franchisor, but use of known name, pretested product, and simplified procedures may enhance volume. Franchisee bears risk of loss, including loss of franchise.	Profit depends on own efforts and judgment.
Transferability	Restricts assignment to anyone other than franchisor.	Free to sell, donate, or leave by will.

A FRANCHISE VERSUS THE INDEPENDENT BUSINESS

Are you trying to decide between buying a franchise or operating as an independent business? The chart on page 78 compares the two types of businesses. The independent business offers freedom of choice, but the franchise offers the security of working with a known product or service and the guidance of the franchisor. This chart should be read with the assumption that the franchisor operates a successful operation that has gained consumer respect and awareness.

FRANCHISEE'S CHECKLIST

Investigate the following before signing a contract or paying any money:

1. Your suitability for the type of business
   - Are you truly interested in this type of enterprise?
   - Do you have the training, experience, or aptitude necessary to run this type of business?
   - Are you prepared for hard work and financial risk?
   - Are you able to manage others?

2. The product or service
   - Is the product or service stable or seasonable, new or nearly obsolete?
   - Is it a proven product or service, and is there a market for it?
   - Are there products or services in competition with it?
   - Are there government regulations or restrictions on the use of the product?
   - Does the product come with warranties or guarantees?
   - Does the product and/or its suppliers have a good reputation?

3. Attendance at trade shows
   - The International Franchise Association sponsors shows throughout the country and carefully screens the exhibitors. It publishes *The Franchise Opportunities Guide,* which contains basic information on more than 2,400 franchise companies. The book can be ordered by calling 800-543-1038. The *Franchise Opportunities Handbook* can be obtained from the U.S. Department of Commerce by calling 202-783-3238.

4. The Franchisor
   - Who are the franchisor's directors, officers, or general partners?
   - What are the business backgrounds of the directors, officers, and partners? Do they have any criminal convictions, civil judgments, or administrative orders?
   - What is the business and franchising experience of the franchisor? How long has it been in business?
   - Is your fee being used to promote the franchisor, or does the franchisor have an established reputation in your locality?
   - Is the franchisor experienced, successful, financially and managerially strong, and reputable in its industry?
   - Is the company public or private?
   - Is the company a subsidiary of a larger company?

5. Services provided by the franchisor
   - What goods, training programs, supervision, advertising, and other services will the franchisor provide?
   - Does the franchisor offer ongoing support? If so, is such support mandatory? How much will it cost?
   - Will the franchisor periodically visit the franchise and provide site-specific comments (display of merchandise, signage, cleanliness of site, appearance of employees, etc.)?
   - What is the nature, extent, and duration of training?
   - What are the costs of training?
   - Is the training of your employees included in any training costs or allowances?
   - Is there a continuing training program?

6. Fees
   - What is the initial license fee? Is it payable in a lump sum or in installments with interest? Is it refundable?
   - Does the initial license fee include the use of the current operation manual, training, and start-up aid?
   - Is the franchisor's license fee competitive with the fee required by competitive franchisors?
   - Are there periodic royalties? How much are they? How are they determined?
   - Are there fees and charges for advertising and promotion?
   - Are there any other hidden costs (accounting fees, lease location expenses, construction supervision fees, etc.)?
   - Will you be indirectly providing the franchisor with other sources of reve-

nue, such as rebates from suppliers for arranging for bulk purchases or rent received as landlord or sublessor of your franchise location?

- Are any of the fees refundable?
- What is the total investment?

7. Premises
   - Are you required to purchase or rent the business premises?
   - Who finds the site for the business premises?
   - What are your costs as a purchaser or lessor?
   - If purchased, how is the site to be financed?

8. Other franchisees
   - How many outlets are currently operating?
   - How many operating franchises will be sold in the coming year?
   - Of the total number of franchises licensed by the franchisor, how many are still in business? How many have failed?
   - Ask other franchisees about the support and training they have received from the franchisor.
   - Ask other franchisees whether the franchisor requires its franchisee to buy costly products and supplies, whether they need them or not.
   - Ask franchisees about sales performance, profitability, and the return on their cash investment.

9. Supplies
   - Does the franchisor require you to purchase or lease goods or services from it or from suppliers it designates?
   - Are the prices you must pay for goods and services competitive with the prices paid by independent businessmen? More? Less?
   - Are there any limitations on the goods or services that you may sell?

10. Termination of the franchise
    - Under what conditions can the franchise be terminated?
    - What are your rights and obligations on the expiration and termination of the franchise? Are there rights of renewal?
    - Does the franchisor have an option or right of first refusal to acquire the franchise in the event you decide to sell your franchise?
    - Are there any covenants not to compete? If so, restrictive covenants must be reasonable in time and geographic scope.

- Can you assign your right or otherwise transfer the franchise?
- If the franchisee dies, will the surviving spouse or children have a specified period of time (e.g., 90 to 270 days) in which to elect to keep the business and satisfy the franchisor's training requirements?
- Some states require the franchisor to acquire the franchisee's inventory in various termination situations. Arkansas requires repurchase of inventory (not equipment, leasehold improvements, or signs) upon any termination without good cause. California requires repurchase of inventory upon either termination or nonrenewal if the relationship is not ended in accordance with the law. Connecticut and Wisconsin require repurchase upon any termination, and Hawaii requires repurchase upon any termination or nonrenewal. Illinois requires repurchase upon nonrenewal because of the "diminution in value of the franchised business caused by expiration of the franchise" if the franchisee either cannot, after expiration of the franchise, conduct substantially the same business under another trademark in the same area or has not been notified at least six months before the expiration date of the franchisor's intent not to renew.

11. Franchisor financing
    - Is the franchisor offering any financing?

12. Territorial protection
    - What territorial protection will you have?
    - Consider the impact of potential population and demographic changes in negotiating the geographic scope of the exclusive territory.
    - Conduct marketing studies, traffic pattern evaluations, and other analyses to evaluate the potential customer reach in the territory.

13. Advertising
    - Is compensation being paid to a public figure whose name is used in the franchise or who endorses the franchise?
    - What advertising and promotions will the franchisor offer?
    - Are there any advertising charges to the franchisee?
    - Evaluate the success of the present marketing campaign and try to determine whether any of the advertising royalty fees will directly benefit you as a franchisee.

14. Financial information
    - What methods of data collection does the franchisor use when preparing projected sales, expenses, and income of the franchised business?
    - Does the franchisor have a recent balance sheet and profit and loss statement that has been audited by an independent certified public accountant?
    - What bookkeeping, accounting, and recording requirements will you have to fulfill?
    - Are there quotas?

15. Trademarks, patents, and copyrights
    - Verify trademarks, trade names, and other commercial symbols of the franchisor.
    - Is there any pending litigation or opposition, or cancellation proceedings involving the trademark, trade name, logo, or other commercial symbol?
    - What is the duration of patents or copyrighted material offered by the franchisor?
    - Does the franchisor intend to renew its patents or copyrights?
    - Consider the strength of the trademark, possible confusion or similarity with other trademarks, the genuineness of the trademark, the extent to which a trademark has acquired a secondary meaning, and the overall image connoted by the trademark.
    - Franchisees should require the franchisor to stand behind its trademark. The franchisor should be obliged to indemnify, defend, and hold harmless franchisees from any intellectual property claim or litigation challenging the validity or use of the mark.
    - Franchisors should compensate franchisees if the trademark must be changed because a court subsequently finds it is not a valid trademark. Compensation should cover increased advertising costs to promote the new trademark and lost revenues during the period the new trademark has not obtained customer acceptance.
    - Franchisees should have the right to terminate the franchise agreement if the trademark is lost. (For further information on patents and trademarks, see Chapter 10.)

Uniform Franchise Offering Circular

The U.S. Federal Trade Commission (FTC) requires all franchise companies to prepare a uniform franchise offering circular (UFOC). It must be provided to all persons interested in buying a franchise. The UFOC is a 23-item prospectus that includes all of the legal and financial information needed for a preliminary review of the franchisor. The UFOC should be reviewed by both your attorney and your accountant before you sign the franchise contract.

The FTC requires franchisors to provide the prospectus and copies of all proposed agreements for the franchise at (1) the first personal meeting with the prospective franchisee; (2) at least ten business days before any binding agreement is signed; or (3) at least ten business days before the franchisor receives any fee or other consideration, whichever is earliest.

THE FTC FRANCHISE RULE: WHO'S COVERED AND WHO'S NOT

If a franchisor is involved in either of the following two types of franchises, it will be subject to the Federal Trade Commission's stringent franchise rules.

1. Traditional franchises in which the franchisee is granted the right to distribute goods or services bearing the franchisor's trademark, service mark, trade name, advertising, or other commercial symbol. The franchisor either exercises significant control over the franchisee or provides significant assistance in the franchisee's method of operation.

2. Business opportunities where the investor sells goods or services supplied by the seller, its affiliate(s), or by suppliers with whom the seller requires the investor to do business; or where the seller secures retail outlets or accounts for the goods or services sold by the investor, secures locations for vending racks or machines, or provides the services of someone who can perform either of these functions. To obtain or commence the venture, the investor must make a required payment to the seller or its affiliate of at least $500 before or within six months after the business operation commences.

The two types of franchises discussed on the previous page may be exempt or excluded from the FTC's franchise rules if the franchise

- is a *fractional franchises*—that is, a relationship adding a new product or service to an established distributor's existing products or services if the franchisee or any of its current directors or executive officers has been in the same type of business for at least two years, and both parties anticipated, or should have, that sales from the franchise would represent no more than 20 percent of the franchisees sales in dollar volume.

- is a *leased department*—that is, a relationship in which the franchisee simply leases space in the premises of another retailer and is not required or advised to buy the goods or services it sells from the retailer or an affiliate of the retailer.

- requires a *minimum investment*—that is, the total of the required payments made by the franchisee within six months is less than $500;

- is established by an *oral agreement* and no material term of the business relationship is in writing;

- is an *employer-employee relationship;*

- is a *general partnership relationship;*

- is a *cooperative association* such as an agricultural cooperative or retailer-owned cooperative chain;

- is a *certification and testing service* such as an organization that authorizes the use of its trademarks to all parties who comply with its standards and pay its fee;

- has a *"single" trademark license,* which includes a license to a single licensee to manufacture trademarked goods, a license of a trademark for a use collateral to that for which the trademark is well known (e.g., a soft drink logo on a T-shirt), and a license granted to settle trademark infringement litigation.

Unless one of these nine exemptions applies, companies covered by the franchise rules must comply with the disclosure and registration requirements of the FTC.

Implied Franchises

Any business arrangement may be considered a franchise if the following three key elements are present: (1) a trademark; (2) a marketing plan; and (3) a franchise fee. For example, an agreement granting a party the exclusive right to sell a product in a stated area may be subject to federal and state franchise laws if (1) the party must spend money to advertise or to maintain a large inventory; (2) the manufacturer recommends marketing methods in an operating manual or in product specifications; and (3) the product's name or distinctive logo is used.

Also, if a business owner allows an employee to start his or her own business in a new location using the owner's name in exchange for a small share of the profits, the owner could be subject to the following: (1) liability to the employee for damages for violation of the registration and prospectus requirements; (2) possible entitlement of the franchisee to rescind the agreement; (3) civil penalties; (4) criminal penalties for willful violations; (5) inability to terminate the relationship except in compliance with franchise laws; and (6) involuntary renewal of the agreement if the franchisee so desires.

WHAT DO STATE FRANCHISE LAWS REQUIRE?

The following states have franchise laws: California, Florida, Hawaii, Illinois, Indiana, Maryland, Michigan, Minnesota, New York, North Dakota, Rhode Island, South Dakota, Texas, Utah, Virginia, Washington, and Wisconsin.

State franchise laws usually require the franchisor to register the offer of its franchise within the state and to provide each prospective franchisee with a disclosure statement, which may be called an *offering prospectus,* a *public offering prospectus,* a *disclosure statement,* or an *offering circular.* This statement contains information about the franchisor, the franchise, and the terms and conditions of the contract.

The state administrative agency reviews all of the following:

- The franchisor's application to register the franchise
- The proposed disclosure statement
- Financial statements
- The franchise's advertising materials
- Information about persons who will engage in the sale of the franchise
- The franchise agreement

- All other agreements that the franchisee must sign to acquire the franchise

Most state franchise regulatory agencies have the power to deny, suspend, or revoke any registration if the offer or sale of the franchise would constitute misrepresentation, deceit, or fraud by the purchasers.

A few states restrict a franchisor from terminating the franchise before the expiration of the franchise agreement or refusing to renew an expired contract. Because franchisees make a substantial investment in developing their franchise business, early termination or non-renewal is not permitted unless the franchisor has "good cause" for its action. California defines good cause as failure to cure a breach of the franchise agreement after notice and the reasonable opportunity to cure. Wisconsin defines it as failure to comply with reasonable requirements imposed on the dealer without discriminating when compared with similarly situated dealers.

Some states require that the franchisor give the spouse and other heirs of a deceased franchisee the opportunity to operate the franchise before the franchisor can terminate it because of the franchisee's death.

The purpose of state review of the franchisor's application is to determine (1) whether the franchisor has fully complied with all legal requirements; (2) whether all documents con-tain all the required information in an under-standable form; (3) whether advertising materials contain any prohibited claims or representations; (4) whether the franchise is fraudulent, deceptive, unfair, or inequitable; and (5) whether the franchisor has sufficient financial resources in which to fulfill its obligations to provide real estate, improvements, equipment, inventory, training, or other items to be included in the establishment and opening of the franchise business.

The state administrative agency may deny or revoke the registration of the franchise offering if the franchisor (1) fails or refuses to comply fully with state law; (2) makes an incomplete or misleading disclosure statement; or (3) engages in any false, fraudulent, or deceptive practices.

Warning: Do not assume that the registration of a franchisor or the preparation of a disclosure statement ensures that the information in the statement is complete, accurate, and free of misleading statements or that the state administrative agency or the FTC has made such a determination or has in any way approved the franchise.

To protect yourself adequately, seek out existing franchisees and ask them to verify the information contained in the disclosure statement.

7

How to Save Time on Tax Recordkeeping

Good financial recordkeeping is crucial to the success of your business for many reasons.

Good records provide the financial data that help you operate more efficiently, thus increasing the profitability of your enterprise. Accurate and complete records enable you, or your accountant, to identify all your business assets, liabilities, income, and expenses, which, when compared with appropriate industry averages, help you pinpoint the strong and weak phases of your business operations.

Good records are essential for the preparation of current financial statements, such as the Income Statement (Profit and Loss) and the Cash Flow Projection. These, in turn, are critical for maintaining good relations with your banker. They also will present a complete picture of your total business operation, which will benefit you as well.

Good records are required for preparing complete and accurate tax documents. For example, poor records often lead to the preparation of income tax returns that result in underpayment or overpayment of taxes. In addition, good records are essential in an IRS audit if you hope to answer questions accurately and to the satisfaction of the IRS.

To be successful, your financial records should be able to provide answers to the following questions:

- How much income are you generating now and how much income can you expect to generate in the future?

- How much cash is tied up in accounts receivable (and thus not available to you), and for how long?

- How much do you owe for merchandise? Rent? Equipment?

- What are your expenses, including payroll, payroll taxes, merchandise, and benefit plans for yourself and your employees (such as health insurance, retirement, etc.)?

- How much cash do you have on hand? How much cash is tied up in inventory? What is your actual working capital budget?

- How frequently do you turn over your inventory?

- Which of your product lines, departments, or services are making a profit, which are breaking even, and which are financial drains?

- What is your gross profit? What is your net profit?

- How does all the financial data listed above compare with last year—or last quarter? How does it compare with the projections in your business plan?

- How does all of the financial data compare with that of your competitors? With that of the industry?

IDENTIFICATION NUMBERS

You or your business must have a taxpayer identification number so that the Internal Revenue Service can process your tax returns. There are two kinds of taxpayer identification numbers: (1) Social Security numbers (SSNs), and (2) employer identification numbers (EINs).

Employer Number

If you operate your business as a sole proprietor (see Chapter 3), you don't need an employer identification number unless you have a Keogh plan or you are required to file employment, excise, fiduciary, or alcohol, tobacco, and firearms tax returns. Otherwise, use your Social Security number.

HOT SITE

The home page of the IRS (http://www.irs.ustreas.gov) is a great resource for tax forms, instructions, and information.

To obtain an EIN, you must file Form SS-4, "Application for Employer Identification Number" (see form at the end of this chapter), with the IRS before you file your first return or statement or make a tax deposit. It takes about four weeks for Form SS-4 to be processed. However, you can obtain an EIN by telephone by calling the numbers listed at the end of this chapter in the instructions for Form SS-4. You can obtain Form SS-4 at your local IRS office or by calling 1-800-TAX-FORM.

You must include your taxpayer identification number (SSN or EIN) on all returns or other documents you send to the IRS. You are also required to furnish that number to anyone who must use your identification number on a return or document that they send to the IRS to report any of the following:

- Interest, dividends, or royalties they have paid to you
- Amounts paid to you (in the course of your business) that total $600 or more for the year
- Any amount paid to you as a dependent care provider
- Any amount paid to you as alimony

If you fail to furnish your identification number as required, you will be subject to penalties imposed by the IRS.

A new EIN is required when any of the following occur:

- A sole proprietorship incorporates.

- A sole proprietorship takes in partners and operates as a partnership.
- A partnership incorporates.
- A partnership is taken over by one of the partners and operated as a sole proprietorship.
- A corporation changes to a partnership or sole proprietorship.
- You purchase or inherit an existing business that you will operate as a sole proprietorship. (You cannot use the EIN of the former owner even if the former owner is your spouse.)
- You are appointed trustee of a trust.
- You represent an estate that receives interest or dividends or operates a business after the owner's death.
- You terminate an old partnership and begin a new one.

If a corporation elects to be taxed as an S corporation, it does not need a new EIN.

Employee and Other Payee Numbers

During the operation of your business, you will ordinarily make certain payments that must be reported on information returns. You must also give the recipient of these payments (the payee) a statement showing the total amount paid during the year. The forms used to report these payments must include the payee's identification number as well as your own identification number.

If you are an employer, you must obtain a Social Security number from each of your employees. When you hire an employee, you should require that person to fill out a Form W-4, "Employee's Withholding Allowance Certificate."

If you make payments to a nonemployee that must be reported on an information return, obtain each individual's (including sole proprietor's) SSN. If you make payments to an organization such as a corporation or partnership, you must get the EIN of the organization.

To get the payee's SSN or EIN, use Form W-9, "Request for Taxpayer Identification Number and Certification" (see the form at the end of this chapter). A sole proprietor must fill in both his or her individual name and SSN or EIN.

BUSINESS TAXES

The type of business you operate determines the taxes you must pay and how you will pay them. There are four general kinds of business taxes:

1. Income tax
2. Self-employment tax
3. Employment taxes
4. Excise taxes

Income Tax

Every business must file an annual income tax return. The form you will use depends on how your business is organized.

Organization	Type of Form to File
Sole proprietorship	Schedule C (Form 1040)
Farming	Schedule F (Form 1040)
Partnership	Form 1065
Corporation	Form 1120 or 1120-A
S corporation	Form 1120S

If you are a sole proprietor or farmer and have more than one business, you must file a separate Schedule C or Schedule F for each business.

Individuals. Income from your business is not subject to withholding. You generally will pay the tax during the year as you earn your income. Sole proprietors, partners, or shareholders of an S corporation pay as they go by making regular payments of estimated tax during the year.

Self-Employment Tax

The self-employment tax is the Social Security tax for individuals who work for themselves, including sole proprietors, self-employed farmers and fishermen, and members of a partnership. This tax is figured and reported on Schedule SE, which is attached to and filed with Form 1040.

Employment Taxes

If you have employees, you will probably be required to pay the following employment taxes:

- Federal income tax withholding
- Social Security and Medicare taxes
- Federal unemployment tax (FUTA)
- State income tax withholding

Federal income, Social Security, and Medicare taxes. You must withhold federal income tax from your employees' wages. For Social Security and Medicare taxes, you withhold part from your employees' wages, and you pay a matching amount yourself.

Tax returns. Social Security, Medicare taxes, and withheld income tax are reported and paid together.

Federal unemployment tax (FUTA). Federal unemployment tax is reported and paid separately from Social Security, Medicare, and withheld income taxes. You pay the FUTA tax only from your own funds. Employees do not pay any portion of this tax or have it withheld from their pay.

Tax return. Form 940, "Employer's Annual Federal Unemployment Tax (FUTA) Return," is used to report federal unemployment tax.

Simplified form. Form 940EZ is a simplified version of Form 940. You can use Form 940EZ if

- you pay employment contributions to only one state,
- you pay all state employment tax by January 31, and
- all wages that were taxable for FUTA tax were also taxable for state unemployment tax.

Excise Taxes

If you manufacture or sell certain products, you may have to pay excise taxes. There are also excise taxes on certain kinds of businesses, certain transactions, and the use of various kinds of equipment, facilities, and products.

Form 720. The federal excise taxes reported on Form 720, "Quarterly Federal Excise Tax Return," consist of several broad categories:

- Environmental taxes imposed on domestic crude oil, imported petroleum products, and certain chemicals sold by producers, manufacturers, or importers
- Facilities and services taxes, including taxes on amounts paid for telephone communications and air transportation
- Fuel taxes, including taxes on the sale or use of gasoline, gasohol, diesel fuel, and special motor fuels
- Manufacturer's taxes on the sale or use of a variety of different products
- Excise taxes on the first retail sale of heavy trucks, trailers, and certain luxury items (passenger cars, boats, aircraft, jewelry, and furs)
- Other excise taxes, including taxes on policies issued by foreign insurers and obligations not in registered form

Form 720 generally must be filed within one month after the end of a calendar quarter.

Form 2290. A federal excise tax is imposed on certain trucks, truck tractors, and buses used on public highways. The tax applies to vehicles having a gross vehicle weight of 55,000 pounds or more. The tax is reported on Form 2290, "Heavy Vehicle Use Tax Return."

ATF Forms. If you produce, sell, or import guns, tobacco, or alcohol products or if you manufacture equipment for their production, you may be liable for one or more excise taxes. These taxes are reported on forms filed with the Bureau of Alcohol, Tobacco and Firearms.

Form 730. If you are in the business of accepting bets or running a betting pool or lottery, you may be liable for federal excise taxes on wagering. Form 730, "Tax on Wagering," is used to report tax on the bets you receive.

Form 11-C. Form 11-C, "Special Tax Return and Application for Registry—Wagering," is used to pay an annual tax and to register your place of business.

DEPOSITING TAXES

The following types of taxes, reported on the forms listed below, are paid by deposit.

Type of Tax	Form on Which Tax Is Reported
Corporate income tax	Form 1120
Social Security and Medicare taxes and withheld income tax (nonagricultural)	Form 941
Social Security and Medicare taxes and withheld income tax (agricultural)	Form 943
Federal unemployment tax (FUTA)	Form 940
Excise tax	Form 720

INFORMATION RETURNS

In the course of your business activities, you may make or receive payments that must be reported to the IRS.

Form 1099-MISC

Form 1099-MISC, "Miscellaneous Income," must be filed to report certain payments you make in the course of your trade or business. These include payments of $10 or more for royalties; payments of $600 or more for rents, prizes, and awards that are not given in return for services rendered; and payments to persons who were not your employees (such as independent contractors).

Form 8300

Form 8300, "Report of Cash Payments over $10,000 Received in a Trade or Business," must be filed if, in the course of your trade or business, you receive more than $10,000 in cash or foreign currency in one or more related transactions. (See form at the end of this chapter.)

HOW GOOD BUSINESS RECORDS CAN SAVE YOU TAXES

Not only are complete records necessary for good business management, but they will ensure that you do not inadvertently lose a tax benefit to which you or your business may be entitled. You should ensure that your record-keeping system will permit you to do the following:

- *Identify sources of receipts.* Your records should identify the sources of your receipts so that you can prove whether they are from nonbusiness sources or are nontaxable.

- *Keep track of deductible expenses.* Expenses may be forgotten by the time you prepare your tax return unless you record them as they occur.

- *Figure depreciation allowances.* You should record depreciable assets in a permanent record. Without a record of the cost of, and other information about, your assets, you cannot figure your depreciation deductions. If the assets are sold or become fully depreciated or if capital improvements are made to them, only a permanent record will show how much of their cost you have not recovered.

- *Take Advantage of capital gain and loss laws.* Your records should show the date an asset was acquired, what it was used for, and whether it was sold, traded, destroyed, or otherwise disposed of. With this information, you may be able to use the capital gain or loss laws. You may also be allowed to put off paying tax on certain gains or allowed to deduct 100 percent of certain losses that otherwise would not be deductible or would be only partly deductible.

- *Determine your earnings for self-employment tax purposes.* The self-employment tax is part of the system for providing Social Security coverage for people who work for themselves. Social Security benefits are paid to you when you retire or become disabled or are paid to your family upon your death. The size of the payment will depend on how much you earn. Your records should show how much of your earnings you pay self-employment tax on.

- *Support items reported on your tax returns.* If any of your tax returns are examined by the Internal Revenue Service, you may be asked to explain the items reported. A complete set of records will speed up the examination and will support your position if any item is challenged. Your records should be supported by sales slips, invoices, receipts, deposit slips, cancelled checks, and similar documentation.

WHAT TAX RECORDS TO SAVE

You should keep all receipts, canceled checks, or other evidence of your deductions for three years. In the event that your returns are challenged or that you find that you are entitled to a refund, your records are the best evidence you will have to support your position.

Audit

The Internal Revenue Service can audit your federal income tax return within three years from the date your return was due or filed, or two years from the date the tax was paid, whichever occurs later. However, if you fail to report more than 25 percent of your gross income, the IRS has six years to collect the taxes or start suit. There is no time limitation if you filed a fraudulent return or if you failed to file a return. It will also be necessary to keep your returns for more than three years if any of the following applies:

- If you average your income, you will need proof of taxable income for the four base-period years.

- If you engage in a property transaction, the basis of new or replacement property may be determined from the basis of the old property.

- If new tax laws come into being, they may provide tax benefits to those who can prove from their records of previous years that they are entitled to the new benefits.

Employees

An employee's record of travel, entertainment, and business gift expenses should be kept in an account book, diary, statement of expense, or similar record and must be supported by adequate documentary evidence.

Charitable Deductions

Contributions are deductible if made to

- an entity that qualifies under Code Sec. 501(c)3;
- the U.S. government or a state, U.S. territorial district, or a municipal government;
- a nonprofit cemetery; or
- a veterans' organization.

Keep records, receipts, canceled checks, and other proof of your charitable deductions. If you contribute property for which you claim a charitable deduction of more than $250, you must attach a statement to your return giving the following information: (1) the name and address of the charity, (2) the date of the contribution, (3) a description of the property and how you acquired it, (4) the approximate date the property was acquired, (5) the property's market value and cost, (6) the terms of your agreement with the charity regarding the sale or use of the property, and (7) a receipt from the charity.

For property gifts over $500, Form 8283 must be completed. Gifts over $5,000 require an appraisal or documentation of valuation if they are a publicly traded security.

The IRS usually keeps returns for six years. You can obtain a copy of your tax return by writing a letter containing your Social Security number and a notarized signature to your local IRS center. You should, however, save copies of your tax returns to help you when you prepare future or amended returns.

BASIC TAX RECORDS

You should keep records of the following for your business:

- *Cash receipts*—used to record the cash that the business receives
- *Cash disbursements*—used to record the firm's expenditures
- *Sales*—used to record and summarize monthly income
- *Purchases*—used to record the purchases of merchandise bought for processing or resale
- *Payroll*—used to record the wages of employees and their deductions, such as those for income taxes and Social Security taxes
- *Equipment*—used to record the firm's capital assets, such as equipment, office furniture, and motor vehicles
- *Inventory*—used to record the firm's investment in stock that is needed for arriving at a true profit on financial statements and for income tax purposes
- *Accounts receivable*—used to record the balances that customers owe to the firm
- *Accounts payable*—used to record what the firm owes its creditors and suppliers

SMALL BUSINESS FINANCIAL STATUS CHECKLIST

Daily

- ❏ Cash on hand
- ❏ Bank balance (Keep business and personal funds separate.)
- ❏ Daily summary of sales and cash receipts
- ❏ Corrections of any errors in recording collections on accounts receivable
- ❏ Record of all monies paid out by cash or check

Weekly

- ❏ Accounts receivable (Take action on slow payers.)
- ❏ Payroll (Records should include name and address of employee, Social Security number, number of exemptions, date ending the pay period, hours worked, rate of pay, total wages, deductions, net pay, and check number.)
- ❏ Taxes and reports to state and federal government (sales, withholding, Social Security, etc.)

Monthly

- ❏ Classify all journal entries according to like elements (these should be generally accepted and standardized for both income and expense), and post to general ledger.
- ❏ Have a profit and loss statement for the month available within a reasonable time—usually 10 to 15 days following the close of the month. This shows the business's income for the month, the expense incurred in obtaining the income, and the profit or loss resulting. From this, take action to eliminate loss (adjust markup? reduce overhead expense? pilferage? incorrect tax reporting? incorrect buying procedures? failure to take advantage of cash discounts?).
- ❏ Prepare a balance sheet to accompany the profit and loss statement. This shows assets (what the business owns), liabilities (what the business owes), and the investment of the owner.
- ❏ Reconcile the bank statement. This procedure ensures that your books are in agreement with the bank's record of the cash balance.
- ❏ Balance the petty cash account. (The actual cash in the petty cash box plus the total of the paid-out slips that have not been charged to a specific expense equals the amount set aside as petty cash.)

- ❑ Check to determine whether all federal tax deposits have been made and that withheld income and FICA taxes (Form 501) and state taxes have been paid.
- ❑ Age all accounts receivable—i.e., 30, 60, 90 days, etc.—past due. (Act on all bad and slow accounts.)
- ❑ Check inventory control to remove dead or slow-moving stock, and order new stock for items in demand.

EMPLOYERS' RECORDS

The items that follow are required for various employment taxes. In addition, your records should also contain your employer identification number, copies of the returns you have filed, and the dates and amounts of deposits you made.

Income Tax Withholding

The specific records you must keep for income tax withholding are as follows:

- Each employee's name, address, and Social Security number
- The total amount and date of each wage payment and the period of time the payment covers
- For each wage payment, the amount subject to withholding
- The amount of withholding tax collected on each payment and the date it was collected
- If the taxable amount is less than the total payment, the reason why it is less
- Copies of any statements furnished by employees relating to nonresident alien status, residence in Puerto Rico or the Virgin Islands, or residence or physical presence in a foreign country
- The fair market value and date of each payment of noncash compensation made to a retail commission salesperson if no income tax was withheld
- For accident or health plans, information about the amount of each payment
- The withholding allowance certificates (Form W-4) filed by each employee
- Any agreement between you and an employee for the voluntary withholding of additional amounts of tax

- The dates in each calendar quarter on which any employee may have worked for you in a capacity that was *not* in the course of your trade or business and the amount paid for that work
- Copies of statements given to you by employees reporting tips received in their work unless the information shown on the statements appears in another item on this list
- Requests by employees to have their withholding tax calculated on the basis of their individual cumulative wages
- The W-5 forms submitted to employees eligible for the earned income credit and who wish to receive their payment in advance rather than when they file their income tax returns

An employee's earnings ledger usually has space for the information required in items 1–4. Verify the employee's U.S. citizenship by having him or her complete Form I–9 (see form in Chapter 11).

Social Security and Medicare Taxes

You must also maintain the following information in your records covering employees' Social Security and Medicare (FICA) taxes:

- The amount of each wage payment subject to Social Security tax
- The amount of each wage payment subject to Medicare tax
- The amount of Social Security and Medicare tax collected for each payment and the date collected
- The reason if the total wage payment and the taxable amount differ

Federal Unemployment Tax Act

The Federal Unemployment Tax Act (FUTA) requires you to maintain the following information in your records:

- The total amount paid to your employees during the calendar year
- The amount of compensation subject to the unemployment tax
- The amount you paid into the state unemployment fund
- Any other information required to be shown on Form 940 (or Form 940-EZ)

You should consult with an accountant for information on how to select accounting periods (calendar, fiscal, or short tax years) and accounting methods (cash or accrual).

PAYROLL RECORDS

Under the Fair Labor Standards Act, employers are required to retain payroll records for specific lengths of time. Time cards, journals, and summaries should be kept for three years. However, it may be advisable to retain these records even longer so that you may use them in case of a wage suit.

The following should be kept for four years: federal tax returns (941, 940, W-3, W-2) and supporting documents, state tax returns (unemployment and wage listing), and supporting documentation.

A current copy of the W-4 claiming the number of exemptions should be kept permanently in each employee's file. You should require each employee to sign a new W-4 every year.

Your employees should be reminded periodically that the amount of tax withheld from each paycheck is determined from information on their most recent Form W-4. Therefore, it is to their benefit to update their Form W-4. The following are situations that could cause a change in the number of personal allowances claimed: (1) change in marital status, (2) birth or death of a dependent, (3) support of a dependent begins or stops, (4) employee or spouse becomes 65 or blind, (5) eligibility for the special withholding allowance changes, and (6) eligibility for additional withholding allowances for credits or deduction changes. Determine if your state requires a permit to pay by check.

HOW TO AVOID IRS PENALTIES

The IRS is targeting small employers because of their high error rate. Problems can be avoided by verifying that your IRS employee income forms (such as 941s) and your Social Security forms (such as W-2s) correspond. Penalties can also be triggered by simple mistakes. Before filing, double-check employees' Social Security numbers and the spelling of their names, and verify your firm's employer identification number.

HOW AND WHEN TO USE THE FORMS IN THIS CHAPTER

Tax Checklist. This guide provides information on the tax filing requirements for partnerships, sole proprietorships, and corporations.

IRS Form SS-4—Application for Employer Identification Number. This form must be filed by every employer who pays wages or is required to have an identification number for use on any return, statement, or other document.

IRS Form W-9—Request for Taxpayer Identification Number and Certification. Anyone who must file an information return with the IRS must obtain the correct taxpayer identification number of the person to whom income is paid or who received a payment or financial benefit arising out of real estate transactions, mortgage interest paid, the acquisition or abandonment of secured property, or contributions made to an IRA.

IRS Form 911—Application for Taxpayer Assistance Order to Relieve Hardship. This form is used to apply for a review by the taxpayer ombudsman of actions being taken by the IRS.

Depreciation Schedule. This schedule is used to compute the depreciation deductions for the current year.

Employee Compensation Record. This sample shows how you should record employees' earnings and deduct them on a weekly basis.

IRS Form 8300—Report of Cash Payments over $10,000 Received in a Trade or Business. This must be filed by each person engaged in a trade or business who receives more than $10,000 in cash in one transaction or two or more related transactions. Carrying $10,000 or more in U.S. or foreign currency or negotiable instruments out of or into the United States is reportable on IRS Form 4790.

Tax Checklist

If You Are a:	Partnership	Sole Propietorship	Partner	S Corp. Shareholder	Corp.	S Corp.
You may be liable for:						
Income tax (I.T.)		X	X	X	X	X
Self-employment tax		X	X			
Estimated tax		X	X	X	X	
Annual return of income	X					
FICA tax & withholding of I.T.	X	X			X	X
Providing information on FICA tax & withholding of I.T.	X	X			X	X
FUTA tax	X	X			X	X
Annual info. returns	X	X			X	X
Excise taxes	X	X			X	X

See your tax adviser for further information regarding the above.

Application for Employer Identification Number

(For use by employers, corporations, partnerships, trusts, estates, churches, government agencies, certain individuals, and others. See instructions.)

▶ Keep a copy for your records.

EIN

OMB No. 1545-0003

Please type or print clearly.

1 Name of applicant (Legal name) (See instructions.)

2 Trade name of business (if different from name on line 1)

3 Executor, trustee, "care of" name

4a Mailing address (street address) (room, apt., or suite no.)

5a Business address (if different from address on lines 4a and 4b)

4b City, state, and ZIP code

5b City, state, and ZIP code

6 County and state where principal business is located

7 Name of principal officer, general partner, grantor, owner, or trustor—SSN required (See instructions.) ▶

8a Type of entity (Check only one box.) (See instructions.)

☐ Sole proprietor (SSN) _____

☐ Partnership   ☐ Personal service corp.

☐ REMIC   ☐ Limited liability co.

☐ State/local government   ☐ National Guard

☐ Other nonprofit organization (specify) ▶ _____

☐ Other (specify) ▶

☐ Estate (SSN of decedent)_____

☐ Plan administrator-SSN _____

☐ Other corporation (specify) ▶ _____

☐ Trust   ☐ Farmers' cooperative

☐ Federal Government/military   ☐ Church or church-controlled organization

(enter GEN if applicable) _____

8b If a corporation, name the state or foreign country (if applicable) where incorporated

State

Foreign country

9 Reason for applying (Check only one box.)

☐ Started new business (specify) ▶ _____

☐ Hired employees

☐ Created a pension plan (specify type) ▶

☐ Banking purpose (specify) ▶ _____

☐ Changed type of organization (specify) ▶ _____

☐ Purchased going business

☐ Created a trust (specify) ▶ _____

☐ Other (specify) ▶

10 Date business started or acquired (Mo., day, year) (See instructions.)

11 Closing month of accounting year (See instructions.)

12 First date wages or annuities were paid or will be paid (Mo., day, year). **Note:** If applicant is a withholding agent, enter date income will first be paid to nonresident alien. (Mo., day, year) . . . . ▶

13 Highest number of employees expected in the next 12 months. **Note:** If the applicant does not expect to have any employees during the period, enter -0-. (See instructions.) . . . ▶

Nonagricultural	Agricultural	Household

14 Principal activity (See instructions.) ▶

15 Is the principal business activity manufacturing? . . . . ☐ Yes   ☐ No
If "Yes," principal product and raw material used ▶

16 To whom are most of the products or services sold? Please check the appropriate box.   ☐ Business (wholesale)
☐ Public (retail)   ☐ Other (specify) ▶   ☐ N/A

17a Has the applicant ever applied for an identification number for this or any other business? . . . . ☐ Yes   ☐ No
Note: If "Yes," please complete lines 17b and 17c.

17b If you checked "Yes" on line 17a, give applicant's legal name and trade name shown on prior application, if different from line 1 or 2 above.
Legal name ▶   Trade name ▶

17c Approximate date when and city and state where the application was filed. Enter previous employer identification number if known.

Approximate date when filed (Mo., day, year)	City and state where filed	Previous EIN

Under penalties of perjury, I declare that I have examined this application, and to the best of my knowledge and belief, it is true, correct, and complete.

Business telephone number (include area code)

Fax telephone number (include area code)

Name and title (Please type or print clearly.) ▶

Signature ▶

Date ▶

Note: Do not write below this line. For official use only.

Please leave blank ▶	Geo.	Ind.	Class	Size	Reason for applying

For Paperwork Reduction Act Notice, see page 4.

Cat. No. 16055N

Form **SS-4** (Rev. 12-95)

General Instructions

Section references are to the Internal Revenue Code unless otherwise noted.

Purpose of Form

Use Form SS-4 to apply for an employer identification number (EIN). An EIN is a nine-digit number (for example, 12-3456789) assigned to sole proprietors, corporations, partnerships, estates, trusts, and other entities for filing and reporting purposes. The information you provide on this form will establish your filing and reporting requirements.

Who Must File

You must file this form if you have not obtained an EIN before and:

● You pay wages to one or more employees including household employees.

● You are required to have an EIN to use on any return, statement, or other document, even if you are not an employer.

● You are a withholding agent required to withhold taxes on income, other than wages, paid to a nonresident alien (individual, corporation, partnership, etc.). A withholding agent may be an agent, broker, fiduciary, manager, tenant, or spouse, and is required to file **Form 1042,** Annual Withholding Tax Return for U.S. Source Income of Foreign Persons.

● You file **Schedule C,** Profit or Loss From Business, or **Schedule F,** Profit or Loss From Farming, of **Form 1040,** U.S. Individual Income Tax Return, **and** have a Keogh plan or are required to file excise, employment, information, or alcohol, tobacco, or firearms returns.

The following must use EINs even if they do not have any employees:

● State and local agencies who serve as tax reporting agents for public assistance recipients, under Rev. Proc. 80-4, 1980-1 C.B. 581, should obtain a separate EIN for this reporting. See **Household employer** on page 3.

● Trusts, except the following:

1. Certain grantor-owned revocable trusts. (See the **Instructions for Form 1041.**)

2. Individual Retirement Arrangement (IRA) trusts, unless the trust has to file **Form 990-T,** Exempt Organization Business Income Tax Return. (See the **Instructions for Form 990-T.**)

3. Certain trusts that are considered household employers can use the trust EIN to report and pay the social security and Medicare taxes, Federal unemployment tax (FUTA) and withheld Federal income tax. A separate EIN is not necessary.

● Estates

● Partnerships

● REMICs (real estate mortgage investment conduits) (See the **Instructions for Form 1066,** U.S. Real Estate Mortgage Investment Conduit Income Tax Return.)

● Corporations

● Nonprofit organizations (churches, clubs, etc.)

● Farmers' cooperatives

● Plan administrators (A plan administrator is the person or group of persons specified as the administrator by the instrument under which the plan is operated.)

When To Apply for a New EIN

New Business.—If you become the new owner of an existing business, **do not** use the EIN of the former owner. IF YOU ALREADY HAVE AN EIN, USE THAT NUMBER. If you do not have an EIN, apply for one on this form. If you become the "owner" of a corporation by acquiring its stock, use the corporation's EIN.

Changes in Organization or Ownership.—If you already have an EIN, you may need to get a new one if either the organization or ownership of your business changes. If you incorporate a sole proprietorship or form a partnership, you must get a new EIN. However, **do not** apply for a new EIN if you change only the name of your business.

Note: *If you are electing to be an "S corporation," be sure you file* **Form 2553,** *Election by a Small Business Corporation.*

File Only One Form SS-4.—File only one Form SS-4, regardless of the number of businesses operated or trade names under which a business operates. However, each corporation in an affiliated group must file a separate application.

EIN Applied For, But Not Received.—If you do not have an EIN by the time a return is due, write "Applied for" and the date you applied in the space shown for the number. **Do not** show your social security number as an EIN on returns.

If you do not have an EIN by the time a tax deposit is due, send your payment to the Internal Revenue Service Center for your filing area. (See **Where To Apply** below.) Make your check or money order payable to Internal Revenue Service and show your name (as shown on Form SS-4), address, type of tax, period covered, and date you applied for an EIN. Send an explanation with the deposit.

For more information about EINs, see **Pub. 583,** Starting a Business and Keeping Records, and **Pub. 1635,** Understanding Your EIN.

How To Apply

You can apply for an EIN either by mail or by telephone. You can get an EIN immediately by calling the Tele-TIN phone number for the service center for your state, or you can send the completed Form SS-4 directly to the service center to receive your EIN in the mail.

Application by Tele-TIN.—Under the Tele-TIN program, you can receive your EIN over the telephone and use it immediately to file a return or make a payment. To receive an EIN by phone, complete Form SS-4, then call the Tele-TIN phone number listed for your state under **Where To Apply.** The person making the call must be authorized to sign the form. (See **Signature block** on page 4.)

An IRS representative will use the information from the Form SS-4 to establish your account and assign you an EIN. Write the number you are given on the upper right-hand corner of the form, sign and date it.

*Mail or FAX the signed SS-4 **within 24 hours** to the Tele-TIN Unit at the service center address for your state. The IRS representative will give you the FAX number. The FAX numbers are also listed in Pub. 1635.*

Taxpayer representatives can receive their client's EIN by phone if they first send a facsimile (FAX) of a completed **Form 2848,** Power of Attorney and Declaration of Representative, or **Form 8821,** Tax Information Authorization, to the Tele-TIN unit. The Form 2848 or Form 8821 will be used solely to release the EIN to the representative authorized on the form.

Application by Mail.—Complete Form SS-4 at least 4 to 5 weeks before you will need an EIN. Sign and date the application and mail it to the service center address for your state. You will receive your EIN in the mail in approximately 4 weeks.

Where To Apply

The Tele-TIN phone numbers listed below will involve a long-distance charge to callers outside of the local calling area and can be used only to apply for an EIN. THE NUMBERS MAY CHANGE WITHOUT NOTICE. Use 1-800-829-1040 to verify a number or to ask about an application by mail or other Federal tax matters.

If your principal business, office or agency, or legal residence in the case of an individual, is located in:	Call the Tele-TIN phone number shown or file with the Internal Revenue Service Center at:
Florida, Georgia, South Carolina	Attn: Entity Control Atlanta, GA 39901 (404) 455-2360
New Jersey, New York City and counties of Nassau, Rockland, Suffolk, and Westchester	Attn: Entity Control Holtsville, NY 00501 (516) 447-4955
New York (all other counties), Connecticut, Maine, Massachusetts, New Hampshire, Rhode Island, Vermont	Attn: Entity Control Andover, MA 05501 (508) 474-9717
Illinois, Iowa, Minnesota, Missouri, Wisconsin	Attn: Entity Control Stop 57A 2306 E. Bannister Rd. Kansas City, MO 64131 (816) 926-5999
Delaware, District of Columbia, Maryland, Pennsylvania, Virginia	Attn: Entity Control Philadelphia, PA 19255 (215) 574-2400
Indiana, Kentucky, Michigan, Ohio, West Virginia	Attn: Entity Control Cincinnati, OH 45999 (606) 292-5467
Kansas, New Mexico, Oklahoma, Texas	Attn: Entity Control Austin, TX 73301 (512) 460-7843

Alaska, Arizona, California (counties of Alpine, Amador, Butte, Calaveras, Colusa, Contra Costa, Del Norte, El Dorado, Glenn, Humboldt, Lake, Lassen, Marin, Mendocino, Modoc, Napa, Nevada, Placer, Plumas, Sacramento, San Joaquin, Shasta, Sierra, Siskiyou, Solano, Sonoma, Sutter, Tehama, Trinity, Yolo, and Yuba), Colorado, Idaho, Montana, Nebraska, Nevada, North Dakota, Oregon, South Dakota, Utah, Washington, Wyoming	Attn: Entity Control Mail Stop 6271-T P.O. Box 9950 Ogden, UT 84409 (801) 620-7645
California (all other counties), Hawaii	Attn: Entity Control Fresno, CA 93888 (209) 452-4010
Alabama, Arkansas, Louisiana, Mississippi, North Carolina, Tennessee	Attn: Entity Control Memphis, TN 37501 (901) 365-5970

If you have no legal residence, principal place of business, or principal office or agency in any state, file your form with the Internal Revenue Service Center, Philadelphia, PA 19255 or call 215-574-2400.

Specific Instructions

The instructions that follow are for those items that are not self-explanatory. Enter N/A (nonapplicable) on the lines that do not apply.

Line 1.—Enter the legal name of the entity applying for the EIN exactly as it appears on the social security card, charter, or other applicable legal document.

Individuals.—Enter the first name, middle initial, and last name. If you are a sole proprietor, enter your individual name, not your business name. Do not use abbreviations or nicknames.

Trusts.—Enter the name of the trust.

Estate of a decedent.—Enter the name of the estate.

Partnerships.—Enter the legal name of the partnership as it appears in the partnership agreement. **Do not** list the names of the partners on line 1. See the specific instructions for line 7.

Corporations.—Enter the corporate name as it appears in the corporation charter or other legal document creating it.

Plan administrators.—Enter the name of the plan administrator. A plan administrator who already has an EIN should use that number.

Line 2.—Enter the trade name of the business if different from the legal name. The trade name is the "doing business as" name.

Note: *Use the full legal name on line 1 on all tax returns filed for the entity. However, if you enter a trade name on line 2 and choose to use the trade name instead of the legal name, enter the trade name on all returns you file. To prevent processing delays and errors,* **always** *use either the legal name only or the trade name only on all tax returns.*

Line 3.—Trusts enter the name of the trustee. Estates enter the name of the executor, administrator, or other fiduciary. If the entity applying has a designated person to receive tax information, enter that person's name as the "care of"

person. Print or type the first name, middle initial, and last name.

Line 7.—Enter the first name, middle initial, last name, and social security number (SSN) of a principal officer if the business is a corporation; of a general partner if a partnership; or of a grantor, owner, or trustor if a trust.

Line 8a.—Check the box that best describes the type of entity applying for the EIN. If not specifically mentioned, check the "Other" box and enter the type of entity. Do not enter N/A.

Sole proprietor.—Check this box if you file Schedule C or F (Form 1040) and have a Keogh plan, or are required to file excise, employment, information, or alcohol, tobacco, or firearms returns. Enter your SSN in the space provided.

REMIC.—Check this box if the entity has elected to be treated as a real estate mortgage investment conduit (REMIC). See the **Instructions for Form 1066** for more information.

Other nonprofit organization.—Check this box if the nonprofit organization is other than a church or church-controlled organization and specify the type of nonprofit organization (for example, an educational organization).

If the organization also seeks tax-exempt status, you must file either **Package 1023** or **Package 1024,** Application for Recognition of Exemption. Get **Pub. 557,** Tax-Exempt Status for Your Organization, for more information.

Group exemption number (GEN).—If the organization is covered by a group exemption letter, enter the four-digit GEN. (Do not confuse the GEN with the nine-digit EIN.) If you do not know the GEN, contact the parent organization. Get Pub. 557 for more information about group exemption numbers.

Withholding agent.—If you are a withholding agent required to file Form 1042, check the "Other" box and enter "Withholding agent."

Personal service corporation.—Check this box if the entity is a personal service corporation. An entity is a personal service corporation for a tax year only if:

● The principal activity of the entity during the testing period (prior tax year) for the tax year is the performance of personal services substantially by employee-owners, and

● The employee-owners own 10% of the fair market value of the outstanding stock in the entity on the last day of the testing period.

Personal services include performance of services in such fields as health, law, accounting, or consulting. For more information about personal service corporations, see the **Instructions for Form 1120,** U.S. Corporation Income Tax Return, and **Pub. 542,** Tax Information on Corporations.

Limited liability co.—See the definition of limited liability company in the **Instructions for Form 1065.** If you are classified as a partnership for Federal income tax

purposes, mark the "Limited liability co." checkbox. If you are classified as a corporation for Federal income tax purposes, mark the "Other corporation" checkbox and write "Limited liability co." in the space provided.

Plan administrator.—If the plan administrator is an individual, enter the plan administrator's SSN in the space provided.

Other corporation.—This box is for any corporation other than a personal service corporation. If you check this box, enter the type of corporation (such as insurance company) in the space provided.

Household employer.—If you are an individual, check the "Other" box and enter "Household employer" and your SSN. If you are a state or local agency serving as a tax reporting agent for public assistance recipients who become household employers, check the "Other" box and enter "Household employer agent." If you are a trust that qualifies as a household employer, you do not need a separate EIN for reporting tax information relating to household employees; use the EIN of the trust.

Line 9.—Check only **one** box. Do not enter N/A.

Started new business.—Check this box if you are starting a new business that requires an EIN. If you check this box, enter the type of business being started. **Do not** apply if you already have an EIN and are only adding another place of business.

Hired employees.—Check this box if the existing business is requesting an EIN because it has hired or is hiring employees and is therefore required to file employment tax returns. **Do not** apply if you already have an EIN and are only hiring employees. For information on the applicable employment taxes for family members, see **Circular E,** Employer's Tax Guide (Publication 15).

Created a pension plan.—Check this box if you have created a pension plan and need this number for reporting purposes. Also, enter the type of plan created.

Banking purpose.—Check this box if you are requesting an EIN for banking purposes only, and enter the banking purpose (for example, a bowling league for depositing dues or an investment club for dividend and interest reporting).

Changed type of organization.—Check this box if the business is changing its type of organization, for example, if the business was a sole proprietorship and has been incorporated or has become a partnership. If you check this box, specify in the space provided the type of change made, for example, "from sole proprietorship to partnership."

Purchased going business.—Check this box if you purchased an existing business. **Do not** use the former owner's EIN. **Do not** apply for a new EIN if you already have one. Use your own EIN.

Created a trust.—Check this box if you created a trust, and enter the type of trust created.

Note: *Do not file this form if you are the grantor/owner of certain revocable trusts. You must use your SSN for the trust. See the Instructions for Form 1041.*

Other (specify).—Check this box if you are requesting an EIN for any reason other than those for which there are checkboxes, and enter the reason.

Line 10.—If you are starting a new business, enter the starting date of the business. If the business you acquired is already operating, enter the date you acquired the business. Trusts should enter the date the trust was legally created. Estates should enter the date of death of the decedent whose name appears on line 1 or the date when the estate was legally funded.

Line 11.—Enter the last month of your accounting year or tax year. An accounting or tax year is usually 12 consecutive months, either a calendar year or a fiscal year (including a period of 52 or 53 weeks). A calendar year is 12 consecutive months ending on December 31. A fiscal year is either 12 consecutive months ending on the last day of any month other than December or a 52-53 week year. For more information on accounting periods, see **Pub. 538,** Accounting Periods and Methods.

Individuals.—Your tax year generally will be a calendar year.

Partnerships.—Partnerships generally must adopt the tax year of either (a) the majority partners; (b) the principal partners; (c) the tax year that results in the least aggregate (total) deferral of income; or (d) some other tax year. (See the **Instructions for Form 1065,** U.S. Partnership Return of Income, for more information.)

REMIC.—REMICs must have a calendar year as their tax year.

Personal service corporations.—A personal service corporation generally must adopt a calendar year unless:

● It can establish a business purpose for having a different tax year, or

● It elects under section 444 to have a tax year other than a calendar year.

Trusts.—Generally, a trust must adopt a calendar year except for the following:

● Tax-exempt trusts,

● Charitable trusts, and

● Grantor-owned trusts.

Line 12.—If the business has or will have employees, enter the date on which the business began or will begin to pay wages. If the business does not plan to have employees, enter N/A.

Withholding agent.—Enter the date you began or will begin to pay income to a nonresident alien. This also applies to individuals who are required to file Form 1042 to report alimony paid to a nonresident alien.

Line 13.—For a definition of agricultural labor (farmworker), see **Circular A,** Agricultural Employer's Tax Guide (Publication 51).

Line 14.—Generally, enter the exact type of business being operated (for example, advertising agency, farm, food or beverage establishment, labor union, real estate agency, steam laundry, rental of coin-operated vending machine, or investment club). Also state if the business will involve the sale or distribution of alcoholic beverages.

Governmental.—Enter the type of organization (state, county, school district, municipality, etc.).

Nonprofit organization (other than governmental).—Enter whether organized for religious, educational, or humane purposes, and the principal activity (for example, religious organization—hospital, charitable).

Mining and quarrying.—Specify the process and the principal product (for example, mining bituminous coal, contract drilling for oil, or quarrying dimension stone).

Contract construction.—Specify whether general contracting or special trade contracting. Also, show the type of work normally performed (for example, general contractor for residential buildings or electrical subcontractor).

Food or beverage establishments.—Specify the type of establishment and state whether you employ workers who receive tips (for example, lounge—yes).

Trade.—Specify the type of sales and the principal line of goods sold (for example, wholesale dairy products, manufacturer's representative for mining machinery, or retail hardware).

Manufacturing.—Specify the type of establishment operated (for example, sawmill or vegetable cannery).

Signature block.—The application must be signed by (a) the individual, if the applicant is an individual, (b) the president, vice president, or other principal officer, if the applicant is a corporation, (c) a responsible and duly authorized member or officer having knowledge of its affairs, if the applicant is a partnership or other unincorporated organization, or (d) the fiduciary, if the applicant is a trust or estate.

Some Useful Publications

You may get the following publications for additional information on the subjects covered on this form. To get these and other free forms and publications, call 1-800-TAX-FORM (1-800-829-3676). You should receive your order or notification of its status within 7 to 15 workdays of your call.

Use your computer.—If you subscribe to an on-line service, ask if IRS information is available and, if so, how to access it. You can also get information through IRIS, the Internal Revenue Information Services, on FedWorld, a government bulletin board. Tax forms, instructions, publications, and other IRS information, are available through IRIS.

IRIS is accessible directly by calling 703-321-8020. On the Internet, you can telnet to fedworld.gov. or, for file transfer protocol services, connect to ftp.fedworld.gov. If you are using the WorldWide Web, connect to http://www.ustreas.gov

FedWorld's help desk offers technical assistance on accessing IRIS (not tax help) during regular business hours at 703-487-4608. The IRIS menus offer information on available file formats and software needed to read and print files. You must print the forms to use them; the forms are not designed to be filled out on-screen.

Tax forms, instructions, and publications are also available on CD-ROM, including prior-year forms starting with the 1991 tax year. For ordering information and software requirements, contact the Government Printing Office's Superintendent of Documents (202-512-1800) or Federal Bulletin Board (202-512-1387).

Pub. 1635, Understanding Your EIN

Pub. 15, Employer's Tax Guide

Pub. 15-A, Employer's Supplemental Tax Guide

Pub. 538, Accounting Periods and Methods

Pub. 541, Tax Information on Partnerships

Pub. 542, Tax Information on Corporations

Pub. 557, Tax-Exempt Status for Your Organization

Pub. 583, Starting a Business and Keeping Records

Package 1023, Application for Recognition of Exemption

Package 1024, Application for Recognition of Exemption Under Section 501(a) or for Determination Under Section 120

Paperwork Reduction Act Notice

We ask for the information on this form to carry out the Internal Revenue laws of the United States. You are required to give us the information. We need it to ensure that you are complying with these laws and to allow us to figure and collect the right amount of tax.

The time needed to complete and file this form will vary depending on individual circumstances. The estimated average time is:

Recordkeeping . . . . 7 min.

Learning about the law or the form . . . . . . 18 min.

Preparing the form . . . . . 45 min.

Copying, assembling, and sending the form to the IRS . . 20 min.

If you have comments concerning the accuracy of these time estimates or suggestions for making this form simpler, we would be happy to hear from you. You can write to the Tax Forms Committee, Western Area Distribution Center, Rancho Cordova, CA 95743-0001. **Do not** send this form to this address. Instead, see **Where To Apply** on page 2.

 Printed on recycled paper

*U.S. Government Printing Office: 1996 - 405-493/40061

Department of the Treasury
Internal Revenue Service

Instructions for the Requester of Form W-9
(March 1994)

Request for Taxpayer Identification Number and Certification

Section references are to the Internal Revenue Code, unless otherwise noted.

These instructions supplement the instructions on the Form W-9, for the requester. The payee may also need these instructions.

Substitute Form W-9

You may use a substitute Form W-9 (your own version) as long as it is substantially similar to the official Form W-9 and conforms to Temporary Regulations section 35a.9999-1, Q/A-36. You may not use a substitute form to require the payee, by signing, to agree to provisions unrelated to TIN certification.

TIN Applied For

If the payee returns the Form W-9 with "Applied For" written in Part I, the payee must provide you with a TIN within 60 days. During this 60-day period, you have two options for withholding on reportable interest or dividend payments. For other reportable payments, if you do not receive the payee's TIN within the 60 days you must backup withhold, until the payee furnishes you with his or her TIN.

Option 1.—You must backup withhold on any withdrawals the payee makes from the account after 7 business days after you receive the Form W-9.

Option 2.—You must backup withhold on any reportable interest or dividend payments made to the payee's account, regardless of whether the payee makes any withdrawals. Backup withholding under this option must begin no later than 7 business days after you receive the Form W-9. Under this option, you must refund the amounts withheld if you receive the payee's certified TIN within the 60-day period and the payee was not otherwise subject to backup withholding during the period.

Payees and Payments Exempt From Backup Withholding

The following is a list of payees exempt from backup withholding and for which no information reporting is required. For interest and dividends, all listed payees are exempt except item **(9)**. For broker transactions, payees listed in items **(1)** through **(13)** and a person registered under the Investment Advisers Act of 1940 who regularly acts as a broker are exempt. Payments subject to reporting under sections 6041 and 6041A are generally exempt from backup withholding only if made to payees described in items **(1)** through **(7)**, except a corporation that provides medical and health care services or bills and collects payments for such services is not exempt from backup withholding or information reporting. Only payees described in items **(2)** through **(6)** are exempt from backup withholding for barter exchange transactions, patronage dividends, and payments by certain fishing boat operators.

(1) A corporation.

(2) An organization exempt from tax under section 501(a), or an IRA, or a custodial account under section 403(b)(7).

(3) The United States or any of its agencies or instrumentalities.

(4) A state, the District of Columbia, a possession of the United States, or any of their political subdivisions or instrumentalities.

(5) A foreign government or any of its political subdivisions, agencies, or instrumentalities.

(6) An international organization or any of its agencies or instrumentalities.

(7) A foreign central bank of issue.

(8) A dealer in securities or commodities required to register in the United States or a possession of the United States.

(9) A futures commission merchant registered with the Commodity Futures Trading Commission.

(10) A real estate investment trust.

(11) An entity registered at all times during the tax year under the Investment Company Act of 1940.

(12) A common trust fund operated by a bank under section 584(a).

(13) A financial institution.

(14) A middleman known in the investment community as a nominee or listed in the most recent publication of the American Society of Corporate Secretaries, Inc., Nominee List.

(15) A trust exempt from tax under section 664 or described in section 4947.

Payments of **dividends and patronage dividends** generally not subject to backup withholding include the following:

● Payments to nonresident aliens subject to withholding under section 1441.

● Payments to partnerships not engaged in a trade or business in the United States and that have at least one nonresident partner.

● Payments of patronage dividends not paid in money.

Cat. No. 20479P

- Payments made by certain foreign organizations.

  Payments of **interest** generally not subject to backup withholding include the following:
- Payments of interest on obligations issued by individuals.

Note: *The payee may be subject to backup withholding if this interest is $600 or more and is paid in the course of your trade or business and the payee has not provided his or her correct TIN to you.*
- Payments of tax-exempt interest (including exempt-interest dividends under section 852).
- Payments described in section 6049(b)(5) to nonresident aliens.
- Payments on tax-free covenant bonds under section 1451.
- Payments made by certain foreign organizations.
- Mortgage interest paid to you.

  Payments that are not subject to information reporting are also not subject to backup withholding. For details, see sections 6041, 6041A(a), 6042, 6044, 6045, 6049, 6050A, and 6050N, and their regulations.

  For more information on backup withholding and your requirements, get **Pub. 1679,** A Guide to Backup Withholding, and **Pub. 1281,** Backup Withholding on Missing and Incorrect TINs.

Names and TINs To Use for Information Reporting

Show the full name and address as provided on the Form W-9 on the appropriate information return. If payments have been made to more than one recipient or the account is in more than one name, enter ONLY on the first name line the name of the recipient whose TIN is shown on the information return. Show the names of any other individual recipients in the area below the first name line, if desired.

For sole proprietors, show the individual's name on the first name line. On the second name line, you may enter the business name if provided. You may not enter only the business name. For the TIN, enter either the individual's SSN or the EIN of the business (sole proprietorship).

Notices From the IRS About Your Payees

We will send you a notice if the payee's name and TIN on the information return you filed do not match our records. You may need to send a "B" Notice to the payee to solicit his or her TIN. See Pub. 1679 and Pub. 1281 for copies of the two different "B" Notices.

Printed on recycled paper

*U.S. Government Printing Office: 1994 — 301-628/00119

Form **W-9**
(Rev. December 1996)
Department of the Treasury
Internal Revenue Service

Request for Taxpayer Identification Number and Certification

Give form to the requester. Do NOT send to the IRS.

Please print or type

Name (If a joint account or you changed your name, see **Specific Instructions** on page 2.)

Business name, if different from above. (See **Specific Instructions** on page 2.)

Check appropriate box: ☐ Individual/Sole proprietor   ☐ Corporation   ☐ Partnership   ☐ Other ▶ ....

Address (number, street, and apt. or suite no.)

Requester's name and address (optional)

City, state, and ZIP code

Part I — Taxpayer Identification Number (TIN)

List account number(s) here (optional)

Enter your TIN in the appropriate box. For individuals, this is your social security number (SSN). However, if you are a resident alien OR a sole proprietor, see the instructions on page 2. For other entities, it is your employer identification number (EIN). If you do not have a number, see **How To Get a TIN** on page 2.

Note: *If the account is in more than one name, see the chart on page 2 for guidelines on whose number to enter.*

Social security number

OR

Employer identification number

Part II — For Payees Exempt From Backup Withholding (See the instructions on page 2.)

▶

Part III — Certification

Under penalties of perjury, I certify that:

1. The number shown on this form is my correct taxpayer identification number (or I am waiting for a number to be issued to me), **and**

2. I am not subject to backup withholding because: **(a)** I am exempt from backup withholding, or **(b)** I have not been notified by the Internal Revenue Service (IRS) that I am subject to backup withholding as a result of a failure to report all interest or dividends, or **(c)** the IRS has notified me that I am no longer subject to backup withholding.

Certification Instructions.—You must cross out item **2** above if you have been notified by the IRS that you are currently subject to backup withholding because you have failed to report all interest and dividends on your tax return. For real estate transactions, item **2** does not apply. For mortgage interest paid, acquisition or abandonment of secured property, cancellation of debt, contributions to an individual retirement arrangement (IRA), and generally, payments other than interest and dividends, you are not required to sign the Certification, but you must provide your correct TIN. (See the instructions on page 2.)

Sign Here   Signature ▶   Date ▶

Purpose of Form.—A person who is required to file an information return with the IRS must get your correct taxpayer identification number (TIN) to report, for example, income paid to you, real estate transactions, mortgage interest you paid, acquisition or abandonment of secured property, cancellation of debt, or contributions you made to an IRA.

Use Form W-9 to give your correct TIN to the person requesting it (the requester) and, when applicable, to:

1. Certify the TIN you are giving is correct (or you are waiting for a number to be issued),

2. Certify you are not subject to backup withholding, or

3. Claim exemption from backup withholding if you are an exempt payee.

Note: *If a requester gives you a form other than a W-9 to request your TIN, you must use the requester's form if it is substantially similar to this Form W-9.*

What Is Backup Withholding?—Persons making certain payments to you must withhold and pay to the IRS 31% of such payments under certain conditions. This is called "backup withholding." Payments that may be subject to backup withholding

include interest, dividends, broker and barter exchange transactions, rents, royalties, nonemployee pay, and certain payments from fishing boat operators. Real estate transactions are not subject to backup withholding.

If you give the requester your correct TIN, make the proper certifications, and report all your taxable interest and dividends on your tax return, payments you receive will not be subject to backup withholding. Payments you receive **will** be subject to backup withholding if:

1. You do not furnish your TIN to the requester, or

2. The IRS tells the requester that you furnished an incorrect TIN, or

3. The IRS tells you that you are subject to backup withholding because you did not report all your interest and dividends on your tax return (for reportable interest and dividends only), or

4. You do not certify to the requester that you are not subject to backup withholding under 3 above (for reportable interest and dividend accounts opened after 1983 only), or

5. You do not certify your TIN when required. See the Part III instructions on page 2 for details.

Certain payees and payments are exempt from backup withholding. See the Part II instructions and the separate **Instructions for the Requester of Form W-9.**

Penalties

Failure To Furnish TIN.—If you fail to furnish your correct TIN to a requester, you are subject to a penalty of $50 for each such failure unless your failure is due to reasonable cause and not to willful neglect.

Civil Penalty for False Information With Respect to Withholding.—If you make a false statement with no reasonable basis that results in no backup withholding, you are subject to a $500 penalty.

Criminal Penalty for Falsifying Information.— Willfully falsifying certifications or affirmations may subject you to criminal penalties including fines and/or imprisonment.

Misuse of TINs.—If the requester discloses or uses TINs in violation of Federal law, the requester may be subject to civil and criminal penalties.

Specific Instructions

Name.—If you are an individual, you must generally enter the name shown on your social security card. However, if you have changed your last name, for instance, due to marriage, without informing the Social Security Administration of the name change, enter your first name, the last name shown on your social security card, and your new last name.

If the account is in joint names, list first and then circle the name of the person or entity whose number you enter in Part I of the form.

Sole Proprietor.—You must enter your **individual** name as shown on your social security card. You may enter your business, trade, or "doing business as" name on the **business name** line.

Other Entities.—Enter the business name as shown on required Federal tax documents. This name should match the name shown on the charter or other legal document creating the entity. You may enter any business, trade, or "doing business as" name on the business name line.

Part I—Taxpayer Identification Number (TIN)

You must enter your TIN in the appropriate box. If you are a resident alien and you do not have and are not eligible to get an SSN, your TIN is your IRS individual taxpayer identification number (ITIN). Enter it in the social security number box. If you do not have an ITIN, see **How To Get a TIN** below.

If you are a sole proprietor and you have an EIN, you may enter either your SSN or EIN. However, using your EIN may result in unnecessary notices to the requester.

Note: *See the chart on this page for further clarification of name and TIN combinations.*

How To Get a TIN.—If you do not have a TIN, apply for one immediately. To apply for an SSN, get **Form SS-5** from your local Social Security Administration office. Get **Form W-7** to apply for an ITIN or **Form SS-4** to apply for an EIN. You can get Forms W-7 and SS-4 from the IRS by calling 1-800-TAX-FORM (1-800-829-3676).

If you do not have a TIN, write "Applied For" in the space for the TIN, sign and date the form, and give it to the requester. For interest and dividend payments, and certain payments made with respect to readily tradable instruments, you will generally have 60 days to get a TIN and give it to the requester. Other payments are subject to backup withholding.

Note: *Writing "Applied For" means that you have already applied for a TIN OR that you intend to apply for one soon.*

Part II—For Payees Exempt From Backup Withholding

Individuals (including sole proprietors) are **not** exempt from backup withholding. Corporations are exempt from backup withholding for certain payments, such as interest and dividends. For more information on exempt payees, see the separate Instructions for the Requester of Form W-9.

If you are exempt from backup withholding, you should still complete this form to avoid possible erroneous backup withholding. Enter your correct TIN in Part I, write "Exempt" in Part II, and sign and date the form.

If you are a nonresident alien or a foreign entity not subject to backup withholding, give the requester a completed **Form W-8,** Certificate of Foreign Status.

Part III—Certification

For a joint account, only the person whose TIN is shown in Part I should sign (when required).

1. Interest, Dividend, and Barter Exchange Accounts Opened Before 1984 and Broker Accounts Considered Active During 1983. You must give your correct TIN, but you do not have to sign the certification.

2. Interest, Dividend, Broker, and Barter Exchange Accounts Opened After 1983 and Broker Accounts Considered Inactive During 1983. You must sign the certification or backup withholding will apply. If you are subject to backup withholding and you are merely providing your correct TIN to the requester, you must cross out item 2 in the certification before signing the form.

3. Real Estate Transactions. You must sign the certification. You may cross out item **2** of the certification.

4. Other Payments. You must give your correct TIN, but you do not have to sign the certification unless you have been notified that you have previously given an incorrect TIN. "Other payments" include payments made in the course of the requester's trade or business for rents, royalties, goods (other than bills for merchandise), medical and health care services (including payments to corporations), payments to a nonemployee for services (including attorney and accounting fees), and payments to certain fishing boat crew members.

5. Mortgage Interest Paid by You, Acquisition or Abandonment of Secured Property, Cancellation of Debt, or IRA Contributions. You must give your correct TIN, but you do not have to sign the certification.

Privacy Act Notice

Section 6109 of the Internal Revenue Code requires you to give your correct TIN to persons who must file information returns with the IRS to report interest, dividends,

and certain other income paid to you, mortgage interest you paid, the acquisition or abandonment of secured property, cancellation of debt, or contributions you made to an IRA. The IRS uses the numbers for identification purposes and to help verify the accuracy of your tax return. The IRS may also provide this information to the Department of Justice for civil and criminal litigation and to cities, states, and the District of Columbia to carry out their tax laws.

You must provide your TIN whether or not you are required to file a tax return. Payers must generally withhold 31% of taxable interest, dividend, and certain other payments to a payee who does not give a TIN to a payer. Certain penalties may also apply.

What Name and Number To Give the Requester

For this type of account:	Give name and SSN of:
1. Individual	The individual
2. Two or more individuals (joint account)	The actual owner of the account or, if combined funds, the first individual on the account [1]
3. Custodian account of a minor (Uniform Gift to Minors Act)	The minor [2]
4. a. The usual revocable savings trust (grantor is also trustee)	The grantor-trustee [1]
b. So-called trust account that is not a legal or valid trust under state law	The actual owner [1]
5. Sole proprietorship	The owner [3]

For this type of account:	Give name and EIN of:
6. Sole proprietorship	The owner [3]
7. A valid trust, estate, or pension trust	Legal entity [4]
8. Corporate	The corporation
9. Association, club, religious, charitable, educational, or other tax-exempt organization	The organization
10. Partnership	The partnership
11. A broker or registered nominee	The broker or nominee
12. Account with the Department of Agriculture in the name of a public entity (such as a state or local government, school district, or prison) that receives agricultural program payments	The public entity

[1] List first and circle the name of the person whose number you furnish. If only one person on a joint account has an SSN, that person's number must be furnished.

[2] Circle the minor's name and furnish the minor's SSN.

[3] You must show your individual name, but you may also enter your business or "doing business as" name. You may use either your SSN or EIN (if you have one).

[4] List first and circle the name of the legal trust, estate, or pension trust. (Do not furnish the TIN of the personal representative or trustee unless the legal entity itself is not designated in the account title.)

Note: *If no name is circled when more than one name is listed, the number will be considered to be that of the first name listed.*

 Printed on recycled paper

*U.S. Government Printing Office: 1997 — 417-677/60044

101

Department of the Treasury – Internal Revenue Service

Application for Taxpayer Assistance Order *(ATAO)*
(Taxpayer's Application for Relief from Hardship)

If sending Form 911 with another form or letter, put Form 911 on top.

Note: If you have not tried to obtain relief from the IRS office that contacted you, use of this form may not be necessary. Use this form only after reading the instructions for When To Use This Form. Filing this application may affect the statutory period of limitations. (See instructions for line 14.)

Section I.   Taxpayer Information

1. Name(s) as shown on tax return

2. Your Social Security Number

4. Tax form

3. Social Security of Spouse Shown in 1.

5. Tax period ended

6. Current mailing address (number & street). For P.O. Box, see instructions   Apt. No.

8. Employer identification number, if applicable.

7. City, town or post office, state and ZIP Code

9. Person to contact

If the above address is different from that shown on latest filed tax return and you want us to update our records with this new address, check here......... ❏

10. Daytime telephone number ( )

11. Best time to call

12. Description of significant hardship *(If more space is needed, attach additional sheets.)*

13. Description of relief requested *(If more space is needed, attach additional sheets.)*

A T A O

14. Signature of taxpayer or Corporate Officer *(See instructions.)*

15. Date

16. Signature of spouse shown in block 1

17. Date

Section II.   Representative Information *(If applicable)*

18. Name of authorized representative (Must be same as on Form 2848 or 8821)

22. Firm name

19. Centralized Authorization File (CAF) number

23. Mailing address

20. Daytime telephone number ( )

21. Best time to call

24. Representative Signature

25. Date

Section III.   (For Internal Revenue Service only)

26. Name of initiating employee

27. ❏ IRS Identified ❏ Taxpayer request

28. Telephone ( )

29. Function

30. Office

31. Date

Cat. No. 16965S

Instructions

When To Use This Form: Use this form to apply for relief from a **significant hardship** which may have already occurred or is about to occur if the IRS takes or fails to take certain actions. A significant hardship normally means not being able to provide the necessities of life for you or your family. Examples of such necessities include, but are not limited to: food, shelter, clothing, or medical care. You may use this form at any time. Instead of using this form, **however, the IRS prefers that requests for relief first be made with the IRS office that most recently contacted you.** In most cases, the relief needed can be secured directly from the appropriate IRS employee. For example, Collection employees handle requests for payment arrangements on late taxes or releases of levy on wages, salaries, or bank accounts; Taxpayer Service employees handle requests for immediate refunds of overpaid taxes; Examination employees handle requests for review of additional tax assessments when the taxpayer has had no opportunity to present proof of claimed deductions.

If an IRS office will not grant the relief requested, or will not grant the relief in time to avoid the significant hardship, you may submit this form. No enforcement action will be taken while we are reviewing your application.

Note: Do not use this application to change the amount of any tax you owe. If you disagree with the amount of tax assessed, see **Publication 1, Your Rights as a Taxpayer.**

Where To Submit This Form: Submit this application to the Internal Revenue Service, Problem Resolution Office, in the district where you live. For the address of the Problem Resolution Office in your district or for more information, call the local Taxpayer Assistance number in your local telephone directory or 1-800-829-1040.

Overseas Taxpayers: Taxpayers residing overseas should submit this application to the Internal Revenue Service., Problem Resolution Office, Assistant Commissioner (International), P.O. Box 44817, L'Enfant Plaza Station, Washington, D.C. 20026-4817.

Caution: Incomplete applications or applications submitted to the incorrect office may result in delays. If you do not hear from us within one week of submitting Form 911, please contact the Problem Resolution Office where you sent your application.

Section I. Taxpayer Information

1. Name(s) as shown on tax return. Enter your name as it appeared on the tax return for each period you are asking for help even if your name has changed since the return was submitted. If you filed a joint return, enter both names.

4. Tax form. Enter the tax form number of the form for which you are requesting assistance. For example, if you are requesting assistance for a problem involving an individual income tax return, enter "1040." If your problem involves more than one tax form, include the information in block 12.

5. Tax period ended. If you are requesting assistance on an annually filed return, enter the calendar year or the ending date of the fiscal year for that return. If the problem concerns a return filed quarterly, enter the ending date of the quarter involved. File only one Form 911 even if multiple tax periods are involved. If the problem involves more than one tax period, include the information in block 12.

6. Current mailing address (number and street). If your post office does not deliver mail to your street address and you have a P.O. box, show your box number instead of your street address.

8. Employer Identification Number. Enter the employer identification number (*EIN*) of the business, corporation, trust, etc., for the name you showed in block 1.

9. Person to contact. Enter the name of the person to contact about the problem. In the case of businesses, corporations, trusts, estates, etc., enter the name of a responsible official.

10. Daytime telephone number. Enter the daytime telephone number, including area code, of the person to contact.

12. Description of significant hardship. Describe the action(s) being taken (or not being taken) by the Internal Revenue Service that are causing you significant hardship. If you know it, include the name of the person, office, telephone number, and/or address of the last contact you had with IRS regarding this problem.

13. Description of relief requested. Be specific. If your remaining income after paying expenses is too little to meet an IRS payment, give the details. Describe the action you want the IRS to take.

14. and 16. Signature(s) If you filed a joint return it is not necessary for both you and your spouse to sign this application for your account to be reviewed. If you sign the application the IRS **may** suspend applicable statutory periods of limitations for the assessment of additional taxes and for the collection of taxes. If the taxpayer is your dependent child who cannot sign this application because of age, **or someone incapable of signing the application because of some other reason,** you may sign the taxpayer's name in the space provided followed by the words "By (your signature), parent (or guardian)." If the application is being made for other than the individual taxpayer, a person having authority to sign the return should sign this form. Enter the date Form 911 is signed.

Section II. Representative Information

Taxpayers: If you wish to have a representative act in your behalf, you must give your representative power of attorney or tax information authorization for the tax form(s) and period(s) involved. (*See Form 2848, Power of Attorney and Declaration of Representative and Instructions or Form 8821, Tax Information Authorization, for more information.*)

Representatives: If you are an authorized representative submitting this request on behalf of the taxpayer identified in Section I, complete blocks 18 through 25, attach a copy of Form 2848, Form 8821, or the power of attorney. Enter your Centralized Authorization File (*CAF*) number in block 19. The CAF number is the unique number that Internal Revenue Service assigns to a representative after a valid Form 2848 or Form 8821 is filed with an IRS office.

(For IRS Use Only)

ATAO Code	How received	Date of Determination	PRO signature

Form **911** (Rev. 1-94)

DEPRECIATION SCHEDULE
FOR YEAR 19_____

Name_____

_____

1. Kind of property (if buildings, state material of which constructed). Exclude land and other nondepreciable property.	2. Date acquired	3. Cost or other basis	4. Depreciation in prior years	5. Method	6. Rate (%) or life (years)	7. Depreciation for this year
_____		$	$			$
_____						
_____						
_____						
_____						
_____						
_____						
_____						
_____						
_____						
_____						
_____						
_____						
_____						
_____						
_____						
_____						
_____						
_____						
_____						
_____						
_____						
_____						
_____						
_____						
_____						
_____						
_____						
_____						
_____						
_____						
_____						

T-2   Prepared by_____

[3]———EMPLOYEE COMPENSATION RECORD

NAME _John E. Marks_

ADDRESS _1 Elm St., Newark, NJ_

PHONE _555 - 6075_

FULL TIME _____

PART TIME ___X___

SOC. SEC. NO. ___567 - 00 - 8901___

DATE OF BIRTH ___12 - 21 - 65___

NO. OF EXEMPTIONS ___Single - 1___

Pay Period Ending	Hours Worked														Total Reg. Hours	Over-time	Earnings				Deductions					Net Pay
	S	M	T	W	T	F	S	S	M	T	W	T	F	S			Regular Rate	Overtime Rate	Total	Social Security	Medicare	Fed. Income Tax	State Income Tax	Other	
1/5/91		5	5	5	5	5				5	5	4	6		40		6.50		$260.00	$16.12	$3.77	$20.00	$6.00		$214.11
1/19/91		4	4	4	4	2			4	3	4	4	3		40		6.50		260.00	16.12	3.77	20.00	6.00		214.11
															80				$520.00	$32.24	$7.54	$40.00	$12.00		$428.22
QUARTERLY TOTALS																									

[C]

105

Form **8300**

(Rev. August 1994)

Department of the Treasury
Internal Revenue Service

Report of Cash Payments Over $10,000
Received in a Trade or Business

▶ See instructions for definition of cash.

Please type or print.

OMB No. 1545-0892

1 Check appropriate boxes if: **a** ☐ amends prior report;   **b** ☐ suspicious transaction.

Part I   Identity of Individual From Whom the Cash Was Received

2 If more than one individual is involved, see instructions and check here . . . . ▶ ☐

3 Last name	**4** First name	**5** M.I.	**6** Social security number

7 Address (number, street, and apt. or suite no.)	**8** Date of birth (see instructions)

9 City	**10** State	**11** ZIP code	**12** Country (if not U.S.)	**13** Occupation, profession, or business

14 Method used to verify identity: **a** Describe identification ▶ ....

   b Issued by .... **c** Number ....

Part II   Person (See Definitions) on Whose Behalf This Transaction Was Conducted

15 If this transaction was conducted on behalf of more than one person, see instructions and check here . . . . . . ▶ ☐

16 Individual's last name or Organization's name	**17** First name	**18** M.I.	**19** Social security number

20 Doing business as (DBA) name (see instructions)	Employer identification number

21 Alien identification: **a** Describe identification ▶ ....

   b Issued by .... **c** Number ....

22 Address (number, street, and apt. or suite no.)	**23** Occupation, profession, or business

24 City	**25** State	**26** ZIP code	**27** Country (if not U.S.)

Part III   Description of Transaction and Method of Payment

28 Date cash received	**29** Total cash received $ .00	**30** If cash was received in more than one payment, check here . . . ▶ ☐	**31** Total price if different from item 29 $ .00

32 Amount of cash received (in U.S. dollar equivalent) (see instructions):

   a U.S. currency $ _____ .00   (Amount in $100 bills or higher $ _____ .00)

   b Foreign currency   _____ .00   (Country ▶ _____)

   c Cashier's check(s)   _____ .00 ⎫

   d Money order(s)   _____ .00 ⎬ Issuer's name(s) and serial number(s) of the monetary instrument(s) ▶ ....

   e Bank draft(s)   _____ .00 ⎭

   f Traveler's check(s)   _____ .00 ⎭

33 Type of transaction

   a ☐ personal property purchased   **f** ☐ debt obligations paid

   b ☐ real property purchased   **g** ☐ exchange of cash

   c ☐ personal services provided   **h** ☐ escrow or trust funds

   d ☐ business services provided   **i** ☐ other (specify) ▶

   e ☐ intangible property purchased

34 Specific description of property or service shown in 33. (Give serial or registration number, address, etc.)

   ▶ ....

Part IV   Business That Received Cash

35 Name of business that received cash	**36** Employer identification number

37 Address (number, street, and apt. or suite no.)	Social security number

38 City	**39** State	**40** ZIP code	**41** Nature of your business

42 Under penalties of perjury, I declare that to the best of my knowledge the information I have furnished above is true, correct, and complete.

Sign Here

_____   _____   _____   ( )

(Authorized signature of business that received cash)   (Title)   (Date signed)   (Telephone number of business)

Cat. No. 62133S   Form **8300** (Rev. 8-94)

Multiple Parties
(Complete applicable parts below if box 2 or 15 on page 1 is checked)

Part I   Continued—Complete if box 2 on page 1 is checked

3 Last name	**4** First name	**5** M.I.	**6** Social security number

7 Address (number, street, and apt. or suite no.)	**8** Date of birth (see instructions)

9 City	**10** State	**11** ZIP code	**12** Country (if not U.S.)	**13** Occupation, profession, or business

14 Method used to verify identity: **a** Describe identification ▶ ....
  b Issued by   **c** Number

3 Last name	**4** First name	**5** M.I.	**6** Social security number

7 Address (number, street, and apt. or suite no.)	**8** Date of birth (see instructions)

9 City	**10** State	**11** ZIP code	**12** Country (if not U.S.)	**13** Occupation, profession, or business

14 Method used to verify identity: **a** Describe identification ▶ ....
  b Issued by   **c** Number

Part II   Continued—Complete if box 15 on page 1 is checked

16 Individual's last name or Organization's name	**17** First name	**18** M.I.	**19** Social security number

20 Doing business as (DBA) name (see instructions)	Employer identification number

21 Alien identification: **a** Describe identification ▶ ....
  b Issued by   **c** Number

22 Address (number, street, and apt. or suite no.)	**23** Occupation, profession, or business

24 City	**25** State	**26** ZIP code	**27** Country (if not U.S.)

16 Individual's last name or Organization's name	**17** First name	**18** M.I.	**19** Social security number

20 Doing business as (DBA) name (see instructions)	Employer identification number

21 Alien identification: **a** Describe identification ▶ ....
  b Issued by   **c** Number

22 Address (number, street, and apt. or suite no.)	**23** Occupation, profession, or business

24 City	**25** State	**26** ZIP code	**27** Country (if not U.S.)

Item You Should Note

The term "cash" includes cashier's checks, bank drafts, traveler's checks, and money orders under certain circumstances. See the **Definitions** section of these instructions and Regulations section 1.6050I-1 for more details.

General Instructions

Who Must File.—Each person engaged in a trade or business who, during that trade or business, receives more than $10,000 in cash in one transaction or two or more related transactions, must file Form 8300. Any transactions conducted between a payer (or its agent) and the recipient in a 24-hour period are related transactions. Transactions are considered related even if they occur over a period of more than 24 hours if the recipient knows, or has reason to know, that each transaction is one of a series of connected transactions. This form may be filed voluntarily for any suspicious transaction (see **Definitions**), even if it does not exceed $10,000.

Exceptions.—Cash is not required to be reported if it is received:

● By a financial institution required to file **Form 4789,** Currency Transaction Report.

● By a casino required to file (or exempt from filing) **Form 8362,** Currency Transaction Report by Casinos, (except for cash received in nongaming businesses).

● By an agent who receives the cash from a principal, if the agent uses all of the cash within 15 days in a second transaction that is reportable on Form 8300 or on Form 4789, and discloses all the information necessary to complete Part II of Form 8300 or Form 4789 to the recipient of the cash in the second transaction.

● In a transaction that occurs entirely outside the United States. See **Pub. 1544,** Reporting Cash Payments Over $10,000 (Received in a Trade or Business), regarding transactions occurring in Puerto Rico, the Virgin Islands, and territories and possessions of the United States.

● In a transaction that is not in the course of a person's trade or business.

When and Where To File.—File Form 8300 by the 15th day after the date the cash was received. If that date falls on a Saturday, Sunday, or legal holiday, you may file the form on the next business day. File the form with the Internal Revenue Service, Detroit Computing Center, P.O. Box 32621, Detroit, MI 48232, or hand carry it to your local IRS office. Keep a copy of each Form 8300 for 5 years from the date you file it.

Statement To Be Provided.—You must provide a written statement to each person named in a required Form 8300 on or before January 31 of the year following the calendar year in which the cash is received. The statement must show the name and address of the business, the total amount of reportable cash received, and that the information was furnished to the IRS. Keep a copy of the statement for your records.

Multiple Payments.—If you receive more than one cash payment on a single transaction or on related transactions, you must report the multiple payments any time you receive a total amount in cash payments that exceeds $10,000 within any 12-month period. Report the amount received within 15 days of the date you receive the payment that causes the total amount to exceed $10,000. (If more than one report is required within 15 days, you may file a combined report. File the combined report no later than the date the earliest report, if filed separately, would be required to be filed.)

Taxpayer Identification Number (TIN).—You are required to furnish the correct TIN of the person or persons from whom you receive the cash and the person or persons on whose behalf the transaction is being conducted, if the transaction is being conducted on behalf of another person or persons. You may be subject to penalties for an incorrect or missing TIN. The TIN for an individual is the individual's social security number. For other persons, including corporations, partnerships, and estates, it is the employer identification number. (See Pub. 1544 regarding exceptions for furnishing TINs of certain nonresident alien individuals and foreign organizations.)

Penalties.—If you are required to file a return, you may be subject to penalties if you fail to file a correct and complete return on time and you cannot show that the failure was due to reasonable cause. You may also be subject to penalties if you fail to furnish a correct and complete statement to each person named in a required report on time. More severe penalties (minimum $25,000) may be imposed if the failure is due to an intentional disregard of the cash reporting requirements. In addition, penalties may be imposed for causing (or attempting to cause) a trade or business to fail to file a required report, for causing (or attempting to cause) a trade or business to file a required report containing a material omission or misstatement of fact, or for structuring (or attempting to structure) transactions to avoid the reporting requirements. These violations may also be subject to criminal prosecution which, upon conviction, may result in imprisonment (up to 5 years) or fines (up to $250,000

for individuals and $500,000 for corporations) or both.

Definitions

Cash.—The term "cash" means the following:

● U.S. and foreign coin and currency received in any transaction.

● A cashier's check, bank draft, traveler's check, or money order having a face amount of not more than $10,000 received in a **Designated Reporting Transaction** as defined below, or received in any transaction in which the recipient knows that such instrument is being used in an attempt to avoid the reporting of the transaction under section 6050I.

Note: *Cash does not include a check drawn on the payor's own account, such as a personal check, regardless of the amount.*

Designated Reporting Transaction.—A retail sale (or the receipt of funds by a broker or other intermediary in connection with a retail sale) of a consumer durable, a collectible, or a travel or entertainment activity.

Retail sale.—Any sale (whether or not the sale is for resale or for any other purpose) made in the course of a trade or business if that trade or business principally consists of making sales to ultimate consumers.

Consumer durable.—An item of tangible personal property of a type suitable under ordinary usage for personal consumption or use that can reasonably be expected to be useful for at least 1 year under ordinary usage, and that has a sales price of more than $10,000.

Collectible.—Any work of art, rug, antique, metal, gem, stamp, or coin.

Travel or entertainment activity.—An item of travel or entertainment that pertains to a single trip or event if the combined sales price of the item and all other items relating to the same trip or event that are sold in the same transaction (or related transactions) exceeds $10,000.

Exceptions.—A cashier's check, bank draft, traveler's check, or money order is not considered to be received in a designated reporting transaction if it constitutes the proceeds of a bank loan or if it is received as a payment on certain promissory notes, installment sales contracts, or down payment plans. See Pub. 1544 for more information.

Person.—Includes an individual, a corporation, a partnership, a trust, an estate, an association, or a company.

Recipient.—The person receiving the cash. Each branch or other unit of a person's trade or business is considered a separate recipient unless the branch receiving the cash (or a central office linking the branches) has reason to know the identity of payers making cash payments to other branches.

Transaction.—Includes the purchase of property or services, the payment of debt, the exchange of a negotiable instrument for cash, and the receipt of cash to be held in escrow or trust. A single transaction may not be broken into multiple transactions to avoid reporting.

Suspicious Transaction.—The term "suspicious transaction" means a transaction in which it appears that a person is attempting to cause Form 8300 not to be filed, or a false or incomplete form to be filed, or where there is an indication of possible illegal activity.

Specific Instructions

Complete all parts. Skip Part II if the individual in Part I is conducting the transaction on his or her behalf only.

Item 1.—If you are amending a prior report, check box 1a. Complete the appropriate items with the amended or correct information only. Complete all of Part IV. Staple a copy of the original report to the amended report.

To voluntarily report a suspicious transaction (see **Definitions**), check box 1b. For a suspicious transaction, you may also telephone the local IRS Criminal Investigation Division. If you do not know the number, please call toll-free 1-800-800-2877.

Part I

Item 2.—If two or more individuals conducted the transaction you are reporting, check the box and complete Part I on any one of the individuals. Provide the same information on the other individual(s) on the back of the form. If more than three individuals are involved, provide the same information on additional sheets of paper and attach them to this form.

Item 6.—Enter the social security number of the individual named. See **Taxpayer Identification Number (TIN)** above.

Item 8.—Enter six numerals for the date of birth of the individual named. For example, if the individual's birth date is July 6, 1960, enter 07 06 60.

Item 13.—Use fully descriptive terms such as plumber or attorney instead of nondescriptive terms such as merchant, businessman, or self-employed.

Item 14.—You must verify the name and address of the individual identified. Verification must be made by examination of a document normally accepted as a means of identification when cashing checks (for example, a driver's license, passport, or other official document). In item 14a, enter the type of document used to verify the identification. In item 14b, identify the issuer of that document. In item 14c, enter the document's number. For example, if the individual has a Utah driver's license, enter "driver's license" in item 14a, "Utah" in item 14b, and its number in item 14c.

Part II

Item 15.—If the transaction is being conducted on behalf of more than one person (for example, if the individual in Part I is buying a vehicle on behalf of two persons), check the box and complete Part II on any one of the persons. Provide the same information requested in Part II on the other person(s) on the back of the form. If more than three persons are involved, provide the same information on additional sheets of paper and attach them to this form.

Items 16 Through 19.—If the person on whose behalf the transaction was conducted is an individual, complete items 16, 17, and 18. Enter his or her social security number in item 19. If the individual is a sole proprietor and has an employer identification number (EIN), enter both the SSN and EIN in item 19. If the person is an organization, put its name in item 16 and its EIN in item 19.

Item 20.—If a sole proprietor or other organization named in items 16 through 18 is doing business under a name other than that entered in items 16-18, enter the doing business as (DBA) name here.

Item 21.—If the person is not required to furnish a TIN (see **Taxpayer Identification Number (TIN)**), complete this item. Enter a general description of the type of official document issued to that person in item 21a (e.g., "passport"), the country that issued the document in item 21b, and the document's number in item 21c.

Part III

Item 28.—Enter the date you received the cash. If you received the cash in more than one payment, enter the date you received the payment that caused the combined amount to exceed $10,000. Also, see **Multiple Payments.**

Item 30.—Check the box if the amount shown in item 29 was received in more than one payment, e.g., as installment payments (see **Multiple Payments**) or payments on related transactions.

Item 31.—Enter the total price of the property, services, amount of cash exchanged, etc. (e.g., the total cost of a vehicle purchased, cost of catering service, exchange of currency) if the total price is different from the amount shown in item 29.

Item 32.—Enter the dollar amount of each form of cash received (see the definition of **Cash**). Show amount of foreign items in U.S. dollars. (For cashier's check, bank draft, traveler's check, and/or money order, provide the name of the issuer and the serial number of each instrument.) The sum of the amounts must equal item 29.

Item 33.—Check the appropriate box(es) that describe the transaction. If the transaction is not specified in boxes a–h, check box i and briefly describe it (e.g., car lease, boat lease, house lease, aircraft rental).

Part IV

Item 36.—Enter the EIN of your business. Enter your SSN only if your business has no EIN.

Item 41.—Describe the nature of your business. Use descriptive terms (attorney, auto dealer, jewelry dealer) rather than nondescriptive terms (business, store).

Paperwork Reduction Act Notice

The requested information is useful in criminal, tax, and regulatory investigations, for instance by directing the Federal Government's attention to unusual or questionable transactions. Trades or businesses are required to provide the information under 26 U.S.C. 6050I.

The time needed to complete this form will vary depending on individual circumstances. The estimated average time is 21 minutes. If you have comments concerning the accuracy of this time estimate or suggestions for making this form more simple, you can write to both the **Internal Revenue Service,** Attention: Reports Clearance Officer PC:FP, Washington, DC 20224; and the **Office of Management and Budget,** Paperwork Reduction Project (1545-0892), Washington, DC 20503. DO NOT send this form to either of these offices. Instead, see **When and Where To File** on page 3.

 Printed on recycled paper   *U.S. Government Printing Office: 1995— 387-095/20004*

8

How to Save Taxes

You can save taxes by maximizing start-up, home office, and charitable deductions; by not trading in equipment; by employing family members; by properly utilizing employee fringe benefits; and by knowing your rights as a taxpayer.

MAXIMIZING DEDUCTIONS

To be deductible, a business expense must be both ordinary and necessary. An *ordinary* expense is one that is commonly accepted in your trade, profession, or field of business. A *necessary* expense is one that is helpful and appropriate for your trade, business, or profession. An expense does not have to be indispensable to be considered necessary.

It is important to separate business expenses from capital expenses and from the expenses used to figure the cost of goods sold.

In addition, you must keep your business expenses separate from your personal expenses. If you have an expense that is partly business and partly personal, separate the personal part from the business part.

Start-Up Costs

When you start a business, all of your costs are treated as capital expenses and are a part of your basis in the business. The costs of specific assets generally can be recovered through depreciation deductions. Other costs generally cannot be recovered until you sell or otherwise go out of business.

However, you can elect to amortize certain costs of setting up your business. These costs are deducted in equal amounts over 60 months or more. To be amortizable, costs must qualify in one of the following three areas:

1. Business start-up costs
2. Organizational costs for a corporation
3. Organizational costs for a partnership

Business start-up costs. These include the costs you incur when you set up an active trade or business or investigate the possibility of creating or acquiring an active trade or business. To be amortizable, a start-up cost must meet the following tests:

- It must be a cost that would be deductible if it were paid or incurred to operate an existing trade or business.

- It must be paid or incurred before you actually begin business operations.

Start-up costs may include the following items:

- A survey of potential markets
- An analysis of available facilities, labor, supplies, and/or equipment
- Advertisements for the opening of the business
- Salaries and wages for employees who are being trained and the people who train them
- Travel and other necessary costs for securing prospective distributors, suppliers, or customers
- Salaries and fees for executives and consultants or for other professional services

Start-up costs do *not* include deductible interest, taxes, and research and experimental costs.

When you sell your business. If you completely dispose of a trade or business before the end of an amortization period, any deferred start-up costs for the trade or business that have not been deducted may be deducted to the extent that they qualify as a loss from a trade or business.

Organizational costs for a corporation. These are costs incurred directly for the creation of a corporation. They include the costs of temporary directors, organizational meetings, state incorporation fees, and accounting services. They also include the cost of legal services, such as drafting the charter, bylaws, terms of the original stock certificates, and minutes of organizational meetings.

However, costs for issuing and selling stock or securities, such as commissions, professional fees, and printing costs, are not organizational costs and may not be amortized. Costs for the transfer of assets to the corporation are capitalized, not amortized.

To qualify for amortization, an organizational cost must be as follows:

- Incident to the creation of the corporation. (The cost must be incurred before the end of the first tax year in which the corporation is in business. A corporation using the cash method may amortize organizational expenses incurred within the first tax year even if it does not pay them in that year.)
- Chargeable to a capital account
- A cost that could be amortized over the life of the corporation if the corporation had a fixed life

Organizational costs for a partnership. These are costs incurred to create a partnership. To be amortizable, an organizational cost must be chargeable to a capital account and must be one that could be amortized over the life of the partnership if the partnership had a fixed life.

The expenses must be for the creation of the partnership trade or business. Organizational expenses include legal and accounting fees for services incident to the organization of the partnership, such as the negotiation and preparation of a partnership agreement and filing fees.

Partnership organizational costs do not include syndication fees. That is, they do not include costs for issuing and marketing interests in the partnership, such as commissions, professional fees, and printing costs. These costs are capitalized and cannot be depreciated or amortized.

Start-up and organizational costs are deducted in equal amounts over a period of not less than 60 months. You can elect a period for start-up costs that is different from the period you elect for organizational costs as long as both are 60 months or more. Once you elect an amortization period, you cannot change it.

To figure your deductions, divide your total start-up or organizational costs by the months in the amortization period. The result is the amount you can deduct each month.

For partnerships on the cash method of accounting, however, no deduction is allowed for an expense that has not been paid by the end of the tax year. Any expense that would have been deductible as an organizational expense in an earlier tax year, if it had been paid, is deductible in the tax year of payment.

The Amortization Period

The amortization period starts with the month you begin business operations. You can amortize only if you actually go into business. If it amortizes organizational costs, a partnership or corporation is deemed to begin business operations when it starts the activities for which it was organized. This can occur either before or after the corporate charter is granted or a partnership agreement is signed. A partnership or corporation begins business when its activities have reached the point where the nature of its business operations is established. For example, if it acquires the assets it needs to operate its business, this may constitute the beginning of business activities.

If you want to amortize your costs, complete Part VI of IRS Form 4562 and attach it to your income tax return. Also attach a separate statement to your return for each type of cost. The statement should

- show the total start-up or organizational costs you will amortize,
- describe why each cost was incurred,
- give the date each cost was incurred,
- state the month your business began operations (or the month you acquired the business), and
- specify the number of months in your amortization period (not less than 60).

Attach Form 4562 and the accompanying statements to your return for the first tax year you are in business. The return must be filed by the due date for the return (including any extensions).

ARE YOU OVERLOOKING ANY BUSINESS DEDUCTIONS?

Merchants and professionals may deduct the following expenses, *subject to certain limitations and requirements:*

- Accounting fees
- Advertising
- Appraisal costs (unless for acquisition of property)
- Attorney fees
- Automobile and truck expenses (prorated between business and personal), including automobile club membership, automobile loan interest, casualty loss (uncompensated damages), gasoline tax, gasoline, insurance judgment for negligent driving, loss on sale of automobile, lubrication and oil, parking, repairs, tires (life of less than one year), and washing
- Bad debts
- Bonuses and awards
- Chamber of commerce dues
- Child-care expenses of employees ($5,000 maximum)
- Commissions
- Computer software costs (purchased or leased)
- Conventions (expenses of attending)
- Depreciation on furniture and fixtures
- Entertainment (80 percent maximum)
- Exploration costs
- Garbage removal
- Gifts for customers (limited to $25 per individual per year)
- Insurance
- Interest
- License fees
- Life insurance ($50,000 maximum for group term coverage for employees)
- Liquidated damages under Fair Labor Standards Act
- Machinery repairs and replacement of parts without prolonging life

- Meals and lodging furnished to employees (80 percent maximum)
- Mortgage prepayment penalty
- Moving expenses of employees
- Night-watch service
- Painting
- Picnics, dances, and entertainment for employees
- Political contributions
- Porter and janitor service
- Postage
- Rent
- Repairs to business property
- Research and exploration costs
- Salaries
- Stationery (letters, bills, envelopes, cards)
- Supplemental unemployment benefit plans
- Tax return preparation
- Taxes (employment, excise, and real estate)
- Telephone
- Theft losses (not compensated by insurance)
- Utilities
- Vacation pay
- Wages (if ordinary, necessary, reasonable, for services performed, and actually paid or incurred)

How to Raise Investment Capital for a Small Corporation

Do you want to issue additional stock in order to expand your corporation? Your shareholders can reduce their risks by investing in your corporation if the stock qualifies under Internal Revenue Code section 1244. If they sell the stock at a profit in a few years, they will get tax-sheltered capital gains treatment. On the other hand, if the investment fails, the investor can write off up to $100,000 on a joint return and $50,000 on a separate return. The write-off is applied against ordinary income.

To qualify for 1244 treatment, your corporation does not have to file or adopt a formal plan so long as

- the majority of the income is from business operations,
- the stock is issued for money or property (other than securities), and
- your corporation has $1 million or less in paid-in capital when the stock is issued.

THE HOME OFFICE DEDUCTION

You may deduct expenses if you use your home for business purposes regularly and exclusively

- as the principal place of business,
- as a place to meet or deal with clients in the normal course of the business, or
- in connection with the business if it is a separate structure not attached to your personal residence.

Regular use means an office used on a continuing basis. Occasional or incidental business use of your office does not meet the regular-use test even if the office is not used for any other purpose.

Exclusive use means a specific part of your home is used for business purposes only. Two exceptions to this rule involve the following:

1. *Storage of inventory* if
   - inventory and product samples are stored for the business,
   - the business is a wholesale or retail business,
   - the home is the only fixed location of the business,
   - the storage space is used on a regular basis, and
   - the space used is separately identifiable space suitable for storage.

2. *Day-care facility.* A taxpayer operating a day-care service out of his or her home may deduct a portion of the dwelling as an office even if the area used for the day-care center is *not* set aside exclusively for the business. A room, for example, can be a living room at night and a day-care playroom by day. The day-care center must be operated as a full-time business, not an occasional one. A school *cannot* be run under the cloak of a day-care center—the services must be primarily custodial.

Home office costs are deductible only to the extent of net income from the business activity. Telephone charges above basic service (i.e., toll calls and additional extensions related to business) are deductible. Deductions that are disallowed because they are in excess of net income can be carried forward. Home office users should save their receipts and other records indefinitely.

Concerning *employee use,* home office deductions for employees (or outside salespersons) are affected by the 2 percent floor on miscellaneous itemized deductions.

WHEN TO TRADE IN BUSINESS EQUIPMENT

The purchase of new business equipment usually is partially financed by trading in old equipment. However, when you trade in equipment, you may create tax disadvantages.

If the market value of the equipment is below its adjusted basis, it may be preferable to sell the equipment to realize an immediate deductible loss. *A loss may not be deducted on a trade-in.* With a trade-in, the potential deduction reflected in the cost basis of the old equipment is not forfeited. The undepreciated basis of the old property becomes part of the basis of the new property and may be depreciated.

In deciding whether to trade or sell where a loss may be realized, determine whether a greater tax deduction will be realized by taking an immediate loss on a sale or by claiming larger depreciation deductions with a trade-in.

If the fair market value of the old equipment exceeds its adjusted basis, a potential gain results. To defer tax on this gain, the equipment must be traded in for new equipment.

NOT ALL CHARITABLE CONTRIBUTIONS ARE DEDUCTIBLE

Charitable contributions to qualified organizations are deductible by individuals and corporations. No deduction, however, is allowed partnerships. But partners can deduct, subject to deduction ceilings, their own contributions plus their distributive share of charitable contributions paid by the partnership during its taxable year.

There are two types of not-for-profit organizations: (1) nonprofit, charitable corporations—for example, churches, nonprofit hospitals, foundations, and the like—and (2) all other nonprofit organizations, such as trade associations. A contribution to an organization in the second group cannot be taken as a charitable contribution even if the organization is not taxed on its income. (You may, however, be able to deduct dues to such groups as "ordinary and necessary business expense.")

An organization qualifies as a charitable organization if it satisfies the tests of the Internal Revenue Code. Ordinarily, such an organization will obtain an IRS ruling to the effect that it satisfies Internal Revenue Code section 170 for qualification as a charitable entity. If it has not done so, then the donor will have to establish the charitable status of the donee.

If you are uncertain about the status of a group that has solicited you for a contribution, you can get your answer from the IRS. It publishes the *Cumulative List of Organizations Described in Section 170(c) of the Internal Revenue Code of 1954*. Request Pub. No. 78 from the Superintendent of Documents, Government Printing Office, Washington, DC 20402. Bimonthly supplements to this list are available from the same source. For the status of an organization not listed in these publications, inquiries may be addressed to the Commissioner of Internal Revenue, Attention: T:R:EO, Washington, DC 20224.

If payments are made to a charity in connection with admission to, or other participation in, fundraising activities such as charity balls, bazaars, banquets, shows, and athletic events, the amount of these payments is deductible only to the extent that it exceeds the fair market value of the value received by the payor. When a charity engages in fundraising activities designed to solicit payments that are in part a gift and in part the purchase price of admission to an event, the charity must clearly indicate to contributors the extent to which such payments are deductible as a charitable gift. Any ticket or receipt provided to a contributor must state the respective amounts of the gift and payment for admission.

EMPLOY YOUR CHILDREN

You can employ your children in your business, pay them a reasonable salary, and deduct their salary as a business expense. The wage earned by the child is earned income taxed at the child's own rate. A child can earn up to $4,000 without paying tax. Children under age 18 who work for a parent are *not* subject to Social Security withholding or employer tax. An additional $2,000 of a child's salary can escape tax if put into an IRA, where the earnings will accumulate tax-deferred.

Your child's compensation will be tax deductible if

- the work is done in connection with your trade or business (or income-producing property),
- the child actually renders services to the trade or business,
- payments to the child are reasonable in relation to the services rendered, and
- payments are actually made.

FRINGE BENEFITS

Fringe benefits constitute one of the main advantages of a corporation over a sole proprietorship. Fringe benefits (such as health insurance, medical reimbursement plans, a company car, a travel expense account, education, and group life insurance) are personal expenses and are nondeductible in a sole proprietorship. In the case of a corporation, however, they are tax deductible. The value of the benefit is tax-free to owner employees if they meet certain conditions. Flexible spending accounts or cafeteria plans are fringe benefits that owner-employees can use to pay for medical expenses and day-care costs. The payments are made with pretax earnings as payroll deductions or employer contributions.

Compensation Package Checklist

The checklist that follows shows the many ways in which you can compensate and provide benefits for yourself and your employees.

The "Employee Benefit Communications Checklist" section contains tips on the ways that you can notify your employees of their benefits and also obtain their feedback regarding their satisfaction with these benefits.

Direct Pay
- ❑ Wages
- ❑ Salaries
- ❑ Commissions
- ❑ Incentives
- ❑ Premiums
- ❑ Overtime
- ❑ Shift differentials
- ❑ Holiday

Employee Benefits Legally Required

❏ Social Security
❏ Workers' compensation
❏ Unemployment insurance
❏ State temporary disability

Pensions

❏ Defined benefit
❏ Fixed benefit
❏ Unit benefit
❏ Defined contribution
  1. Money purchase
  2. Profit sharing
     • Thrift plan
     • Employee stock ownership plan (ESOP)
     • Individual retirement account (IRA)
❏ SEP-IRA (Simplified Employee Pension–Individual Retirement Account)
❏ SARSEP-IRA (Salary Reduction Simplified Employee Pension–Individual Retirement Account)
❏ Money purchase/Target benefit
❏ 401(k) plan
❏ REAL-VEBA (multiple employer welfare plan)

Group Insurance

❏ Life
❏ Medical
❏ Dental
❏ Vision care
❏ Prescription drugs
❏ Major medical
❏ Short-term disability
❏ Long-term disability
❏ Health maintenance organizations (HMOs)

Supplementary Insurance

❏ Term life
❏ Ordinary life
❏ Travel-accident
❏ Accidental death and dismemberment (AD&D)
❏ Homeowners
❏ Automobiles

Payment for Time Not Worked

❏ Personal business
❏ Severance/layoff
❏ Military duty

❏ Lunch period
❏ Vacations
❏ Holidays
❏ Bereavement
❏ Jury/witness
❏ Clean-up allowance
❏ Supplemental unemployment
❏ Guaranteed annual wage
❏ Relief break

Employee Services

❏ Employee meals
❏ Social-recreational programs
❏ Legal services
❏ Christmas bonus
❏ Employee suggestion program
❏ Membership in professional trade associations
❏ Travel clubs
❏ Credit unions
❏ Discount purchases
❏ Credit cards
❏ Income tax services
❏ Preretirement counseling
❏ Relocation expenses
❏ Food services
❏ Work-study programs
❏ Scholarships for dependent children
❏ Matched donations—universities and colleges

Capital Accumulation

❏ Cash profit sharing
❏ Service bonuses/awards
❏ Performance bonuses
❏ Employee savings/thrift plan
❏ Nonqualified stock purchase plan
❏ Tax-deferred annuities
❏ Payroll-based stock ownership (PAYSOP)
❏ Stock bonuses
❏ IRAs
❏ Keogh plans (HR-10)

Executive Capital Accumulation

❏ Phantom stock plan
❏ Incentive growth plan
❏ Performance shares/units
❏ Excess personal liability insurance
❏ Key person life insurance

❏ Education benefits
❏ Nonqualified supplemental pension plan
❏ Stock options
❏ Stock appreciation rights
❏ Stock purchase plan (executive)
❏ Split-dollar life insurance
❏ Cash bonus plan
❏ Apartment/suites
❏ Deferred profit sharing
❏ Directors'/officers' liability protection
❏ Executive group life insurance
❏ Deferred compensation plan
   1. Qualified
   2. Nonqualified

Perquisites

❏ Legal assistance
❏ Company automobile
❏ Extra vacation
❏ Vacation villas
❏ Special parking privileges
❏ Personal expense accounts
❏ Spouse traveling on company business
❏ Loans/mortgages
❏ Club memberships
❏ Chauffeur
❏ Airplane(s)
❏ Estate planning
❏ Financial counseling
❏ Home entertainment allowance
❏ Physical examinations
❏ Executive dining room
❏ Sabbaticals (with pay)
❏ Special executive medical expense reimbursement

Personnel Policies and Practices Requiring Additional Expenditures

❏ Orientation and training
❏ Banking services
❏ Tuition refund
❏ Broker/consultant
❏ Relocation expenses
❏ House financing
❏ Medical facilities
❏ Employee benefit booklets
❏ Employee benefit statements
❏ Administrative costs (other)
❏ Employee benefits consultant

Laws Pertaining to Employee Benefits

The complexity of employee benefits law stems from the broad scope of legislation and Internal Revenue Service regulations governing benefits administration, including the following:

• Age Discrimination in Employment Act
• Americans with Disabilities Act (See Chapter 17.)
• Civil Rights Act of 1964—Title VII (maternity-disability benefits)
• Employee Retirement Income Security Act of 1974 (ERISA)
• Fair Labor Standards Act (Equal Pay Act Amendment) (See Chapter 11.)
• Federal and state unemployment insurance
• Foreign Corrupt Practices Act of 1977
• Health Maintenance Organization Act (HMO)
• Older Workers' Benefit Protection Act (See section in this chapter.)
• Revenue Acts of 1978
• Social Security Act
• State temporary disability statutes—California, Hawaii, New Jersey, New York, Puerto Rico, and Rhode Island
• State workers' compensation laws
• Tax Equity and Fiscal Responsibility Act of 1982 (TEFRA)
• 401(k) Internal Revenue Code
• 501(c) Internal Revenue Code

Employee Benefits Communication Checklist

You can notify your employees of benefits by means of the following:

• Summary plan descriptions
• Computerized statements
• Notices on bulletin boards
• Annual reports
• Booklets and brochures
• Films and filmstrips
• Employee publications
• Posters
• Benefit manuals
• Closed-circuit TV
• Word-of-mouth

- Reports (other than annual reports)
- Employee meetings
- Slide presentations
- Pay envelope inserts
- Paycheck deduction stubs
- Regular employee meetings
- Letters to employees' homes
- Personal counseling sessions

You can use the following ways to obtain feedback from your employees regarding their benefits:

- Attitude surveys
- Suggestions systems
- Face-to-face contacts
- Union contacts
- Telephone hot line
- Question-and-answer formats (employee publications)

Fringe Benefits That Are Tax-Free to Employees

The following employee fringe benefits are tax-free to employees unless otherwise noted:

- *No-additional-cost service.* This includes hotel accommodations; telephone services; and transportation by aircraft, train, bus, subway, and cruise liner. The value of the service is excluded from an employee's gross income if the service is offered to the public *and* the employer incurs no additional cost by offering the service to the employee.
- *Qualified employee discounts.* This applies to goods and services that the employer generally offers to the public.
- *Working-condition fringe benefits.* Goods and services that the employer generally offers to the public are tax-free to the employee if they would have been deductible as a business expense had the employee paid for the expense.
- *De minimis fringe benefits.* These are minimal benefits, such as occasional personal use of office equipment by the employee.
- *On-premises athletic facilities.* Such facilities are tax-free to employees if the facility generally is only used by employees, their spouses, and their children.

- *Day-care services.* These services can be paid for by the employees with pretax earnings or employer contributions.
- *Educational assistance.* This includes tuition, fees, books, and supplies. Employer assistance payments of up to $5,250 are excluded from employees' gross income.
- *Employee achievement awards up to $400 for nonqualified plans and $1,600 for qualified plans per year.* An example of such an award is a watch given to an employee for length of service or safety achievement.
- *Meals and lodging.* Meals provided on the employer's business premises for the employer's convenience are tax-free; lodging must be a condition of employment.
- *Accident and health insurance* (See "Medical Savings Accounts" below.)
- *Group-term life insurance up to $50,000 coverage*
- *Cafeteria plans.* These are explained in the next section. They are programs providing two or more benefits consisting of cash and qualified benefits and permit the employee to choose the benefit he or she considers most valuable.
- *Deferred compensation.* This refers to a situation in which employees agree to work now and defer receipt of their salary until a future date. The payment may be tax deferred or taxable to the employees currently, depending on the arrangement.
- *Employer-provided vehicle.* The cost of a vehicle used by an employee for business or personal purposes may be taxable or tax-free to the employee, depending on the arrangement.
- *Qualified retirement plans.* These are tax deferred to the employee until the funds are withdrawn.

Welfare Benefit Plans

The choice of business form affects the availability and taxability of welfare benefit plans. The wrong choice can result in a large tax liability. "Welfare benefits" are plans established or maintained by the employer to provide certain benefits (other than pension or retirement benefits) such as health insurance, disability insurance, life and accident insurance, vacation plans, and supplemental unemployment plans. The definition of "employee" excludes sole proprietors, partners, and certain shareholders of S corporations who are treated as self-employed.

The objective is to have benefits excluded from taxable income and be deductible by the employer as a business expense.

Health insurance.

Sole proprietorships. Health insurance benefits are not taxable for nonowner employees. Owner employees can deduct 40 percent (to be increased to 80 percent by 2006) of the cost of health insurance premiums paid for them, their spouse, and their dependents. The net remaining premium cost can be treated as an itemized deduction subject to limitations. Reimbursements received from health insurance plans by owner employees are excluded from gross income.

C corporations. Gross income of shareholder employees and nonshareholder employees does not include employer-provided health insurance and monies received from health insurance plans as reimbursement for medical expenses except for self-insured discriminatory plans established to benefit highly compensated employees (one of the five highest-paid officers, a shareholder who owns more than 10 percent of stock, or one among the highest-paid 25 percent of all employees).

S corporations, partnerships, and LLCs. When an employee is also a partner, an LLC member, or a 2 percent-plus shareholder of an S corporation, the employee is treated as self-employed. Thus, his or her health insurance premium is not a deductible business expense but is included in gross income, and the employee is entitled to a deduction of 40 percent of the premium value.

Life insurance and death benefits.
The value of the premiums paid by the employer are included in the employee's gross income except when the insurance is group term (not whole life), the individual is a current employee, the plan is nondiscriminatory and available to all employees, and the insurance cost for policies over $50,000 is included in the employee's gross income.

The premiums paid for S corporations, shareholders, LLC members, sole proprietors, and partners are not deductible but are included in gross income.

Disability benefits.

Sole proprietorship. Disability insurance for nonowner employees is deductible. Unlike health insurance, no proportion of the premium is allowed as a business deduction for owner employees.

C corporations. Employees, whether shareholders or not, are entitled to exclude from their income the value of a disability policy provided by the employer.

S corporations, partnerships, and LLCs. Shareholders and partners in these business forms are not entitled to deductions.

Cafeteria Plans

A cafeteria plan differs from traditional employee benefit plans in allowing employees to customize their benefit package. Any plan that allows employees to choose between receiving taxable compensation and funding one or more tax-free benefits is a cafeteria plan. An older employee usually chooses a deferred 401(k) retirement plan, while a younger employee might select a life or health insurance benefit. The plan must be maintained by an employer solely for the benefit of its employees and must be written, available to all eligible employees, and include two or more benefits consisting of cash and qualified benefits. A *qualified benefit* is any benefit that is not includable in the gross income of the employee by an express statutory exclusion (except educational assistance programs, scholarships, van pooling, or excludable fringe benefits). Except for section 401(k) arrangements, a cafeteria plan may not include a plan that enables employees to defer compensation. Thus, unused contributions to the plan in one year may not be carried over to a subsequent year. However, plans may pay employees in cash for unused elective vacation days so long as the employees receive the cash by the end of the plan year or the employees' tax year.

Medical Savings Accounts

The uninsured, self-employed, and those who work for employers with 50 or fewer employees are eligible for Medical Savings Accounts (MSAs). Contributions are deductible from taxable income whether or not the taxpayer itemizes.

To avoid a 15 percent withdrawal penalty, the funds must remain in the account until it is used to pay medical bills. However, funds not spent are automatically rolled over into succeeding years, earning interest tax-free until they are spent or otherwise withdrawn.

MSAs must be set up in conjunction with a qualified health insurance policy, either straight indemnity or some kind of managed-care plan. For an individual policy, the deductible must be at least $1,500 and no more than $2,250. For a family policy, the range is $3,000 to $4,500.

The law limits the amount of contributions that may be excluded from taxes. For individual policies, the limit is 65 percent of the deductible, or $1,462.50 for a $2,250 deductible policy. For families, the limit is 75 percent, or $3,375 for a $4,500 deductible policy. Also, funds may be withdrawn without penalty for any purpose at age 65. Unlike IRAs, there is no age at which taxable withdrawals must be made.

Savings Incentive Match Plan

The Savings Incentive Match Plan for Employees (SIMPLE) (see the form at the end of this chapter) is available to any business with fewer than 100 employees. Either a 401(k) plan or an IRA can be set up. In order to qualify

- employee contributions must be limited to $6,000 per year;
- the company must agree to (1) match an employee's contribution dollar-for-dollar up to 3 percent of the employee's salary, or (2) contribute 2 percent of each employee's salary regardless of the employee's contribution (for this requirement, salaries are capped at $150,000);
- the total of an employee's contribution and the company's contribution can't be more than $10,500;
- the company can't maintain any other retirement plan; and
- all contributions must vest immediately.

If a plan discriminates in favor of highly compensated employees as to either eligibility to participate or benefits enjoyed, it will lose its nontaxable status for highly compensated employees. Therefore, if lower-paid employees do not participate or participate only marginally, the tax-free benefits are lost to key or highly compensated employees. Benefits to nonkey employees or those not highly compensated remain nontaxable even if the plan fails the discrimination tests.

A plan that provides health benefits will not be treated as discriminatory if

- contributions on behalf of each participant either equal 100 percent of the health benefits cost for the majority of similarly situated, highly compensated participants or are at least 75 percent of the health benefits cost for similarly situated participants having the highest-cost health benefits coverage, and
- contributions in excess of those described above bear a uniform relationship to compensation.

A separate nondiscrimination test applies to key employees. If key employees receive more than 25 percent of the nontaxable benefits provided to all participants under the plan, benefits received by the key employees will be taxed to them. (See the chart at the end of this chapter for reporting requirements.)

Older Workers' Benefit Protection Act

Under the Older Workers' Benefit Protection Act, employers

- must provide older workers with benefits at least equal to those provided for younger workers unless the employer can prove that the cost of providing an equal benefit is greater for an older worker than for a younger worker;
- may provide early retirement incentives within certain limits;
- may have a defined pension plan that provides payments constituting the subsidized portion of early retirement benefits;
- may have pension benefit plans that establish minimum ages as a condition of eligibility for early or normal retirement benefits;
- may reduce long-term disability benefits by pension benefits not attributable to employee contributions when these disability benefits have been paid to an individual after the individual voluntarily elected to receive them or when an individual has reached either age 62 or normal retirement age;
- may pay Social Security supplements under defined benefit pension plans; and
- may provide minimum ages for benefit eligibility and pension plans.

The Effect of the ADA on Employee Benefit Plans

The Americans with Disabilities Act (ADA) generally prohibits employers from discriminating against the disabled in employment, public accommodations, and public service (see Chapter 17). Within the context of nondiscrimination in employment, an employer may not discriminate against an individual with a disability in regard to the terms, conditions, and privileges of employment. Employers should be aware that the terms, conditions, and privileges of employment include employee benefit plans.

The ADA generally requires that employees with disabilities be accorded equal access to whatever health coverage the employer provides to other employees. Certain plan features, such as a preexisting condition exclusion or a limitation on the number of times a particular procedure may be performed in a year, will not be considered discriminatory even if they adversely affect individuals with a disability as long as the plan features are not used as a subterfuge to evade the purpose of the legislation.

TAXPAYERS' BILL OF RIGHTS

- The IRS must furnish a statement describing taxpayers' rights and obligations and the procedures for appeal, refund claims, and collections when contacting a taxpayer about a tax deficiency or an audit.

- Taxpayers can make audio recordings of examination interviews provided they give proper notice.

- The IRS is prohibited from imposing production quotas on IRS employees directly involved in the collection process.

- Taxpayers can make installment payment agreements with the IRS for tax deficiencies when certain financial conditions exist.

- The waiting period after the IRS notifies a taxpayer of its intent to impose a levy on the taxpayer's property is 30 days.

- Taxpayers can recover legal fees if the IRS position is unjustified. The taxpayer must first try to remedy the problem through proper procedures.

- The amount of weekly wages exempt from a levy is equal to the taxpayer's standard deduction plus personal exemptions divided by 52.

- The taxpayer's principal residence is exempt from a levy unless a district director or assistant district director of the IRS approves the levy or the Secretary of the Treasury determines the tax collection is in jeopardy.

- Banks must hold accounts for 21 days before surrendering levies to the IRS.

- The IRS must release seized property promptly when the tax liability is paid or when an installment agreement is made.

- Tax problems that are not resolved through normal channels can be handled by the Problem Resolution Office of the IRS, which must arrange for an immediate review of the case. During the review the IRS will not take any enforcement action. (See Form 911 at the end of Chapter 7.)

- IRS examinations must take place at a reasonable time and place convenient to the taxpayer and the IRS.

- A taxpayer can be represented by an attorney, certified public accountant, or an enrolled agent. At the taxpayer's request, the IRS must suspend an interview to allow the taxpayer to exercise the right to consultation.

- Taxpayers can sue the government if the IRS wrongfully fails to release a lien or if an IRS employee disregards tax laws while collecting tax.

- A penalty cannot be imposed on a tax deficiency resulting from erroneous advice provided in writing by an IRS employee.

HOW AND WHEN TO USE THE FORMS IN THIS CHAPTER

Reporting and Disclosure Guide for Employee Benefit Plans. This guide will help you determine your reporting and disclosure responsibilities under the Employee Retirement Income Security Act (ERISA). Generally, you must file reports with the government and provide plan information directly to participants and beneficiaries.

IRS Form 5305-SIMPLE. This is a model Savings Incentive Match Plan for Employees of Small Employers (SIMPLE) plan document that employers may use in combination with SIMPLE IRAs to establish a SIMPLE plan. Although you are not required to file this form with the IRS, you must keep it for your records.

To Plan Administrators:

This guide is designed to help you determine your reporting and disclosure responsibilities under the Employee Retirement Income Security Act (ERISA). In general, you must file reports with the government and provide plan information directly to participants and beneficiaries.

For a complete description of the reporting and disclosure requirements, consult the regulations on reporting and disclosure requirements.

Although this guide is a quick reference to the reporting and disclosure requirements, it does not in any way replace regulations issued on the subject. These should be referred to for specific details. Reports required only for such special events as plan mergers, etc., are not covered in this guide.

For more information contact:

U. S. Department of Labor
Pension and Welfare Benefits Administration
Division of Reporting and Disclosure
Room N5669
200 Constitution Ave., N. W.
Washington, D.C. 20210
(202) 219-8515

and

Pension Benefit Guaranty Corporation
Standard Termination Processing Division
1200 K Street, N.W., Suite 930
Washington, D.C. 20005-4026
(202) 326-4000

Key:	**DOL**	Department of Labor
	IRS	Internal Revenue Service
	PBGC	Pension Benefit Guaranty Corporation

Forms	**With 100 or more participants**
Summary Plan Description[1]	**DOL Initial**-SPD within 120 days after plan is subject to ERISA. **Amended**-A summary of material modifications or updated SPD is due 210 days after end of plan year in which a change was made.
Annual Return/ Report Form 5500 *See Note - pg 4	**IRS**-By last day of the 7th month after end of plan year.
Annual Return/ Report Form 5500-C[2] *See Note - pg 4	
Registration Statement Form 5500-R *See Note -pg 4	
Schedule A Insurance Information	**IRS** - For insured plans, filed with Form 5500.
Schedule B Actuarial Information	**IRS** - If subject to minimum funding standards, filed with Form 5500.
Schedule C Trustee/Service Provider Information	**IRS** - For service provider, trustee and termination information, filed with Form 5500.
Schedule SSA Identification of Separated Participants with Deferred Vested Benefits	**IRS** - If plan has participants with deferred vested benefits separated during plan year, filed with Form 5500.
Summary Annual Report *Not required to be filed with the DOL*	**Participants**- Nine months after end of plan year.

1   **Participants-Initial**-SPD within 120 days after plan is subject to ERISA. New participants within 90 days after becoming covered by the plan. **Amended** - A summary of material modification or updated SPD is due 210 days after end of plan year in which a change was made. SPD must be updated every five years if there are material modifications; 10 years in any event.

2   The Form 5500-C must be filed: A) The initial plan year (the year the plan begins); B) The year a final report would be filed; C) At least once every three years with the Form 5500-R filed for each plan year for which the 5500-C is not filed. (For Annual Return of One-Participant (Owners and Their Spouses) Pension Benefit Plan, file Form 5500-EZ with the IRS by the last day of the 7th month after the end of the plan year.) See the instructions to the appropriate forms under the heading "What to File."

With fewer than 100 Participants

DOL-Initial-SPD within 120 days after plan is subject to ERISA.
Amended-A summary of material modification or updated SPD is due 210 days after end of plan year in which a change was made.

IRS - By last day of the 7th month after end of plan year.

IRS - By last day of the 7th month after end of plan year for which Form 5500-C is not required to be filed.

IRS - For insured plans, filed with Form 5500-C/R.

IRS - If subject to minimum funding standards, filed with Form 5500-C/R.

IRS - If plan has participants with deferred vested benefits separated during plan year, filed with Form 5500-C/R.

Participants - Nine months after end of plan year.[3]

Regardless of the Number of Participants

Form: **Notice of Failure to Meet Minimum Funding Standards**

DOL - For plans subject to the minimum funding standards, other than multiemployer plans, the employer must provide notice to **participants and beneficiaries** (including alternate payees) -within 60 days of a failure to make a required payment or, if a waiver from the minimum funding standards was pending relating to the payment, within 60 days after the date of a denial of the waiver.

Forms

With 100 or more participants

Summary Plan Description[4]	**DOL Initial** - SPD within 120 days after plan is subject to ERISA. **Amended** - A summary of material modifications or updated SPD is due 210 days after end of plan year in which a change was made
Annual Return/ Report Form 5500 *See Note	**IRS**-By last day of the 7th month after end of plan year.
Annual Return/ Report Form 5500-C[5] *See Note	
Registration Statement Form 5500-R *See Note	
Schedule A Insurance Information	**IRS** - For insured plans, filed with Form 5500.
Schedule C Trustee/ Service Provider Information	**IRS** - For service provider, trustee and termination information. filed with Form 5500.
Summary Annual Report Not required to be filed with the DOL	**Participants**- Nine months after end of plan year.

NOTE: If the plan has between 80 and 120 participants (inclusive) at the beginning of the plan year, the plan administrator may filed the same type of form that was filed for the previous year. Such forms can be Form 5500 or Form 5500-C/R, whichever applies.

4   **Participants-Initial**-SPD within 120 days after plan is subject to ERISA. New participants within 90 days after becoming covered by the plan. **Amended**-A summary of material modification or updated SPD is due 210 days after end of plan year in which a change was made. SPD must be updated every five years if there are material modifications. 10 years in any event.

5   The Form 5500-C must be filed: A) The initial plan year (the year the plan begins); B) The year a final report would be filed; C) At least once every three years with the Form 5500-R filed for each plan year for which the 5500-C is not filed. See the instructions to the appropriate forms under the heading "What to File."

6   These plans, for the plan year the Form 5500-R is filed, must either furnish participants with a copy of the Form 5500-R and a copy of a disclosure notice or a notice that participants may submit a written request to obtain a copy of the Form 5500-R. See DOL regulation 29 CFR 2520.104b-10.

3   These plans. for the plan year the Form 5500-R is filed, must either furnish participants with a copy of the Form 5500-R and a copy of a disclosure notice or a notice that participants may submit a written request to obtain a copy of the Form 5500-R. See DOL regulation 29 CFR 2520.104b-10.

With fewer than 100 participants which are not:

    (1) Fully insured,
    (2) Unfunded or
    (3) Combination of insured and unfunded

DOL- Initial-SPD within 120 days after plan is subject to ERISA. **Amended** - A summary of material modification or updated SPD is due 210 days after end of plan year in which a change was made.

IRS - By last day of the 7th month after end of plan year.

IRS - By last day of the 7th month after end of plan year for which Form 5500-C is not required to be filed.

IRS - For insured plans, file with Form 5500-C/R.

Participants - Nine months after end of plan year.[6]

ADDENDUM: Certain categories of plans have been exempted from most or all of the reporting and disclosure requirements, while other plans meeting certain conditions are exempted from some of the requirements. Administrators should refer to the applicable section published in Title 29, Part 2520 - Rules and Regulations for Reporting and Disclosure. These plans include: apprenticeship plans - section 2520.104-22; pension and welfare plans for certain selected employees - sections 2520.104-23 and 2520.104-24; certain dues-financed pension and welfare plans - sections 2520.104-27 and 2520.104-26; welfare plans participating in certain group insurance arrangements - sections 2520.104-21 and 2520.104-43; certain unfunded welfare plans - sections 2520.104-20 and 2520.104-44; certain fully insured pension plans - section 2520.104-44; and certain simplified employee pension plans - sections 2520.104-48 and 2520.104-49.

Forms	With fewer than 100 Participants
PBGC-1 Annual Premium Filing	**PBGC**-For PBGC-covered defined benefit plans, by the 15th day of the 8th full calendar month following the month in which the plan year began. Plans with 500 or more participants for the prior plan year must file the estimated flat rate premium (Form 1-ES) by the last day of the second full calendar month following the close of the prior plan year.
Notice of ReportableEvent	**PBGC**-For covered defined benefit plans, file for some reportable events by 30 days after the event occurs.
Notice of Failure to Make Required Contributions PBGC Form 200	**PBGC**-For covered defined benefit plans with aggregate missed contributions of more than $1 million, file no later than 10 days after contribution due date.
Notice of Security Requirement Due to Amendment Increasing Benefits	**PBGC**-For defined benefit plans amended to increase benefits by more than $10 million, file within 30 days after amendment.
Notice of Intent to Terminate[7]	**Participants**-At least 60 and no more than 90 days before proposed plan termination date. If possible insurers not known at this time, supplemental notice no later than 45 days before date of distribution.
Notice of Plan Benefits[8]	**Participants**-No later than the date Form 5500 filed with PBGC.
Standard Termination Notice PBGC Form 500[9]	**PBGC**-On or before the 120th day after the proposed termination date. If possible insurers not known at this time, supplemental notice no later than 45 days before date of distribution.
Post-Distribution Certification PBGC Form 501[10] or 602[11]	**PBGC**-No later than the 30th day after distribution of plan assets completed.

fewer than 100 participants	Forms	With 100 or more participants
PBGC-For defined benefit plans by the 15th day of the 8th full calendar month following the month in which the plan year began.	**Notice of Intent to Terminate-** No form for participants; **PBGC Form 600 for PBGC**[12]	**Participants and PBGC**-At least 60 and (except with PBGC approval) no more than 90 days before proposed termination date. (Issue to participants by time of PBGC notice.)
Same	**Distress Termination Notice PBGC Form 601**[13]	**PBGC**-On or before the 120th day after the proposed plan termination date.
Same	**Notice of Request to Bankruptcy Court to Approve Termination**[14]	**PBGC**-Concurrently with the request to Bankruptcy Court.
Same	**Notice of Plan's Funding Status and Limits on PBGC Guarantee**	**Participants**-No later than two months after due date for annual report for previous plan year.
Same	**Advance Notice of Reportable Events**	**PBGC**-For privately-held companies in controlled groups with aggregate unfunded vested benefits over $50 million and aggregate funded vested benefit percentage under 90 percent. file for some reportable events at least 30 days in advance of occurrence.
Same		
Same		
Same		

NOTE: If a plan finds itself in the situation where a termination will (or may) occur, they should contact PBGC for full instructions regarding their filing obligations. The plan should not rely solely on the brief overview of the filing requirements in this pamphlet.

5, 6, 7, 8 Standard Terminations

9, 10, 11, 12, 13, 14 Distress Terminations

Savings Incentive Match Plan for Employees of Small Employers (SIMPLE)

(for Use With a Designated Financial Institution)

OMB No. 1545-1502

**DO NOT File with
the Internal
Revenue Service**

_____ establishes the following SIMPLE

Name of Employer

plan under section 408(p) of the Internal Revenue Code and pursuant to the instructions contained in this form.

Article I—Employee Eligibility Requirements (Complete appropriate box(es) and blanks—see instructions.)

1 General Eligibility Requirements. The Employer agrees to permit salary reduction contributions to be made in each calendar year to the SIMPLE individual retirement account or annuity established at the designated financial institution (SIMPLE IRA) for each employee who meets the following requirements (select either **1a** or **1b**):

a ☐ **Full Eligibility.** All employees are eligible.

b ☐ **Limited Eligibility.** Eligibility is limited to employees who are described in both **(i)** and **(ii)** below:

    (i) Current compensation. Employees who are reasonably expected to receive at least $ _____ in compensation (not to exceed $5,000) for the calendar year.

    (ii) Prior compensation. Employees who have received at least $ _____ in compensation (not to exceed $5,000) during any _____ calendar year(s) (insert 0, 1, or 2) preceding the calendar year.

2 Excludable Employees (OPTIONAL)

    ☐ The Employer elects to exclude employees covered under a collective bargaining agreement for which retirement benefits were the subject of good faith bargaining.

Article II—Salary Reduction Agreements (Complete the box and blank, if appropriate—see instructions.)

1 Salary Reduction Election. An eligible employee may make a salary reduction election to have his or her compensation for each pay period reduced by a percentage. The total amount of the reduction in the employee's compensation cannot exceed $6,000* for any calendar year.

2 Timing of Salary Reduction Elections

a For a calendar year, an eligible employee may make or modify a salary reduction election during the 60-day period immediately preceding January 1 of that year. However, for the year in which the employee becomes eligible to make salary reduction contributions, the period during which the employee may make or modify the election is a 60-day period that includes either the date the employee becomes eligible or the day before.

b In addition to the election periods in **2a**, eligible employees may make salary reduction elections or modify prior elections _____ _____ (If the Employer chooses this option, insert a period or periods (e.g. semi-annually, quarterly, monthly, or daily) that will apply uniformly to all eligible employees.)

c No salary reduction election may apply to compensation that an employee received, or had a right to immediately receive, before execution of the salary reduction election.

d An employee may terminate a salary reduction election at any time during the calendar year. ☐ If this box is checked, an employee who terminates a salary reduction election not in accordance with **2b** may not resume salary reduction contributions during the calendar year.

Article III—Contributions (Complete the blank, if appropriate—see instructions.)

1 Salary Reduction Contributions. The amount by which the employee agrees to reduce his or her compensation will be contributed by the Employer to the employee's SIMPLE IRA.

2 Other Contributions

a Matching Contributions

    (i) For each calendar year, the Employer will contribute a matching contribution to each eligible employee's SIMPLE IRA equal to the employee's salary reduction contributions up to a limit of 3% of the employee's compensation for the calendar year.

    (ii) The Employer may reduce the 3% limit for the calendar year in **(i)** only if:

        (1) The limit is not reduced below 1%; **(2)** The limit is not reduced for more than 2 calendar years during the 5-year period ending with the calendar year the reduction is effective; and **(3)** Each employee is notified of the reduced limit within a reasonable period of time before the employees' 60-day election period for the calendar year (described in **Article II, item 2a**).

b Nonelective Contributions

    (i) For any calendar year, instead of making matching contributions, the Employer may make nonelective contributions equal to 2% of compensation for the calendar year to the SIMPLE IRA of each eligible employee who has at least $ _____ (not more than $5,000) in compensation for the calendar year. No more than $160,000* in compensation can be taken into account in determining the nonelective contribution for each eligible employee.

    (ii) For any calendar year, the Employer may make 2% nonelective contributions instead of matching contributions only if:

        (1) Each eligible employee is notified that a 2% nonelective contribution will be made instead of a matching contribution; and

        (2) This notification is provided within a reasonable period of time before the employees' 60-day election period for the calendar year (described in **Article II, item 2a**).

3 Time and Manner of Contributions

a The Employer will make the salary reduction contributions (described in **1** above) to the designated financial institution for the IRAs established under this SIMPLE plan no later than 30 days after the end of the month in which the money is withheld from the employee's pay. See instructions.

b The Employer will make the matching or nonelective contributions (described in **2a** and **2b** above) to the designated financial institution for the IRAs established under this SIMPLE plan no later than the due date for filing the Employer's tax return, including extensions, for the taxable year that includes the last day of the calendar year for which the contributions are made.

For Paperwork Reduction Act Notice, see Instructions.   Cat. No. 23063F   Form **5305-SIMPLE** (10-96)

Article IV—Other Requirements and Provisions

1 **Contributions in General.** The Employer will make no contributions to the SIMPLE IRAs other than salary reduction contributions *(described in **Article III, item 1**)* and matching or nonelective contributions *(described in **Article III, items 2a** and **2b**).*

2 **Vesting Requirements.** All contributions made under this SIMPLE plan are fully vested and nonforfeitable.

3 **No Withdrawal Restrictions.** The Employer may not require the employee to retain any portion of the contributions in his or her SIMPLE IRA or otherwise impose any withdrawal restrictions.

4 **No Cost Or Penalty For Transfers.** The Employer will not impose any cost or penalty on a participant for the transfer of the participant's SIMPLE IRA balance to another IRA.

5 **Amendments To This SIMPLE Plan.** This SIMPLE plan may not be amended except to modify the entries inserted in the blanks or boxes provided in **Articles I, II, III, VI,** and **VII.**

6 **Effects Of Withdrawals and Rollovers**

a An amount withdrawn from the SIMPLE IRA is generally includible in gross income. However, a SIMPLE IRA balance may be rolled over or transferred on a tax-free basis to another IRA designed solely to hold funds under a SIMPLE plan. In addition, an individual may roll over or transfer his or her SIMPLE IRA balance to any IRA on a tax-free basis after a 2-year period has expired since the individual first participated in a SIMPLE plan. Any rollover or transfer must comply with the requirements under section 408.

b If an individual withdraws an amount from a SIMPLE IRA during the 2-year period beginning when the individual first participated in a SIMPLE plan and the amount is subject to the additional tax on early distributions under section 72(t), this additional tax is increased from 10% to 25%.

Article V—Definitions

1 **Compensation**

a **General Definition of Compensation.** Compensation means the sum of the wages, tips, and other compensation from the Employer subject to federal income tax withholding (as described in section 6051(a)(3)) and the employee's salary reduction contributions made under this plan, and, if applicable, elective deferrals under a section 401(k) plan, a SARSEP, or a section 403(b) annuity contract and compensation deferred under a section 457 plan required to be reported by the Employer on Form W-2 (as described in section 6058(a)(8)).

b **Compensation for Self-Employed Individuals.** For self-employed individuals, compensation means the net earnings from self-employment determined under section 1402(a) prior to subtracting any contributions made pursuant to this plan on behalf of the individual.

2 **Employee.** Employee means a common-law employee of the Employer. The term employee also includes a self-employed individual and a leased employee described in section 414(n) but does not include a nonresident alien who received no earned income from the Employer that constitutes income from sources within the United States.

3 **Eligible Employee.** An eligible employee means an employee who satisfies the conditions in **Article I, item 1** and is not excluded under **Article I, item 2.**

4 **Designated Financial Institution.** A designated financial institution is a trustee, custodian, or insurance company (that issues annuity contracts) for the SIMPLE plan that receives all contributions made pursuant to the SIMPLE plan and deposits those contributions to the SIMPLE IRA of each eligible employee.

Article VI—Procedures for Withdrawal *(The designated financial institution will provide the instructions (to be attached or inserted in the space below) on the procedures for withdrawals of contributions by employees.)*

Article VII—Effective Date

This SIMPLE plan is effective _____ .(See instructions.)

*   *   *   *   *

Name of Employer _____

By: Signature _____   Date

Address of Employer _____

Name and title

The undersigned agrees to serve as designated financial institution, receiving all contributions made pursuant to this SIMPLE plan and depositing those contributions to the SIMPLE IRA of each eligible employee as soon as practicable. Upon the request of any participant, the undersigned also agrees to transfer the participant's balance in a SIMPLE IRA established under this SIMPLE plan to another IRA without cost or penalty to the participant.

Name of designated financial institution _____

By: Signature _____   Date

Address _____

Name and title

*****This amount will be adjusted to reflect any annual cost-of-living increases announced by the IRS.**

Model Notification to Eligible Employees

I. Opportunity to Participate in the SIMPLE Plan

You are eligible to make salary reduction contributions to the _____
SIMPLE plan. This notice and the attached summary description provide you with information that you should consider before you decide whether to start, continue, or change your salary reduction agreement.

II. Employer Contribution Election

For the _____ calendar year, the employer elects to contribute to your SIMPLE IRA *(employer must select either (1), (2), or (3)):*

☐ **(1)** A matching contribution equal to your salary reduction contributions up to a limit of 3% of your compensation for the year;

☐ **(2)** A matching contribution equal to your salary reduction contributions up to a limit of _____% *(employer must insert a number from 1 to 3 and is subject to certain restrictions)* of your compensation for the year; or

☐ **(3)** A nonelective contribution equal to 2% of your compensation for the year (limited to $160,000*) if you are an employee who makes at least $ _____ *(employer must insert an amount that is $5,000 or less)* in compensation for the year.

III. Administrative Procedures

If you decide to start or change your salary reduction agreement, you must complete the salary reduction agreement and return it to _____ *(employer should designate a place or individual)* by _____ *(employer should insert a date that is not less than 60 days after notice is given).*

Model Salary Reduction Agreement

I. Salary Reduction Election

Subject to the requirements of the SIMPLE plan of _____ *(name of employer)* I authorize _____ % or
$ _____ (which equals _____ % of my current rate of pay)
to be withheld from my pay for each pay period and contributed to my SIMPLE IRA as a salary reduction contribution.

II. Maximum Salary Reduction

I understand that the total amount of my salary reduction contributions in any calendar year cannot exceed $6,000.*

III. Date Salary Reduction Begins

I understand that my salary reduction contributions will start as soon as permitted under the SIMPLE plan and as soon as administratively feasible or, if later, _____. *(Fill in the date you want the salary reduction contributions to begin. The date must be after you sign this agreement.)*

IV. Duration of Election

This salary reduction agreement replaces any earlier agreement and will remain in effect as long as I remain an eligible employee under the SIMPLE plan or until I provide my employer with a request to end my salary reduction contributions or provide a new salary reduction agreement as permitted under this SIMPLE plan.

Signature of employee _____

Date _____

***This amount will be adjusted to reflect any annual cost-of-living increases announced by the IRS.**

Section references are to the Internal Revenue Code unless otherwise noted.

Paperwork Reduction Act Notice

You are not required to provide the information requested on a form that is subject to the Paperwork Reduction Act unless the form displays a valid OMB control number. Books or records relating to a form or its instructions must be retained as long as their contents may become material in the administration of any Internal Revenue law. Generally, tax returns and return information are confidential, as required by section 6103.

The time needed to complete this form will vary depending on individual circumstances. The estimated average time is:

Recordkeeping	3 hr., 38 min.
Learning about the law or the form	2 hr., 26 min.
Preparing the form	47 min.

If you have comments concerning the accuracy of these time estimates or suggestions for making this form simpler, we would be happy to hear from you. You can write to the Tax Forms Committee, Western Area Distribution Center, Rancho Cordova, CA 95743-0001. **DO NOT** send this form to this address. Instead, keep it for your records.

General Instructions

Note: *The instructions for this form are designed to assist in the establishment and administration of the SIMPLE plan; they are **not** intended to supersede any provisions in the SIMPLE plan.*

Purpose of Form

Form 5305-SIMPLE is a model Savings Incentive Match Plan for Employees of Small Employers (SIMPLE) plan document that an employer may use in combination with SIMPLE IRAs to establish a SIMPLE plan described in section 408(p). It is important that you keep this form for your records. **DO NOT** file this form with the IRS. For more information, see **Pub. 560,** Retirement Plans for the Self-Employed, and **Pub. 590,** Individual Retirement Arrangements (IRAs).

Instructions for the Employer

Which Employers May Establish and Maintain a SIMPLE Plan?

You are eligible to establish and maintain a SIMPLE plan only if you meet both of the following requirements:

1. Last calendar year, you had no more than 100 employees (including self-employed individuals) who earned $5,000 or more in compensation from you during the year. If you have a SIMPLE plan but later exceed this 100-employee limit, you will be treated as meeting the limit for the two years following the calendar year in which you last satisfied the limit. If the failure to continue to satisfy the 100-employee limit is due to an acquisition or similar transaction involving your business, special rules apply. Consult your tax advisor to find out if you can still maintain the plan after the transaction.

2. You do not maintain during any part of the calendar year another qualified plan with respect to which contributions are made, or benefits are accrued, for service in the calendar year. For this purpose, a qualified plan (defined in section 219(g)(5)) includes a qualified pension plan, a profit-sharing plan, a stock bonus plan, a qualified annuity plan, a tax-sheltered annuity plan, and a simplified employee pension (SEP) plan.

Certain related employers (trades or businesses under common control) must be treated as a single employer for purposes of the SIMPLE requirements. These are: **(1)** a controlled group of corporations under section 414(b); **(2)** a partnership or sole proprietorship under common control under section 414(c); or **(3)** an affiliated service group under section 414(m). In addition, if you have leased employees required to be treated as your own employees under the rules of section 414(n), then you must count all such leased employees for the requirements listed above.

What is a SIMPLE Plan?

A SIMPLE plan is a written arrangement that provides you and your employees with a simplified way to make contributions to provide retirement income for your employees. Under a SIMPLE plan, employees may choose whether to make salary reduction contributions to the SIMPLE plan rather than receiving these amounts as part of their regular compensation. In addition, you will contribute matching or nonelective contributions on behalf of eligible employees (see **Employee Eligibility Requirements** below and **Contributions** on page 5). All contributions under this plan will be deposited into a SIMPLE individual retirement account or annuity established for each eligible employee with the designated financial institution named in Article VII (SIMPLE IRA).

The information provided below is intended to help you understand and administer the rules of your SIMPLE plan.

When to Use Form 5305-SIMPLE

A SIMPLE plan may be established by using this Model Form or any other document that satisfies the statutory requirements. Thus, you are not required to use Form 5305-SIMPLE to establish and maintain a SIMPLE plan. Further, do not use Form 5305-SIMPLE if:

1. You do not want to require that all SIMPLE plan contributions initially go to a financial institution designated by you. (e.g., you want to permit each of your eligible employees to choose a financial institution that will initially receive contributions.);

2. You want employees who are nonresident aliens receiving no earned income from you that constitutes income from sources within the United States to be eligible under this plan; or

3. You want to establish a SIMPLE 401(k) plan.

Completing Form 5305-SIMPLE

Pages 1 and 2 of Form 5305-SIMPLE contain the operative provisions of your SIMPLE plan. This SIMPLE plan is considered adopted when you have completed all appropriate boxes and blanks and it has been executed by you and the designated financial institution.

The SIMPLE plan is a legal document with important tax consequences for you and your employees. You may want to consult with your attorney or tax advisor before adopting this plan.

Employee Eligibility Requirements (Article I)

Each year for which this SIMPLE plan is effective, you must permit salary reduction contributions to be made by all of your employees who are reasonably expected to receive at least $5,000 in compensation from you during the year, and who received at least $5,000 in compensation from you in any 2 preceding years. However, you can expand the group of employees who are eligible to participate in the SIMPLE plan by completing the options provided in Article I, items 1a and 1b. To choose full eligibility, check the box in Article I, item 1a. Alternatively, to choose limited eligibility, check the box in Article I, item 1b, and then insert $5,000 or a lower compensation amount (including zero) and 2 or a lower number of years of service in the blanks in (i) and (ii) of Article I, item 1b.

In addition, you can exclude from participation those employees covered under a collective bargaining agreement for which retirement benefits were the subject of good faith bargaining. You may do this by checking the box in Article I, item 2.

Salary Reduction Agreements (Article II)

As indicated in Article II, item 1, a salary reduction agreement permits an eligible employee to make a salary reduction election to have his or her compensation for each pay period reduced by a percentage (expressed as a percentage or dollar amount). The total amount of the reduction in the employee's compensation cannot exceed $6,000* for any calendar year.

Timing of Salary Reduction Elections

For a calendar year, an eligible employee may make or modify a salary reduction election during the 60-day period immediately preceding January 1 of that year. However, for the year in which the employee becomes eligible to make salary reduction contributions, the period during which the employee may make or modify the election is a 60-day period that includes either the date the employee becomes eligible or the day before.

You can extend the 60-day election periods to provide additional opportunities for eligible employees to make or modify salary reduction elections using the blank in Article II, item 2b. For example, you can provide that eligible employees may make new salary reduction elections or modify prior elections for any calendar quarter during the 30 days before that quarter.

You may use (but are not required to) the **Model Salary Reduction Agreement** on page 3 to enable eligible employees to make or modify salary reduction elections.

Employees must be permitted to terminate their salary reduction elections at any time. They may resume salary reduction contributions if permitted under Article II, item 2b. However, by checking the box in Article II, item 2d. you may prohibit an employee who terminates a salary reduction election outside the normal election cycle from resuming salary reduction contributions during the remainder of the calendar year.

Contributions (Article III)

Only contributions described below may be made to this SIMPLE plan. No additional contributions may be made.

Salary Reduction Contributions

As indicated in Article III, item 1, salary reduction contributions consist of the amount by which the employee agrees to reduce his or her compensation. You must contribute the salary reduction contributions to the designated financial institution for the employee's SIMPLE IRA.

Other Contributions
Matching Contributions

In general, you must contribute a matching contribution to each eligible employee's SIMPLE IRA equal to the employee's salary reduction contributions. This matching contribution cannot exceed 3% of the employee's compensation. See **Definition of Compensation**, below.

You may reduce this 3% limit to a lower percentage, but not lower than 1%. You cannot lower the 3% limit for more than 2 calendar years out of the 5-year period ending with the calendar year the reduction is effective.

Note: *If any year in the 5-year period described above is a year before you first established any SIMPLE plan, you will be treated as making a 3% matching contribution for that year for purposes of determining when you may reduce the employer matching contribution.*

In order to elect this option, you must notify the employees of the reduced limit within a reasonable period of time before the applicable 60-day election periods for the year. See **Timing of Salary Reduction Elections** above.

Nonelective contributions.—Instead of making a matching contribution, you may, for any year, make a nonelective contribution equal to 2% of compensation for each eligible employee who has at least $5,000 in compensation for the year. Nonelective contributions may not be based on more than $160,000* of compensation.

In order to elect to make nonelective contributions, you must notify employees within a reasonable period of time before the applicable 60-day election periods for such year. See **Timing of Salary Reduction Elections** above.

Note: *Insert $5,000 in Article III, item 2b(i) to impose the $5,000 compensation requirement. You may expand the group of employees who are eligible for nonelective contributions by inserting a compensation amount lower than $5,000.*

Effective Date (Article VII)

Insert in Article VII, the date you want the provisions of the SIMPLE plan to become effective. You must insert January 1 of the applicable year unless this is the first year for which you are adopting any SIMPLE plan. If this is the first year for which you are adopting a SIMPLE plan, you may insert any date between January 1 and October 1, inclusive of the applicable year. Do not insert any date before January 1, 1997.

Other Important Information About Your SIMPLE Plan

Timing of Salary Reduction Contributions

Under the Internal Revenue Code, for all SIMPLE plans, the employer must make the salary reduction contributions to the designated financial institution for the SIMPLE IRAs of all eligible employees no later than the 30th day of the month following the month in which the amounts would otherwise have been payable to the employee in cash. The Department of Labor has indicated that most SIMPLE plans are also subject to Title I of the Employee Retirement Income Security Act of 1974 (ERISA). The Department of Labor has informed the IRS that, as a matter of enforcement policy, for these plans, salary reduction contributions must be made to the SIMPLE IRA at the designated financial institution as of the earliest date on which those contributions can reasonably be segregated from the employer's general assets, but in no event later than the 30-day deadline described above.

Definition of Compensation

"Compensation" means the amount described in section 6051(a)(3) (wages, tips, and other compensation from the employer subject to federal income tax withholding under section 3401(a)). Usually, this is the amount shown in box 1 of **Form W-2**, Wage and Tax Statement. For further information, see **Pub. 15** (Circular E), Employer's Tax Guide. Compensation also includes the salary reduction contributions made under this plan, and, if applicable, compensation deferred under a section 457 plan. In determining an employee's compensation for prior years, the employee's elective deferrals under a section 401(k) plan, a SARSEP, or a section 403(b) annuity contract are also included in the employee's compensation.

For self-employed individuals, compensation means the net earnings from self-employment determined under section 1402(a) prior to subtracting any contributions made pursuant to this SIMPLE plan on behalf of the individual.

Employee Notification

You must notify eligible employees prior to the employees' 60-day election period described above that they can make or change salary reduction elections. In this notification, you must indicate whether you will provide:

This amount will be adjusted to reflect any annual cost-of-living increases announced by the IRS.

1. A matching contribution equal to your employees' salary reduction contributions up to a limit of 3% of their compensation;

2. A matching contribution equal to your employees' salary reduction contributions subject to a percentage limit that is between 1 and 3% of their compensation; or

3. A nonelective contribution equal to 2% of your employees' compensation.

You can use the **Model Notification to Eligible Employees** on page 3 to satisfy these employee notification requirements for this SIMPLE plan. A **Summary Description** must also be provided to eligible employees at this time. This summary description requirement may be satisfied by providing a completed copy of pages 1 and 2 of Form 5305-SIMPLE (including the Article IV Procedures for Withdrawals and transfers from the SIMPLE IRAs established under this SIMPLE plan).

If you fail to provide the employee notification (including the summary description) described above, you will be liable for a penalty of $50 per day until the notification is provided. If you can show that the failure was due to reasonable cause, the penalty will not be imposed.

Reporting Requirements

You are not required to file any annual information returns for your SIMPLE plan, such as Forms 5500, 5500-C/R, or 5500-EZ. However, you must report to the IRS which eligible employees are active participants in the SIMPLE plan and the amount of your employees' salary reduction contributions to the SIMPLE plan on Form W-2. These contributions are subject to social security, medicare, railroad retirement, and federal unemployment tax.

Deducting Contributions

Contributions to this SIMPLE plan are deductible in your tax year containing the end of the calendar year for which the contributions are made.

Contributions will be treated as made for a particular tax year if they are made for that year and are made by the due date (including extensions) of your income tax return for that year.

Choosing the Designated Financial Institution

As indicated in Article V, item 4, a designated financial institution is a trustee, custodian, or insurance company (that issues annuity contracts) for the SIMPLE plan that would receive all contributions made pursuant to the SIMPLE plan and deposit the contributions to the SIMPLE IRA of each eligible employee.

Only certain financial institutions, such as banks, savings & loan associations, insured credit unions, insurance companies (that issue annuity contracts), or IRS-approved nonbank trustees may serve as a designated financial institution under a SIMPLE plan.

You are not required to choose a designated financial institution for your SIMPLE plan. However, if you do not want to choose a designated financial institution, you cannot use this form (See **When to Use Form 5305-SIMPLE** on page 4).

Instructions for the Designated Financial Institution

Completing Form 5305-SIMPLE

By completing Article VII, you have agreed to be the designated financial institution for this SIMPLE plan. You agree to maintain IRAs on behalf of all individuals receiving contributions under the plan and to receive all contributions made pursuant to this plan and to deposit those contributions to the SIMPLE IRAs of each eligible employee as soon as practicable. You also agree that upon the request of a participant, you will transfer the participant's balance in a SIMPLE IRA to another IRA without cost or penalty to the participant.

Summary Description

Each year the SIMPLE plan is in effect, you must provide the employer the information described in section 408(l)(2)(B). This requirement may be satisfied by providing the employer a current copy of Form 5305-SIMPLE (including instructions) together with your procedures for withdrawals and transfers from the SIMPLE IRAs established under this SIMPLE plan. The summary description must be received by the employer in sufficient time to comply with the **Employee Notification** requirements on page 5.

If you fail to provide the summary description described above, you will be liable for a penalty of $50 per day until the notification is provided. If you can show that the failure was due to reasonable cause, the penalty will not be imposed.

*U.S. Government Printing Office: 1996 - 417-677/40207

9

Sales Contracts and Warranties

Whether you are buying or selling goods, you should be familiar with the methods for discerning price, delivery terms, remedies for a breach of contract, warranties, letters of intent, and the Door-to-Door Sales Act.

CONTRACT FORMATION

Contracts for the sale of goods for $500 or more are not enforceable unless in writing. *Goods* mean (1) all things that are movable at the time of "identification to the contract," (2) unborn young of animals, (3) growing crops, and (4) minerals. A written contract may be enforced even if the price, time, place of payment or delivery, general quantity of goods, or particular warranties are omitted. The only requirements are that the writing must be a contract for the sale of goods, that it is signed by the party to be charged, and that it specifies a quantity.

ORAL AGREEMENTS

Oral contracts between merchants upon which a written confirmation is subsequently made are binding if the merchant receiving the written confirmation fails to object to its contents within ten days after receipt.

If goods are to be specially manufactured and are not ordinarily resalable in the ordinary course of the seller's business, an oral agreement will be binding if the seller has made a substantial beginning on, or a commitment to, acquiring the goods called for in an agreement.

PRICE TERMS

A contract of sale may be created without a price being specified. The methods and terms used to determine price are as follows:

- *Cost plus*—the seller's overhead and profit margins
- *Market price*—the selling price on an organized mercantile or other exchange
- Price in a trade journal
- Government-related price
- Price by leading suppliers
- Price by appraisal
- *Price to be agreed upon*—a fair market price
- *Price set by seller*—uses the good-faith standard
- *Escalator clauses*—use the standard price indices published by the U.S. Department of Labor, the Department of Commerce, or other recognized entities reflecting overall economic trends, including price rises (such as the consumer price index or wholesale price index)
- Gold or foreign currency clauses

DELIVERY TERMS

In the absence of a specific agreement, the place of delivery will be the locale of the goods where they were identified in the agreement at the time the agreement was made. If the goods were not identified in the agreement at the time the agreement was made, the place of delivery will be the seller's place of business, or if the seller has no place of business, his or her home unless otherwise agreed.

The most frequently used delivery terms are as follows:

- *FOB (place of shipment)*. Unless otherwise agreed, the seller must ship the goods and bear the expense of putting the goods in the hands of the shipper. The seller must notify the buyer of the shipment and obtain and deliver necessary documents of title to enable the buyer to obtain possession. The buyer must provide the seller with proper shipping instructions.

- *FOB (place of destination)*. Unless otherwise agreed, the seller must at its own expense transport the goods to the place of destination, give the buyer reasonable notification to enable it to take delivery, tender delivery at a reasonable time, and keep the goods available for a reasonable time to permit the buyer to take possession.

- *FOB (car or other vehicle)*. In addition to putting the goods in the possession of the carrier, the seller must load them on board the truck, car, or other vehicle used by the carrier.

- *FOB (vessel)*. The seller must place the goods on board the vessel designated by the buyer and furnish a proper bill of lading in an appropriate case.

- *FAS (vessel)*. The seller must, at its own expense, deliver the goods alongside the vessel designated by the buyer or on the dock designated in the manner usual in the particular port and obtain a receipt in exchange for which the carrier is obligated to issue a bill of lading.

- *CIF*. The price stated includes the cost of goods, insurance, and freight (CIF) to the named destination. The seller is obligated to load the goods, obtain a receipt showing that the freight has been paid or provided for, obtain a negotiable bill of lading, insure the goods to the account of the buyer, and forward all necessary documents to the buyer with commercial promptness.

- *C&F of CF*. These terms are equivalent to CIF except that the price includes only the cost of goods plus freight to the named destination. Insurance is not included.

RISK OF LOSS

Unless otherwise provided for in the sales contract, risk of loss is determined under the following standards:

- *Goods to be delivered to carrier*. If the seller is required to deliver the goods to a carrier, the risk of loss shifts to the buyer when the seller duly delivers the goods to the carrier.

- *FOB—place of shipment*. Risk of loss shifts to the buyer when the goods are placed in the hands of the shipper.

- *FOB—destination*. Risk of loss shifts to the buyer at the time and place of delivery or the time and place where tender of delivery is made to the buyer.

- *Seller to deliver*. If the seller must deliver the goods to the destination, the risk of loss shifts to the buyer when the delivery is tendered to it so as to enable it to take possession.

- *Sale or return*. If the goods are sold to the buyer for resale rather than for use, with the understanding that they may be returned, the risk of loss is on the buyer until they're returned.

- *Sale on approval*. If the goods are sold to a buyer primarily for its own use rather than for resale and the agreement calls for a sale on approval, the risk of loss shifts to the buyer when the buyer accepts the goods. Failure to notify the seller within a reasonable amount of time of rejection of the goods is deemed to be acceptance.

- *Goods fail to conform*. When delivered goods fail to conform to the requirements of the agreement, the risk of loss remains on the seller until the nonconformity is cured or the nonconforming goods are accepted by the buyer.

- *Buyer revokes acceptance*. If the buyer initially accepts the goods but subsequently (and justifiably) revokes their acceptance, the buyer may treat the risk of loss as having rested on the seller to the extent of any deficiency in its insurance coverage.

- *Repudiation.* If the buyer repudiates the agreement before title to the goods passes to it, the seller may treat the risk of loss as having rested on the buyer for a commercially reasonable time. However, the buyer's liability is limited to the extent of any deficiency in the seller's insurance coverage.

- *Nonconforming goods.* When the goods tendered fail to conform to the agreement to an extent that the buyer would be entitled to reject the tender of delivery, the risk of loss remains on the seller until it has cured the defect or the buyer has accepted the goods.

Excused Performance

When goods are destroyed before the risk of loss shifts from the seller to the buyer, the agreement will be void if they were identified to the agreement before their destruction and the destruction was not the fault of either party. If goods that were identified in the agreement when the agreement was made are so deteriorated that they no longer conform to the requirements of the agreement or have been partially destroyed without the fault of either party, the buyer has the option of treating the contract as void or accepting the goods with allowance for the deterioration or destruction.

The seller will be excused from performance if it becomes commercially impracticable as the result of a contingency whose nonoccurrence was a basic assumption on which the agreement was founded.

Deposits, Prepayments, and Liquidated Damages

The seller is entitled to keep the buyer's deposit if the buyer refuses to accept the goods or otherwise breaches the agreement, provided the deposit does not exceed either 20 percent of the buyer's obligation or $500 (whichever is smaller) unless the buyer has received a benefit or the seller has incurred damages.

SELLER'S REMEDIES

Depending upon the circumstances, a seller can choose from a myriad of approaches when dealing with a problem buyer.

When the seller learns of a buyer's insolvency, the seller may take any of the following actions:

- *Stop delivery* unless (1) the goods have been received by the buyer; (2) acknowledgment has been made by the buyer's warehouseman; (3) the goods have been reshipped by the carrier (which constitutes an acknowledgment to the buyer that the carrier holds the goods for the buyer); or (4) the carrier has notified the buyer, in which case it was holding the goods as a warehouseman for the buyer rather than as a carrier.

  The seller must notify the carrier in time to enable it to act with reasonable diligence and stop the shipment. If a negotiable document of title is involved, it should be presented to the carrier with the order to stop shipment.

- *Withhold delivery* if the goods have not been shipped and wait for the buyer to prepay even though the contract called for shipment on credit.

- *Reclaim the goods* if they were received while the buyer was insolvent provided demand is made within ten days. The ten-day limitation does not apply if the buyer falsely represented its solvency to the seller within three months of delivery.

When the buyer repudiates the agreement, the seller may take any of the following actions:

- *Withhold delivery.*
- *Stop delivery* if the goods have not been delivered to the buyer, provided the shipment meets the quantity requirements spelled out in the Uniform Commercial Code—i.e., carload, truckload, ship, and the like.
- *Identify and sell conforming goods* as well as recover damages for the difference between the resale price and the contract price.
- *Recover damages for repudiation.* When there is an established market price, the damages are the difference between the market price and the contract price at the time and place of the tentative delivery together with incidental damages less any expenses saved as a result of the buyer's breach. Incidental damages include commercially reasonable charges, expenses, or commissions incurred in stopping shipment; transportation or care of goods after the breach; and resale or return of the goods and any other commercially reasonable

charges, expenses, or commissions resulting from the breach. If there is no established market at a place specified for tender, the market price at another locale is substituted, although adjustment is made for transportation differentials. When the damages computed by the difference between contract price and market price are adequate, the seller may recover the profit that it would have made from full performance.

Cancellation after the buyer's repudiation does not extinguish the seller's right to proceed against the buyer for damages.

If the contract is repudiated by the buyer after acceptance, the seller may maintain an action for the contract price. An action for the price may also be maintained when the seller has been unable to resell goods identified in the agreement at a reasonable price or the circumstances indicate that efforts to resell would be fruitless. When the seller maintains an action for the price, it must remain prepared to deliver the goods. However, if an opportunity arises to sell the goods, the buyer may do so and deduct the resale price from its claim.

A resale must be made in good faith and in a commercially reasonable manner.

- *Suspend performance and await withdrawal of the repudiation* for a commercially reasonable time and if a withdrawal is made, demand adequate assurance of performance.

The seller must suspend performance if it has not finished the goods and the completion of the goods or the completion of its performance would result in a material increase in damages.

When the buyer fails to cooperate as required by the agreement (i.e., fails to specify assortment or give needed instruction, etc.), a seller may take the following actions:

- *Delay its performance* without incurring any liability for breach by reason of late delivery.

- *Proceed to perform* in a commercially reasonable manner.

- *Treat the failure to cooperate as a breach* of the agreement.

If the buyer refuses to accept conforming goods or wrongfully withdraws acceptance of conforming goods, the seller may resell the goods and recover damages. Damages constitute the difference between the contract price and the resale price less any expenses saved as a result of the breach but including any costs incurred in reselling.

Resale

Resale costs may include reasonable commission charges, transportation charges, and other incidental expenses. The buyer must be notified of the sale and the seller must use reasonable efforts to get the highest possible price for the goods.

For goods resold at auction, the sale must be held at the usual place or market for selling such goods if one is available. The goods must be available for inspection prior to or at the sale.

Damages

Damages are measured by the difference between market price (at the time and place specified for delivery) and the contract price, provided such damages are adequate to put the seller in as good a position as it would have been if the buyer had accepted the goods. Otherwise, it is entitled to at least the profits that it would have made if the buyer accepted the goods and fully performed the agreement.

The seller may also choose between an action for the price for goods that are not readily resalable or may cancel the contract.

WHAT TO DO IF YOUR SUPPLIER DOES NOT DELIVER

You have four possible remedies if your supplier fails to make delivery or repudiates the contract:

1. *Substitute goods.* You, as the buyer, can obtain substitute goods (cover) and recover damages on the difference between the higher cost of cover and the lower contract price. You can also recover incidental damages, such as brokerage fees, and consequential damages, such as loss of profits during any delay.

2. *Market price.* You can recover damages based on the difference between the higher market price and the lower contract price plus incidental and consequential damages.

3. *Specific performance.* Under some circumstances, you may obtain specific performance or seizure by the sheriff *(replevin)*. Specific performance is permitted where the goods are unique or were the subject of a long-term requirement contract. The

buyer can replevy goods if they have already been identified in the contract and if it is unable to obtain cover.

4. *Recovery of goods.* The buyer can recover goods identified in the contract if it has paid part or all of the price and the seller becomes insolvent within ten days after receipt of the first installment of the price. Insolvency occurs where the seller ceases to pay its debts as they become due or is insolvent under federal bankruptcy law.

LETTERS OF INTENT

Letters of intent are preliminary agreements that state proposed terms for a final contract. However, courts have found letters of intent to be binding even though both parties may not have intended them to be legally binding.

Letters of intent are used when a document must be presented to a potential creditor, an investor, or a corporation's board of directors before final agreement has been reached. Letters of intent facilitate the negotiation of complex deals.

Warning: If you do not want to be legally bound by a letter of intent, you should not use language such as "agreement in principal" or "memorandum of intent," and do not charge nonrefundable fees. Letters of intent should contain a disclaimer that there will be no legally binding obligations, including a legal duty to continue negotiations, until an agreement is approved.

CANCELLATION OF DOOR-TO-DOOR SALES

The Door-to-Door Sales Act covers the sale, lease, or rental of consumer goods or services in which (1) the seller personally solicits the sale, including a sale in response to the buyer's invitation, and (2) the contract is signed at a place other than the seller's place of business. Consumer goods or services refer to those purchased, leased, or rented for personal, family, or household purposes, including courses of instruction or training.

Buyer's Right to Cancel

The buyer may cancel a door-to-door sale up until midnight of the third business day after the contract is signed. The sale can be canceled by mailing or delivering a signed and dated copy of the cancellation notice or any other written notice or by sending a telegram. Cancellation occurs when the written notice of cancellation is given to the seller. Notice of cancellation, if mailed, becomes effective when deposited in a mailbox.

The seller must inform the buyer at the time he or she signs the contract of the right to cancel. Until the seller has complied with the law, the buyer may cancel the sale by notifying the seller in any manner and by any means. The time period to cancel begins when the seller complies with the law.

The seller must give the buyer a fully completed receipt or copy of any contract at the time of signing. The receipt or contract must set out (1) the sales date, (2) the seller's name and address, and (3) a statement in ten-point boldface type describing the buyer's right to cancel. A detachable duplicate notice of cancellation must be attached to the contract or receipt.

Return of Down Payment

If the buyer cancels, the seller must return any property traded in, payments made, and promissory notes provided by the buyer and must do so within ten business days after receiving the cancellation notice. If the seller refuses to return the buyer's payment within ten days, the buyer is entitled to a court award, reasonable attorney fees, and court costs, in addition to the return of his or her payment.

The buyer must make available to the seller at his or her home, in substantially as good condition as when received, any goods delivered; or the buyer may, if he or she wishes, follow the seller's instructions and ship the goods at the seller's expense and risk.

If the buyer makes the goods available to the seller and the seller does not pick them up within 20 days of the date of notice of cancellation, the buyer may keep or dispose of the goods without any further obligation. If the buyer fails to make the goods available to the seller or agrees to return the goods to the seller and fails to do so, then the buyer will remain liable to perform his or her contractual obligations.

Until the seller has complied with the law, the buyer may keep the delivered goods as security for his or her payment.

Exceptions

The Door-to-Door Sales Act does not apply

- if the buyer made prior negotiations at the seller's store;
- if the buyer contacted the seller because the goods or services were needed for an emergency and he or she gave the seller a dated and signed handwritten statement describing the situation and waiving his or her right to cancel;
- if conducted entirely by mail or telephone;
- if the buyer requests the seller to visit his or her home for repairs or maintenance;
- to real estate sales or rentals or to the sale of insurance, securities, or commodities; and
- if the purchase price does not exceed $25 and only one delivery is necessary.

FEDERAL WARRANTY REQUIREMENTS

For products costing more than $15, federal law requires that the following information be included if a written warranty is supplied to the consumer:

- Who is entitled to the protection
- Identification of the parts covered by the warranty
- Indication of what will be done to correct defects or failures (including which items or services will be paid for by the warrantor and which expenses must be borne by the consumer)
- The date that the warranty becomes effective (unless it is the date of purchase)
- Steps the consumer must follow to obtain performance under the warranty (including a statement of the warrantor's name and mailing address, the name and address of a department responsible for warranty obligations, or a telephone number that the con-

sumer may use without charge to obtain information)

NEW HOME WARRANTIES

The following three types of warranties should be in contracts for newly constructed single-family homes, condominiums, and cooperatives:

1. For one year, the home must be free from defects due to failure to construct in a skillful manner. The workmanship and materials must meet or exceed the State Uniform Fire Prevention and Building Code or locally accepted building practices.

2. For two years, the following systems must be free from defects:
   - Plumbing systems: Gas supply lines and fittings; water supply, waste, and vent pipes and their fittings; septic tanks and their drain fields; and water, gas, and sewer service piping and their extensions to the tie-in of a public utility connection or on-site well and sewage disposal systems.
   - Electrical systems: All wiring, electrical boxes, switches, outlets, and connections up to the public utility connection.
   - Heating, cooling, and ventilation systems: All duct work; steam, water, and refrigerant lines; registers; convectors; radiation elements; and dampers.

3. For six years, the following load-bearing portions of the home must be free from defects that make it unsafe, unsanitary, or otherwise unlivable: foundation footings and systems, beams, girders, lintels, columns, walls and partitions, floor systems, and roof-framing systems.

Most construction contract warranty clauses require the owner to *notify* the contractor of any nonconforming work within the above stated time periods in order to trigger the contractor's obligation to make repairs at no additional cost to the homeowner. Builders can exclude or modify warranties by providing a "limited warranty." Most construction contracts incorporate by reference the American Institute of Architects Document A201, which contains many of the specific requirements that define the obligations of the homeowner and general contractor. The document requires that any disputes arising out of the construction contract be submitted to binding arbitration conducted according to the Construction Industries Rules of the American Arbitration Association.

HOME IMPROVEMENT CONTRACT CHECKLIST

Home improvement contracts for the repairing and remodeling of residential property, including driveways, swimming pools, siding, insulation, roofing, windows, terraces, patios, landscaping, fences, porches, garages, solar energy systems, flooring, basements, burglar alarms, texture coating, air-conditioning, and heating equipment, should contain the following:

❑ The name, address, telephone number, and license number, if applicable, of the contractor

❑ The approximate dates when work will begin and be substantially completed, including whether time is of the essence for completion

❑ A description of the work to be performed; the materials to be provided including the make, model number, or any other identifying information; and the price for the work and materials

❑ A notice to the owner that the contractor or subcontractor may have a claim against the owner's property under the lien law for nonpayment

❑ A statement that the contractor must deposit all payments received prior to completion in an escrow account or post a bond, contract of indemnity, or irrevocable letter of credit guaranteeing return or proper application of the payments

❑ A schedule of progress payments (if the contract provides for progress payments) showing the amount of each payment and specifically identifying the state of completion of work or service performed, including any materials to be supplied before each progress payment is due

❑ A notice that the owner may cancel the contract until midnight of the third business day after the day on which the owner signs the agreement (This clause does not apply if the owner has initiated the contact, the home improvement is needed to meet a bona fide emergency, and the owner provides a statement waiving his or her right to cancel.)

HOW AND WHEN TO USE THE FORMS IN THIS CHAPTER

Construction Contract. This form can be used for virtually any form of new building construction based upon an architect's drawings and specifications. The form includes a statement of the buyer's cancellation rights.

Distributorship Agreement. This form can be used for virtually any type of product and for distributorships involving either foreign sales or foreign products.

CONSTRUCTION CONTRACT

THIS AGREEMENT made this   day of   , 199   ,

by and Between   doing business as   ,

of   , (hereinafter called the Contractor) and residing at

(hereinafter called the Owner)

WITNESSETH,

That the Owner and the Contractor, for the considerations hereinafter named agree as follows:

1. Scope of the Work

The Contractor shall furnish all of the material and perform all of the work for the construction of a

at   as

shown on the Drawings and described in the Specifications dated   and prepared by

, Architect, all in accordance with the Contract herein and attachments.

2. Time of Completion

The work shall be commenced on   and completed

3. Contract Sum

The Owner shall pay the Contractor for the performance of the Contract subject to the additions and

deductions provided therein, the sum of   dollars ($).

4. Progress Payments

The Owner shall make payments on account of the contract, as follows: $ upon signing

this contract; $ upon completion of the framing and roofing; $ upon

hanging of drywall; $ upon final completion of the contract.

5. Contract Documents

Attached hereto and made a part of this contract are the following:

❑   Schedule A – Itemization of price

❑   Schedule B – Description of material

❑   Schedule C – Lease

❑   Schedule D – Note and mortgage

❑   Schedule E – Contract . . . Dwelling built on seller's land

6. Surveys and Easements

The Owner shall furnish all surveys unless otherwise specified. Easements for permanent structures or permanent changes in existing facilities shall be secured and paid for by the Owner, unless otherwise agreed.

7. Contractor's Right to Terminate Contract

Should the work be stopped by any public authority for a period of thirty (30) days or more, through no fault of the Contractor, or should the work be stopped through act of neglect of the Owner for a period of seven (7) days, or should the Owner fail to pay the Contractor upon seven (7) days after it is due, then the Contractor upon seven (7) days' written notice to the Owner, may stop work or terminate the contract and recover from the Owner payment for all work executed and any loss sustained and reasonable profit and damages.

8. Owner's Liability Insurance

The Owner shall maintain liability insurance in the amount of at least $500,000, with a policy meeting contractor's requirements.

9. Fire Insurance with Extended Coverage

The Owner shall effect and maintain fire insurance with extended coverage upon the entire structure on which the work of this Contract is to be done to one hundred percent of the insurable value thereof, including items of labor and materials connected therewith whether in or adjacent to the structure insured, materials in place or to be used as part of the permanent construction including surplus materials, shanties, protective fences, bridges, temporary structures, miscellaneous materials and supplies incident to the work, and such scaffoldings, stagings, towers, forms, and equipment as are not owned or rented by the Contractor, the cost of which is included in the cost of the work. Certificates of such insurance shall be filed with the Contractor if he so desires. If the Owner fails to effect or maintain insurance as above and so notifies the Contractor, the Contractor may insure his own interests to the Owner. If the Contractor is damaged by failure of the Owner to maintain such insurance or to so notify the Contractor, he may recover as stipulated in the contract for recovery of damages.

10. Arbitration

Any disagreement arising out of this contract or from the breach thereof shall be submitted to arbitration, and judgment upon the award rendered may be entered in the court of the forum, state or federal, having jurisdiction. It is mutually agreed that the decision of the arbitrators shall be in a condition precedent to any right of legal action that either party may have against the other. The arbitration shall be held under the Standard Form of Arbitration Procedure of The American Institute of Architects or under the Rules of the American Arbitration Association.

11. Changes and Determinations by Contractor

The Contractor reserves the right to make such changes and/or substitutions in the construction as may be necessary because of the unavailability of materials through Contractor's ordinary and usual sources of supply or as may be required by law provided the changes are of equal or better quality. Unless otherwise agreed upon by the building on the plot to fit into the general pattern of the development. The Contractor shall determine the grading and elevations of the plot and determine the elevations of foundations, driveways, and walks to conform with topographical conditions.

12. Color and Other Selections

Whenever Owner has the right to make selection styles, colors, patterns, fixtures, and/or materials, Owner shall do so within seven (7) days after written demand therefore from Contractor. In the event the Owner fails to make such selections within such period, the Contractor shall have the right to use its own judgment in the selection of colors, fixtures, and materials and the Owner shall accept same. Such written demand shall be by ordinary mail sent to Owner at the address set forth above.

13. Completion, Inability to Complete

Contractor shall not be liable if it is unable to complete construction or for any delays in completion of construction occasioned by: (i) governmental restrictions or manufacture, sale, distribution, and/or use of necessary materials; (ii) Contractor's inability to obtain necessary materials because of strikes, lockouts, fires, floods, earthquakes or other acts of God, military operations and requirements, national emergencies, etc.; (iii) the failure of necessary utilities to be installed to service the property.

14. Work by Other Than Contractor

Owner shall not authorize or permit any work to be performed or any materials to be installed or supplied to the property by any person or persons not employed by or under the contract to the Contractor, without the prior written consent of the Contractor.

15. Restriction on Assignability

This agreement is binding upon the heirs, executors, and administrators of the respective parties, and it is expressly understood and agreed that neither Owner nor Contractor will assign this Contract without the written consent of the other.

16. Default

In the event of default by Owner, Owner shall pay to Contractor reasonable attorney's fees, collection charges, and interest at the rate of 18% per annum. Owner agrees that acceptance of a payment after default shall not be deemed a waiver by contractor of any action or right which he may have by reason of such default.

17. Address for Notices and Payments

Owner shall deliver all payments required herein and all notices to Contractor at   .
All notices and change orders by Owner shall be in writing. Owner will notify Contractor by five (5) days' written notice of any change of address.

18. Entire Agreement

This Contract of sale contains the entire agreement between the Contractor and Owner and nothing is binding on either of them which is not contained in this Contract. This Contract is intended to bind the Contractor and Owner and those who succeed to their interests.

19. Signatures

Unless all of the persons whose names appear at the beginning of this Contract sign it on or before the day of   , 199   , this Contract shall not become effective.

"YOU THE BUYER MAY CANCEL THIS TRANSACTION AT ANY TIME PRIOR TO MIDNIGHT OF THE THIRD BUSINESS DAY AFTER THE DATE OF THIS TRANS-ACTION—SEE THE ATTACHED NOTICE OF CANCELLATION FORM FOR AN EXPLANATION OF THIS RIGHT."

_____

_____

_____

DISTRIBUTORSHIP AGREEMENT

AGREEMENT made this day of _____ , 199___ , between a domestic business corporation incorporated in the State of _____ , doing business at the following address: _____ , Town of _____ , County of _____ , State of _____ (hereinafter referred to as "the Company"), and _____ , a corporation incorporated in the State of _____ , doing business at _____ , Village of _____ , County of _____ , State of _____ (hereinafter referred to as "the Distributor").

WHEREAS the Distributor desires to be appointed by the Company as Distributor of the Company's _____ (hereinafter referred to as the "Product") in the territory hereinafter described, subject to the provisions set forth herein.

NOW THEREFORE in consideration of the premises and the mutual covenants herein set forth, it is agreed by and between the parties as follows:

I. OPERATIONAL REQUIREMENTS

The Distributor shall purchase B's from the Company for the purpose of resale within the territories set forth in Exhibit "A" attached hereto and made a part hereof and is not the Company's agent or employee for any purpose whatsoever. The Distributor is not given the authority to bind the Company in any contracts or agreements whatsoever. The Distributor accepts such appointment and agrees as follows:

A. To develop the market for the Product in the above-mentioned territories with due diligence and to appoint sufficient subdistributors in said territories to aggressively promote the sale of the Product throughout the assigned territory. All said subdistributors in said territories to aggressively promote the sale of PBS throughout the assigned territory. All said subdistributors which the Distributor appoints are the sole responsibility of the Distributor.

B. To keep posted on all information, bulletins, and price changes in connection with the Product which may be issued to the Distributor from time to time.

C. To conform faithfully to the Company's sales plans and policies.

D. To refrain from any transactions whatsoever in the territories of other Distributors and territories reserved by the Company.

E. To refrain from selling or offering for sale any items manufactured by others which are similar or functionally the same as Product.

II. PRICES

The Distributor's cost will be _____ percent of the Company's F.O.B. factory published price for the Product and any after market accessories. The current retail price of the Product is $ _____ U.S. funds. Distributor shall sell the Product for no less than $ _____ U.S. funds. All shipping and collection costs including taxes, exchange, license fees, stamps, and all charges thereon are the Distributor's responsibility. The Company shall have the right, from time to time without notice, to fix and to change its published prices.

III. ACCEPTANCE ORDERS

While the Company will endeavor to accept all orders for reasonable quantities submitted by the Distributor hereunder, it is expressly agreed that all orders are subject to written acceptance by the Company, as in its sole discretion it shall determine, and no order shall be the commitment of the Company until written acceptance thereof has been mailed to the Distributor by the Company, and such acceptance shall be subject to all of the provisions of both this Agreement and the Company's acknowledgment.

IV. PAYMENT TERMS

Full payment in the form of cash, certified funds, or an irrevocable letter of credit must accompany all orders. Full payment as aforesaid is due prior to delivery of orders. In the event any order submitted by the Distributor is cancelled by the Distributor for any reason before shipment, the Distributor shall pay any loss or damage to the Company. The Company will not be liable for failure to perform under this Agreement, if such failure shall be due to fire or to labor, material or car shortage, or to strikes, lock-outs, public enemies, Acts of God, or causes beyond Company's control. This Agreement shall not be assignable by the Distributor either by voluntary act or by operation of law.

V. TERMS OF AGREEMENT

This agreement shall be effective from   , 199   for a period of   year(s) and can be renewed by mutual agreement. If either party to this Agreement shall violate any of its terms and conditions, the other party, at its option may, upon   days written notice to the violator, by certified or registered mail, terminate this Agreement. The Agreement may, at the option of the Company, be terminated immediately if the Distributor becomes insolvent; violates the laws, regulations, rules, or statutes of any government; ceases doing business; makes an assignment for the benefit of creditors; or commits an act of bankruptcy. The Company's failure to exercise any right hereunder shall not operate as a waiver of such right and all remedies contained herein shall be cumulative. Distributor agrees that for a period of years following the termination of this Agreement, the Distributor shall not market or sell the Product or any similar product.

VI. CONFLICT OF LAWS

Any part of this Agreement that is contrary to any federal, state, or local law shall not be applicable and shall not invalidate any other part of this Agreement. In the event of disputes or legal interpretation of the terms of this Agreement, the laws of the State of   shall govern and be binding upon the parties hereto.

VII. ENTIRE AGREEMENT

This Agreement contains the entire understanding of the parties and there are no commitments, agreements, or understandings between the parties other than those expressly set forth herein. This agreement shall not be altered, waived, modified, or amended except in writing signed by the parties hereto and notarized.

VIII. ARBITRATION

Any controversy or claim arising out of or relating to this contract or the breach thereof shall be settled by arbitration to be held in the City of _____, State of _____, U.S.A., in accordance with the Rules of the American Arbitration Association, and judgment upon the award rendered by the arbitrators may be entered in any Court having jurisdiction thereof.

IX. SECRECY

Distributor agrees not to disclose or use, except as required in Distributor's duties, at any time, any information disclosed to or acquired by Distributor during the term of this contract. Distributor agrees that all confidential information shall be deemed to be and shall be treated as a sole and exclusive property of the Company.

X. GOVERNING LAW

This Agreement shall be governed by and be construed in accordance to the laws of the State of _____, United States of America.

XI. SUPPORT SERVICES

Company will support services relating to after sale, customer complaints, and Applications Engineering.

XII. NOTICES

Any and all notices herein shall be in writing and shall be sent by certified mail, return receipt requested, to the addresses set forth at the head of this Agreement.

IN WITNESS WHEREOF, the parties hereto have executed this Agreement the day and year first above written.

BY: _____

BY: _____

EXHIBIT A

The territory for Distributor shall consist of:

10

Patents and Trademarks

TRADEMARKS

A *trademark* is a word, phrase, symbol, design, or a combination of these, that identifies and distinguishes the source of the goods or services of one party from those of others. A *service mark* is the same as a trademark except that it identifies and distinguishes the source of a service rather than a product. Throughout this chapter the terms *trademark* and *mark* are used to refer to both trademarks and service marks. A mark for goods ordinarily appears on a product or on its packaging, whereas a service mark appears in advertising for the service.

A trademark should be distinguished from a copyright or a patent. A *copyright* protects an artistic or literary work, whereas a *patent* protects an invention.

How to Establish Trademark Rights

Although you can use a mark without registering it with the federal Patent and Trademark Office (PTO), federal registration provides important benefits for trademark holders. For example, the person who obtains federal registration for a mark is presumed to be the owner of the mark for the goods or services specified in the registration and is entitled to the exclusive nationwide use of that mark. A federal registration can thus provide significant advantages to a party involved in a court proceeding.

Two related but distinct types of rights exist in a mark: the right to register and the right to use. Generally, the first party who either uses a mark in commerce or files an application with the PTO has the ultimate right to register that mark. The PTO's authority is limited to determining the right to register. The right to use a mark can be more complicated to determine. This is particularly true when two parties have begun use of the same or similar mark without the knowledge of one another and when neither has a federal registration. Only a court can render a decision about the right to use, such as issuing an injunction or awarding damages for infringement. The PTO cannot provide advice concerning rights in a mark; only a private attorney can provide such advice.

Unlike copyrights or patents, trademark rights can last indefinitely if the owner continues to use the mark to identify its goods or services. The term of a federal trademark registration is ten years, with ten-year renewal terms. Between the fifth and sixth year after the date of initial registration, however, the registrant must file an affidavit with the required filing fee setting forth certain information to keep the registration alive. If no affidavit is filed, the registration will be canceled.

An applicant may apply for federal registration in three principal ways:

1. An applicant who has already used a mark in commerce may file based on that use (a *use* application).

2. An applicant who has not yet used the mark may apply based on a bona fide intention to use the mark in commerce (an *intent-to-use* application).

For the purposes of obtaining federal registration, *commerce* means all commerce that may lawfully be regulated by the U.S. Congress (e.g., interstate commerce or commerce between the United States and another country). The *use in commerce* must be a bona fide use in the ordinary course of trade and not made merely to reserve a right in a mark. If an applicant files based on having a bona fide intention to use in commerce, the applicant will have to use the mark in commerce and submit an allegation of use to the PTO.

3. Under certain international agreements, an applicant may file in the United States based on an application or registration in another country.

An application to the PTO must be filed in the name of the owner of the mark, usually an individual, a corporation, or a partnership. The owner controls the nature and quality of the goods or services identified by the mark. The owner may submit and prosecute its own application for registration or may be represented by an attorney, but the PTO cannot help select an attorney.

Applicants not living in the United States must designate, *in writing,* the name and address of a domestic representative—a person residing in the United States "upon whom notices of process may be served for proceedings affecting the mark." Applicants do this by submitting a signed statement that the named person at the address indicated is appointed as the applicant's domestic representative under § 1(e) of the Trademark Act. The named person will then receive all communications from the PTO unless the applicant is represented by an attorney in the United States.

A U.S. registration provides protection only in the United States and its territories. If the owner of a mark wishes to protect a mark in other countries, the owner must seek protection in each country separately under the relevant laws. The PTO cannot provide information or advice concerning protection in other countries. Interested parties may inquire directly in the applicable country or its U.S. offices or through an attorney.

Searches for Conflicting Marks

An applicant is not required to conduct a search for conflicting marks prior to applying to the PTO. However, it may be useful. In evaluating an application, an examining attorney conducts a search and notifies the applicant if a conflicting mark is found. The application fee, which covers processing and search costs, will not be refunded even if a conflict is found and the mark cannot be registered.

The PTO does not conduct searches for the public to determine if a conflicting mark is registered or is the subject of a pending application except when acting on an application. However, a variety of ways to obtain such information includes (1) performing a search in the PTO's public search library, (2) visiting a patent and depository library, or (3) employing either a private trademark search company or a trademark attorney.

The Registration Process

The PTO is responsible for the federal registration of trademarks. When an application is received, the PTO reviews it to determine if it meets the minimum requirements for receiving a filing date. If the application meets the filing requirements, the PTO assigns it a serial number and sends the applicant a receipt about two months after filing. If the minimum requirements are not met, the entire mailing, including the filing fee, is returned to the applicant.

About four or five months after filing the application, an examining attorney at the PTO reviews the application and determines whether the mark may be registered. If the examining attorney determines that the mark can't be registered, the attorney will issue a letter listing the grounds for refusal and any corrections required in the application. The examining attorney may also contact the applicant by telephone if only minor corrections are required. The applicant must respond to any objections within six months of the mailing date of the letter or the application will be abandoned. If the applicant's response does not overcome all objections, the examining attorney will issue a final refusal. The applicant may then appeal to the Trademark Trial and Appeal Board, an administrative tribunal within the PTO.

A common ground for refusal is the likelihood of confusion between the applicant's mark and a registered mark. Marks that merely describe the applicant's goods or services or a feature of the goods or services, as well as marks consisting of geographic terms or surnames, may also be refused. Marks may be refused for other reasons as well.

If there are no objections or if the applicant overcomes all objections, the examining attorney will approve the mark for publication in the *Official Gazette,* a weekly publication of the PTO. The PTO will send a Notice of Publication to the applicant. Any party who believes it may be damaged by the registration of the mark has 30 days from the date of publication to file an opposition to registration. An opposition is similar to a formal proceeding in the federal courts but is held before the Trademark Trial and Appeal Board. If no opposition is filed, the application enters the next stage of the registration process, as described next.

If the application was based upon the *actual use of the mark in commerce prior to approval for publication,* the PTO will register the mark and issue a registration certificate about 12 weeks after the date the mark was published, assuming no opposition to register was filed.

If, instead, the mark was published based upon the applicant's statement of having a *bona fide intention to use the mark in commerce,* the PTO will issue a Notice of Allowance about 12 weeks after the date the mark was published, again provided no opposition was filed. The applicant then has six months from the date of the Notice of Allowance to either (1) use the mark in commerce and submit a Statement of Use, or (2) request a six-month Extension of Time to File a Statement of Use. The applicant may request additional extensions of time only as noted in the instructions on the back of the extension form. If the Statement of Use is filed and approved, the PTO will then issue the registration certificate.

It is difficult to provide precise estimates of how long it takes from the filing of an application to the receipt of a certificate of registration in any particular case because numerous factors can arise during the examination process that can lengthen the process. For example, if an application is refused because of a prior pending conflicting application, the later-filed application could be suspended for several months or possibly one or two years until the prior-pending conflicting application is either registered or abandoned. Other factors, such as whether the application has been filed based on an intent to use or based on a foreign application, or whether a Notice of Opposition is filed by a third party, can cause delays. However, if there are no (or relatively minor) substantive or procedural problems and the application is based on "use in commerce," and no Notice of Opposition is filed by a third party, it may be possible to obtain a registration within 10 to 12 months of the application filing date. Intent-to-use (ITU) applications that have little or no major problems, and that are not opposed by third parties, could receive a Notice of Allowance within 10 to 12 months of the filing date. However, the ITU application would not be registered until the applicant files an acceptable Statement of Use along with specimens showing the mark in use in commerce.

Marks Not Subject to Registration

A trademark cannot be registered if it

- consists of or comprises immoral, deceptive, or scandalous matter or matter that may disparage or falsely suggest a connection with persons living or dead, institutions, beliefs, or national symbols or bring them into contempt or disrepute;

- consists of or comprises the flag or coat of arms or other insignia of the United States, or of any state or municipality, or of any foreign nation or any simulation of these;

- consists of or comprises a name, portrait, or signature identifying a particular living individual, except by his or her written consent, or the name, signature, or portrait of a deceased president of the United States during the life of his widow, if any, except by the written consent of the widow;

- consists of or comprises a mark that so resembles a mark registered in the Patent and Trademark Office, or a mark or trade name previously used in the United States by another and not abandoned, as to be likely when applied to the goods of another person to cause confusion, mistake, or to deceive.

Service, Certification, and Collective Marks

The Trademark Act also provides for the registration of the following:

- *Service mark.* This is a mark used in the sale or advertising of services to identify the services of one person and distinguish them from the services of others. Titles, character names, and other distinctive features of radio or television programs may be registered as service marks notwithstanding that they, or the programs, may advertise the goods of the sponsor.

- *Certification mark.* This is a mark used on or in connection with the products or services of one or more persons other than the owner of the mark to certify regional or other origin, material, mode of manufacture, quality, accuracy, or other characteristics of such goods or services or that the work or labor on the goods or services was performed by members of a union or other organization.

- *Collective mark.* This is a trademark or service mark used by the members of a cooperative, an association, or other collective group or organization. Marks used to indicate membership in such organizations may be registered as collective membership marks.

Anyone who claims rights in a mark may use the ™ (trademark) or ˢᴹ (service mark) designation with the mark to alert the public to the claim. It is not necessary to have a registration, or even a pending application, to use the designations. The claim may or may not be valid. The registration symbol ® may only be used when the mark is registered with the PTO; it is improper to use it before the registration issues. Omit all symbols from the mark in the drawing you submit with your application; the symbols are not considered part of the mark.

Trademark Assistance Center. In order to provide improved service to trademark applicants, registrants, and the general public, the Patent and Trademark Office has implemented a pilot program called the Trademark Assistance Center. The center provides general information about the trademark registration process and responds to inquiries about the status of specific trademark applications and registrations. The location of the center is 2900 Crystal Drive, Room 4B10, Arlington,

Virginia 22202-3513. Assistance may be obtained in person or by dialing 703-308-9000, Monday through Friday, 8:30 AM to 5:00 PM EST except for holidays. Assistance concerning trademark and patent matters is also available at 703-308-HELP or 800-PTO-9199; recorded information is available at 703-557-INFO. Automated information about the status of trademark applications and registrations is available at 703-305-8747.

HOT SITE

Trademark information available on the PTO home page (http://www.uspto.gov/) includes the *Basic Facts about Trademarks* booklet along with forms in the booklet. Also offered are current fee schedules; fact sheets; the *Trademark Manual of Acceptable Identifications and Classifications for Goods and Services;* and the *Trademark Trial and Appeal Board Manual of Procedure.* The *Trademark Manual of Acceptable Identifications and Classifications for Goods and Services* has thousands of listings for goods and services that the PTO routinely accepts, along with the proper international classification for the goods and services. Applicants are encouraged to use this resource in drafting identifications for goods and services. The PTO home page is formatted in WordPerfect 5.1 for Windows (convertible to Word) and in Pagemaker 5.0.

PATENTS

You have a great idea, and you think you need a patent. Below are answers to frequently asked questions about obtaining a patent. If you need additional information, call 800-PTO-9199.

What is a patent? A patent is granted by the federal government to an inventor "to exclude others from making, using, offering for sale or selling the invention throughout the United States or importing the invention into the United States."

The three types of patents are the following:

1. *Utility* patents may be granted to anyone who invents or discovers any new and useful process, machine, article of manufacture, or compositions of matter, or any new useful improvement to any of these.

2. *Design* patents may be granted to anyone who invents a new, original, and ornamental design for an article of manufacture.

3. *Plant* patents may be granted to anyone who invents or discovers and asexually reproduces any distinct and new variety of plant.

Methods of doing business, a mere idea or suggestion, or printed matter cannot be patented.

Frequently Asked Questions

How long does patent protection last? Utility and plant patents are granted for a term that begins on the date of the grant and ends 20 years from the date the patent application was first filed. Design patents are granted for a term of 14 years from the date of the grant. A patent holder loses exclusive rights to the invention when the term expires or when periodic maintenance fees are not paid.

Who owns the patent rights? Patents are granted only to the true inventor, who may sell all or part of his or her interest in the patent application or patent to anyone by a properly worded assignment. Only the true inventor may apply for a patent with the U.S. Patent and Trademark Office.

How do I get a patent? Inventors can apply in writing to the Commissioner of Patents and Trademarks using one of two types of patent applications.

1. A **nonprovisional** application, which begins the examination process that may lead to a patent, must include the following:
   - A specification (a satisfactory description of the invention with at least one claim). For an inventor, claims are the most important part of a nonprovisional application because they are used to judge the patentability of an invention. A concisely written claim describes an invention without unnecessary details and recites all essential features necessary to distinguish the new invention from what is old. Claims continue to be important once a patent is granted because questions of infringement are judged by the courts on the basis of claims.
   - A drawing where necessary
   - An oath or declaration
   - The filing fee required by law

2. A **provisional** application establishes a filing date but does not begin the examination process. It provides the inventor with a one-year period to further develop the invention, determine marketability, acquire funding or capital, or seek licensing agreements. To obtain a patent, the inventor must file a nonprovisional application within 12 months of the filing date of the provisional application.

   A provisional application must include the following:
   - A cover sheet identifying the application as a provisional application, the name of the inventor, and other bibliographic data
   - A partial type of specification (a satisfactory description without claims)
   - A drawing where necessary
   - The filing fee required by law

Both types of applications are held in confidence and may be used to apply for either a utility or a plant patent. An application for a design patent must be filed as a nonprovisional application.

The terms *patent pending* or *patent applied for* may be used by a manufacturer or seller of an article to inform the public that a pending provisional or nonprovisional application for that article is on file. The law imposes a fine on those who use these terms falsely.

A valid patent may not be obtained if the invention was in public use or on sale in this country for more than one year prior to the filing of a patent application. Your own use and sale of the invention for more than a year before the application is filed will also bar the right to a patent.

How much does it cost to obtain a patent? The cost for a patent varies by type of patent, whether the applicant is a small entity (individual inventor, nonprofit organization, or a small business concern) or a corporation and several other factors. For a utility patent, the basic filing fee, the issue fee, and the maintenance fees during the patent term will total approximately $4,000 for a small entity. Charges for design and plant patents are slightly lower. Fees are adjusted annually.

Should I hire a lawyer? The patent application process can be complex, and the Patent and Trademark Office cannot assist in the preparation of application papers. It is advisable to engage the services of a patent attorney or agent.

Applicants should also consult local telephone directories for the names of patent attorneys or agents in their area.

What is the Disclosure Document Program? Under the Disclosure Document Program, the PTO accepts and preserves for a two-year period papers disclosing an invention pending the filing of a patent application. This disclosure is accepted as evidence of the date of conception of the invention but provides no patent protection. For more information, contact 703-308-4357.

Important contacts for PTO customers

Toll-free Number 800-PTO-9199
Help Line (General Information
    Services Division) 703-308-4357
Copyright Office,
    Library of Congress 202-707-3000
Patent Copy Sales 703-305-4350
Office of Public Affairs 703-305-8341

What about patent promotion organizations? The Patent and Trademark Office has no control over, and does not maintain information about, patent promotion organizations. Before using one of these organizations, you should check the reputation of any firm by consulting the better business bureau in your area or asking your patent attorney or agent.

How do I get help marketing my invention? The Patent and Trademark Office cannot assist in the development and marketing of an invention but will publish, at a patent owner's request and expense, a notice in the weekly *Official Gazette* that the patent is available for licensing or sale. You may want to consult chambers of commerce, banks, industrial development organizations, or similar groups for help in promoting your invention. Consult directories in your local library or write to state authorities for the names and addresses of such organizations.

Is my patent good in foreign countries? A U.S. patent protects your invention in this country only. Normally, a license must be obtained from the Commissioner of Patents and Trademarks before you can file for a patent in another country unless that filing occurs more than six months after the filing in this country. In that case, no license is necessary unless you are informed otherwise by the Patent and Trademark Office.

Do I need to do a patent search before I apply? Many inventors do make a search of issued patents to be sure that someone else has not already patented their idea. You may do this, or you may hire someone to do it for you, at the Patent Search Room of the Patent and Trademark Office in Arlington, Virginia. The Search Room is open to the public from 8:00 AM to 8:00 PM, EST, Monday through Friday, except for federal holidays. The PTO's Scientific and Technical Information Center, which contains a vast collection of technical literature, is also open to the public. A Files Information Unit is also available for the public to inspect open records, such as those for issued patents; applicants and their attorneys may examine their own cases.

Collections of patents and patent-related materials may also be examined at any Patent and Trademark Depository Library (PTDL) throughout the country.

PTDLs maintain collections of current and previously issued patents, as well as patent and trademark reference materials. While these reference collections vary from library to library, all PTDLs provide direct, computerized access to PTO data. Copying facilities are available for a fee along with technical staff assistance. The partnership libraries in Sunnyvale, California, and Detroit, Michigan, offer video teleconferencing and complete search collections.

Invention Evaluation Checklist

To determine whether your idea has commercial merit, you should determine how the following items relate to your idea:

- ❑ Legality
- ❑ Safety (particularly in view of the current rash of product liability lawsuits)
- ❑ Environmental impact under federal and state laws
- ❑ Potential market and marketing research needed to sell the invention
- ❑ Product life cycle
- ❑ Ease of usage by potential customers
- ❑ Product visibility (particularly if it will be sold at the retail level)
- ❑ Service needs and whether independent service companies can handle potential problems
- ❑ Durability
- ❑ The function your invention will fulfill and the need for that function
- ❑ Production requirements
- ❑ Nature of demand and whether it is stable, seasonal, or otherwise cyclical
- ❑ Distribution requirements
- ❑ Existing competition and the ease with which larger, entrenched companies can develop a competitive product
- ❑ Investment costs needed to develop your invention and bring it to market
- ❑ Trend of demand in the market to which you will promote your invention
- ❑ Product-line potential
- ❑ Promotional needs
- ❑ Price and whether your invention will be cost-efficient for users
- ❑ Whether it can be protected from legal copying
- ❑ Payback period needed to recover costs absorbed while developing your invention and bringing it to market
- ❑ Profitability per projected sale
- ❑ Product interdependence (particularly if your invention incorporates an existing patented product)
- ❑ Research and development costs

Establishing Novelty

To receive a patent, your invention must be "novel." Novelty is one of the most crucial and difficult determinations to make. You must do two things: (1) analyze the device or invention according to specified standards, and (2) determine whether anyone else has already patented your invention. The only sure way to accomplish this is to make a search of Patent Office files.

Analyzing your device should be done according to the following standards of what is patentable:

- Any new, useful, and unobvious process (primarily industrial or technical), machine, manufacture, composition, or matter (generally chemical compounds, formulas, and the like); or any new, useful, and unobvious improvements to the preceding

- Any new and unobvious original and ornamental design for an article of manufacture, such as a new auto-body design (Note that a design patent may not always turn out to be valuable because a commercially similar design can easily be made without infringing the patent.)

- Any distinct and new variety of plant, other than a tube-propagated one, that is asexually reproduced

Another way to analyze your product is to consider it in relation to what is *not* patentable. The following are unpatentable:

- An idea (as opposed to a mechanical device)

- A method of doing business (such as the assembly-line system) (However, any structural or mechanical innovations employed in the method of doing business might constitute patentable subject matter.)

- Printed matter (covered by copyright law)

- An inoperable device

- An improvement in a device that is obvious or the result of mere mechanical skill (such as a new assembly of old parts or an adaptation of an old principle—aluminum window frames, for example, instead of the conventional wood)

Applications for patents on machines or processes for producing fissionable material can be filed with the Patent and Trademark

Office. In most instances, however, such applications might be withheld if the subject matter affects national security and for that reason should not be made public.

The invention should also be tested for novelty by the following criteria:

- Whether known or used by others in this country before the invention by the applicant

- Whether patented or described in a printed publication in this or a foreign country before the invention by the applicant

- Whether described in a printed publication more than one year prior to the date of the patent application in the United States

- Whether in public use or on sale in the country more than one year prior to the date of the patent application in the United States

These points are important. For example, if you describe a new device in a printed publication or use it publicly or place it on sale, you must apply for a patent within one year of publication or the first sale; otherwise, you lose any right to a patent.

Although marking your product "patent pending" after you have applied has no legal protective effect, it often tends to ward off potential infringers.

HOT SITE

The IBM Patent Server (http://patent. womplex.ibm.com) provides access to over 26 years of U.S. PTO patent descriptions as well as the past 17 years of images. The first entries date back to January 5, 1971. You can search, retrieve, and study over 2 million patents.

HOW AND WHEN TO USE THE FORMS IN THIS CHAPTER

The **Limited Disclosure Agreement** protects the applicant for a patent from disclosure by those to whom it is considering licensing the intention.

The **Exclusive Licensing Agreement** is designed to be used for the marketing, manufacture, and research and development of a patented product.

LIMITED DISCLOSURE AGREEMENT

THIS AGREEMENT, dated the day of   , 199   by and between
                    Inc., a   corporation having an office and place of business at
                    ,   ("P") and   , Inc., a
corporation having its principal office and place of business at   ("B").

WITNESSETH:

WHEREAS, P   is the owner and holder of certain United States patent applications pertaining to   , and is the owner and holder of certain proprietary technical information and expertise in the processing of   thereof and certain other processes (said patent applications, proprietary technical information, expertise and processes being hereinafter referred to as the "Processes"); and

WHEREAS, B   is desirous of obtaining information concerning the Processes for the purposes of evaluation and negotiation with P   for a license agreement pertaining to the Processes; and

WHEREAS, P   is unwilling to divulge any information to B   concerning the Processes without the protection against disclosure or use provided to it by this agreement.

NOW, THEREFORE, for and in consideration of the premises and for other good and valuable consideration, the receipt and sufficiency of which is acknowledged, P and B agree as follows:

1. For a period of   days from the date hereof, P   agrees to permit designated officers, directors, or employees (collectively "Representatives") of B   to visit its facilities at times to be mutually agreed upon, and to discuss with representatives of P   certain matters related to the Processes.

2. B   agrees that it will treat as confidential all information derived from such visits and discussions and will not divulge to others the Processes or any information disclosed or furnished by   relating to the Processes. Furthermore, B   shall (i) advise each of its Representatives who is to receive any such information of the confidential nature thereof, and of the restrictions imposed by this Limited Disclosure Agreement, and (ii) require each of its Representatives who is to receive any such information to agree in writing to be bound by the terms and conditions of this Limited Disclosure Agreement. Copies of the agreement of each B   Representative shall be furnished to P

3. B   agrees that it will not make any commercial use of any information furnished by representatives of P   without the prior written consent of P   . This restriction shall be binding upon B   , its officers, directors, shareholders, employees, and agents.

4. Without limiting the foregoing, and as an inducement to P   to disclose information to the Representatives of B   , hereunder, B   consents to the issuance of an injunction against it by any court of competent jurisdiction in the event the court determines that there has been a breach of the obligations imposed on B   hereunder.

IN WITNESS WHEREOF,   and   have executed this Limited Disclosure Agreement as of the day and year first above written.

By _____
Vice President

By _____

EXCLUSIVE LICENSING AGREEMENT

THIS AGREEMENT made this   of   , 199   between   ,
INC., incorporated in the State of   having its principal office at   Street,
                    , (hereinafter referred to as "Licensor") and   and having their prin-
cipal office at   , (hereinafter referred to as "Licensee").

W I T N E S S E T H:

WHEREAS, Licensee has invented a   machine (hereinafter referred to as "the
machine") identified and described in Exhibit "A" attached hereto, which is intended to be leased to vendors
to be used by them for the purpose of   ;

WHEREAS, Licensor as a result of its additional design work desires to acquire interests in the machine
and the right to letters patent of the United States and foreign countries that may be granted thereon;

WHEREAS, Licensor has commenced, and will reasonably pursue, applying for all feasible patents at
the earliest possible time;

WHEREAS, the Licensor and Licensee desire to have the machine marketed for consumer use exclusively by Licensee;

WHEREAS, the Licensee desires the Licensor to manufacture the machine for Licensee's use and
Licensor has asserted that it can manufacture the machine to a quality and for a price that will be competitive
with other manufacturers and not hamper Licensee's ability to market the machine;

WHEREAS, the Licensor has agreed to manufacture and the Licensee is desirous of selling and leasing
the machines; and

WHEREAS, the Licensee and Licensor desire that further research investigations be conducted with
respect to developing and manufacturing the machine.

NOW, THEREFORE, in consideration of mutual covenants and promises herein contained, the parties
agree as follows:

1. Assignment. In consideration of One Dollar ($1.00), the exclusive right granted to Licensee to market
the machine, and other consideration, receipt of which is acknowledged by Licensee, Licensee assigns to
Licensor any claims to a patent that it may have, and to all rights of priority thereto pursuant to the
International Convention for the Protection of Industrial Property; and in any patents on the machine (and/
or the improvements) that may be granted in the United States or any foreign country, and in any
applications for such patent, and to each reissue or extension of the patent.

2. License. The Licensor hereby grants to the Licensee full and exclusive license and authority to market
the machine, together with any and all improvements thereto developed by Licensor in the future for
consumer uses.

3. Cooperation. Licensee agrees to cooperate with Licensor such that Licensor may enjoy to the fullest
extent the rights conveyed hereunder. Included within the scope of this duty is cooperation in such
proceedings involving the United States and foreign applications and patents as opposition, cancellation

proceedings, priority contests, public use proceedings, court action, and the like. Licensor agrees to take such action as is necessary against third parties to protect and defend its patent rights and the exclusive rights of licensee to market the machines.

4. Warranty. Licensee warrants and represents that a) it has not entered into any assignment, contract, or understanding in conflict herewith; b) it has at no time filed, or caused to be filed, applications for patents, or obtained in its name, or caused to be obtained in the name of others, any patents in the United States or elsewhere based on or covering the machine; c) the design, engineering, development and manufacturing specifications of the machine developed by Licensor and Licensee are secret, have not been developed or revealed, and shall not be disclosed or revealed except (if the payment pursuant to paragraph 7 is made) as necessary for the purposes of marketing the machine, securing investors in Licensee, or engaging another to manufacture the machine in accordance with paragraph 12;. d) it shall have its officers, employees, agents, franchisees, and lessees sign a limited disclosure and covenant against competition agreement; e) its lease agreements shall require the lessees to obtain any and all parts for any machine manufactured   by the Licensor from Licensor.

5. Research project. Licensor has commenced and shall continue to conduct a research project in order to develop the machine and a prototype "test bed module." Licensor shall devote as much time and attention to the project as is reasonably necessary for is success.

6. Compensation. In consideration of Licensor's development of the prototype "   ,"
Licensee has paid Licensor   dollars ($), receipt of which is hereby acknowledged.

7. Engineering costs. Prior to releasing the test bed module to Licensee pursuant to paragraph 6, and in exchange for the release of said module and a complete set of all plans, drawings specifications, and bill of materials prepared to date, Licensee will reimburse Licensor for engineering costs to date, at a rate not exceeding   dollars ($) per hour and up to dollars ($).

8. Goods to Be Supplied. As soon as practical but not later than 60 days after the receipt of any order for the said machines and a deposit of 33⅓ percent of the cost of the machine, the Licensor shall deliver to a common carrier pursuant to paragraph 9 or any other person whom Licensee may designate in such order. with such number of the said machine as such order may require. Licensor shall stand ready to supply parts for machines ordered from it at reasonable costs.

9. Delivery. All machines to be supplied by the Licensor hereunder shall be delivered to such common carrier as the Licensee may designate, and in default of such designation to such common carrier as the Licensor may see fit, consigned to the Licensee or to such other person as the order may designate at the address therein mentioned. The cost of transportation shall be borne and paid by the Licensee.

10. Payment. The Licensee shall pay to the Licensor within 30 days after such delivery of the machines by the common carrier as aforesaid at the address designated pursuant to paragraph 9, the balance due for every machine so delivered (less the deposit as set forth in paragraph 8). Licensee shall pay 18 percent per annum interest and reasonable attorney's fees on all overdue balances.

11. Ownership of Patents. All patents shall be the sole and exclusive property of the Licensor, subject to exclusive license hereby granted.

12. Right of Licensee to Have Machine Manufactured by Others; Minimum Order. If Licensor's delivered cost per machine is within 5 percent of competitor's prices and the quality of the manufactured machines proves functional in application, Licensee will elect to have Licensor manufacture all machines it requires. Otherwise Licensee shall have the right to appoint another to manufacture the machine for Licensee's use and to require Licensor to enter into one or more licensing agreements for the manufacture of the machine in consideration of the royalty payment set forth in paragraph 13.

13. Royalties. Licensee shalt pay the Licensor a royalty for each and every machine manufactured for Licensee which is not manufactured by the Licensor. This royalty shall be a one-time payment per machine of _____ dollars ($ ____), plus insurance costs of up to and not exceeding dollars ($ ____) per machine that Licensor may incur in connection with the marketing and consumer use of the machine. Licensee shall at all times keep an accurate account of sales and shall render a full statement of same in writing to the Licensor for each calendar quarter within thirty (30) days of the end of such calendar quarter and concurrently with the rendering of such statement pay to the Licensor the amount of royalties accrued during the corresponding calendar quarter. Licensee agrees that the Licensor shall have the right to examine the books of Licensee.

14. Termination. Licensor and Licensee shall have the right to terminate/cancel this Agreement by giving written notice of termination/cancellation being effective fifteen (15) days following receipt of such notice or twenty (20) days after such notice is mailed, whichever is earlier:

a) Liquidation of Licensee or Licensor, or

b) Insolvency or bankruptcy of Licensee or Licensor whether voluntary or involuntary, or

c) Appointment of a trustee or receiver for Licensee or Licensor, or

d) Failure of Licensee to make the payments herein provided for or failure of Licensor or Licensee to perform any of the agreements contained herein for thirty (30) days.

15. Consequences of Termination/Cancellation. The parties agree that termination/cancellation under the terms of paragraph 14 hereof for reasons other than Licensee's failure to make the payments herein provided for does not divest the Licensee of the exclusive license to market the machines or have them manufactured by another.

16. No Waiver of Default. The Waiver of any default under this Agreement by either party shall not constitute a Waiver of the right to terminate/cancel this Agreement for any subsequent or like default, and the exercise of the right of termination/cancellation shall not impose any liability by reason of termination/cancellation nor have the effect of waiving any damages to which the terminating/canceling party might otherwise be entitled.

17. Notices. All notices, requests, demands, and other communications under this Agreement or in connection therewith shall be given to or be made upon the respective parties hereto at the above stated addresses. All notices, requests, demands, and other communications given or made in accordance with the provisions of this Agreement shall be in writing, shall be forwarded by registered mail, and shall be deemed to have been given when deposited postage prepaid, addressed as specified in the preceding sentence.

18. Arbitration. Any controversy or claim arising out of or relating to this Agreement, or the breach thereof, shall be settled by arbitration in the State of _____ , in accordance with the Commercial Arbitration Rules of the American Arbitration Association, and judgment upon the award rendered by the Arbitrator(s) may be entered in any court having jurisdiction thereof.

19. Benefit. This Agreement shall be binding upon and inure to the benefit of the heirs, legal representatives, successors, and assigns of the parties hereto.

In witness whereof the parties have executed this Agreement.

INC.

By: _____
      President

11

You and Your Employees

Employment discrimination and unlawful discharge lawsuits are at the heart of the new civil rights movement. However, proper personnel procedures can minimize the likelihood of employee suits and create better overall employer-employee relations.

HIRING AN INDEPENDENT CONTRACTOR INSTEAD OF AN EMPLOYEE

The independent contractor relationship benefits the employer as well as the contractor. However, if an independent contractor is reclassified by the IRS as an employee in a payroll audit, the employer becomes liable for all withholding taxes and possible nonpayment penalties. IRS auditors disregard the independent contractor status whenever possible.

Employers of independent contractors, on the other hand, have less paperwork and are not required to do the following:

- Withhold income taxes and Social Security taxes (FICA) from employees' wages
- Pay one-half of the FICA tax
- Pay unemployment taxes (FUTA)
- Pay other state and local taxes, such as unemployment and workers' compensation
- Provide the same fringe benefits offered to employees, such as insurance coverages, vacation days, sick days, and pensions

The independent contractor receives the tax benefits of a self-employed businessperson such as travel, entertainment, and home office deductions (see Chapter 8); Keogh plans; and depreciation of work-related assets. No taxes are withheld from the earnings of independent contractors, who are responsible for the payment of their own taxes, are not entitled to any fringe benefits, and receive a Form 1099-MISC from the business.

Common Law Rules

The primary factors distinguishing an independent contractor from an employee are whether the employer "controls" the worker and the basis upon which the worker is paid.

Under common law applied by most state courts, independent contractors are those who

- work on their own—decide how work is to be done without employer direction or instruction except as to the end result;
- do not receive any job training from the employer;
- hire their own assistants if needed;
- are hired to do one particular job at a time and do not work for the same employer year after year;
- work for more than one employer or, at the very least, are not required to work full-time for one employer;
- set their own pace and the sequence of services performed;
- do not submit oral or written reports;
- are paid on a commission or per-job basis (not an hourly wage);

- pay for their own business or traveling expenses;
- furnish their own tools and materials;
- have an investment in their own business;
- assume responsibilities for good or bad decisions and their effect on their own personal gains or losses;
- provide services to the general public; and
- cannot be fired if contract specifications are met.

Statutory Employees

The Internal Revenue Code lists four occupational groups that are considered independent contractors under the common law rules just described, but they are treated as statutory employees for tax purposes.

1. *Agent drivers or commission drivers.* This includes workers who distribute meat, vegetables, fruit, bakery products, beverages (other than milk), or laundry/dry-cleaning.
2. *Full-time life insurance salespeople.* They must work for one company.
3. *Homemakers.* They must work at home for one employer doing needlework or making clothing, bedspreads, buttons, quilts, gloves, and the like.
4. *Traveling or city salespeople.* They must sell for one principal employer.

Statutory employees receive special treatment when they deduct unreimbursed business expenses. They can use Schedule C to deduct their expenses instead of Schedule A, which means they are not subject to the 2 percent adjusted gross income limitation on miscellaneous itemized deductions. The statutory employee box must be checked on Schedule C and on the employee's W-2.

The statutory employee must receive a W-2 form and not a 1099-MISC. The employer pays one-half of FICA, and the other half is withheld from the employee's wages. (Schedule SE is not filed with Schedule C.)

Statutory Nonemployees

The Internal Revenue Code provides that the following individuals are not employees:

- *Qualified real estate agents.* These people are licensed and paid on a commission basis. Their contract must state they are not employees for federal tax purposes.

- *Direct sellers.* They sell consumer products away from the premises of a permanent retail establishment, are paid on a commission basis, and have a contract stating they are not employees for federal tax purposes.

Safe Harbor

If a worker is neither a common law independent contractor nor a statutory employee, that person may qualify as an independent contractor under existing "safe harbor" rules. A business may treat a worker as an independent contractor for employment tax purposes if the following conditions are met:

- A reasonable basis exists for not treating the worker as an employee.
- The business has not treated the worker or others performing substantially similar work as employees during any period after December 31, 1977.
- Amounts paid to the worker have been reported and filed on Form 1099 on a timely basis.

Certain technical workers, including engineers, designers, draftspeople, computer programmers, and systems analysts, cannot use the safe harbor treatment. The status of these workers is determined under the common law rules.

Employers' Precautions

If you hire independent contractors, take the following precautions to prevent a disfavorable audit from the IRS:

- Draft a written contract that provides for and/or contains (1) the type of services to be performed, (2) the place of work, (3) payment, (4) duration of the contract, (5) an arbitration clause, and (6) a covenant against competition.
- The worker should bill you for services rendered.
- As much independence as possible should be given to the worker (e.g., hours worked, supervision on the job, and the location where the work is to be performed).
- The worker should be required to provide his or her own tools, supplies, training, and transportation.

- If in doubt, file Form SS-8, "Information for Use in Determining Whether a Worker Is an Employee for Purposes of Federal Employment Taxes and Income Tax Withholding," with your IRS district director.

Employers' Penalties for Using Interns

The U.S. Fair Labor Standards Act (FLSA) restricts the kinds of tasks that unpaid interns or trainees may perform. Interns are classified as nonemployees exempt from minimum wage provisions if employers do not derive any immediate advantage by using them. Even though the training may include tasks performed for the business, it must be comparable to a learning experience found in a vocational school program. The FLSA applies to all companies that have at least two employees directly engaged in interstate commerce and annual sales of $500,000 or more. The act also covers public agencies and medical and educational institutions.

The factors considered by the courts and the Labor Department in classifying an intern as a nonemployee under the FLSA are as follows:

- If billing clients for work performed by interns gave the company an "immediate advantage"
- If the unpaid intern displaces a regular worker
- Whether the training benefits the intern
- Whether the intern is entitled to a job at the conclusion of the training program
- Whether there is an understanding that the intern is not entitled to wages for time spent in training

The legality of intern contracts specifying that the intern will accept a small stipend or college credit in lieu of a minimum wage is being challenged by a class action lawsuit. The Labor Act applies even if the student is working for a school program and is paid in college credits.

THE HIRING PROCESS

Is Your Employment Application a Danger Spot?

Have you looked at your employment application lately? It may contain many illegal questions. The employee selection process is responsible for more discrimination charges than any other area of employment practice. Do *not* ask questions that refer to race, color, creed, sex, age, disability, marital status, or national origin. Only basic questions regarding an individual's personal, educational, and employment background are permissible.

Employers run the risk of encouraging unlawful discrimination and providing evidence that may be used against them if they inquire into or solicit information regarding the following:

- Prior married name
- Marital status
- Spouse's name
- Age (or date of birth) unless this is a bona fide occupational qualifications
- Sex unless it is a bona fide occupational qualification
- Color of eyes or hair
- Height and weight unless they are bona fide occupational qualifications
- Number and age of children
- Willingness to work on Saturdays or Sundays
- Lowest salary acceptable
- Credit references or indebtedness
- Arrest record
- Conviction record (except traffic violations) unless it is relevant for a bona fide occupational qualification
- Military experience and type of discharge
- Physical defects or disability, or being related to someone with a disability
- Name of person to contact in case of an emergency
- Maiden name

(See "Employment Application" at the end of this chapter.)

IMMIGRATION REFORM AND CONTROL ACT OF 1986

The Immigration Reform and Control Act of 1986 is the most comprehensive reform of U.S. immigration laws since 1952. It requires employers to keep records and verify an employee's identity and eligibility to work. Stiff penalties are imposed on those employing aliens who are not authorized to work in the United States.

The law requires that employers take the following precautions:

- Have employees fill out their portion of Form I-9 when they start employment.

- Check documents establishing an employee's identity and eligibility to work.

- Complete the employer's section of Form I-9.

- Retain Form I-9 for at least three years. (If you employ the person for more than three years, you must retain the form until one year after the person leaves your employment.)

- Present the form for inspection to an Immigration and Naturalization Service (INS) or Department of Labor (DOL) officer upon request on at least three days' advance notice.

When Form I-9 Must Be Completed

If you employ persons to perform labor or services in return for wages or other pay, you must complete Form I-9 within three business days of the date of the hire. (If you employ the person for less than three days, you must complete Form I-9 before the end of the employee's first working day.)

You do not need to complete Form I-9 for the following:

- Persons you employ for domestic work in a private home on an intermittent or sporadic basis

- Persons who provide labor for you if they are employed by a contractor providing contract services (e.g., employee leasing firms)

- Persons who are independent contractors

Unlawful Discrimination

The immigration law also prohibits discrimination. If you have four or more employees, you may not discriminate against any individual (other than an unauthorized alien) in hiring, discharging, recruiting, or referring for a fee because of that person's national origin or, in the case of a citizen or a person intending to become a citizen, because of his or her citizenship status.

Employers found to have engaged in discriminatory practices will be ordered to cease the prohibited practice. They may also be ordered to hire, with or without back pay, individuals directly injured by the discrimination and pay a fine of up to $1,000 for each individual discriminated against (up to $2,000 for each such individual in cases of employers previously fined). The court may also order the employer to keep certain records regarding the hiring of applicants and employees. If a court decides that the losing party's claim has no reasonable basis in fact or law, the court may award attorney fees to the prevailing parties other than the United States.

Penalties

There are civil as well as criminal penalties for violation of the federal immigration law. If an investigation reveals that an employer has violated the law with respect to employees hired after November 6, 1986, the INS may take action. When the INS intends to impose those penalties, it first issues a notice of intent to fine. Employers who receive the notice may request a hearing before an administrative law judge. If a hearing is not requested within 30 days, a penalty will be imposed.

Hiring or continuing to employ unauthorized employees. Employers determined to have knowingly hired unauthorized employees (or to be continuing to employ persons knowing that they are or have become unauthorized) may be fined as follows:

- *First violation*—not less than $250 and not more than $2,000 for each unauthorized employee

- *Second violation*—not less than $2,000 and not more than $5,000 for each unauthorized employee

- *Subsequent violations*—not less than $3,000 and not more than $10,000 for each unauthorized employee

Failing to comply with recordkeeping requirements. Employers who fail to properly complete, retain, and present for inspection Form I-9 as required by law may face civil fines of not less than $100 and not more than $1,000 for each employee for whom the form was not completed, retained, or presented. In determining penalties, consideration will be given to the size of the business, good-faith efforts to comply, the seriousness of the violation, and whether the violation involved unauthorized employees.

Requiring indemnification. Employers found to have required a bond or indemnity from an individual against liability under the new law may be fined $1,000 and ordered to make restitution either to the person who was required to pay the indemnity or, if that person cannot be located, to the U.S. Treasury.

Recruiting unauthorized seasonal agricultural workers outside the United States. Employers who knowingly recruit unauthorized workers outside the United States to perform seasonal agricultural labor may face the same penalties imposed on employers who hire unauthorized workers unless the workers recruited have been granted Special Agricultural Worker (SAW) status.

Engaging in a pattern or practice of knowingly hiring or continuing to employ unauthorized employees. Employers convicted for having engaged in a pattern or practice of knowingly hiring unauthorized aliens after November 6, 1986, may face fines of up to $3,000 per employee and/or six months imprisonment. The same penalties apply to engaging in a pattern or practice of recruiting unauthorized seasonal agricultural workers outside the United States. Criminal sanctions are reserved for serious or repeated violations.

Engaging in fraud or false statements or otherwise misusing visas, immigration permits, and identity documents. Persons who use fraudulent identification or employment eligibility documents or documents that were lawfully issued to another or who make a false statement or attestation for purposes of satisfying the employment eligibility requirements may be imprisoned for up to five years or fined or both.

DISCRIMINATION LAWS

Title VII of the Civil Rights Acts of 1964 and 1991

Coverage. Title VII covers private and public employers with 15 or more employees, labor organizations, and employment agencies.

Exemptions. Private clubs that are exempt from taxation and churches acting as employers who employ persons of a particular religion in all activities are exempt from Title VII.

Prohibited conduct. Discrimination in enumerated employment conditions and decisions, including hiring based on race, color, religion, sex, or national origin, is prohibited.

Disparate treatment. Intentionally different treatment because of race, color, religion, sex, or national origin (e.g., purposeful refusal to hire blacks or women) is prohibited.

Disparate impact. Title VII prohibits neutral selection criteria that have the effect of disproportionately screening out members of protected classes. Such criteria may include tests, education requirements, credit checks, and subjective decision-making criteria. Once plaintiffs show disparate impact in *unintentional* discrimination cases, the burden shifts to the employer to demonstrate job relatedness and business necessity.

BFOQ defense. Employers may discriminate on the basis of sex, age, religion, or national origin (not race or color) if there is a bona fide occupational qualification (BFOQ) for doing so.

Remedies. Compensatory and punitive damages are capped in sex, religion, and disability cases at $50,000 for employers with 15 to 100 employees. When the plaintiff can show that the discriminatory motive fueled an adverse employment action, the employer may be liable for a part of the employee's attorney fee even if the employer proves that it would have taken the same action even without any discriminatory motive.

Age Discrimination in Employment Act (ADEA)

Coverage. This act includes private employers with 20 or more employees, state and local governments, employment agencies, and unions with 25 or more members. The act protects workers age 40 or older, although it provides limited exceptions for public safety personnel, high-level managers, and tenured university faculty.

Prohibited conduct. Employment discrimination is prohibited; it includes the failure or refusal to hire an individual because of age and any preference, limitation, specification, or discrimination based on age in any notices or advertisements for employment.

Remedies. Included among ADEA's remedies are back pay; front pay in certain circumstances in lieu of reinstatement; attorney fees and costs to the prevailing party; and double back-pay liquidated damages for a willful violation.

National Labor Relations Act (NLRA)

Coverage. The NLRA covers private employers who meet the National Labor Relation Board's (NLRB) jurisdictional standards based on their volume of interstate commerce (most private employers qualify) and labor organizations.

Prohibited conduct. The following conduct is prohibited under the act: (1) interfering with, restraining, or coercing employees who engage in union or organizational activity or who act in concert with respect to issues involving wages, hours, or other terms and conditions of their employment; (2) discriminating against employees in regard to hire or terms of employment in order to encourage or discourage union membership; or (3) interrogating applicants concerning their union activity and refusal to hire applicants because of their union activity.

Rehabilitation Act of 1973

Coverage. This act applies to any private employer who has federal contracts or subcontracts for $2,500 or more. Federal contractors are required to institute affirmative action programs in order to employ qualified handicapped individuals. The act is administered by the Office of Federal Contract Compliance within the U.S. Department of Labor. It does not provide employees a private right of action.

Prohibited conduct. Discrimination against "otherwise qualified" handicapped individuals in programs and activities receiving federal financial assistance as well as the executive branch of the federal government is prohibited. The act defines "handicapped individual" as

> any person who (i) has a physical or mental impairment which substantially limits one or more of such person's major life activities, (ii) has a record of such an impairment, or (iii) is regarded as having such an impairment. . . . Such term does not include any individual who is an alcoholic or drug abuser whose current use of alcohol or drugs prevents such individual from performing the duties of the job in question or whose employment, by reason of such current alcohol or drug abuse, would constitute a direct threat to property or the safety of others. Provided a handicapped individual is able to perform the requirements of the job, with reasonable accommodations if necessary, they will not be subject to "adverse employment action."

Examples of adverse employment include a refusal to hire a protected individual, the termination of a protected individual, or any reassignment of a protected individual (even though there is no loss in pay or benefits) if that action is taken as a result of the individual's handicapped condition and the individual is physically and mentally capable of performing the work in question. Employees with AIDS, HIV, or an HIV-related illness who show no symptoms of disease are entitled to the protection of this statute.

Vietnam Era Veterans Readjustment Assistance Act of 1974

Coverage. Contractors and subcontractors holding contracts with the federal government in excess of $10,000 for the procurement of personal property or for nonpersonal services (including construction) must take affirmative action to employ qualified disabled veterans and veterans of the Vietnam era under such contracts and subcontracts.

Written plans for affirmative action are required if the contractor or subcontractor employs 50 or more workers and receives a contract of $50,000 or more.

Executive Order 11246

Coverage. Contracts with the federal government in the amount of $10,000 or more must contain an equal employment opportunity clause barring discrimination based on race, color, religion, sex, and national origin. The clause must be binding on the contractor or subcontractor for the life of the contract. Contracts for less than $10,000 may be aggregated during a 12-month period to bring a contractor or subcontractor within the scope of the executive order.

Each contractor with 50 or more employees and a contract of $50,000 or more is required to develop an affirmative action compliance program for each of its establishments.

Executive Order 11246 is administered and enforced by the Office of Federal Contract Compliance.

The Civil Rights Act of 1866

Coverage. This act applies to private and public employers (except federal employers) and protects whites, blacks, and members of certain ethnic groups, including Jews, Hispanics, and persons of Arabian ancestry from racial discrimination.

Prohibited conduct. Discrimination based on race in making or enforcing all contracts, including employment contracts, is prohibited. The Supreme Court has explained that the statute prohibits on the basis of race "the refusal to enter into a contract with someone as well as the offer to make a contract only on discriminatory terms. [It] does not extend . . . to conduct by the employer after the contract relation has been established, including breach of the terms of the contract or imposition of discriminatory working conditions." In addition, the Supreme Court held that the guarantee of the right to enforce contracts "does not . . . extend beyond conduct by an employer which impairs an employee's ability to enforce through legal process his or her established contract rights."

Remedies. Included in the act's remedies are back pay that is not restricted to the two-year limit of Title VII; compensatory damages and punitive damages in proper cases; attorney fees and costs; and equitable relief.

The Civil Rights Act of 1991

This act creates no new substantive rights but makes it easier for employees to prove employment discrimination. It establishes the right to a jury trial and new remedies (see Title VII of the Civil Rights Act of 1964) and the right to jury trial that previously were unavailable in certain cases of intentional employment discrimination. It amends Title VII of the Civil Rights Act of 1964, the Civil Rights Act of 1866, the Americans with Disabilities Act of 1990, the Age Discrimination in Employment Act of 1967, and the Attorneys Fees Awards Act of 1976.

The Americans with Disabilities Act of 1990

(See complete coverage of this act in Chapter 17.)

Additional Laws against Discrimination

Family and Medical Leave Act of 1993. This act applies to employers with 50 or more employees and requires that employees receive up to 12 weeks of unpaid leave without interruption of health benefits and an equivalent job upon return to work in the event of the birth of a child, receiving a foster or adopted child, or the need to care for oneself, a child, a spouse, or a parent.

Reconstruction ERA Civil Rights Act Sections 1981, 1983, and 1985. This act protects the right of employees to enter into and enforce employment contracts. It prohibits conspiracies to deprive people of equal protection, immunities, and privileges under the law.

Medical Employment Termination Act. Remedies to employees terminated without cause are provided by this act.

Federal Equal Pay Act of 1963. This act prohibits discrimination in pay on the basis of sex.

Federal Employee Retirement Income Security Act of 1974. This act regulates pension and welfare plans and prohibits interference with individual rights.

Immigration and Nationality Act. This act prohibits discrimination against noncitizen employees in hiring, recruitment, referral, or discharge.

Uniformed Services Employment and Reemployment Rights Act of 1994. This act prohibits discrimination on the basis of a person's service in the uniformed services of the United States or any state.

State laws may also prohibit

- discrimination in employment on the basis of a person's age, race, creed, color, national origin, sex, disability, marital status, or status as an ex-offender;
- discrimination in pay on the basis of sex;
- discrimination on the basis of a person's political activities outside of working hours, a person's legal use of consumable products, an individual's legal recreational activities outside of working hours, and an individual's membership in a labor organization or exercise of rights under the National Labor Relations Act; and
- retaliatory actions against an employee because of whistle-blower activity.

RIGHTS OF EMPLOYEES WITH AIDS

Employers must comply with federal and state antidiscrimination laws and health and safety laws in dealing with employees with AIDS. Employers usually may not

- terminate or discriminate against an employee or job applicant based solely on the fact the employee has the AIDS virus;
- ask a job applicant whether he or she has AIDS;
- refuse a qualified job applicant employment because the applicant has AIDS unless the condition would interfere with the person's ability to perform the job; or
- discriminate against AIDS-infected employees in firing, demotions, transfers, job assignments, benefits, disability leave, compensation, or related matters.

If a coworker refuses to work with an AIDS-infected worker, the coworker must establish that his or her apprehension is reasonable and in good faith in order to be protected from discipline.

Employers must have policies that comply with

- all requirements of the Vocational Rehabilitation Act, the Americans with Disabilities Act, Title VII parallels, and existing Equal Employment Opportunity Commission (EEOC) guidelines;
- Occupational Safety and Health Administration Rules governing exposure to blood-borne pathogens;
- employee privacy rights; and
- employee benefit provisions.

ARE YOU GUILTY OF SEX DISCRIMINATION?

Federal and state laws prohibit employment discrimination on the basis of sex. Additionally, state laws prohibit employment discrimination based on marital status (married, single, separated, divorced, or widowed). These laws prohibit

- sex and marital status discrimination in the hiring, firing, and promotion of employees (preemployment questions about a woman's ability to type, for example, may be discriminatory if that woman is seeking a managerial or professional position);
- sexual harassment by either a supervisor or coworker when a term or condition of employment is in some way tied to the employee's acquiescence (a corporate employer may be liable for its supervisor's sexual harassment of an employee even if it lacks knowledge of the harassment);
- sex or marital status discrimination by employers based on "customer preference," such as airlines that employ women as flight attendants because of the preferences of male passengers;
- job qualifications, such as minimum height and weight requirements, that discriminate against women and are not related to job performance; and
- retaliation by an employer, union, or employment agency against someone who has opposed discriminatory employment practices.

Compensation

State and federal laws also prohibit

- paying women less than men for equal work;
- sex and marital status discrimination in the provision of fringe benefits, including insurance, leave time, and vacation; and not providing maternity care coverage and pregnancy disability benefits if other kinds of health insurance and disability benefits are provided; and
- requiring women to contribute greater amounts to retirement systems than men or paying women lesser amounts than men upon retirement.

Working Mothers

Additional legal prohibitions include

- preemployment inquiries concerning sex, marital status, child-bearing ability, and parental duties unless based upon a bona fide occupational qualification;
- harassing or firing a pregnant employee capable of performing her job;
- forcing a pregnant employee to take a maternity leave while she is still capable of performing her job;
- treating employees disabled by pregnancy differently than employees disabled by any other condition; and
- sex discrimination in the provision of leaves of absence for child care.

Exceptions

- Federal fair employment laws do not apply to employers or unions with less than 15 employees.
- State fair employment law does not apply to employers or unions with less than four employees.
- An employer may use sex as a legitimate consideration if an employee of a particular sex is required for the job (a bona fide occupational qualification), such as requiring a male actor for a part written specifically for a man.

Company Policy on Sexual Harassment

The Civil Rights Act of 1991 permits employees to seek both compensatory and punitive damages for sexual harassment in the workplace. To avoid such problems, companies should establish and promulgate to all of their employees clearly worded company policies prohibiting sexual harassment. The following guidelines should be used in establishing a sexual harassment policy:

- Memos explaining the policy in concise terms should be circulated at least once a year.
- Sexual harassment should be thoroughly defined in the statement. The EEOC guidelines define sexual harassment as "unwelcome sexual advances, requests for sexual favors and other verbal or physical conduct of a sexual nature." The statement should specifically warn against the use of sexually explicit language and the display of sexually oriented posters.
- Establish a simple procedure for receiving and investigating sexual harassment complaints. The policy should guarantee that there will be no retaliation by the employer or the accused against the victim.
- The punishment should match the crime. The policy should state, for example, that a reprimand will be instituted in the first case and immediate dismissal will result from repeated offenses.
- Complaints should be handled in-house if at all possible. Victims of sexual harassment have the option of submitting their complaints as an internal grievance, instituting a lawsuit, or filing complaints with either the federal EEOC or a state's division of human rights.
- Sexual harassment training sessions are available from government agencies and private consultants. These training sessions stress the prevention of sexual harassment and can help in developing a sound company policy.

Written sexual harassment policies should be implemented to prevent sexual harassment, educate employers and employees about their responsibilities and rights, improve morale, enhance professionalism, increase productivity, encourage victims to come forward, and ensure that management takes prompt and effective corrective action to eradicate sexual harassment. Sexual harassment policies should, at a minimum, cover the following four items:

1. A written sexual harassment policy statement that includes the following:
   - An unequivocal statement that the employer will not tolerate, condone, or allow sexual harassment by any owner, employee, manager, supervisor, coworker, customer, independent contractor, or other nonemployee who conducts business with the employer
   - A statement that any employee who believes sexual harassment may be occurring is required to report the conduct to the appropriate human resources or other management employee
   - A definition of sexual harassment that includes specific examples of prohibited behavior, whether or not directed specifically to any individual. For example:
     - *Verbal:* Sexual innuendoes, suggestive or insulting comments or sounds, teasing jokes of a sexual nature, sexual propositions, or threats; continuing to express personal interest after being informed that interest is unwelcome
     - *Visual:* Sexually suggestive objects, pictures, or letters; leering, whistling, or obscene gestures
     - *Physical:* Unwanted physical contact, including touching, pinching, brushing the body, impeding or blocking movement, sexual intercourse, or assault

2. Procedures for implementation, including an educational and training program covering the company's sexual harassment policies on an ongoing regular basis for all levels of employees

3. A complaint procedure that includes the following:
   - The option of reporting any perceived sexual harassment to the employee's supervisor, other management person, or human resources representatives
   - Measures to ensure reasonable confidentiality about the charge.
   - Measures to ensure protection for the complainant or other participants in the complaint investigation from retaliation
   - Informing the complainant of his or her legal rights when a complaint of sexual harassment is made
   - A prompt, thorough and impartial investigation of the complaint
   - Informing the complainant of the results of the investigation and, if harassment if found, of the remedial options available through the employer
   - Appropriate disciplinary measures against any employee who violates the sexual harassment policy or retaliates against an employee who reports perceived sexual harassment, up to and including termination
   - Follow-up procedures to ensure subsequent acts of harassment or retaliation are not occurring

4. Procedures for preventing and acting against known or suspected harassment, whether or not a complaint has been filed

DRUG TESTING

Drug testing may expose employers to lawsuits for privacy violations, defamation, and negligence. The Drug-Free Workplace Act requires federal contractors and grantees to certify that they will provide drug-free workplaces. This certification is a precondition to receiving a grant or contract from a federal agency. The certification must provide that the employer will take the following actions:

- Fire or refuse to hire an individual who is a current user of illegal drugs
- Ban the use of alcohol or illegal drugs in the workplace by all employees
- Require that employees not be under the influence of alcohol or illegal drugs in the workplace
- Require employees to conform to the requirements of the Drug-Free Workplace Act
- Hold alcoholic or drug-addicted employees to the same standards as all other employees even if their unsatisfactory job performance is caused by their drug addiction or alcoholism
- Test employees for drug use (A drug test will not be considered a medical examination.)
- Require employees to comply with Department of Defense, Nuclear Regulatory Commission, and Department of Transportation drug policy and testing regulations

Employees have challenged discipline and termination based on the results of a drug test. Their lawsuits have alleged violation of their privacy rights, defamation, negligent testing procedures, and negligent infliction of emotional distress.

The following states have constitutional provisions ensuring a citizen's right of privacy: Alaska, Arizona, California, Florida, Hawaii, Illinois, Louisiana, Montana, South Carolina, and Washington. Connecticut, Iowa, and Utah have express provisions regarding drug and alcohol testing. Lawsuits for invasion of privacy involve the intrusive nature of drug testing, the compulsion to reveal private medical information, faulty and inaccurate testing procedures, and improper justification for imposing the tests.

In New Jersey, random drug testing of employees is considered to be a violation of the right to privacy. California requires that an employer demonstrate a "compelling interest" before conducting drug tests.

DISCRIMINATION AGAINST MINORITIES

Many employment practices that may appear neutral are in fact discriminatory against blacks, Hispanics, and other minorities. Such practices are illegal if they are not necessary to the employer's business. These practices include the following:

- Use of hiring or promotion standards that are not related to the job, such as an arbitrary height requirement or a college degree for unskilled workers
- Use of certain hiring or promotion tests that often contain ethnically or racially biased questions
- Preemployment inquiries about arrest and conviction records (See "Is Your Employment Application Illegal?" in this chapter.)
- A requirement that employees meet arbitrary health and fitness requirements, such as passing a special test for sickle-cell anemia

Employment discrimination also occurs if minority employees are forced into jobs with a slim chance for promotion, while white employees are given jobs where promotions regularly occur.

A pattern or practice of discrimination may exist when the percentage of minority employees in a particular job category or company is substantially below the percentage of qualified minority applications or minority members of the labor market in the geographic area. Such imbalances are particularly questionable when the company's hiring or promotion standards are vague or when recruitment occurs by word of mouth between present employees and their friends or relatives.

HOW TO TERMINATE EMPLOYEES PROPERLY

Dos and Don'ts for Investigating Employee Misconduct

Employee guidelines, such as the following, should be used so that employers conduct thorough investigations of an employee's misconduct and avoid lawsuits for defamation and invasion of privacy:

- Do ascertain whether legal counsel should be involved, especially if the employee's termination may be challenged.
- Do conduct a complete investigation.
- Do obtain corroborating statements from other employees.
- Do allow the employee to give an explanation of the events.
- Do conduct a prompt interrogation.
- Do obtain a signed admission of improper conduct from the employee (if possible).
- Do advise your other employees that you are not at liberty to disclose the reason for the employee's discipline or dismissal.
- Do not threaten your employees with prosecution or loss of their jobs.
- Do not touch your employees or make threatening gestures while you are questioning them.
- Do not restrain your employees from leaving the room while interrogating them.
- Do not ask employees about private matters unrelated to their misconduct.
- Do not give false or inaccurate reasons for termination.

Precautions to Prevent Wrongful Discharge Suits

The following procedures should be implemented by all employers to reduce the risks of liability exposure in discrimination suits for wrongful discharge:

- Provide written policies and rules to inform employees of the type of conduct that will result in disciplinary action and discharge.

- Establish a review procedure to verify that all discharges are for legitimate, nondiscriminatory business reasons.

- Document all personnel actions regarding the employee's disciplinary history, including performance evaluations and counseling notes.

- Conduct exit interviews (see form at the end of this chapter) with all terminated employees to confirm the reasons for their termination and to determine whether the employee believes that the termination was for unlawful reasons. The exit interview is a prime opportunity to obtain statements from the employee (e.g., admissions of inadequate performance or misconduct).

- Be sure that the dismissal is consistent with past practice and in compliance with all procedures and policies in personnel manuals.

- Alternative dispute resolution mechanisms, such as mediation and arbitration, should be used to resolve employee discrimination complaints.

- Liability insurance policies should be reviewed by the employer's legal counsel to make sure the policy covers discrimination claims.

- Policies and procedures contained in handbooks, manuals, job requisition orders, and corporate codes of ethics should state a strong and comprehensive policy against discrimination in the workplace.

- Managers and supervisors should be trained to avoid discriminatory acts. They should be sensitized to harassment or stereotyping and should learn how to deal with disabled employees in compliance with the Americans with Disabilities Act.

- Obtain a release and waiver from the employee stating that the release and waiver is "voluntary and knowing" and provides for severance pay, outplacement services, nondisparagement, confidentiality, group health insurance coverage, waiver of unemployment, and accrued vacation pay, and states that the employee has consulted with his or her own attorney.

Employers may obtain waivers of the Age Discrimination in Employment Act if the waivers meet the following seven requirements:

1. They are part of an agreement between the employee and the employer.

2. They are written in ordinary English.

3. They refer specifically to rights or claims arising under ADEA.

4. They do not cover rights or claims that may arise after the date waivers are executed.

5. They can be exchanged but only if the employer provides additional consideration (compensation in addition to benefits and severance pay they would get anyway).

6. Employees are given 21 days (45 days if leaving because of buy-out incentives or mass layoffs) to decide whether to sign the waivers.

7. Employees are advised in writing to consult with an attorney before signing the waivers.

Accused of Discrimination?

The EEOC investigates charges of employment discrimination, determines whether a reasonable basis exists for charges, and seeks to informally conciliate unlawful employment practices. Information supplied by the employer to the EEOC during an investigation can provide the basis for court action by either the employee or the EEOC. If your business is charged with employment discrimination, make sure you comply with the following:

- Do not independently contact the EEOC. Contact your attorney immediately to handle the charges.

- As soon as you receive the EEOC charge, make a thorough investigation.

- Your staff should be courteous at all times when dealing with the EEOC investigator.

- Your attorney should be present during any interviews of management personnel because their statements can bind you as the employer.

Representation by an attorney from the inception of a discrimination charge can prevent lawsuits and large monetary awards.

Retaliatory Discharge

Employees have a right to sue for retaliatory discharge if they are fired because of their efforts to compel their employers to comply with the law. Courts have held that employers may not discharge an employee who (1) insists that an employer comply with the Occupational Safety and Health Act (OSHA) standards or the food and drug laws; (2) furnishes evidence to law enforcement officials regarding criminal violations of co-employees; (3) refuses to give perjured testimony on an employer's behalf, violate a statute, commit a crime, or illegally alter pollution control records; (4) refuses the sexual advances of supervisors; (5) promotes unionism; (6) serves on a jury; (7) exercises his or her rights under workers' compensation law; (8) acts as an election official; or (9) cooperates with an official investigation.

Not covered under this right of action are employees who are discharged because of a private dispute, even if the employer's actions appear arbitrary or unfair. The issue may involve such matters as internal management disputes, taking excessive sick leave, an employee-shareholder discharged for exercising the right to examine the company's books, an employee who impugns the company's integrity, a refusal to take psychological stress evaluations, attendance at night school, or misuse of Christmas funds.

Whistle-Blowers

The False Claims Act, also known as the "Lincoln Law," "Informer's Act," or the "qui tam" statute, permits a private individual with knowledge that the federal government is being defrauded to file suit on behalf of the government to recover compensatory damages, stiff civil penalties, and treble punitive damages. The civil case is commenced by filing a claim with the government. Even if the government chooses not to intervene, criminally or civilly, the whistle-blower can still pursue the action and recover a share of the government's ultimate recovery, costs, and attorney fees. The whistle-blower will be required to pay the prevailing party's attorney fees and expenses if the case is lost or if it was frivolous, vexatious, or harassing. Examples of whistle-blower suits include the following:

- An employer sells blood plasma to the federal government for treating Medicare and Medicaid patients and veterans. The em-

ployee was harassed, threatened, intimidated, and eventually dismissed after she complained to her boss that the product was improperly tested for the presence of HIV and hepatitis C before it was sold to the government. The employer's contract with the government guaranteed that the product would be properly tested. The employee's reporting of the faulty testing was protected under the act, and her allegation of retaliatory discharge was sufficient.

- A nursing home's failure to provide adequate nutrition to patients in violation of the Nursing Home Reform Act while billing Medicare or Medicaid for nursing home services constituted a false claim within the meaning of the act.

- The lack of supervision of a store's cash register constitutes a knowingly submitted false claim where food stamps were exchanged for cash instead of food.

Employers May Be Jailed

An employer who discharges or penalizes an employee who, upon notice to his or her employer, is absent as a result of a subpoena to attend a criminal trial as a witness, has acted in criminal contempt of court and is subject to punishment.

MORE LABOR LAWS

Employees are protected by the following federal labor laws:

- *The Davis-Bacon and Related Acts* require payment of prevailing wage rates and fringe benefits for federally financed or assisted construction.

- *The Walsh-Healey Public Contracts Act* requires payment of minimum wage rates and overtime pay in contracts to provide goods to the federal government.

- *The Service Contract Act* requires payment of prevailing wage rates and fringe benefits in contracts to provide services to the federal government.

- *The Contract Work Hours and Safety Standards Act* sets overtime standards for service and construction contracts.

- *The Migrant and Seasonal Agricultural Worker Protection Act* protects farm workers by imposing certain requirements on agricultural employers and associations and by requiring the registration of crew leaders who must also provide the same worker protections.

- *The H-2A Provisions of the Immigration and Nationality Act* provides for the enforcement of contractual obligations of job offers that have been certified to by employers of temporary alien nonimmigrant agricultural workers.

- *The Wage Garnishment Law* limits the amount of an individual's income that may be legally garnished and prohibits the firing of an employee whose pay is garnished for payment of a single debt.

- *The Employee Polygraph Protection Act* prohibits most private employers from using any type of lie detector test either for pre-employment screening of job applicants or for testing current employees.

- *The Immigration Nursing Relief Act of 1989* provides for the enforcement of employment conditions attested to by employers of H-1A temporary alien nonimmigrant registered nurses.

- *The Immigration Act of 1990* provides for enforcing employment conditions attested to by employers seeking to employ alien crew members to perform specified longshore activity at U.S. ports.

- *The H-1B Provisions of the Immigration and Nationality Act* govern enforcement of labor condition applications filed by employers wishing to employ aliens in specialty occupations, and as fashion models of distinguished merit and ability, on H-1B visas.

- *Section 221 of the Immigration Act of 1990* governs the filing and enforcement of attestations by employers seeking to use aliens admitted as students on F-1 visas in off-campus work.

- *The Fair Labor Standards Act* establishes minimum wages, overtime pay, recordkeeping (see Chapter 7), and child labor standards. The equal pay provisions of FLSA prohibit wage differentials based on sex; between men and women employed in the same establishment; and on jobs that require equal skill, effort, and responsibility and that are performed under similar working conditions. These provisions, as well as other statutes prohibiting discrimination in employment, are enforced by the Equal Employment Opportunity Commission. More

detailed information is available from EEOC offices, which are listed in most telephone directories under U.S. Government, Department of Labor.

HOW TO ELIMINATE THEFT

To reduce theft by your employees, take the following steps:

- Review bookkeeping and other operations periodically.
- Do not give one employee responsibility over both accounts payable and accounts receivable.
- Obtain advice from an accountant on appropriate procedures and controls.
- Conduct annual independent audits.
- Require employees to sign for the use of office equipment and supplies.
- Change locks periodically on file cabinets and doors, and change computer passwords.
- Thoroughly screen job applicants by checking their references.
- Publish a code of ethics.
- Obtain fidelity bonds.
- Monitor the use of rubber signature stamps.

INTELLECTUAL PROPERTY PROTECTION

If your business creates and utilizes patentable inventions, trade secrets, and copyrights (see Chapter 10), you should use employment agreements to protect your existing and future intellectual property rights.

Patents

Most patents are awarded to employed inventors who assign the patents to their employers. However, the employer's ownership of its employees' inventions is not automatic. Without a written agreement, whether an invention discovered on company time belongs to the employee or the employer depends on the employee's status.

Employment agreements should require employees to disclose all inventions to the employer; assign all inventions to the employer; and cooperate in pursuing patents for inventions on behalf of the employer, including maintaining the duty to confidentiality about the invention. Some states, such as Illinois and California, have statutes that prohibit employers from unfairly receiving the benefit of inventions developed by their employees on their own time.

Trade Secrets

To prevent your company's trade secrets from being disclosed by employees, an employment agreement must specifically enumerate and define trade secrets. Typically, such a provision should refer to "inventions, ideas, technical data, products, product specifications, services, processes, machinery, apparatus, prices, discounts, manufacturing costs, and computer and information systems used in management, engineering, manufacturing, marketing, purchasing, finance operations, or otherwise."

Copyrights

As a result of the work-for-hire doctrine contained in the Copyright Act of 1976, an employer automatically becomes the owner of works authored by its employees in the scope of their employment. This is true even in the absence of a written employment agreement. An independent contractor or consultant, however, does not come under the work-for-hire doctrine, and the employer will not own the copyright of the works created unless it has entered into a written agreement specifically providing for ownership by the employer.

IS YOUR EMPLOYEE A FUTURE COMPETITOR?

As a general rule, an employee may compete with a former employer after the termination of employment or may work for a competitor. However, an employee may not compete with a former employer fraudulently, by misappropriating trade secrets or confidential information, or by violating an enforceable anticompetitive covenant.

Solicitation of Former Employer's Customers

Before leaving employment, an employee may notify the employer's customers that he or she is severing relations with the employer and going into his or her own business but may not solicit them as customers for the new business or divert orders from the employer to the new business. The same rule applies to group resignations: Employees may resign en masse by prearrangement, but they cannot solicit their employer's customers for their new business while they are still working for the employer.

Enforceability of Covenants against Competition

Covenants against competition will be enforced only if reasonably limited in time and geographical area and only to the extent necessary to protect the employer from unfair competition that stems from the employee's use or disclosure of trade secrets or confidential customer lists or if the employee's services are unique or extraordinary.

Are Customer Lists Trade Secrets?

An employee may solicit a former employer's customers in the absence of either an express contract to the contrary or any secret or confidential character of the employment. In the absence of a written contract forbidding competition, a former employee may use lists of customers made up from memory. But even though employees, after leaving the service of their employers, may solicit customers, they have no right to make a list of customers before leaving and, on leaving, take them to a rival concern. Even though employees may get most of their customers from contacts made while working for a former employer, they will not be restrained if those contacts could have been obtained merely by looking up names in a telephone or city directory or by going to any advertised location.

If customers' identities can be ascertained independently as prospective users or customers of a service or product, trade secret protection generally will not attach, and courts will not enjoin an employee from soliciting a former employer's customers. But an injunction will be granted if the employer's list of customers was obtained through years of effort and advertising, involving time, money, and enterprise, and the customers are not located in well-advertised locations.

Former employees will not be enjoined from soliciting customers of a former employer if there is no evidence that the employer expended any sums on advertising or other efforts to secure customer patronage; if the former employees explained how they found customers (frequently by reference to publicly available sources or prior existing trade or social contacts); or if the former employer's business did not involve long-standing, loyal customer and supplier relationships but rather a series of "one-shot" transactions based on the price of the items being offered.

WORKERS' COMPENSATION

Workers' compensation is employer-paid insurance that provides cash benefits and medical care for workers who become disabled because of an injury or sickness suffered because of their job. If death results, benefits are payable to the surviving spouse and dependents.

Employers without workers' compensation insurance are subject to fines, criminal prosecution, and civil liability. Employees of businesses conducted for profit and certain farm workers must be covered by workers' compensation insurance; but independent contractors are not covered. (See Chapter 17 for a discussion of how the Americans with Disabilities Act affects workers' compensation.)

Penalties

Failure to provide workers' compensation insurance coverage can result in

- fines,
- criminal prosecution,
- personal liability of the employer for any workers' compensation benefits due injured workers, and
- an employee's exercising the option to sue the employer rather than file a compensation claim.

Duties

Employers must perform the following duties:

- Post a notice of compliance in a conspicuous place at each job site.
- Provide immediate emergency medical treatment for employees who sustain on-the-job injuries.
- Furnish further medical attention if an injured worker is unable to select a doctor or advises the employer in writing of a desire not to do so.
- Complete a report of the injury and mail it to the nearest workers' compensation board office. A copy of the report should also be mailed to the employer's insurance company. An employer who refuses or neglects to make an injury report may be guilty of a misdemeanor, punishable by a fine.
- Make a written report of every accident resulting in personal injury that causes a loss of time from regular duties beyond the working day or shift on which the accident occurred or that requires medical treatment beyond first aid or more than two treatments by a doctor or persons rendering first aid. (See the "Employer's Report of Injury" form at the end of this chapter.)
- Comply with all requests for further information regarding injured workers by the workers' compensation board or the insurance company—that is, statements of the employee's earnings before and after the accident, reports of the date of the employee's return to work, or other reports that may be required to determine the employee's work status following the injury.

How Employees Avoid Workers' Compensation Laws

Workers' compensation benefits usually are the exclusive remedy of injured employees against their employer. However, there are a number of exceptions where the "conditions of compensation" do not exist, enabling employees or their survivors to sue an employer or a third party.

Third Parties. A third party such as a property owner, a manufacturer of machinery, or a subcontractor that is liable for the employee's injuries can be sued. That third party in turn can sue the employer for contribution or indemnification. New York limits the third-party liability of employers to cases involving grave injuries.

Uninsured employers. If an employer doesn't have workers' compensation insurance coverage, injured employees may bring a civil suit against the employer. Some states permit both a civil suit and a compensation claim.

No employer-employee relationship. One must be in the service of an employer under an appointment or contract of hire or an apprenticeship—express or implied, oral or written. If the services are voluntary, there may be no employer-employee relationship. Similarly, the required relationship does not exist if the injured person is employed as or by an independent contractor.

Excluded employment. Certain employees are not covered by the state workers' compensation legislation. For example, farm workers, corporate officers, working partners, domestics, railroad laborers, those employed by businesses employing less than a minimum number of employees, and casual employees are typically not covered.

Excluded injuries. Although most physical injuries are covered by workers' compensation, claims for some other types of injuries are not. They include false imprisonment, malicious prosecution, defamation, invasion of privacy, deprivation of civil rights, and emotional distress. In these instances the employee may commence a civil action.

Injury outside the course of employment. If the employee's injuries are inflicted outside the course or scope of employment, workers' compensation acts do not apply.

Employer's intentional misconduct. Certain states increase awards by one-half when an employee is injured by the "serious and willful" misconduct of the employer. In certain states, if the employer exposes the employee to toxic chemicals and knows of the danger, yet fails to correct it or warn the employee, a civil suit or criminal prosecution may be permitted.

Dual capacity doctrine. An employer may be held liable to an injured employee on the basis that it occupied a second capacity in addition to that of an employer. Dual capacity exists where the nonemployer aspect of the employer's activity generates a different set of obligations than the employer's duties to its employees. These situations can arise, for example, if an employer manufactures a product that causes harm to the employee or if a doctor treats a nurse. The doctrine applies where the employer takes on an obligation separate and distinct from that involved in the employment.

Corporate employees. Where the employee's injuries arise from the acts of a separate subsidiary of the employee's corporate employer, the parent is liable for the injury; the subsidiary is viewed as an entity separate and distinct from the parent. Also, where a corporation is consolidated rather than merged, separate entities may be involved.

Fellow employee. An employee may be permitted to sue a coworker for injuries caused by willful misconduct or intoxication.

Injured Workers Protected from Retaliation

Although workers' compensation laws provide remedies to injured employees, they also protect employers because they provide employees their only remedy against employers for job-related injuries. To protect employees from employers who use the exclusive remedy protection to harass injured employees, the following states prohibit employers from punishing, retaliating against, or discharging employees who exercise their rights under workers' compensation laws: Arizona, California, Hawaii, Maine, Maryland, Minnesota, Missouri, New Jersey, New York, North Carolina, Ohio, Oklahoma, Texas, and Wisconsin.

The burden of proof in a retaliatory discharge suit is on the employee. However, the employee does not have to prove that the workers' compensation claim is the sole reason for the discharge. The test is whether the employer's action is rooted substantially or significantly in the employee's exercise of rights.

A basic case often can be shown by the proximity of time between the filing of the claim and the date of discharge, especially when coupled with a satisfactory work record. Once a basic case is established, the burden shifts to the employer to show that he or she based the discharge on nonretaliatory motives.

California law entitles employees to 50 percent additional compensation (not to exceed $10,000). New York law provides for reinstatement, payment of back wages, and penalties ranging from $100 to $500. Employees who have testified or are about to testify in a workers' compensation proceeding are also protected by New York law.

Some states, such as California, make retaliation a criminal offense. However, certain courts have used such criminal statutes as a basis for denying an employee's civil cause of action for a retaliatory discharge.

Some states, such as Alabama, North Carolina, Florida, Mississippi, and New Mexico, do not recognize retaliatory discharge as a cause of action.

Besides termination, retaliation may take the form of more subtle types of discriminatory treatment, such as demotion or salary reduction. Injured employees are protected from discriminatory conduct immediately after an injury and before a formal workers' compensation claim is filed. An employee's cause of action may be valid even though all the employee did was give notice to the employer of a claim.

HOW AND WHEN TO USE THE FORMS IN THIS CHAPTER

Employment Application. This form should be completed by all job applicants before they are interviewed. It should be retained even if the applicant is not hired.

Independent Contractor Agreement. This form should be completed, signed, and notarized by all salespeople working for a real estate broker. It spells out the rights and duties of the broker and salesperson. There are two optional paragraphs that may also be used.

Contract with Consultant. This contract should be used when a consultant is hired on an independent contractor basis. The agreement protects the business owner from the use of trade secrets by the consultant. It also contains clauses regarding payment, restrictions on competition, how the agreement can be terminated, and the place of work.

Employment Agreement. This agreement contains a clause restricting the employee from revealing trade secrets and from competing with the employer. The employee is required to surrender all records upon termination of employment.

Employer's Report of Injury. This form should be completed and filed with the state workers' compensation board immediately after an employee is injured on the job. Failure to do so may result in penalties.

Employee Manual. Such a manual provides better communication and employer-employee relations. However, it should be used with caution because it may constitute a contract that gives employees a right to sue for unlawful discharge. The manual contains clauses regarding administrative policies, wages and salaries, benefits, and discipline. The acknowledgment should be signed by the employee as proof that a copy of the manual was received.

Performance Appraisal Report. This is completed on various occasions by a supervisor and should be signed by both the supervisor and employee.

Exit Questionnaire. This should be completed by an employee whenever he or she leaves employment.

Form I-9. This is the Immigration and Naturalization Service's Employment Eligibility Verification form that must be filled out by all employers.

Employer Recordkeeping Requirements. These include the length of time records are required to be preserved, the notices that must be conspicuously posted, and the statutes setting out those requirements.

EMPLOYMENT APPLICATION

Date of Application

APPLICATION FOR EMPLOYMENT

We are an equal opportunity employer. We will take affirmative action to ensure that during the interview process and employment, applicants and employees are treated without discrimination based on race, color, religion, sex, age, national origin, handicap, or marital status. We only hire individuals authorized for employment in the United States.

Instructions: In filling out your application, you are requested to furnish complete and accurate information concerning your employment. All applications are verified. A false or incomplete application will not be considered and can be used as a reason for discharge.

PERSONAL INFORMATION

Name:

      (Last)   (First)   (Middle Initial)

Social Security No.:

Present Address:

      (No., Street)   (City)   (State)   (Zip)

How long?

Telephone No.:

Are you a U.S. citizen?   Yes   No

If not, do you have a legal right to work permanently in the United States?   Yes   No

Is your age at least 18?   Yes   No

If not 18, can you submit a work permit?   Yes   No

JOB INTEREST

Position(s) applied for:

Have you ever been employed by our company?   Yes   No

From   to

Have you previously applied for employment at our company?   Yes   No   If yes, when?

Rate of pay expected: $ per hour

Would you work full-time?   part-time?   Specify day and hours if part-time:

Are you available to work overtime when necessary?   Yes   No

EMPLOYMENT APPLICATION
(continued)

EDUCATION AND TRAINING

Type of School	Name of School	No. of Years Attended	Graduated (yes or no)	Major Courses Degree
Elementary:				
High School:				
College:				
Graduate:				
Trade or Business:				
Correspondence:				
Other Training:				

OCCUPATIONAL HISTORY

Employer—Name and Address; Start with Present or Last	Immediate Supervisor	Your Job or Position	Dates Held	Salary or Wage	Reason for Leaving
				from to	
				from to	
				from to	

MILITARY SERVICE RECORD

Have you served in the U.S. armed forces?   Yes   No

Date of entry: Branch of service:

Date of discharge: Final rank:

Indicate service school attended or special training received:

SPECIAL SKILLS

Typing Speed	Shorthand or Speed Writing	Other Equipment Operated:
wpm	wpm	

EMPLOYMENT APPLICATION
(continued)

MISCELLANEOUS

Is there any additional information involving a change of your name or assumed name that will permit us to check your work record? If yes, please explain.

Have you ever been convicted of a crime?   Yes   No

If yes, please explain.

Amount of time lost from work during the past two years. Please explain.

PLEASE READ THIS STATEMENT CAREFULLY

I hereby affirm that the information given by me on this application for employment is complete and accurate. I understand that any falsification or omission will be immediate ground for dismissal. I authorize a thorough investigation to be made in connection with this application concerning my character, general reputation, personal characteristics, employment and educational background, any criminal record, and mode of living, whichever may be applicable. I hereby authorize the release of documents and personal interviews with third parties, such as prior employers, family members, business associates, financial sources, friends, neighbors, or others with whom I am acquainted. I further understand that I have the right to make a written request within a reasonable period of time for a complete and accurate disclosure of the nature and scope of this investigation.

It is understood that, as a condition of initial or continued employment, I agree to submit to such lawful examinations, medical, substance abuse, or other, as may be required by the company. The company will pay the reasonable cost of any such examination that may be required.

If I am hired, I agree that my employment and compensation can be terminated with or without cause and without notice, at any time, at the option of this company or myself. I understand that no manager or other representative other than a vice-president, and in writing, has the authority to enter into any agreement for employment for any specified period of time, or to make any agreement contrary to the foregoing.

I have read and affirm as my own the above statements.

Date _____

_____
Signature

INDEPENDENT CONTRACTOR AGREEMENT

THIS AGREEMENT, made this   day of   , 199   ,

by and between   (insert name of broker)

with business address at No.   (Street, Ave.)

in the   of   ,

hereinafter referred to as the "Broker" and

(insert name of Salesman)   with address at

(Street, Ave.)   in the

of   in the state of

hereinafter referred to as the "Salesman".

WITNESSETH:

WHEREAS, said Broker is now, and has been, engaged in business as a general real estate broker in the State of and is qualified to, and does, operate a general real estate business and is duly qualified to and does procure the listings of real estate for sale, lease or rental; and,

WHEREAS said Broker maintains an office in the

of   , equipped with furnishings and other equipment necessary and incidental to the proper operation of said business, suitable to serving the public as a real estate broker; and,

WHEREAS, the Salesman is duly licensed and registered as a real estate Salesman under the laws of the State of   ; and

WHEREAS, said Salesman is now, and has been, engaged in business as a real estate salesman; and

WHEREAS, it is deemed to be to the mutual advantage of said Broker and said Salesman to form an independent contractor relationship pursuant to the terms and conditions hereinafter set forth:

NOW, THEREFORE, for and in consideration of the foregoing premises and of the mutual covenants hereinafter contained, it is mutually agreed as follows:

1. Broker agrees to make available to the Salesman all current listings of the office, except such as the Broker for valid and usual business reasons may place exclusively in the temporary possession of some other Salesman, and agrees, upon request, to assist the Salesman in his work by advice and instruction and agrees to provide full cooperation in every way possible. Broker may, from time to time, conduct sales meetings and property inspections for Salesmen to assist them in obtaining listings and to improve their knowledge of the local and general real estate market including information as to the availability of mortgage financing. Attendance by Salesman at such sales meetings and/or property inspections shall not be required by the Broker.

2. Broker agrees that the Salesman may share with other Salesmen all the facilities of the office now operated by said Broker, in connection with the subject matter of this contract, which office is now maintained   at

184

In this regard, Salesman understands that all automobile, entertainment, and home telephone costs shall be his own nonreimbursable expenses and that no particular desk or office facilities will be set aside for him but such desk and office facilities shall be used generally by all sales personnel.

3. Salesman agrees to work diligently and with his best efforts to sell, lease, or rent any and all real estate listed with the Broker, to solicit additional listings and customers of said Broker, and otherwise promote the business of serving the public in real estate transactions to the end that each of the parties hereto may derive the greatest profit possible. Broker shall not require of the Salesman that he devote a required amount or prescribed schedule of selling or "floor" time at the Broker's office or at any outside sale or lease location.

4. Salesman agrees to conduct his business and regulate his habits so as to maintain and to increase the goodwill and reputation of the Broker and the Salesman, and the parties hereto agree to act in an ethical manner and to conform to and abide by all laws, rules, and regulations, which are applicable to real estate brokers and real estate salesmen. The Broker is desirous that the Salesman join as a member the local, state, and national Boards of REALTORS® but in no way is any such membership to be considered a requirement or a prior or continuing condition to the validity or force and effect of this agreement. In the event, Salesman shall pay at his own nonreimbursable expense any admission and membership fees connected therewith. Furthermore, if Salesman chooses to apply for professional licenses or to take educational courses and/or examinations, any fees pertaining thereto shall also be the nonreimbursable expense of the Salesman.

5. The Commission to be charged for any services performed hereunder shall be determined in each instance by the Broker and client. The Broker shall advise the Salesman of the terms of such commission agreement relating to a transaction in which Salesman participates. When the Salesman shall perform any service hereunder, whereby a commission is earned, said commission shall, when collected by Broker, be divided promptly between the Broker and Salesman in accordance with Broker's schedule of commissions to be paid his Salesmen. This schedule shall be kept on file in Broker's office and current copies thereof shall be distributed to all Salesmen. Variations in the schedule of payments to be paid Salesmen may be made by Broker in specific instances provided the rate of division in each such instance is agreed upon in advance by the Broker and the Salesman. In the event that two or more Salesmen participate in such a service, or claim to have done so, the amount of the Salesman's commission apart from the amount accruing to the Broker shall be divided between such participating Salesmen according to an agreement between them or, failing such an agreement, as determined by arbitration pursuant to the rules and regulations of the Practice and Ethics Committee of the Board of REALTORS®, Inc. In no event shall the Broker be personally liable to the Salesman for the default in the payment of any commission by a client.

6. Suits for the collection of real estate commissions shall, as required by state law, be maintained only in the name of the Broker.

7. In all respects, it is the mutual desire of both the Broker and the Salesman that each be deemed an independent contractor and the Salesman not be deemed a servant, employee, or partner of the Broker.

This contract and the association created hereunder may be terminated by either party hereto at any time upon notice given to the other but the respective rights of the Broker and Salesman to any commissions which accrued prior to such notice of termination shall not be divested by such termination.

8. After termination of this contract the Salesman shall not use to his own advantage or the advantage of any other person or corporation, confidential information gained from the business of the broker or his files and office records. This paragraph, however, shall not be construed to be a noncompetitive covenant, which, after such termination, restricts or limits the Salesman in any area or for any period of time from engaging in the sale of real estate.

IN WITNESS WHEREOF, the parties hereto have hereunto set their hands and seals, the day and year first above written.

_____
BROKER

_____
SALESMAN

ACKNOWLEDGMENT BY BROKER IF AN INDIVIDUAL

STATE OF

COUNTY OF $\Big\}$ SS:

On this   day of   , 199   , before me, the subscriber, personally appeared

to me personally known and known to me to be the same person described in and who executed the within Instrument, and he or she duly acknowledged to me that he or she executed the same.

_____

ACKNOWLEDGMENT BY BROKER IF A CORPORATION

STATE OF

COUNTY OF $\Big\}$ SS:

On this   day of   , 199   , before me, the subscriber, personally came

, to me known who, being by me duly sworn, did depose and say that he or she resides in   , the corporation described in and which executed the above Instrument; that he or she knows the seal of said corporation; that the seal affixed to said instrument is such corporate seal; that is was so affixed by order of the Board of Directors of said corporation; and that he or she signed his or her name thereto by like order.

_____

ACKNOWLEDGMENT BY SALESMAN (INDIVIDUAL ONLY)

STATE OF

COUNTY OF $\Big\}$ SS:

On this   day of   , 199   , before me, the subscriber, personally appeared

, to me personally known and known to me to be the same person described in and who executed the within Instrument, and he or she duly acknowledged to me that he or she executed the same.

_____

OPTIONAL PARAGRAPHS TO BE USED ONLY IN
THE CIRCUMSTANCES CITED BELOW

*OPTIONAL PARAGRAPH A.
(Insert after Paragraph 6 of the Independent Contractor Agreement
and then renumber succeeding paragraphs)

The Broker and Salesman agree that any monies which may from time to time be advanced by the Broker to the Salesman shall not constitute a wage, salary, or compensation as an employee. The Salesman agrees that any such advance is made to him only as a loan to relieve temporary economic hardship. The Broker shall keep an account showing the current balances of the outstanding indebtedness owed by the Salesman and commissions due to the Salesman. The unpaid amount of such loan advances shall be deducted from commissions earned by and due to the Salesman and commissions due to the Salesman. The unpaid amount of such loan advances shall be deducted from commissions earned by and due the Salesman. At any time, however, the Broker may demand payment by the Salesman of any net balance of indebtedness owed and Salesman shall repay such amount within thirty (30) days thereafter. Upon failure of the Salesman to repay such amount within thirty days after demand, interest at the rate of 6% shall accrue on the unpaid sums computed from the end of said thirty-day period until payment is received. The Broker may require the Salesman who receives loan advances to sign a separate loan agreement or promissory note as further evidence of the indebtedness owed by the Salesman to the Broker.

NOTE* Paragraph A is an optional paragraph and should be inserted in the independent contractor agreement *only* if the Broker advances money to the contracting Salesman. *If the Broker intends to make no advances to the contracting Salesman, the draft of the independent contractor agreement should contain no reference to "advances" or words such as draws, loans, etc.*

*OPTIONAL PARAGRAPH B
(Insert after Paragraph 6 of the Independent Contractor Agreement
and then renumber succeeding paragraphs)

The Broker and Salesman agree that the inclusion of the Salesman within the coverage of a workers' compensation policy shall in no way affect, diminish, or change the independent contractor status existing between the Broker and the Salesman.

NOTE* This Paragraph B is an optional paragraph and should be used *only* if the Broker deems it advisable to have coverage for sales personnel under the Workers' Compensation Act. *If no coverage is in force there should be no reference to such coverage in the independent contractor agreement.*

CONTRACT WITH CONSULTANT

THIS AGREEMENT, made this   day of   , 199   , between   doing business at   (herein referred to as "C") and   of   (herein referred to as "Consultant").

A.   C is in the business of   and in the conduct of said business desires to have the following services, as a Consultant, to be performed by Consultant: .

B. Consultant agrees to perform the services for C under the terms and conditions set forth in this agreement.

In consideration of the mutual promises set forth herein it is agreed by and between C and Consultant as follows:

1. NATURE OF EMPLOYMENT

Consultant will perform consulting, advisory, and programming services on behalf of C with respect to all matters and relating to or affecting   . As a part of Consultant's services, Consultant shall suggest to employees of C and review their findings concerning   and make suggestions thereon.

2. PLACE OF WORK

Consultant's services will be rendered largely at   , but Consultant will, on request, come to C's address of   , or such other places designated by C to meet with representatives of C.

3. TIME DEVOTED TO WORK

In the performance of the services, the aforesaid services and the hours Consultant is to work on any given day will be entirely within Consultant's control and C will rely upon Consultant to put in such number of hours as is reasonably necessary to fulfill the spirit and purpose of this contract. This arrangement will probably take about   days of work per week although there undoubtedly will be some weeks during which Consultant may not perform any services at all or, on the other hand, may work practically the full week.

4. PAYMENT

C will pay Consultant.

5. DURATION

After the term hereof has once commenced, it shall continue thereafter until terminated by either party by ten (10) days' written notice to the other party.

6. STATUS OF CONSULTANT

The Consultant is engaged as an independent contractor and shall be treated as such for all purposes, including but not limited to Federal and State taxation, withholding, unemployment insurance, and workers' compensation. Consultant will not be considered an employee of C for any purpose.

7. SERVICES FOR OTHERS

Inasmuch as Consultant will acquire or have access to information which is of a highly confidential and secret nature, it is expected that Consultant will not perform any services for any other person or firm without C's prior written approval.

8. SERVICES AFTER TERMINATION

Consultant agrees that, for a period of five (5) years following the termination of this agreement, Consultant will not perform any similar services for any person or firm engaged in the business of

, the Counties of   and

and State of   .

9. SECRECY

a) Consultant agrees not to disclose or use, except as required in Consultant's duties, at any time, any information disclosed to or acquired by Consultant during the term of this contract. Consultant shall disclose promptly to C all inventions, discoveries, formulas, processes, designs, trade secrets, and other useful technical information and know-how made, discovered, or developed by Consultant (either alone or in conjunction with any other person) during the term of this contract. Consultant agrees that he shall not, without the written consent of C, disclose to third parties or use for his own financial benefit or for the financial or other benefit of any competitor of C, any information, data, and know-how, manuals, disks, or otherwise, including all programs, decks, listings, tapes, summaries of any papers, documents, plans, specifications, or drawings.

b) Consultant shall take all reasonable precautions to prevent any other person with whom Consultant is or may become associated from acquiring confidential information at any time.

c) Consultant agrees that all confidential information shall be deemed to be and shall be treated as the sole and exclusive property of C.

d) Upon termination of this contract, Consultant shall deliver to C all drawings, manuals, letters, notes, notebooks, reports, and all other materials (including all copies of such materials), relating to such confidential information or the business of C which are in the possession or under the control of Consultant. Consultant shall sign secrecy agreements provided by C.

10. ARBITRATION

Any controversy or claim arising out of or relating to this contract, or the breach thereof, shall be settled by arbitration in accordance with the Rules of the American Arbitration Association, and judgment upon the award rendered by the Arbitrator(s) may be entered in any court having jurisdiction thereof.

IN WITNESS WHEREOF, the parties hereto have executed this agreement the day and year first above written.

_____

_____

EMPLOYMENT AGREEMENT

AGREEMENT made this   day of   , 199   , by and between   (hereinafter referred to as "C") doing business at   and   of   , (hereinafter referred to as "Employee").

WITNESSETH:

WHEREAS, C is engaged in the County of   , State of   , and its vicinity in   ; and whereas, the parties hereto acknowledge that the goodwill, continued patronage, and names and addresses of its customers constitute the principal asset of C—the same having been acquired through the outlay of considerable time, money, and effort; and

WHEREAS, the Employee has been employed by C on the terms and conditions hereinafter set forth and in connection with his employment he has become or will become acquainted with many of the said customers, their names, addresses, and requirements, and will become acquainted with other and future customers, and with other of C's business and confidential matters, and

WHEREAS, the parties hereto are desirous of providing for the continuance of said employment and desire in connection therewith to reduce to writing their agreement, including the mutual covenants heretofore entered into orally, NOW, THEREFORE, THIS AGREEMENT WITNESSETH:

1. C agrees to employ the Employee as a(n)   at an agreed salary of   per hour. The term of this agreement commences on the   day of   , 199   , for a period of six (6) weeks and shall continue thereafter by agreement of the parties.

2. The Employee agrees to serve C diligently and to the best of his ability and further covenants as follows:

   a) That he will not during his employment or after the end thereof, irrespective of the time, manner, or cause of its termination, directly or indirectly, disclose to any person, firm, or corporation, the name, address, or requirements of any customers of C or any of its branches, and that he will not divulge any during his period of employment. Inasmuch as Employee will acquire or have access to information which is of a highly confidential and secret nature, it is expected that Employee will not perform any services for any other person or firm without C's prior written approval.

   b) That upon the termination of his employment, irrespective of the time, manner, or cause of said termination, he will surrender to C all lists, books, and records of or in connection with C's customers or business and all other property belonging to C.

   c) That he will not for a period of five (5) years after the end or termination of his employment, irrespective of the time, manner, or cause of the said termination of his employment, directly or indirectly, either as principal, agent, employee, employer, stockholder, co-partner, or in any other individual or representative capacity whatever, solicit, serve, or cater to, or engage, assist, be interested in, or connected with any other person, firm, or corporation soliciting, serving, or catering to any of the customers served by him or by any other employee of C or any of its branches or dealers during his employment with C.

d) Employee's services will be rendered largely at _____, but employee, upon request, may come to other locations requested by C.

e) Any controversy or claim arising out of or relating to this contract, or the breach thereof, shall be settled by arbitration in accordance with the Rules of the American Arbitration Association, and judgment upon the award rendered by the Arbitrator(s) may be entered in any court having jurisdiction thereof.

IN WITNESS WHEREOF, the parties have executed this agreement on the date above written.

_____

_____

WORKERS' COMPENSATION BOARD

Send this notice directly to Chairman, Worker's Compensation Board at address shown on reverse side within ten (10) days after accident occurs. Copy also should be sent to your insurance carrier.

PLEASE PRINT OR TYPE — INCLUDE ZIP CODE IN ALL ADDRESSES — EMPLOYEE'S SS# MUST BE ENTERED BELOW

W.C.B. CASE NO.	CARRIER CASE NO.	CODE NO.	WC. POLICY NUMBER	DATE OF ACCIDENT	EMPLOYEE'S S.S. NO.

(ENTER CASE NUMBERS, IF KNOWN, IN ABOVE SPACES)

	(a) NAME	(b) MAIL ADDRESS	(c) OSHA CASE OR FILE NO.
1. EMPLOYER			
(d) LOCATION (if different from mail address)			(e) E.R. NO.
2. INSURANCE CARRIER			
3. INJURED PERSON	(First Name) (Middle Initial) (Last Name)	(Home Address Give Number and Street, City, State, Zip Code and Apt. No.)	

EMPLOYER

4. Nature of business: (State principal products manufactured or sold or services rendered) _____

5. Address where accident occured (*Include county*) _____

ACCIDENT

6. Date of accident: _____ 19____, Day of Week _____ Hour of Day _____ A.M. _____ P.M.
   If occupational illness, date of initial diagnosis: _____ 19____

7. (a) Date disability began: _____ 19____
   (b) *Was injured paid in full for this day?* _____

8. Name of Department (where regularly employed) and foreman _____

9. When did you or foreman first know of injury? _____

10. Names and addresses of witnesses: _____

INJURED PERSON

11. (a) Marital status: _____ (b) Sex _____

12. Age: _____ 13. Did you have on file employment certificate or permit? _____

14. Occupation: (a) Job title for which employed: _____
    (b) Occupation when injuried: _____

15. (a) How long employed by you? _____ (b) Piece or time worker? _____
    (c) Hours per day: _____ (d) Days per week: _____

16. Earnings in your employ: (a) Rate per: Hours $_____ Day $_____ Week $_____ Month $_____
    (b) Total earnings paid during year prior to date of accident: (include bonuses paid, value of board, lodging, etc.)
    $_____ Average per week: $_____
    (c) Bonuses or premiums paid and included in item 16(b) above: $_____ (d) Estimated value of board,
    lodging, or other advantages in addition to wages: (included in item 16(b) above) $_____
    (e) Calendar weeks in past 52 in same kind of work as at time of injury: _____

NATURE OF INJURY OR OCCUPATIONAL DISEASE

17. State nature of injury and part or parts of body affected: (as "Injury to Chest," etc.) _____

18. Did you provide medical care? _____

19. Name and address of doctor: _____

20. Name and address of hospital: _____

21. Probable length of disability: _____

22. (a) Has employee returned to work? _____ (b) If so, give date: _____
    (c) At what occupation? _____ (d) At what weekly wage? $_____

NOTE: Form C-11 must be filed each time there is any change in the employment status as reported in item 22 above.

FATAL CASES

23. Has injured died? _____ (a) If so, give date of death: _____
    (b) Name and address of nearest relative: _____

24. (a) What was employee doing when accident occurred? (Describe briefly as "loading truck," "operating press," "shoveling dirt," "painting with spray gun," "walking downstairs," etc.) _____
    (b) Where did accident occur? (Specify whether on the employer's premises, and indicate if in street, factory yard, on loading platform, in factory, etc.) _____

CAUSE OF ACCIDENT OR OCCUPATIONAL DISEASE

25. How was accident or occupational disease sustained? (Describe fully, stating whether injured person slipped, fell, was struck, etc., and what factors led up to or contributed to accident. Use additional sheets, if necessary.) _____

_____

26. (a) What specific machine, tool, appliance, gas, liquid, or other substance or object was most closely connected with this accident or occupational disease? _____

(b) If mechanical apparatus or vehicle, what part of it? (State if gears, pulley, motor, etc.) _____

_____

27. Were mechanical guards or other safeguards (such as goggles) provided? _____ (a) Were they in use at time of accident? _____ (b) Was machine, tool, or object defective? _____ If so, in what way? _____

_____

	Enter "X" in this box if accident was reported on Form C-2.1
	Enter "X" in this box if accident was previously reported on Form C-2.5

DATE OF THIS REPORT: _____

FIRM NAME: _____

SIGNED BY: _____

TEL. NO. _____ Official Title

THE WORKERS' COMPENSATION BOARD EMPLOYS AND SERVES THE HANDICAPPED WITHOUT DISCRIMINATION.

C-2   C-2   C-2   C-2   C-2

EMPLOYEE MANUAL

1. ADMINISTRATIVE POLICIES

Hours

Normal working hours are from nine to five, with one hour for lunch, for a total of 35 hours a week.

Security

Please lock all doors if you are in the office alone, and make sure that the doors are locked if you are the last to leave.

Reimbursement for Expenses

Major expenses such as travel may be put on a personal credit card and reimbursed at a later date by the business manager. Airline tickets and hotel reservations may be ordered on the company account through our travel agent.

First Aid

(Location of)

Fire Extinguishers

(Location of)

II. WAGES AND SALARIES

_____ pays wages and salaries in accordance with a Wage and Salary Administration Program which bears a fair and reasonable relationship to rates existing in the community and which ensures comparable pay for jobs of comparable responsibility within _____ .

Salary and wage surveys for all job classifications are conducted periodically by the Personnel Department. Adjustments in salary levels are granted when warranted by prevailing economic conditions.

Starting Salaries

Starting salaries will normally be at the minimum of the range, except when otherwise recommended by the department manager, with the concurrence of the Personnel Manager.

Salary Increases

All increases in salary will be based on the recommendations of your supervisor.

There are three types of salary changes:

1. *Annual Increase*
   a) An evaluation does not necessarily mean that you will be granted a salary increase. You must have outstanding performance to be eligible for an increase. If you move from one job classification to another, your supervisor may request, with written justification, that your increase be delayed.

2. *Change in Job Classification*
   a) Transfer or promotion to a new position.
   b) Reevaluation of job by Personnel Manager.

3. *Salary Adjustments*

   a) Cost-of-living increases and/or an overall increase given to all employees as a result of a change in the salary scale.

   b) Realign salary to marketplace demand.

   c) Alter salary to correspond to permanently increased job responsibilities.

Shift Differential

A shift differential will be paid to all permanent, full-time, and part-time employees. A shift differential of forty cents per hour will be paid where the scheduled hours worked are between 5:00 p.m. and 8:00 a.m. The shift differential will be added to the base hourly rate of pay when computing overtime pay.

Non-Scheduled Call-Out

If you are called out of your home by   to provide services after the end of your regularly scheduled hours of work, you will be compensated with a minimum of two hours pay at your regular rate. This benefit will be provided only when you have been called out by your immediate supervisor or department head.

Temporary Work Assignment

If you do another person's job for a full day in their absence, and their job is more highly paid than yours, you will be compensated for your own salary step within that job group.

Paydays, Pay Periods, Paychecks

Paydays are every other   .

Pay periods cover a fourteen-consecutive-day time period always beginning on a Sunday and ending two Saturdays later. Paydays always follow the conclusion of a pay period and will include all earnings for that pay period.

The check stub is your record of hours, wages paid, deductions, and year-to-date earnings. If you have questions concerning your pay, please direct them to your supervisor. Normally, a shortage in pay amounting in one or more day's pay will be adjusted within 48 hours after written notice of such shortage is given to your supervisor.

Paychecks will not be released to anyone other than you without your written permission.

Your final paycheck may be picked up in the Personnel Department after all equipment and supplies belonging to   are returned.

If your paycheck is lost or stolen, it is your responsibility to report this fact immediately to your department manager and the payroll office. You will be required to sign a statement certifying that the payroll check was lost or stolen, which will be retained by payroll. Then a replacement check will be issued.

Overtime Pay

There may be times when it will be necessary to work overtime, which only managers will have the right to determine. Hourly employees will be paid for overtime indicated on the time sheet when it exceeds fifteen minutes and is properly approved and authorized by the department manager. If you are required to work

196

overtime, you will be given as much advance notice as possible. However, in the case of emergencies, you will be expected to work overtime whether or not advance notice is given.

Overtime pay will be paid at the rate of time and one-half for all consecutive hours worked in excess of forty hours of actual work per week. You may be granted time off in lieu of overtime pay. This time off should be taken within the same pay period.

The following absences are not to be considered as time worked for overtime payment purposes:

a) sickness

b) leave of absence (for any reason)

c) vacations

Holiday time, however, will be counted as time worked for purposes of overtime pay.

Deductions from Pay

is required by law to make deductions for Federal and State withholding Taxes and Social Security. You are reminded that must also pay Social Security Tax in an amount equal to that being deducted from your paycheck, up to a maximum set by law. Additional deductions for payroll savings, charitable contributions, etc., can be made with your written approval.

Annual Performance Evaluation

An annual performance evaluation of you will be made in writing by your department manager or supervisor and acknowledged by you. This policy provides the opportunity for you to meet privately with your supervisor to review the previous period's performance, receive guidance and counseling, plan individual development, and discuss mutual work-related problems. The evaluation, which normally takes place near your anniversary date, provides a permanent record of development and progress and may serve as a basis for retention, promotion, and wage increases.

Anniversary Date of Employment

For permanent full-time or part-time employees, the date that you are hired is your anniversary date of employment. This date will be used to calculate your eligibility for holidays, vacations, sick time, and certain other fringe benefits. It will also be considered for purposes of scheduling holidays and vacations, promotions, transfers, and retrenchment.

If you move from part-time to full-time employment, your full-time anniversary date is used to calculate time-off benefits.

Exit Interview

wants to know why employees resign; consequently, prior to leaving, you will be requested to participate in a confidential exit interview with a representative of the Personnel Department. The continuation of benefits, the collection of keys, ID cards, uniforms, etc., and arrangements for final paychecks will be handled during the interview.

III. BENEFITS

Parking

Holidays

As a general practice, the company observes all national holidays observed by the U.S. Postal Service:

—New Year's Day, January 1

—Washington's Birthday, third Monday in February

—Memorial Day, last Monday in May

—Independence Day, July 4

—Labor day, first Monday in September

—Columbus Day, second Monday in October

—Veteran's Day, November 11

—Christmas Day, December 25

Vacation

All full-time, permanent employees accrue one day of paid annual leave at the end of each month, available at the end of the first six months of employment. No more than 20 days paid annual leave may be accrued. At the end of the second year of employment, an additional day of annual leave will be accrued per year. Additional days will be accrued with seniority according to the following schedule:

Years of Employment	Days Annual Leave for That Year
First	12
Second	12
Third	13
Fourth	14
Fifth	15
Sixth	20
Seventh	20
Eighth	20
Ninth	20
Tenth	20

At the end of six months of employment, any employee may elect to receive one day's additional salary in lieu of each day of annual leave accrued and not taken. However, all employees must take at least five days of vacation (not in cash) each year.

Employees who desire to take accrued annual leave must request approval of their supervisor. No annual leave will be granted without prior approval.

Sick Leave

All full-time, permanent employees accrue one day of sick leave at the end of each month, beginning at the end of the first month of employment. No more than 30 days sick leave may be accrued.

Salary equivalent will not be paid in compensation for untaken sick leave. Sick leave may be taken only for bona fide illness, medical visits, or pregnancy.

Personal Leave

An employee may request up to five days per year of Personal leave for such emergencies as family illness or funerals. The employee's supervisor will decide if such leave may be granted. In such cases the time absent from the job will be paid but will not count against the employee's vacation time or sick leave.

Leave of Absence without Pay

In case of extended illness or pregnancy, and after an employee's sick leave and vacation are exhausted, an employee may request up to 45 days of unpaid temporary leave of absence without forfeiting his or her job. If the employee fails to return to work after the expiration of a 45-day leave of absence, he or she will be discharged. In unusual situations, the employee may apply to the Executive Committee for an extension. The committee's ruling on that request will be final and binding.

Jury Duty

Employees will be excused to serve jury duty. Time absent to serve jury duty will be paid at full salary.

Workers' Compensation

The company carries an insurance policy providing coverage for physical damages and loss of work time to an employee who sustains an accident on the job. If you are injured on the job, please notify your supervisor and the business office so that the appropriate forms can be completed.

Group Insurance

Details of Employee Benefit plans—(life, medical, and limitations, hospitalization, waiting periods, etc.)

IV. PERSONNEL POLICIES

Hiring

We are committed to a policy of equal employment opportunity for all, regardless of race, creed, color, national origin, sex, or age. It is our policy to promote such equality to all job levels and in all aspects of employment, including recruitment, hiring, advertising, promotion, transfer solicitation for employment, rates of pay, layoffs, or termination.

It is our policy to communicate this to everyone, including employees, outside recruiting services, and employment agencies, and all other unions, vendors, or associations with whom we are in contact. All advertising for vacancies shall include the statement that we are an "EOE, M/F" employer.

Performance Appraisal

Upon completion of the three-month probationary period, all employees receive a verbal and written evaluation at least annually thereafter.

Discipline

In the event of employee conduct which necessitates disciplinary action, one of the following penalties will be imposed depending on the seriousness of the offense and on the employee's previous disciplinary record:

—A verbal warning;

—A written warning;

—Suspension without pay, not to exceed five days; or

—Discharge

Resignations

All employees who voluntarily leave the company, are asked to give the company at least two weeks' notice. No severance pay is given to resigning employees, and those who fail to give the two weeks' notice will forfeit their accrued vacation pay.

Employees discharged for cause will receive no severance pay or accrued vacation pay.

Grievance Procedure

Any employee who has a question about interpretation or application of company policy, or feels that he or she has been treated unfairly by the company, may use the following procedure.

V. DISMISSAL FOR CAUSE

Recommendation for dismissal and dismissal itself are the responsibilities of your immediate supervisor. You may be dismissed immediately for a serious act.

The following offenses are deemed serious enough to warrant immediate dismissal:

1. making a false statement on the application for employment or pre-employment physical form;

2. theft, or removing from the premises without proper authorization, any property or the property of another employee;

3. being absent and failing to notify your supervisor according to the provisions set forth in these policies;

4. fighting, or attempting bodily injury to another employee, visitor, or patient;

5. using abusive or threatening language to supervisors, fellow employees, or patients;

6. sexual harassment

7. being insubordinate or refusing to carry out the orders of your supervisor;

8. gambling on property;

9. giving out information of a confidential nature to unauthorized personnel;

10. unauthorized possession of firearms or explosives on premises;

11. any conduct detrimental to patient care or operations;

12. attempting to obtain money from the company on the basis of false statements;

13. failure to maintain proper licensure, registration, or certification required by state, federal, or local law; or

14. receiving three reprimand slips within any twelve-month period.

ACKNOWLEDGMENT

Date _____ , 199

I acknowledge receipt of my personal copy of the Personnel Policy Handbook, which supersedes all previously issued employee manuals. I am aware that the handbook summarizes the employee relations policies and practices currently in force.

I understand and agree to comply with the policies as stated in the Manual. I understand the needs of the changing economic and social conditions, as well as Federal and State legislation, may bring about policy and procedure changes from time to time. I am aware that I will be notified of such changes by the Personnel Department.

_____
Signature of Employee

_____
Date

IMPORTANT:

Please sign, detach, and deliver this acknowledgment within five days to the Personnel Office.

PERFORMANCE APPRAISAL REPORT

Employee's Name	Job Title		Department
Supervisor's Name	Date of Interview	Date Employed	Months Under Your Supervision

INSTRUCTIONS TO SUPERVISORS:

- Become thoroughly familiar with procedure on performance appraisal located in the employee manual.
- Consider only one trait or quality at a time. Don't let your judgment concerning one trait influence your judgment of other traits.
- The evaluation **should** encompass the entire period of time since the last appraisal. Recent happenings or isolated incidents should be minimized.
- Both supervisor and employee should have a common understanding of acceptable standards for the job being evaluated. Be certain that both employee and **supervisor** are familiar with the job description because the evaluation must embrace the entire job.
- Check only one degree of achievement for each category.
- Comments are essential to the appraisal. Use comments to explain your ratings, and to make specific suggestions for improvement and development.

RATING

TRAIT TO BE EVALUATED							COMMENTS
QUANTITY OF WORK Produces acceptable volume of work							
TIMELINESS Completes assignments on or ahead of schedule							
ATTITUDE Shows interest, enthusiasm, and cooperation							
ADAPTABILITY Learns new duties and adjusts to new situations							
PLANNING & ORGANIZATION Works in an orderly way							
PUNCTUALITY & ATTENDANCE Lateness and Absenteeism at a minimum							
RELATIONSHIPS WITH OTHERS Effectively works and deals with other people							
COMMUNICATION Effectively relates ideas and keeps others informed							

TRAIT TO BE EVALUATED							COMMENTS
QUALITY OF WORK Produces an acceptable grade of work							
INITIATIVE Eagerly performs jobs with self-confidence							

OVERALL JOB EFFECTIVENESS:

Better than most; overall
performance excellent ☐

Meets full, normal
requirements of job ☐

Need some improvement;
work sometimes less than
acceptable ☐

Performance unsatisfactory;
needs considerable improvement ☐

PROBATION EVALUATION ONLY: Do you recommend that this probationary employee be made a permanent employee?

YES ☐   NO ☐

SUPERVISOR REMARKS: Discuss unusual ratings above, and recommend steps for development and career advancement. (Attach an additional sheet if necessary.)

EMPLOYEE REMARKS: (Attach an additional sheet if necessary.)

_____   _____
Supervisor's signature   Employee's signature

Employee's signature—which is voluntary—indicates that employee has seen and discussed this report, and does not imply agreement with it.

EXIT QUESTIONNAIRE

You recently terminated your employment with _____, and we'd like to know why you left. We want to improve our personnel practices and make our company a better place to work. Your answers will be kept confidential.

1. Why did you leave?

2. When you were first employed, were your duties and responsibilities clearly explained to you? Comments: Yes   No

3. Were the conditions of work, salary, hours of work, and other benefits clearly explained to you? Comments: Yes   No

4. Did you understand the importance of your job?   Yes   No

5. Did you feel your work was appreciated?   Yes   No

6. Were working conditions satisfactory?   Yes   No

7. Was your pay adequate?   Yes   No

8. Was overall treatment both fair and impartial?   Yes   No
   If no, please explain:

9. Was your supervisor a fair person?   Yes   No

10. Was your supervisor competent?   Yes   No
    Comments:

11. When you needed information to do your job, were you able to get it easily?
    Comments: Yes   No

12. Did you feel as if you were part of the company?   Yes   No
    If no, please explain:

13. Could we have done anything to prevent your leaving?   Yes   No

14. Comments:

15. How do you feel about your progress here?

16. What do you like about your new job?

17. Would you consider working for _____ again?   Yes   No

18. If you could tell the president of the company exactly how you feel about the way the company is run, what would you tell him or her?

Name _____ Department _____

Supervisor _____ Date of Interview _____

U.S. Department of Justice
Immigration and Naturalization Service

OMB No. 1115-0136

Employment Eligibility Verification

Please read instructions carefully before completing this form. The instructions must be available during completion of this form. **ANTI-DISCRIMINATION NOTICE.** It is illegal to discriminate against work eligible individuals. Employers CANNOT specify which document(s) they will accept from an employee. The refusal to hire an individual because of a future expiration date may also constitute illegal discrimination.

Section 1. Employee Information and Verification. To be completed and signed by employee at the time employment begins

Print Name: Last	First	Middle Initial	Maiden Name

Address *(Street Name and Number)*		Apt. #	Date of Birth *(month, day year)*

City	State	Zip Code	Social Security #

I am aware that federal law provides for imprisonment and/or fines for false statements or use of false documents in connection with the completion of this form.

I attest, under penalty of perjury, that I am (check one of the following):
- ☐ A citizen or national of the United States
- ☐ A Lawful Permanent Resident (Alien # A_____)
- ☐ An alien authorized to work until ____/____/____
  (Alien # or Admission #_____)

Employee's Signature	Date *(month/day/year)*

Preparer and/or Translator Certification. *(To be completed and signed if Section 1 is prepared by a person other than the employee.)* I attest, under penalty of perjury, that I have assisted in the completion of this form and that to the best of my knowledge the information is true and correct.

Preparer's/Translator's Signature	Print Name

Address *(Street Name and Number, City, State, Zip Code)*	Date *(month, day/year)*

Section 2. Employer Review and Verification. To be completed and signed by employer. Examine one document from List A OR examine one document from List B **and** one from List C as listed on the reverse of this form and record the title, number and expiration date, if any, of the document(s)

List A	OR	List B	AND	List C
Document title: _____		_____		_____
Issuing authority: _____		_____		_____
Document #: _____		_____		_____
Expiration Date *(if any)*: ___/___/___		___/___/___		___/___/___
Document #: _____				
Expiration Date *(if any)*: ___/___/___				

CERTIFICATION - I attest, under penalty of perjury, that I have examined the document(s) presented by the above-named employee, that the above-listed document(s) appear to be genuine and to relate to the employee named, that the employee began employment on *(month/day/year)* ____/____/____ and that to the best of my knowledge the employee is eligible to work in the United States. (State employment agencies may omit the date the employee began employment).

Signature of Employer or Authorized Representative	Print Name	Title

Business or Organization Name	Address *(Street Name and Number, City, State, Zip Code)*	Date *(month/day/year)*

Section 3. Updating and Reverification. To be completed and signed by employer

A. New Name *(if applicable)*	B. Date of rehire *(month/day/year)* *(if applicable)*

C. If employee's previous grant of work authorization has expired, provide the information below for the document that establishes current employment eligibility.

Document Title:_____ Document #:_____ Expiration Date *(if any)*: ___/___/___

I attest, under penalty of perjury, that to the best of my knowledge, this employee is eligible to work in the United States, and if the employee presented document(s), the document(s) I have examined appear to be genuine and to relate to the individual.

Signature of Employer or Authorized Representative	Date *(month/day/year)*

Form I-9 (Rev. 11-21-91) N

LISTS OF ACCEPTABLE DOCUMENTS

LIST A		LIST B		LIST C
Documents that Establish Both Identity and Employment Eligibility	**OR**	**Documents that Establish Identity**	**AND**	**Documents that Establish Employment Eligibility**

LIST A

Documents that Establish Both Identity and Employment Eligibility

1. U.S. Passport (unexpired or expired)

2. Certificate of U.S. Citizenship (INS Form N-560 or N-561)

3. Certificate of Naturalization (INS Form N-550 or N-570)

4. Unexpired foreign passport, with I-551 *stamp or* attached INS Form I-94 indicating unexpired employment authorization

5. Alien Registration Receipt Card with photograph (INS Form I-151 or I-551)

6. Unexpired Temporary Resident Card (INS Form I-688)

7. Unexpired Employment Authorization Card (INS Form I-688A)

8. Unexpired Reentry Permit (INS Form I-327)

9. Unexpired Refugee Travel Document (INS Form I-571)

10. Unexpired Employment Authorization Document issued by the INS which contains a photograph (INS Form I-688B)

OR

LIST B

Documents that Establish Identity

1. Driver's license or ID card issued by a state or outlying possession of the United States provided it contains a photograph or information such as name, date of birth, sex, height, eye color, and address

2. ID card issued by federal, state, or local government agencies or entities provided it contains a photograph or information such as name, date of birth, sex, height, eye color, and address

3. School ID card with a photograph

4. Voter's registration card

5. U.S. Military card or draft record

6. Military dependent's ID card

7. U.S. Coast Guard Merchant Mariner Card

8. Native American tribal document

9. Driver's license issued by a Canadian government authority

For persons under age 18 who are unable to present a document listed above:

10. School record or report card

11. Clinic, doctor, or hospital record

12. Day-care or nursery school record

AND

LIST C

Documents that Establish Employment Eligibility

1. U.S. social security card issued by the Social Security Administration (*other than a card stating it is not valid for employment*)

2. Certification of Birth Abroad issued by the Department of State (*Form FS-545 or Form DS-1350*)

3. Original or certified copy of a birth certificate issued by a state, county, municipal authority or outlying possession of the United States bearing an official seal

4. Native American tribal document

5. U.S. Citizen ID Card (*INS Form I-197*)

6. ID Card for use of Resident Citizen in the United States (*INS Form I-179*)

7. Unexpired employment authorization document issued by the INS (*other than those listed under List A*)

Illustrations of many of these documents appear in Part 8 of the Handbook for Employers (M-274)

Form I-9 (Rev. 11-21-91) N

206

U.S. Department of Justice
Immigration and Naturalization Service

OMB No. 1115-0136

Employment Eligibility Verification

INSTRUCTIONS
PLEASE READ ALL INSTRUCTIONS CAREFULLY BEFORE COMPLETING THIS FORM.

Anti-Discrimination Notice. It is illegal to discriminate against any individual (other than an alien not authorized to work in the U.S.) in hiring, discharging, or recruiting or referring for a fee because of that individual's national origin or citizenship status. It is illegal to discriminate against work eligible individuals. Employers **CANNOT** specify which document(s) they will accept from an employee. The refusal to hire an individual because of a future expiration date may also constitute illegal discrimination.

Section 1 - Employee. All employees, citizens and noncitizens, hired after November 6, 1986, must complete Section 1 of this form at the time of hire, which is the actual beginning of employment. **The employer is responsible for ensuring that Section 1 is timely and properly completed.**

Preparer/Translator Certification. The Preparer/Translator Certification must be completed if Section 1 is prepared by a person other than the employee. A preparer/translator may be used only when the employee is unable to complete Section 1 on his/her own. However, the employee must still sign Section 1 personally.

Section 2 - Employer. For the purpose of completing this form, the term "employer" includes those recruiters and referrers for a fee who are agricultural associations, agricultural employers, or farm labor contractors.

Employers must complete Section 2 by examining evidence of identity and employment eligibility within three (3) business days of the date employment begins. If employees are authorized to work, but are unable to present the required document(s) within three business days, they must present a receipt for the application of the document(s) within three business days and the actual document(s) within ninety (90) days. However, if employers hire individuals for a duration of less than three business days, Section 2 must be completed at the time employment begins. **Employers must record: 1)** document title; **2)** issuing authority; **3)** document number, **4)** expiration date, if any; and **5)** the date employment begins. Employers must sign and date the certification. Employees must present original documents. Employers may, but are not required to, photocopy the document(s) presented. These photocopies may only be used for the verification process and must be retained with the I-9. **However, employers are still responsible for completing the I-9.**

Section 3 - Updating and Reverification. Employers must complete Section 3 when updating and/or reverifying the I-9. Employers must reverify employment eligibility of their employees on or before the expiration date recorded in Section 1. Employers **CANNOT** specify which document(s) they will accept from an employee.

- If an employee's name has changed at the time this form is being updated/ reverified, complete Block A.

- If an employee is rehired within three (3) years of the date this form was originally completed and the employee is still eligible to be employed on the same basis as previously indicated on this form (updating), complete Block B and the signature block.

- If an employee is rehired within three (3) years of the date this form was originally completed and the employee's work authorization has expired **or** if a current employee's work authorization is about to expire (reverification), complete Block B and:
  - examine any document that reflects that the employee is authorized to work in the U.S. (see List A **or** C),
  - record the document title, document number and expiration date (if any) in Block C, and
  - complete the signature block.

Photocopying and Retaining Form I-9. A blank I-9 may be reproduced provided both sides are copied. The Instructions must be available to all employees completing this form. Employers must retain completed I-9s for three (3) years after the date of hire **or** one (1) year after the date employment ends, whichever is later.

For more detailed information, you may refer to the INS Handbook for Employers, (Form M-274). You may obtain the handbook at your local INS office.

Privacy Act Notice. The authority for collecting this information is the Immigration Reform and Control Act of 1986, Pub. L. 99-603 (8 U.S.C. 1324a).

This information is for employers to verify the eligibility of individuals for employment to preclude the unlawful hiring, or recruiting or referring for a fee, of aliens who are not authorized to work in the United States.

This information will be used by employers as a record of their basis for determining eligibility of an employee to work in the United States. The form will be kept by the employer and made available for inspection by officials of the U.S. Immigration and Naturalization Service, the Department of Labor, and the Office of Special Counsel for Immigration Related Unfair Employment Practices.

Submission of the information required in this form is voluntary. However, an individual may not begin employment since employers are subject to civil or criminal penalties if they do not comply with the Immigration Reform and Control Act of 1986.

Reporting Burden. We try to create forms and instructions that are accurate, can be easily understood, and which impose the least possible burden on you to provide us with information. Often this is difficult because some immigration laws are very complex. Accordingly, the reporting burden for this collection of information is computed as follows: **1)** learning about this form, 5 minutes; **2)** completing the form, 5 minutes; and **3)** assembling and filing (recordkeeping) the form, 5 minutes, for an average of 15 minutes per response. If you have comments regarding the accuracy of this burden estimate, or suggestions for making this form simpler, you can write to both the Immigration and Naturalization Service, 425 I Street, N.W., Room 5304, Washington, D. C. 20536; and the Office of Management and Budget, Paperwork Reduction Project, OMB No. 1115-0136, Washington, D.C. 20503.

Form I-9 (Rev. 11-21-91) N

EMPLOYERS MUST RETAIN COMPLETED I-9
PLEASE DO NOT MAIL COMPLETED I-9 TO INS

EMPLOYER RECORDKEEPING REQUIREMENTS

STATUTE	RECORDS REQUIRED TO BE KEPT	LENGTH OF TIME
Federal Fair Labor Standards Act (FLSA); Equal Pay Act; NY Workers' Compensation Law NY Unemployment Insurance Law NY Labor Law NY Wage Payment Laws	Payroll records, including employee's name, address, social security number, date of birth, sex, job title, regular workday and workweek, overtime hours, rate paid for regular and overtime hours, total straight time earnings and amount paid as a premium for overtime hours (records regarding actual payments to employees should be segregated according to payroll period)	3 years (6 years under New York Wage Payment Laws)
Fair Labor Standards Act	Agreements with employees; certificates and notices listed or named in any applicable section of the Act, such as a Certificate of Age obtained in connection with the employment of a minor, and sales and purchase records (in total volume figures)	3 years
Fair Labor Standards Act	Wage rate tables or schedules; work schedules and time records or time sheets; order, shipping, and billing records related to purchases and sales; records of any additions or subtractions made to or from employees' paychecks	2 years
Age Discrimination in Employment Act (ADEA); Civil Rights Act of 1964; Americans With Disabilities Act (ADA)	Job applications and resumes; employment advertisements; job orders to employment agencies or labor organizations; employee aptitude tests and results of physical examinations; records regarding hiring, promotion, discipline, discharge, and employee benefit plans; requests for reasonable accommodation	1 year from date of making of record or the personnel action involved, whichever is later
Civil Rights Act of 1964	Employer Information Report EEO-1 (only required for employers with 100 or more employees)	1 year
Occupational Safety and Health Act (OSHA)	Log and summary of all recordable occupational injuries and illnesses (OSHA form 200); Annual summary of occupational injuries and illnesses; supplementary record of occupational injuries and illnesses (OSHA Form 101) [not required if state workers' compensation report contains same information]	5 years following end of year to which records relate
OSHA Hazard Communication Standard, 29 C.F.R. §1910.1200; NY Right-To-Know Law	Written Hazard Communication Program; labels for containers of hazardous chemicals; Material Safety Data Sheets (MSDS) for all hazardous chemicals used in the workplace; records of employees who handle toxic substances (New York law)	As long as hazardous chemicals are used in the workplace (employee records must be kept 40 years under New York law)
Internal Revenue Code	IRS Forms W-4 (Employee's Withholding Allowance Certificate) and W-5 (Earned Income Advanced Pay Certificate for Employees earning less than $24,396 annually); other forms that employees may elect to file with respect to the withholding of Federal income tax from their wages, e.g., Form W-4E, claiming complete exemption from withholding of tax from wages	4 years from due date or payment of tax to which record relates, whichever is later; forms filed by employees must be kept for 4 years after the form becomes inoperative
Employee Retirement Income Security Act (ERISA)	Plan documents, Summary Plan Descriptions, Annual Reports (IRS Form 5500), Summary Annual Reports, and descriptions of plan amendments	Specific ERISA requirements may vary according to the type of employee benefit plan; employers are advised to consult their plan advisor for the requirements applicable to their plans
Executive Order 11246	Affirmative Action Documents	Not specified (should keep at least 3 years)
Immigration Reform and Control Act (IRCA)	I-9 Forms	3 years after worker is hired or 1 year after termination, whichever is later

STATUTE	REQUIRED PERMIT OR LICENSE
N.Y. Labor Law	Permit to employ minors.
N.Y. Wage Permit Laws	Permit to pay wages by check.
N.Y. Workers' Compensation Law	License to operate as self-insurer.

STATUTE	NOTICE REQUIRED TO BE POSTED IN A CONSPICUOUS LOCATION
Federal Fair Labor Standards Act; Federal Equal Pay Act	Federal Minimum Wage Law & Equal Pay Act Notices published by the U.S. Department of Labor
Notices Pertaining to Employment Discrimination: Age Discrimination in Employment Act Title VII of the Civil Rights Act of 1964 Americans With Disability Act Executive Order 11246*	The notice-posting requirements of all four statutes are satisfied by displaying the "Equal Employment Opportunity is ... the Law" Poster published by the Equal Employment Opportunity Commission. ——————— * Applies only to Federal contractors and subcontractors and requires that employers take certain Affirmative Action to provide employment opportunities for women and certain minorities.
Family and Medical Leave Act	Notice of rights afforded employees under the law.
Occupational Safety & Health Act	A. Notice of Act's Requirements B. Annual Summary of Occupational Illness and Injuries (summary is to be prepared on OSHA Form No. 200 and posted from February 1 to March 1 each year).
N.Y. State Minimum Wage Laws	Notice Summarizing Provisions of the Law
N.Y. Wage Payment Laws	Employee Handbook or Notice outlining company policy on sick leave, vacation, personal leave, holidays and hours.
N.Y. Unemployment Insurance Law	Notice that the Employer is subject to the Law
N.Y. Human Rights Law	Notice of Rights afforded individuals under the Law
N.Y. Workers' Compensation Law	A. Notice of Employees of Workers' Compensation Law, Form C-105* B. Notice to Employees re: Privilege of Selecting Own Physician* C. Notice of Compliance with Law's Requirement of Security for Payment of Compensation* D. Notice of Provision for Payment of Disability Benefits* E. Occupational Injury or Illness Report** ——————— * Notice requirements A-D may be satisfied by one (1) poster. ** Required to be prepared within ten (10) days after the occurrence of any occupational illness or injury resulting in a loss of work time in excess of the day on which the injury or illness first occurred.

Special Laws Affecting Small Business

The number of state and federal laws that can affect a business is so large that it is impossible to cover all of them within the covers of any one book. There are, however, certain federal and state laws that affect almost all small businesses. They include laws governing your duty to report product hazards, your right to obtain federal agency records, your duty to report environmental hazards, your duty to obtain medical certification of commercial drivers, updating your corporate records, commercial arbitration clauses, and immigration laws.

DUTY TO REPORT
PRODUCT HAZARDS

Importers, manufacturers, and distributors of consumer products must notify the Consumer Products Safety Commission (CPSC) within 24 hours if a product fails to comply with a safety rule or has a defect that could create a substantial product hazard. A "substantial product hazard" is a product defect that, because of the pattern of the defect, the number of defective products distributed, and the severity of the risk, has a substantial risk of causing injury to the public.

Violation of this rule may result in civil penalties being imposed by the CPSC and lawsuits by an injured consumer for damages, court costs, and attorney fees.

To contact the CPSC, check your local phone directory under U.S. Government, or contact the Office of the Secretary, CPSC, Washington, DC 20207, 800-638-2772 (toll-free except in Washington, D.C.).

HOW TO OBTAIN
FEDERAL RECORDS

By exercising your rights under the Freedom of Information Act (FOIA), you can (1) learn if the Federal Bureau of Investigation has a file on you; (2) obtain information from the Department of Labor about a work-related accident at a nearby job site or manufacturing plant; (3) obtain information about an investigation of motor-vehicle defects from the Department of Transportation; (4) obtain details from the Consumer Products Safety Commission about a toy that is being investigated as a safety hazard; or (5) review the Social Security Administration's latest inspection report on conditions in a nursing home certified for Medicare.

Exemptions

The FOIA gives you the right of access to the official files of federal agencies except for (1) classified national defense and foreign relations information; (2) internal agency personnel rules and practices; (3) material prohibited from disclosure by another law; (4) trade secrets and other confidential business information; (5) certain interagency or intraagency communications; (6) personnel; medical and other files involving personal privacy; (7) certain investigatory records compiled for law enforcement purposes; (8) matters relating to the supervision of financial institutions; and (9) geological information on oil wells.

The FOIA does not apply to Congress, courts, and records of state or local governments. However, most state governments have FOIA-type laws. Information about state laws can be obtained from the attorney general of your home state.

Where to Request Information

No one office handles all FOIA requests. Each request for information must be made to the appropriate agency. For assistance, you can contact the nearest Federal Information Center or obtain the *Consumers Resource Handbook.* Another fine resource tool is the *U.S. Government Manual,* which describes programs within each federal agency and lists the names and addresses of top personnel. The manual is available at most libraries, or it can be purchased from the Superintendent of Documents, U.S. Government Printing Office, Washington, DC 20402.

Some of the larger departments and agencies have several FOIA offices. Some of these larger agencies structure their offices according to the function they perform; other agencies simply structure the offices on a regional basis. For example, to obtain information regarding a work-related accident, you should contact the Department of Labor at its office in the region where the accident occurred.

How to Request Information

Write a letter of request to the agency's specific FOIA office. You must describe the material you want as specifically as possible. If the agency cannot identify the material based on a vague request, it is under no obligation to you. An agency is not required by the FOIA to do research, to compile or analyze data, or to answer questions.

Identify the records that you want as accurately as possible and reasonably describe the records sought. Any information that you can furnish about the time, place, persons, events, subjects, or other details of the records will be helpful to the agency's personnel. Stating the reasons for your request may persuade an agency to give you access to records it might otherwise deny as legally exempt.

Costs

An agency may charge only for the cost of searching for the material and making copies. Search fees range from $4 to $26 per hour. The copying charge is $.25 per copy or less. If you wish to avoid copying charges, you may ask to visit the agency in person to examine its records. You may receive a waiver or reduction of fees if you can show that the information you are seeking will primarily benefit the general public.

Time Necessary

Federal agencies must answer requests for information within ten working days of receipt. If you have not received a reply within ten days, you may write a follow-up letter or telephone the agency. If the agency needs more than ten working days in which to find or examine the records or consult other agencies, it must inform you before the deadline.

Refusal to Grant Information

If an agency denies your request, it must be able to prove that the information is covered by one of the nine exemptions listed earlier. The reasons for denial must be given to you in writing, along with a notice of your right to appeal. You should exercise your appeal right by promptly notifying the agency that you wish to appeal. Most agencies require that appeals be made within 30 to 45 days after you receive a notification of denial. The appeal itself should ask the agency to review your FOIA request and change its decision. You should explain why you believe the denial was wrong. Refer to all previous communications you may have had with the agency.

The agency has 20 working days to respond to your letter of appeal. It may also take an extension of up to ten working days. If your appeal is denied, you may file an FOIA lawsuit in the U.S. district court where you live, where you have your principal place of business, where the documents are kept, or in the District of Columbia. If you win a substantial portion of your case, the court may award you court costs and attorney fees.

DRUG TESTING OF DRIVERS

Federal regulations require drivers who operate a commercial motor vehicle to take a medical examination every two years and to obtain a doctor's certification stating that they are medically qualified to drive. Among the criteria for medical certification is a determination by the employer that a driver is not using a controlled substance without a prescription. Drug tests may be required as part of medical examinations if a doctor thinks it is necessary in order to make that determination.

The regulations also require the driver's employer to assure itself that the driver is medically qualified, and the employer must keep the driver off the road if he or she lacks a current medical certificate, is using controlled substances, or is otherwise not medically qualified to drive.

Commercial motor vehicles are defined as self-propelled or towed vehicles used on public highways to transport passengers or property in interstate commerce that (1) have a gross vehicle weight rating or gross combination weight rating of more than 10,000 pounds; (2) are designed to transport more than 15 passengers, including the driver; or (3) are used in transporting hazardous materials.

KEEP YOUR CORPORATE MINUTES UP-TO-DATE

Your corporate minutes should be reviewed on a regular basis by the corporate directors, officers, and advisers. It is extremely important that the minutes contain accurate and up-to-date information. Accurate, well-maintained corporate minutes can provide insulation from personal liability and can document executive compensation.

If your corporation is being sued, the minutes will protect the corporation's employees and officers from personal liability. If the minutes demonstrate that the employees acted in good faith and in their corporate capacity, the plaintiff will be prevented from "piercing the corporate veil." Also, employees and officers may be entitled to reimbursement by the corporation for legal fees incurred in their defense.

Corporate minutes can also protect executive compensation. Your corporation can deduct compensation paid to corporate officers (e.g., salary or bonuses) as a business expense if it is a reasonable amount for the services rendered. The deduction may be denied if the IRS determines that the compensation was unreasonable or a disguised dividend. To ensure the deductibility of compensation paid, the corporation's minutes should show that the board of directors took the following steps:

- Specified the salaries of all officers and the procedures for salary adjustments and bonuses.

- Established dividend and return on capital investment policies.

- Prepared job descriptions for each officer.

- Specified any additional responsibilities for officers over and above their usual duties.

Corporate minutes can also be used to avoid the penalty for excess accumulated earnings by detailing the following:

- Expansion plans that justify a retention of earnings

- Extenuating business circumstances, such as a threat of a labor strike

- The intention to retain earnings only to cover working capital for the year

Minutes should detail the board of directors' decisions as to the election of officers, acceptance of contracts, approval for mergers, compliance with governmental regulations, and authorization of loans.

A good resource to assist in this record-keeping is *The Corporate Forms Kit* by Ted Nicholas, published by Upstart Publishing Company.

ENVIRONMENTAL REPORTING REQUIREMENTS

State and federal environmental statutes require companies to advise governmental agencies of past and present environmental problems.

The Clean Water Act requires persons in charge of vessels or facilities to notify the National Response Center as soon as they have knowledge of a discharge of oil or a hazardous substance in a reportable quantity. Criminal sanctions may be imposed upon employees and corporate officers who fail to make a required report.

The Comprehensive Environmental Response Compensation and Liability Act (CERCLA) imposes a reporting requirement on parties responsible for a vessel or a facility if there is a discharge of hazardous substances in quantities set by the Environmental Protection Agency (EPA). In addition, the owner or operator of a facility at which a release occurred must also notify potentially injured parties by publication in local newspapers in the affected area.

Under section 304 of the Emergency Planning and Community Right-to-Know Act of 1986, the release of a reportable quantity of any "extremely hazardous substance" or CERCLA hazardous substance must be reported to the local Emergency Planning Committee and the state Emergency Response Commission. Immediate telephonic notice and a follow-up written report are required.

In addition to federal legislation, most states have environmental laws. Typical of the state approach is New Jersey's, which requires reporting spills or releases that may be detected during audits. The New Jersey Spill Compensation and Control Act specifically requires any person who has discharged hazardous substances or who is in any fashion responsible for the hazardous substances that may have been discharged to notify the New Jersey Department of Environmental Protection (NJDEP). The Hazardous Substances Discharge Reports and Notices Act requires owners of industrial establishments or real property that may have housed an industrial establishment to report known or suspected discharges of hazardous substances occurring either above or below ground.

HOW TO AVOID EPA SANCTIONS

A business that conducts voluntary audits and discovers violations of environmental law can avoid EPA sanctions if the violation is reported to the EPA within ten days; the problem is corrected and measures are taken to ensure that it won't reoccur; and the audit meets the EPA's specifications. (If it doesn't meet the specifications, the violator can still get a 75 percent reduction in its fines.) Sanctions cannot be avoided if (1) the violation causes serious harm or seriously endangers human health or the environment; (2) the same or a similar violation has occurred at the same plant within the past three years; (3) the problem is part of a "pattern of violations" over the past five years; (4) company officials have been "consciously involved in or willfully blind to" the problem; (5) the violation was identified as part of a

monitoring or sampling procedure required by law; (6) the company is already being inspected by the EPA or a local environmental agency; or (7) the company doesn't report the violation until after it has been reported by a whistleblower or a third party.

COMMERCIAL ARBITRATION CLAUSES

Arbitration is a method by which disputes can be resolved quickly and inexpensively. Little or no discovery is allowed, congested trial dockets are avoided, and grounds for challenge on appeal are limited. Inclusion of an arbitration clause in a commercial contract usually permits each side to a dispute to save time and money. However, if all parties do not agree that a particular dispute should be arbitrated, problems may arise.

The Federal Arbitration Act strongly favors arbitration by ensuring that an arbitration procedure will be speedy and will not be subjected to delay and obstruction in the courts. A well-drafted arbitration clause will cover the following issues:

- The number and qualifications of the arbitrators
- Issues the arbitrators are authorized to decide
- The rules of evidence and procedure that will apply
- Who will bear the cost of arbitration
- The venue (where the arbitration will be held)
- Time limits during which either party can seek arbitration

IMMIGRATION LAW

Although immigration law is beyond the scope of this guide, you should be aware of a few immigration laws that apply to your business, especially if you have employees. The Immigration and Nationality Act has employment-based preferences for permanent resident visas that significantly increase the number of aliens allowed to enter permanently to work.

The first preference is given to aliens with extraordinary ability in the sciences, arts, education, business, or athletics; outstanding professors and researchers; and multinational executives and managers. The second preference includes aliens who are members of the professions holding advanced degrees or the equivalent or who have exceptional ability in the sciences, arts, or business. There is another preference for aliens who invest either $1 million or $500,000 in a commercial U.S. enterprise, depending on the area where the enterprise is located (rural areas or areas with a high unemployment rate require less investment). The investment may be made in a new enterprise, a restructured existing business, or a distressed business. The enterprise must create full-time employment for at least ten U.S. citizens or lawfully admitted permanent residents, excluding the investing immigrant and his or her spouse and children. However, if the enterprise is distressed, the employment creation requirement is waived as long as the preinvestment level of employment is maintained.

The North American Free Trade Agreement (NAFTA) between Canada, Mexico, and the United States allows temporary entry of nationals of one country into another country for business purposes.

The Immigration and Nationality Act prohibits discrimination against employees because of citizenship in hiring, recruitment, referral, or discharge. The Immigration Reform and Control Act subjects employers to civil fines or criminal prosecution for hiring persons not authorized to work in the United States. For further information, see Chapter 11 and consult with an immigration law specialist.

13

Estate Planning Strategies

No one wants to pay a cent more for estate taxes than is absolutely necessary. No one wants ungrateful relatives to receive all or part of his or her estate. However, most people are needlessly paying estate taxes and leaving their estates to ungrateful relatives because they neglected to utilize basic estate planning techniques.

With proper planning, you can avoid or reduce estate taxes and probate costs. Most people, for example, do not have a will and therefore are not taking advantage of their right to designate who will receive their personal and business property when they die.

HOT SITE

Estate Planning/Elder Legal Survival

(http://www.friran.com/elder_law.html)

Whether you are 22 or 92, president of a multimillion-dollar corporation or president of a home-based corporation, now is the time to start your estate planning. A carefully constructed estate plan is important for everyone, especially the small business owner, because it permits you to distribute your property to whom and in what amounts you wish. Equally important, an estate plan permits you to take advantage of a variety of tax-minimizing techniques that can increase your family's security.

Careful planning can (1) ensure distribution of property to intended beneficiaries, (2) minimize the burden of federal and state estate taxes, (3) allocate the tax burden in the manner most consistent with your wishes, and (4) ensure the orderly continuation of your business.

Because of frequent changes in the estate and gift tax laws, it is especially important for you to review any existing estate plans.

ESTATE PLANNING CHECKLIST

When owners of a small business prepare an estate plan, they must develop one that incorporates both business and nonbusiness assets. With that in mind, the following checklist was designed to have you review all of your needs and assets.

To properly implement your estate plan, do the following:

❏ Determine the value of your estate, which includes all of the property you own or have a controlling interest in.

❏ Set up a home filing system, household inventory, and record book.

❏ Rent a safe-deposit box.

❏ Have a will drawn up (see "Why You Need a Will" in this chapter) or update your current will. Appoint competent and trustworthy guardians for your children and trustees or executors (see "How to Choose an Executor or Trustee" in this chapter).

❏ Prepare a buy-sell agreement concerning corporate stock (see "How to Restrict the Transfer of Stock" in this chapter).

- ❑ Execute a health care proxy and a living will.
- ❑ Consider transferring real estate to your heirs and retain a life estate.
- ❑ Determine whether a life insurance super-trust will serve your needs.
- ❑ Determine whether a revocable trust, an irrevocable trust, a power of attorney, or a combination of these will be best for you.
- ❑ Make gifts to reduce your taxable estate.
- ❑ Set up a deferred retirement plan.
- ❑ Review with your advisers the estate planning aspects of your pension plans, joint bank accounts, annuities, real estate, stocks, bonds, insurance policies, and personal property (see "Perils and Pitfalls of Joint Ownership" in this chapter).
- ❑ Consider a family partnership (see Chapter 3).

ESTATE AND GIFT TAXES

The federal government and some state governments impose an estate tax on a deceased person's adjusted gross estate. An estate tax is not an inheritance tax; it is levied on the whole estate before the assets are distributed to the heirs. An inheritance tax (imposed by some states) is paid by the heirs or by the beneficiaries on the share of the estate that they receive.

For federal estate tax purposes, the gross estate includes probate and nonprobate assets such as cash, bonds, stocks, interest, dividends, personal effects, life insurance, wages, real estate, and business interests. The estate tax is based on the fair market value of these assets at the time of death. Deductions, such as marital and charitable deductions, are subtracted from the gross estate amount, leaving the taxable estate, which is used to determine the amount of the estate tax due. Credits can be used to reduce the estate tax. The major credit is the unified credit of $192,800, which is applied on a dollar-for-dollar basis against potential gift and estate taxes. The unified credit makes estates up to $600,000 exempt from federal estate tax.

The federal and estate tax exemption will increase to $625,000 in 1998; $650,000 in 1999; $675,000 in 2000; $675,000 in 2001; $700,000 in 2002; $700,000 in 2003; $850,000 in 2004; $950,000 in 2005; and $1,000,000 in 2006.

There are four ways to avoid paying estate taxes:

1. Keep property out of your gross estate by gifting property and creating irrevocable trusts.
2. Maximize estate tax deductions.
3. Maximize tax credits.
4. Use life insurance to pay any estate tax by creating an irrevocable life insurance trust.

Unlimited Marital Deduction

There are no limits on the amount of property that qualifies for the gift and estate tax marital deduction. Although all federal estate taxes are avoided at the death of the first spouse if the marital deduction is used, the tax is merely deferred until the death of the surviving spouse.

If the spouse is given only the right to receive the income from property payable at least annually, the property can be treated as qualified terminable interest property (QTIP), and the entire value of the estate may qualify for the marital deduction. This creates great flexibility in planning for situations in which it may not be desirable to give the spouse total rights in the property.

For example, assume one spouse has little knowledge of and/or interest in a family-owned business. If, on the death of the business's operator, the other spouse is left to manage the business, the business will suffer. This jeopardizes the business, the surviving spouse's income, and the residual interests of the children, who will inherit the business from the wife.

With the option of the QTIP, an alternative arrangement can be made for carrying on the business so that the surviving spouse receives income, and management of the enterprise is put into the hands of the children or other knowledgeable persons.

A QTIP is also useful where the survivor may not have the knowledge, experience, or inclination to manage any assets—even cash. By providing in the will or living trust for the creation of a QTIP trust, the assets can be competently managed for the security of the surviving spouse and for ensuring their preservation for ultimate beneficiaries.

A gift tax is imposed on the donor. The annual exclusion for gifts is $10,000 for each donee ($20,000 if husband and wife each make a gift). A husband and wife with three children, for example, can make gifts totaling $60,000 a year ($20,000 to each child) every year without paying a gift tax or using any part of the unified credit.

Charitable Gifts

Seven ways to make charitable gifts. They are as follows:

1. An *outright gift* of cash, marketable securities, mutual funds, life insurance, or real estate is one means of making a charitable gift.

2. A *bequest* in a will is fully deductible for federal and state estate tax purposes. Donors have several options if they are considering a bequest: They can leave a percentage of the residuary estate or a specific dollar amount, or they can specify that a bequest be made upon certain conditions, such as the death of another beneficiary.

3. A *charitable remainder trust,* either an annuity trust or a unitrust, provides a way for a donor to receive income for life and then establish a fund. After the death of the surviving income beneficiary, the trust property is used to create a fund to fulfill the donor's charitable wishes.

4. A *charitable lead trust* forms the principal of a fund. After a period of time, the remainder interest passes to such noncharitable beneficiaries as members of the donor's family, but the fund lasts forever.

5. A *life insurance policy* and tax-deductible gifts of the premiums each year are another form of charitable giving.

6. *Retirement funds* are a sixth means of making a gift. Assets in retirement accounts and other qualified pension plans can provide the resources to establish a fund. Consider bequeathing undistributed assets in retirement accounts to charity, because these assets, if left to heirs, will be taxed three times: as an estate, as an excise, and as income to noncharitable beneficiaries.

7. A *gift of residence* is a final type of gift. Here the donor receives a current tax benefit while retaining the right to use the property for life or for a term of years.

IS A LIVING TRUST RIGHT FOR YOU?

The trust is one the most useful estate planning tools. A trust is a written agreement granting a person or institution (trustee) legal title to real or personal property that is held for the benefit of another (beneficiary).

A trust must have the following:

- A *grantor* or *settler* who creates the trust by executing a trust agreement

- A *trustee*—an individual or institution, such as a bank, who holds legal title to the trust, invests the trust assets (personal property or real property), and makes distributions of the trust principal and income as directed in the trust agreement

- *One or more beneficiaries* who receive the trust income and principal as directed in the trust document

Living trusts, also known as *inter vivos trusts,* can offer many advantages, including estate tax savings; proper management of assets; avoidance of probate; elimination of the need for guardianships, life estates, or joint ownership; and assurance of privacy.

There are two types of living trusts:

1. *Revocable trusts* can be revoked or amended by the grantor. Property in a revocable trust is treated as if it belongs to the grantor. Interest earned on the account is taxed to the grantor. The principal and any accumulated interest in the trust at the time of the grantor's death is part of the grantor's estate for estate tax purposes.

2. *Irrevocable trusts* cannot be changed, but tax and Medicaid advantages may outweigh this loss of control. The principal and interest in an irrevocable trust is not considered for estate tax purposes, and the grantor does not pay income tax on interest earned by the trust property unless it is paid to the grantor.

Through a *charitable trust,* you can take an immediate tax deduction for stocks or real estate and still receive dividends or reside in your home. The amount of the deduction depends on your life expectancy. You can also avoid tax on the gain if the property has appreciated in value.

A trust can avoid the costs, delays, and publicity attendant on probate. Assets that have been transferred to the trust are not included in the probate estate for calculating attorney or executor fees. Trust property usually passes more quickly to beneficiaries than probate property; and unlike probate court files, trust documents and property are not on public record.

Trusts can ease the transfer of financial management from a disabled elderly person without the need to institute costly guardianship or conservatorship proceedings; a revocable trust allows the grantor to test the abilities of a prospective trustee, guardian, or personal representative.

Another option to consider is the durable power of attorney, which is explained in detail in a later section of this chapter. It can be used in conjunction with a "stand-by trust" and permits the grantor to defer funding the trust until it is actually needed and thus avoid the expense of an active trustee until the trust becomes necessary. Even if you have established a living or irrevocable trust, you will still need a will to cover any assets that may not have been placed in the trust and as an added safeguard in the event the trust is revoked.

Income Splitting

If you wish to split your income with a family member or relieve yourself of liability for income taxes on certain property, you may do so by conveying the property in trust to that family member. This is particularly useful where a minor child is involved and allows you to avoid tax on part of your income.

To obtain tax-saving benefits of the trust, you should be aware of the following:

- The transfer of income-producing property rather than income must be involved. With certain exceptions, the grantor must not retain the right to receive income from the trust property.

- The grantor may not remain the owner of the trust property and must give up control over it. Nor may the grantor retain administrative powers enabling him or her to obtain, by dealing with the trust, financial benefits that would not be available in an arm's-length transaction.

- The grantor must not have the authority to regain possession of the trust principal within ten years of the transfer of the trust.

Taxation will not result, however, if the reversion takes effect only on the death of the income beneficiary.

Irrevocable Life Insurance Trust

An *irrevocable life insurance trust,* also known as a *supertrust,* is a trust that owns a life insurance policy. The grantor makes an annual gift to the trust that is used to pay the insurance premium. When the grantor dies, the proceeds are paid to the trust, which in turn pays them to the beneficiaries according to the instructions in the trust agreement. Life insurance proceeds are not subject to an estate tax if the grantor does not own the policy or have powers of ownership.

Second-to-die life insurance policies insure two people (a husband and wife or two business partners) but pay benefits only after the second death, when the estate tax exposure is the greatest. There are also *first-to-die* life insurance policies that can be used to fund corporate buy-sell agreements.

WHY YOU NEED A WILL

If you and your spouse were to die together, would you want a stranger to sell your house and business for much less than their true worth, administer your estate, control your children's money, and be their guardian? Do you want your estate to pay more estate taxes and expenses than is absolutely necessary, leaving as little as possible for your children?

If you answered these questions "no," you need a will.

A person's major asset is usually his or her home. With inflation rapidly driving up home values and mortgage insurance covering the mortgage, many homeowners have a much larger estate than they may think they have.

If you and your spouse own your home or your business together, one of you automatically gets ownership on the other's death. But what if you both die together? That business or home you worked so hard to maintain would be sold, and the proceeds would be controlled by a stranger until your children reach age 18, at which time they could spend the remaining proceeds as they wish.

Owning your business or home jointly with your spouse does not mean you don't need a will. Dying without a will may allow your estate to go to someone you don't wish to be your beneficiary and result in unnecessary estate taxes, delays in settling the estate, and added expenses. Finally, your estate assets may not receive proper management and protection.

What a Will Does

A properly drawn will ensures that at your death your property will be distributed to those you have chosen to be your beneficiaries. Your will can dispose of real and personal property in the proportions and to the persons you wish; you appoint competent and trustworthy executors (see "How to Choose an Executor or Trustee"), trustees, and guardians for your children.

A spouse's will can provide that some money will go into a testamentary trust instead of directly to the other spouse in order to avoid estate taxes on the second spouse's death.

You can disinherit your children, but you cannot disinherit your spouse. Your spouse usually has a right to at least one-third of the value of your estate unless a prenuptial or postnuptial agreement is signed (see "Divorce Planning" in Chapter 16).

Making a will is a privilege, and if it is not executed in strict compliance with state law, it may be declared to be invalid and your property will pass as if you had no will.

Testamentary Trusts

Do you envision your children squandering your estate on expensive cars and vacations? Would you like your children's inheritance managed for them until they reach the age of 25 or even 35?

The answer is *not* to leave your estate directly to your children or to a guardian but to provide in your will for a testamentary trust to be managed by a bank or trusted friend. If your estate is left to a guardian for your child, the guardian must turn the property over to the child when the child reaches 18 and can do with it as he or she wishes. When drafting a testamentary trust in your will, consider the following characteristics of your children and grandchildren:

- Their ages
- Their educational needs—the costs of undergraduate, graduate, and technical school

- The best age at which to distribute trust income and principal in a lump sum or installments
- Their ability to manage money with awareness of disabilities, alcoholism, and gambling problems
- Their financial needs and earning capabilities
- The effect distributions may have on their eligibility for disability benefits or Medicaid for any who are disabled
- The need to safeguard assets from creditors and ex-spouses for those who are divorced, on the verge of bankruptcy, or being sued

The trust can provide for either specific monthly payments; payments at the discretion of the trustee for the children's support, medical expenses, and education; or partial distributions of principal at certain ages (e.g., one-third at 25 years of age, one-third at 35 years of age and one-third at 45 years of age).

You should discuss these considerations with your attorney before executing a will.

Does Your Will Need Updating?

If you have a will, you should review it with your attorney whenever there is a change in your family (a birth or death) or your residence; the executor, guardian, or trustee named in your will becomes unavailable; you or your beneficiaries' financial worth increases dramatically; your marital status or that of a family member changes; or the status of your business undergoes a change.

HOW TO CHOOSE AN EXECUTOR OR TRUSTEE

It is especially important for the small business owner to choose a competent and trustworthy executor or trustee. Otherwise, even careful estate planning may be rendered useless.

The *executor,* the person who carries out the instructions in your will and who pays the estate's debts and taxes, can be any person or institution (such as a trust company) you choose. However, a competent executor should be

- experienced and competent in business matters;
- familiar with your business, finances, and property;
- able and willing to act as your executor;

- able to spend the time necessary to perform his or her duties;
- able to work with the estate's attorney and accountant; and
- able to provide for the continuation of your business.

You should consider naming alternate executors and co-executors.

Executor's Duties

The executor's responsibilities include the following:

- Meeting with the funeral director, cemetery representative, and clergy to make burial and funeral arrangements.
- Collecting the following documents to establish rights for insurance, pensions, Social Security, and ownership: will, birth and marriage certificates, Social Security number, citizenship papers, insurance policies (life, health, accident, and property), bank books and statements, deeds, leases, car title/registration, income tax returns, veterans discharge certificates, disability claims, unpaid bills, property tax bills, and credit card information.
- Notifying the post office; relatives; friends; employer; insurance agents (life, health, and accident); religious, fraternal, civic, and veterans organizations; unions; newspapers regarding notices; your attorney; and your accountant.
- Collecting, preserving, and appraising the personal property of the estate.
- Securing the residence and reviewing the insurance coverage.
- Paying all valid debts including funeral costs, fees and expenses incurred in administration, estate taxes, income and other taxes, medical bills, and utilities.
- Applying for Social Security benefits and employer identification number.
- Distributing the money and property in accordance with the will.

Trustees' Duties

The responsibilities of a trustee include the following:

- Read a copy of the trust agreement, keep it with the trust records, and review it annually.
- Deposit checks or bank drafts funding the trust and attach a photocopy of these to Schedule A of the trust agreement.
- Obtain a federal employer identification number for the trust.
- Consult with your financial adviser about the types of accounts (brokerage firm, management account, bank account) to open and deposit funds. Under the prudent investor rule, trustees must formulate an overall investment strategy that takes into account general economic conditions, inflation, the beneficiaries' needs, the duration of the trust, and the tax impact. Trustees usually must diversify the investments and can designate outside experts to handle their duties.
- Consult with your attorney or accountant for further information about the annual fiduciary tax returns (IRS form 1041) and equivalent state forms that are due on or about April 15 of the year following the opening of the trust and each subsequent year.
- Consider a change of trustee when there is a change of circumstances.
- Review with an attorney the requirements for closing the trust (i.e., releases and final tax returns).

POWERS OF ATTORNEY

The *principal,* by signing a power of attorney, authorizes another person—known as the *agent* or *attorney-in-fact*—to act on the principal's behalf to perform any number of specified acts. The power is only valid during the principal's lifetime. A separate health care proxy must be signed to authorize the agent to make health care decisions.

The three types of powers of attorney are as follows:

- The *durable general power of attorney* continues to be effective on the incapacity of the principal.

- The *nondurable general power of attorney* ceases to be effective on the incapacity of the principal.

- The *springing power of attorney* takes effect at a specified time or upon the occurrence of a specified contingency, such as the incapacity of the principal.

Powers of attorney have a variety of features that are described below.

Multiple agents. If more than one agent is designated to act, the principal may indicate either that each agent must act separately or that all agents must act together.

Successor agent. The principal may designate a successor agent who will become an agent if all other named agents are unable or unwilling to serve.

Retirement benefit transactions. The agent may be authorized to contribute to, withdraw from, and deposit funds in any type of retirement benefit or plan; select and change payment options and exercise any other election; make rollover contributions from one plan to another; and execute any documents or take any other necessary action. The agent can make or change a beneficiary designation but may not designate himself or herself as beneficiary unless the agent is the principal's spouse, child, grandchild, parent, brother, or sister.

Gift transactions. The agent may be authorized to make gifts from the principal's property in amounts aggregating $10,000 per year to the principal's spouse and to each of the principal's children, more remote descendants, and parents. Gifts can be made outright or to a trust for the sole benefit of one or more of these permissible donees, including an existing trust or a trust that the agent is authorized to create. Gifts may only be made for purposes that are in the best interest of the principal, specifically including the minimization of taxes. The agent may also satisfy pledges made by the principal to charitable and other organizations.

The agent may prepare, execute, consent to, and file any return or other document needed with regard to any such gift and may execute any deed, assignment, agreement, trust agreement, or other necessary instrument. The agent may also prosecute and defend any claim existing in favor of or against the principal, and may hire and compensate attorneys, accountants, and others needed to carry out these acts.

Tax matters. The agent may be permitted to prepare, sign, and file tax returns on behalf of the principal. The agent may execute any power of attorney required by the IRS or other taxing authority and is also empowered to represent the principal or to designate another person to represent the principal before the IRS and any other taxing authority.

Health Care Decision Making

Living wills are written declarations instructing a patient's family and doctor about life-prolonging medical procedures when the patient's condition is terminal and no chance of recovery is apparent. Under constitutional and common law, patients have the right to refuse medical treatment.

A living will gives individuals the opportunity to express their wishes in advance as they may not be able to make them known when it becomes necessary to do so.

Life-prolonging procedures include the use of machines for those who cannot breathe on their own, performing operations or prescribing antibiotics that cannot realistically increase the chances for recovery, starting the heart mechanically when it has stopped beating, or feeding by tube. Individuals can direct that the only treatment rendered be the relief of pain.

A nursing home that ignored a living will and refused to remove a feeding tube until it was ordered to by a court could not collect $14,000 in medical bills that had accrued during the court battle.

Health care proxies recognize a person's right to appoint a health care agent that he or she trusts to decide about medical treatment in the event that he or she becomes unable to decide personally. Unless specified otherwise, the agent will have the same authority that the patient would have in deciding about treatment. The authority encompasses the right to forgo treatment or to consent to needed treatment. The agent's authority begins only when a physician determines that the patient has lost the capacity to decide about treatment.

Do-not-resuscitate orders are a direction not to revive a patient if his or her breathing or heartbeat stops (e.g., mouth-to-mouth resuscitation, chest compression, electric shock, open heart massage, or injecting a heart with medication). A patient's estate was allowed to sue a hospital that saved his life, in spite of a do-not-resuscitate order, for negligence and battery. The patient suffered a stroke after resuscitation, but lived for two more years. His estate sued for his medical bills and the pain and suffering resulting from the stroke.

HOW TO RESTRICT THE TRANSFER OF STOCK

As a shareholder, would you like veto power over the admission of new shareholders? Would you like to ensure the continuation of your business in the event a partner or shareholder dies or decides to sell his or her interest? Would you like an arrangement guaranteeing that there would be a willing buyer should a shareholder or partner die or decide to sell his or her shares?

You can achieve all this by having all shareholders or partners sign a buy-sell agreement. Buy-sell agreements usually require shareholders to offer their shares to the corporation and/or the other shareholders at an agreed-upon price before selling to an outsider. Some buy-sell agreements provide that shareholders may be prohibited from transferring their shares unless the board consents to or approves the purchase.

Restrictions on a transfer of corporate shares are effective against third-party buyers only if the restrictions are noted conspicuously on the stock certificates.

Determination of the selling price may be based on the book value of the shares from the latest balance sheet or shareholder agreement, capitalization of earnings, a fixed price, a formula relating to principles of sales or revenues, arbitration, or appraisal. The valuation method must, however, be more than simply an "agreement to agree." The agreed price is also useful in establishing the tax basis of your stock for estate tax purposes.

Buy-sell agreements usually provide for the manner of payment and a specific payment plan. Plans can be funded by insurance.

If a buy-sell agreement is conditioned on the death or disability of a shareholder, the shareholder should be covered by life and disability insurance so that the corporation will have adequate funds with which to purchase the shareholder's shares.

PERILS AND PITFALLS OF JOINT OWNERSHIP

If you are considering making your adult child a joint owner of your real estate or your business to avoid probate, beware! Many potential legal complications and tax liabilities are involved in this simple but risky move. If a person owns an asset in "joint tenancy with the right of survivorship" with a child or with a spouse, the asset automatically passes to the survivor upon the person's death.

Various risks are involved when a husband and wife add a child's name to the title of an asset. If the child were to be divorced, the asset could be the subject of a property settlement. If the child is sued by creditors or becomes bankrupt, the property might be ordered to be sold. If the child was in an automobile accident and rendered mentally incompetent, the parents could not sell without the approval of a court guardian. If both parents died as a result of a common accident and the child died shortly afterwards, the child's heirs (i.e., spouse and children) would receive the proceeds of the sale rather than the parents' heirs.

By adding the child to the title the parents also surrender their freedom to do as they wish with the property. If the parents decide to sell the house, the child could withhold consent. If one of the parents should die and the survivor decided to remarry, the child could prevent the new spouse from being added to the title.

Joint ownership does not avoid estate taxes. When a couple owns property jointly, one-half of the total value of the property will be included in the estate of the first to die. When the joint owners are married, the marital deduction eliminates any tax on the property. However, when the entire property is in the estate of the second spouse, it will be subject to tax in the absence of proper estate planning. Joint title ownership merely delays the tax. Joint property interest will also increase the gross estate of the first to die for purposes of the installment payment of the estate taxes on a small business.

HOW AND WHEN TO USE THE FORMS IN THIS CHAPTER

Document Checklist; Business Data; Personal Data. The time you spend filling out these forms will greatly reduce the time your attorney will have to spend obtaining information from you when preparing to draft your will.

Family Tree. This form should be kept with your original will.

DOCUMENT CHECKLIST

PERSONAL DOCUMENTS

( )   COPY OF YOUR WILL

( )   COPY OF YOUR SPOUSE'S WILL

( )   PERSONAL BALANCE SHEET

( )   LAST YEAR'S INCOME TAX RETURN

( )   COPY OF TRUST AGREEMENTS

( )   ANY OTHER SIGNIFICANT AGREEMENTS

( )   COPIES OF PERSONAL LIFE, MEDICAL, AND DISABILITY INSURANCE CONTRACTS

CORPORATE DOCUMENTS

( )   CURRENT BALANCE SHEET

( )   PROFIT AND LOSS STATEMENTS FOR PAST FIVE YEARS

( )   PENSION TRUST AGREEMENT—MOST RECENT VALUATION

( )   PROFIT-SHARING TRUST AGREEMENT—MOST RECENT ACCOUNTING

( )   BUY-SELL AGREEMENT

( )   CORPORATE MINUTE BOOK

( )   COMPENSATION AND EMPLOYMENT AGREEMENTS

( )   LIST OF SHAREHOLDERS

( )   CORPORATE LIFE INSURANCE CONTRACTS

( )   ANY OTHER SIGNIFICANT CORPORATE DOCUMENTS

( )   EMPLOYEE INFORMATION CENSUS

( )   EMPLOYEE BENEFIT BOOKLETS

BUSINESS DATA

FULL LEGAL NAME: _____

ADDRESS: _____

_____

BUSINESS NOW OPERATES AS:

❑ PROPRIETORSHIP   ❑ CORPORATION

❑ PARTNERSHIP   ❑ SUBCHAPTER S CORPORATION

PRINCIPAL BUSINESS ACTIVITY: _____

IN WHAT YEAR DID THIS BUSINESS BEGIN OPERATION? _____

DATE OF INCORPORATION IF IT BEGAN OTHER THAN AS A CORPORATION: _____

FISCAL YEAR ENDING: _____

WHAT IS YOUR FUNCTION IN THE BUSINESS? _____

PRESENT BOOK VALUE:_____ ESTIMATED VALUE: _____

WHAT IS YOUR ESTIMATE OF THE LOWEST PRICE FOR WHICH THE ENTIRE BUSINESS MIGHT BE SOLD AS A GOING CONCERN TODAY? _____

WHAT WOULD YOU SELL YOUR INTEREST FOR?_____

PRESENT OWNERS:

(A) _____ OWNS _____ % COMMON _____ % PREFERRED

(B) _____ OWNS _____ % COMMON _____ % PREFERRED

(C) _____ OWNS _____ % COMMON _____ % PREFERRED

(D) _____ OWNS _____ % COMMON _____ % PREFERRED

(E) _____ OWNS _____ % COMMON _____ % PREFERRED

NUMBER AND CLASSES OF SHARES:

_____

_____

_____

_____

CORPORATE AGREEMENTS

BUY-SELL: _____

SHAREHOLDER: _____

VOTING TRUST:_____

OTHER: _____

BUSINESS DATA
(continued)

BUSINESS ATTORNEY

    NAME: _____

    ADDRESS: _____

    TELEPHONE: _____

BUSINESS ACCOUNTANT

    NAME: _____

    ADDRESS: _____

    TELEPHONE: _____

KEY EMPLOYEES

NAME	DATE OF BIRTH	POSITION	DATE OF EMPLOYMENT	SALARY BONUS	COST OF REPLACEMENT

PLANS, FUTURE, STABILITY, PROBLEMS:

_____

_____

_____

_____

_____

_____

_____

_____

_____

BUSINESS DATA
(continued)

LIFE INSURANCE ON OFFICERS AND KEY EMPLOYEES

INSURED	AMOUNT	TYPE	COMPANY	DATE OF ISSUE	OWNER	BENEFICIARY	W/P-D.I.

Note any assignments or ratings.

BUSINESS DATA
(continued)

CORPORATE BENEFITS

GROUP LIFE INSURANCE   COMPANY: _____

     SCHEDULE: _____

GROUP HOSPITAL AND SURGICAL   COMPANY: _____

     FEATURES:_____

GROUP MAJOR MEDICAL   COMPANY: _____

     DEDUCTIBLE: _____

     COINSURANCE: _____

     MAXIMUM: _____

DISABILITY INCOME   COMPANY: _____

     GROUP/INDIVIDUAL: _____

     AMOUNTS: _____

     SALARY CONTINUATION PLAN: _____

PENSION PLAN   I.D.#: _____ EFFECTIVE DATE: _____

     TYPE: _____

     PRESENT EVALUATION—INVESTMENT AND RESULTS: _____

     _____

     INSURANCE: _____

     ADMINISTRATION: _____

PROFIT-SHARING PLAN   I.D.#: _____ EFFECTIVE DATE: _____

     FORMULA: _____

     INSURANCE: _____

     KEY MAN: _____

     PRESENT WORTH: _____

     INVESTMENT AND RESULTS: _____

     _____

HEALTH AND ACCIDENT REIMBURSEMENT PLAN: _____

_____

STOCK OPTIONS: _____

_____

BONUS PLAN: _____

_____

WIDOW'S DEATH BENEFIT: _____

_____

BUSINESS DATA
(continued)

CORPORATE BENEFITS
(continued)

DEFERRED COMPENSATION: _____

_____

SECTION 79: _____ YES _____ NO   FOR WHOM: _____

_____

SALARY CONTINUATION PLAN: _____

_____

EXCESS SALARY AND EXPENSE REIMBURSEMENT AGREEMENT: _____

_____

_____

OTHER:

_____

_____

_____

_____

BUSINESS DATA
(continued)

INSURANCE

HEALTH INSURANCE

	COMPANY	INSURED	MONTHLY DISABILITY INCOME	
			ACCIDENT	SICKNESS
#1				
#2				
#3				
#4				
#5				

MEDICAL EXPENSE INSURANCE

	COMPANY NAME OR SERVICE-TYPE PLAN	INSURED	(CHECK APPROPRIATE COVERAGES)		
			BASIC HOSPITAL	SURGICAL	MAJOR MEDICAL
#1					
#2					
#3					
#4					

LIFE INSURANCE

	COMPANY	TYPE OF POLICY	FACE AMOUNT	ISSUE AGE	PREMIUM	(A/S/Q/M) MODE	OWNER/ BENEFICIARY
#1							
#2							
#3							
#4							
#5							
#6							

PERSONAL DATA

CLIENT: _____ DATE OF BIRTH: _____

PLACE OF BIRTH: _____ CITIZENSHIP: _____

HOME ADDRESS: _____ PHONE: _____

_____

BUSINESS ADDRESS: _____ PHONE: _____

_____

MARITAL STATUS: _____ SOCIAL SECURITY NO.: _____

CONSULTANTS FOR BUSINESS AND FINANCIAL PLANNING

ATTORNEY   NAME: _____ PHONE: _____

ADDRESS: _____

ACCOUNTANT   NAME: _____ PHONE: _____

ADDRESS: _____

TRUST OFFICER   NAME: _____ PHONE: _____

ADDRESS: _____

OTHER BANK OFFICER   NAME: _____ PHONE: _____

ADDRESS: _____

LIFE UNDERWRITER   NAME: _____ PHONE: _____

ADDRESS: _____

GENERAL INSURANCE   NAME: _____ PHONE: _____

ADDRESS: _____

CLIENT'S FAMILY

SPOUSE: _____ DATE OF BIRTH: _____

OCCUPATION: _____ SPECIAL HEALTH NEEDS: _____

SOCIAL SECURITY NO.: _____ PLACE OF BIRTH: _____

CHILDREN

NAME	PLACE OF BIRTH	DATE OF BIRTH	OCCUPATION	AMOUNT OF SUPPORT

PERSONAL DATA
(continued)

CLIENT'S PARENTS, BROTHERS, AND SISTERS

NAME   RELATIONSHIP   DATE OF BIRTH   CONDITION OF HEALTH

_____

_____

_____

_____

SPOUSE'S PARENTS, BROTHERS, AND SISTERS

NAME   RELATIONSHIP   DATE OF BIRTH   CONDITION OF HEALTH

_____

_____

_____

_____

WILLS AND MARITAL AGREEMENTS

   DO YOU HAVE A WILL? _____ SPOUSE? _____

TRUSTS

   HAVE YOU CREATED A LIVING TRUST? _____

   TRUSTEE: _____ BENEFICIARY: _____

   HAS YOUR SPOUSE CREATED A LIVING TRUST? _____

   TRUSTEE: _____ BENEFICIARY: _____

   ARE ANY MEMBERS OF YOUR IMMEDIATE FAMILY BENEFICIARIES
     OF A TRUST? _____

   WHO WILL BE GUARDIANS AND SUCCESSOR GUARDIANS
     OF YOUR CHILDREN? _____

   WHO WILL BE TRUSTEES AND SUCCESSOR TRUSTEES OF
     YOUR ESTATE?_____

CUSTODIANSHIPS

   HAVE YOU OR YOUR SPOUSE MADE A GIFT UNDER THE UNIFORM GIFT
     TO MINORS ACT?_____

   CUSTODIANS: _____ DONEES: _____

GIFTS AND INHERITANCES

   DO YOU OR YOUR SPOUSE EXPECT TO RECEIVE ANY GIFTS
     OR INHERITANCES? _____

PERSONAL DATA
(continued)

IF SO, PLEASE EXPLAIN. _____

EDUCATION/MILITARY EXPERIENCE

  COLLEGE: _____ DATES: _____ DEGREE: _____

  MILITARY SERVICE BRANCH: _____

  SERVICE-RELATED BENEFITS: _____

PERSONAL AND FAMILY PROPERTY

PROPERTY	HUSBAND	OWNERSHIP (X) WIFE	JOINT	FAIR MARKET VALUE	ORIGINAL COST	PRESENT INDEBTEDNESS
REAL ESTATE						
RESIDENCE	___	___	___	___	___	___
OTHER	___	___	___	___	___	___
_____	___	___	___	___	___	___
SECURITIES						
CORPORATE BONDS	___	___	___	___	___	___
MUNICIPAL BONDS	___	___	___	___	___	___
GOVERNMENT BONDS	___	___	___	___	___	___
COMMON STOCK	___	___	___	___	___	___
PREFERRED STOCK	___	___	___	___	___	___
OTHER	___	___	___	___	___	___
MORTGAGES, ACCOUNTS RECEIVABLE, NOTES RECEIVABLE						
MORTGAGES	___	___	___	___	___	___
ACCOUNTS RECEIVABLE	___	___	___	___	___	___
NOTES RECEIVABLE	___	___	___	___	___	___

PERSONAL DATA
(continued)

FAMILY INCOME

	CLIENT	SPOUSE	DEPENDENT CHILDREN
ANNUAL INCOME			
SALARY, BONUS			
REAL ESTATE			
DIVIDENDS			
INVESTMENTS			
CLOSE CORP. STOCK			
INTEREST			
BONDS			
SAVINGS ACCOUNTS			
TRUST INCOME			
OTHER			

EXPECTED FUTURE INCOME

NEXT YEAR: _____ NEXT FIVE YEARS: _____

OBJECTIVES REQUIRING ADDITIONAL INCOME

  EDUCATION FUND

NAME OF CHILD	AGE	NO. YEARS REQUIRED	ESTIMATED EXPENSES

OTHER OBJECTIVES

_____

INCOME AND CAPITAL NEEDS

AT WHAT AGE WOULD YOU LIKE TO RETIRE? _____

ESTIMATED REQUIRED MONTHLY INCOME AT RETIREMENT: _____

ESTIMATED REQUIRED MONTHLY INCOME IF DISABLED: _____

PERSONAL DATA
(continued)

EXPECTED SOURCES OF FUNDS

	RETIREMENT	DISABILITY
SOCIAL SECURITY	_____	_____
OTHER GOVERNMENT PENSION	_____	_____
INDIVIDUAL RETIREMENT ACCOUNT	_____	_____
PENSION PLAN	_____	_____
PROFIT-SHARING PLAN	_____	_____
TAX-DEFERRED ANNUITY	_____	_____
NONQUALIFIED DEFERRED COMPENSATION	_____	_____
NONQUALIFIED ANNUITY	_____	_____
LIFE INSURANCE CASH VALUES	_____	_____
INDEPENDENT INCOME	_____	_____
OTHER	_____	_____

PERSONAL AND FAMILY PROPERTY

	OWNERSHIP (X)					
PROPERTY	HUSBAND	WIFE	JOINT	FAIR MARKET VALUE	ORIGINAL COST	PRESENT INDEBTEDNESS
PERSONAL PROPERTY						
PERSONAL POSSESSIONS	_____	_____	_____	_____	_____	_____
AUTOS	_____	_____	_____	_____	_____	_____
HOME FURNISHINGS	_____	_____	_____	_____	_____	_____
OTHER	_____	_____	_____	_____	_____	_____
JEWELS/FURS	_____	_____	_____	_____	_____	_____
COLLECTIONS	_____	_____	_____	_____	_____	_____
OTHER	_____	_____	_____	_____	_____	_____
BANK ACCOUNTS AND CASH						
SAVINGS ACCOUNT	_____	_____	_____	_____	_____	_____
CHECKING ACCOUNT	_____	_____	_____	_____	_____	_____
READY CASH	_____	_____	_____	_____	_____	_____
OTHER	_____	_____	_____	_____	_____	_____

PERSONAL DATA
(continued)

ANY OTHER PERSONAL ASSETS

_____ _____ _____ _____ _____ _____ _____

_____ _____ _____ _____ _____ _____ _____

_____ _____ _____ _____ _____ _____ _____

INSURANCE

HEALTH INSURANCE

| | COMPANY | INSURED | MONTHLY DISABILITY INCOME | |
			ACCIDENT	SICKNESS
#1				
#2				
#3				
#4				
#5				

MEDICAL EXPENSE INSURANCE

(CHECK APPROPRIATE COVERAGES)

	COMPANY NAME OR SERVICE-TYPE PLAN	INSURED	BASIC HOSPITAL	SURGICAL	MAJOR MEDICAL
#1					
#2					
#3					
#4					

LIFE INSURANCE

	COMPANY	TYPE OF POLICY	FACE AMOUNT	ISSUE AGE	PREMIUM	(A/S/Q/M) MODE	OWNER/ BENEFICIARY
#1							
#2							
#3							
#4							
#5							
#6							

237

PERSONAL DATA
(continued)

PROJECTION OBJECTIVES

(1) INCOME TO WIDOW AND CHILDREN ($/MONTH)

(2) INCOME TO WIDOW ALONE ($/MONTH)   _____

(3) CASH FUND FOR LAST EXPENSES   _____

(4) CASH FUND FOR EMERGENCIES   _____

(5) CASH FUND FOR MORTGAGE   _____

(6) CASH FUND FOR EDUCATION   _____

(7) CASH FUND FOR OTHER NEEDS   _____

(8) PRIORITY OF OBJECTIVES   _____

    (Enter question numbers 1–7 in order of importance.) _____

       1. _____

       2. _____

       3. _____

       4. _____

       5. _____

       6. _____

       7. _____

PATERNAL
SIDE

GRANDFATHER

GRANDMOTHER

FATHER OF DECEDENT

MATERNAL
SIDE

GRANDFATHER

GRANDMOTHER

MOTHER OF DECEDENT

** PARENTHESIS INDICATES
THAT INDIVIDUAL
PRE-DECEASED THE
DECEDENT NAMED HEREIN.

STATE OF NEW YORK
COUNTY OF   ss:

_____ being duly sworn,
states that the charts contained on this paper are true and correct and based
upon the information and belief (personal knowledge) of the undersigned.

Sworn to before me on _____

_____
NOTARY PUBLIC

FORM FT-1 (FAMILY TREE)

┌─────────────────────────┐
│ CROSS OUT CLASS   │
│ NOT APPLICABLE   │
└─────────────────────────┘

CHILDREN
–or–
BROTHERS AND
SISTERS

GRANDCHILDREN
–or–
NIECES AND
NEPHEWS

GREAT
GRANDCHILDREN
–or–
GRANDNIECES AND
GRANDNEPHEWS

DECEDENT

SPOUSE   NAME

☐ DECEASED   DATE

☐ DIVORCED   DATE/STATE

☐ NEVER MARRIED

** PARENTHESIS INDICATES
THAT INDIVIDUAL
PRE-DECEASED THE
DECEDENT NAMED HEREIN.

STATE OF NEW YORK   ss:
COUNTY OF

_____ being duly sworn,
states that the charts contained on this paper are true and correct and based
upon information and belief (personal knowledge) of the undersigned.

Sworn to before me on _____

_____
NOTARY PUBLIC

240

14

Real Estate Strategies

Even in poor economic times, real estate ownership is an attractive investment for many small businesses. Chief among its attractions is the ability to leverage the purchase by acquiring property with other people's money. In fact, careful shopping and the right circumstances may even enable you to acquire real estate without paying anything down.

As attractive as any investment may be, there are always hidden dangers that may surface later and prove overwhelmingly costly to the buyer. Among those dangers are potential nuisance suits, zoning laws, potential housing discrimination charges, the claims of squatters, and possible environmental liability.

HOT SITE

Real Estate Legal Survival

(http://www.real_estate.html)

BUYING REAL ESTATE

You should get answers to the following questions *before signing* a purchase agreement:

- What services is the seller providing to the tenants (e.g., heat, parking, gas, electricity, oil, water, garbage collection, snow plowing, and general maintenance)?

- Is the seller holding security deposits or cleaning deposits? A seller commits a crim-

inal misdemeanor in some states for failing to transfer security deposits to the buyer and/or failing to inform the tenants of the buyer's identity.

- Are there any written leases? What are their terms? Because you will be bound by any leases between the seller and his or her tenant(s), you should study the lease terms carefully and note expiration dates, the landlord's rights to enter the property, the tenant's responsibility to comply with the Americans with Disabilities Act (see Chapter 17), rental amounts, the tenant's right to sublet or assign the lease, and whether the lease is renewable. If there is no written lease, you can evict the tenant or raise the rent after giving 30 days' notice.

- Is the property operating profitably? Require the seller to provide you with an operating statement showing rental income and all operating expenses.

- How expensive are utility and heating costs? Ask for fuel bills for the past two years. Are the utilities separately metered?

- Does the seller have any service contracts on appliances or equipment? Are they assignable?

- Who are the employees or agents of the seller, and what are the terms of their employment?

- What personal property (equipment, supplies, and appliances) is included with the sale?

- Are there any liens against the real estate or any of the personal property you expect to receive?
- Is there any work or remodeling in progress? If so, will it be completed before the closing? Has the seller made all decorations and alterations required by the lease?
- Are there any legal actions pending against the seller?
- What repairs must tenants make?
- Are the rents paid up to date?
- Is the present mortgage assumable? Will the interest rate increase if the mortgage is assumed?
- Is there a tenants' association?
- Is the property zoned for the use to which you intend to put the property?
- What are the relevant building and housing codes? Have any complaints been lodged against the seller for alleged violations of those codes?
- Are there any assessments for special improvements to the property?
- What is the assessed value of the property? What is the equalization rate?
- Is a certificate of occupancy required, and does the seller have one?
- Is there rent control?
- What are the sewer charges and water rates?

Avoid Costly Mistakes When Purchasing Rental Property

If you are considering buying rental property, avoid the following seven costliest mistakes.

Mistake #1: Bad location. The property should be in an area where the demand for rental housing exceeds the supply and there is access to public transportation, churches, schools, and stores to ensure good rents and a good resale price.

Mistake #2: Failure to check utility costs. Under the Truth-in-Heating Law, sellers and landlords of residential buildings, including one- and two-family residences, condominiums, cooperatives, and apartments, must provide prospective buyers and tenants with a summary or a copy of heating and/or cooling bills for the preceding two years and a statement of the type and location of insulation installed by the current owner and previous owners. Determine whether the utilities are separately metered.

Mistake #3: Zoning or building code violations. Determine whether the building and planned renovations conform to zoning ordinances, building codes, deed restrictions, and loan requirements of the bank, the Veterans Administration (VA), or the Federal Housing Administration (FHA). Also, inquire as to whether a certificate of occupancy is necessary.

Mistake #4: Assuming personal property stays with the real estate. The contract of sale should state which appliances, equipment, furnishings, and other personal property are included with the sale.

Mistake #5: Defective or dangerous property. The contract of sale should contain a clause that the sale is contingent on an inspection by a professional inspector, licensed engineer, or licensed architect. Ascertain whether the property contains lead paint, asbestos, or other hazardous materials.

Mistake #6: Assuming there are no leases. The seller should be required to furnish copies of all leases, tenant applications, and move-in/move-out checklists prior to closing. Since the purchaser will be bound by any leases between the seller and his or her tenants, the purchaser should study the terms of the lease very carefully for such items as the expiration date, rental amount, the tenant's right to sublet, and whether the lease is renewable. If there are no leases, the contract should specify whether the units must be vacant at the time of closing, include assurances that the seller will not enter into any new leases, specify the amounts of security or cleaning deposits, list the names of the tenant(s), and specify the amount of the monthly rent.

Mistake #7: Expecting to close on the closing date. The closing date stated in the contract is merely a target date unless it is specified that "time is of the essence."

For further information on purchasing real estate, see Robert Friedman's book *How to Survive Legally as a Landlord* (Victoria Square Publishing Company, Inc.).

VACANT LAND

If you are looking for a vacant lot on which to build, take the following precautions:

- Check with the town planning board to determine what type of development is planned in the area.
- Determine whether there are oil or gas leases on the property.
- Determine which utilities (gas, electric, water, and sewer) will service the property.
- Ask the owner if a percolation test has been done for a sewage disposal system. If not, have a percolation test contingency clause inserted in the contract of sale.
- Check with the town building or zoning department to find out which building and other permits are required and the zoning requirements that will have to be satisfied (e.g., minimum square footage, minimum lot size, and minimum frontage).
- Check to see if the property is in a flood zone.
- Determine whether state, county, and local subdivision regulations have been met.
- Make sure that the contract of sale indicates the lot's dimensions and size. The contract should also require the seller to have the lot staked by a surveyor.
- Check for signs of hazardous waste dumping by having an environmental study done.
- Insert a contract provision stating that the contract is subject to your attorney's approval as to form and content.

FINANCING REAL ESTATE

If you have less available cash than you believe you will need to make a down payment on property—even if you have no available cash—don't be discouraged. The lack of a cash down payment should not be a hindrance to buying real estate.

There are 12 techniques that will enable you to buy commercial or rental properties without a cash down payment. These methods can be used either to finance the entire purchase or in combination with a first mortgage or an assumed mortgage. They are as follows:

1. *Professional services.* Enter into a contract with the seller to provide him or her with professional services (e.g., medical, legal, accounting, plumbing, etc.) that the seller may need in the future.

2. *Partnership.* If you and one or more other persons expect to create a partnership to buy property, your effort and expertise in forming a partnership could serve as your contribution for your interest in the partnership. By organizing a partnership, you receive an ownership position and the cash is furnished by your partners (see the "Cotenancy Agreement" form at the end of this chapter).

3. *Corporate stock.* Form a real estate investment corporation and issue stock to the other investors for their equity in the property—and issue stock to yourself based on the work you expended promoting and forming the corporation.

4. *Second mortgage.* Give the seller a second mortgage on your residence or other real estate you presently own.

5. *Assign rents.* Assign the rents (in whole or in part) of the property to the seller, giving the seller the right to impound them if you are in default on a mortgage the seller has given you in lieu of a down payment.

6. *Advertise for a private loan.* Look for a private lender who is interested in receiving a high interest rate on a first or second mortgage.

7. *Use your commission.* If you are a real estate broker, the seller may be willing to apply the commission owed you as all or part of the down payment.

8. *Real estate equity.* Your equity in other investment property may be used as a down payment by deeding an undivided interest to the seller. This may qualify as a nontaxable exchange. The seller would obtain a partial interest in your property in exchange for your obtaining full ownership of the seller's property. The seller then becomes your partner in the original property.

9. *Installment down payment.* Acquire the property now, but arrange to make the down payment in installments over the first year of ownership.

10. *Broker as lender.* Ask if your real estate broker would like to make a good investment at a high interest rate by holding a second mortgage in the amount of the sale's commission. The broker may prefer holding the mortgage to losing a good sale.

11. *Friend as lender.* Consider the possibility of borrowing from family, friends, business associates, or your retirement plan.

12. *Shared equity arrangement.* This technique, although easily set in motion, involves several planning procedures and is described in the following subsection.

Before embarking on the use of any of these 12 techniques, make certain it is economically feasible. Review the particular cash-flow and tax consequences carefully. You should consult a real estate attorney for details regarding these and any other financing techniques.

NEED HELP IN PURCHASING REAL ESTATE?

If you lack the income necessary to qualify for a mortgage loan and the down payment necessary to purchase real estate, you may be able to attract help from others through a shared equity financing arrangement (SEA).

How SEA Works

In the following example, we will assume that a parent wants to help a child purchase a commercial building. An SEA, however, can be used where any person—a friend, relative, or business associate—wants to help another person.

The parents and the child buy the property as co-owners, each with a one-half ownership interest in the building. On the purchase of a $100,000 building, the parents make the $25,000 down payment (one-fourth of the $100,000 purchase price) and are responsible for one-third of the $75,000 mortgage. The $25,000 down payment plus the $25,000 share of the mortgage gives them one-half interest in the home. The parents pay one-third of the monthly mortgage payment and one-half of the property taxes.

The child would be responsible for paying two-thirds of the $75,000 mortgage and that $50,000 share of the mortgage provides a one-half ownership interest. The parents lease the property to the child, who must pay the parents a fair monthly rental for the exclusive use of the building. The child also pays two-thirds of the monthly mortgage payment and one-half of the property taxes.

Tax Deductions

Both the parents and the child, as co-owners, are entitled to take tax deductions on the property. The parents are entitled to landlords' tax deductions on their one-half share of the property (i.e., depreciation, repairs, and insurance) as well as deductions on one-third of the mortgage interest payments and one-half of the property taxes. The child is entitled to deductions of two-thirds of the mortgage interest payments and one-half of the property taxes. Any person can rent to relatives and take deductions for rental-related expenses; but for tax purposes, relatives must pay a fair rental value—determined by taking into account such factors as comparable rents in the area and whether substantial gifts, other than holiday or birthday gifts, were made to a relative at or about the time of the lease or were made periodically during the year.

Advantages

SEA makes mortgage financing easier to obtain because banks consider parents' income, as well as the child's, when evaluating the mortgage loan application. Both the parents and child sign the mortgage.

If this technique is used to enable a child to buy residential property, then the child obtains the benefits of tax deductions on interest and property taxes instead of making just nondeductible rental payments. Parents also receive rental income from the child.

An attorney can provide you with complete details on how to set up an SEA and the tax benefits and risks involved.

THE BENEFITS OF PRIVATE MORTGAGES

Given the relatively weak market for commercial real estate, property owners who want to sell real property must make it as salable as possible. One of the difficulties faced by an interested buyer is the unwillingness of most banks to provide mortgage funding.

Knowledgeable sellers, therefore, are increasingly beginning to offer qualified buyers purchase money mortgages. In addition to dramatically increasing the marketability of the real estate, private mortgages offer many other advantages to both the buyer and seller.

For example, the closing period is much shorter as the mortgage approval delays attendant on institutional mortgages are avoided. The buyer is saved the expense of the bank attorney's fee, title insurance premiums, and other bank charges. Private mortgages are more flexible than institutional mortgages. The buyer and seller can negotiate the interest rate and all other terms. The buyer will enjoy interest deductions on income tax because it pays for the property with cheaper inflated dollars. The seller benefits from the purchase money mortgage because it too will enjoy income tax savings as it earns interest income.

Arrangements for the Mortgage

The terms of a private mortgage should be detailed in the purchase contract and should specify

- the interest rate,
- late charges,
- attorney fees on default,
- prepayment penalties,
- assumability of the mortgage,
- the payment grace period,
- the first or second mortgage,
- the balloon payment, and
- the buyer's agreement to submit to a credit check.

The private mortgage will be drawn up by the buyer's or seller's attorney in accordance with the purchase agreement and will be recorded with the county clerk on the closing date. The mortgage gives the seller, as mortgagee, security for the loan by creating a lien on the mortgagor's property. In addition to providing the property as security for the loan, the mortgagor also personally obligates itself for the loan by signing a promissory note. The mortgage continues to be a lien on the real estate until it is paid in full.

A balloon payment mortgage should be used if the seller wishes to hold the mortgage for a short period of time. An example would be a mortgage that runs for a term of five years with monthly payments that are as low as those used in a self-liquidating 20-year mortgage. At the end of the five years, the borrower makes a large "balloon" payment to pay off the balance.

LEGAL JARGON OF THE PURCHASE CONTRACT

To help you better understand and negotiate contracts of sale, we have set forth the following definitions of the legal terminology commonly found in these contracts:

Title. A title is evidence of the owner's right to possess and use real estate. The seller should deliver a *marketable title*—that is, one that is acceptable to the buyer because it is free and clear of encumbrances.

Encumbrances. This term refers to the legal interests of others that diminish the value of the property, such as mortgages, judgments, liens, leases, deed restrictions, and easements.

Lien. A lien is the legal right or claim upon property that attaches to the property until a debt is satisfied, such as a tax lien or mechanic's lien.

Easement. An easement is a right-of-way authorizing access by the public or an individual on, over, or through land. A common example of an easement is an electric company's easement to maintain power lines.

Deed restriction. This refers to a clause in a deed that limits the use of land, such as a restriction against the sale of liquor or a restriction on the size, value, or placement of the types of buildings that can be constructed on the property.

Mortgage. A mortgage is a written instrument that creates a lien upon real estate as security for the payment of a debt. The person holding the mortgage, the *mortgagor*, has security for the loan because a lien is created against the land. (See "Can the Bank Foreclose Your Mortgage?" in this chapter.)

Assumption of mortgage. An assumption occurs when a buyer agrees to be personally liable for payment of an existing mortgage.

Search. Also known as an *abstract of title,* this is a historical digest of every document that has been recorded concerning a particular piece of property, including deeds, easements, mortgages, rights-of-way, oil and gas leases, estate proceedings, tax liens, and judgments. Excerpts from each legal document are arranged chronologically and state the names of the parties involved, the type of document, and the date the document was signed and recorded.

Survey. This is a blueprint drawn by a surveyor showing the measurements, boundaries, and area of the property. It also shows fences, driveways, streams, and all buildings located on the property.

Deed. A deed is a document, signed by the seller, that transfers ownership of real estate. It contains the names of the buyer and seller and a legal description of the property sold.

The most common, as well as the most advantageous, type of deed is the *warranty deed,* which promises that the seller has the right to sell the property, that the seller owns the property, and that the property is free of encumbrances. If the purchase agreement contains no language as to the type of deed, the seller need only provide a *quit claim deed* or a *bargain and sales deed, without covenant against grantor,* which simply transfers ownership of the property without any warranties by the seller that the title is good.

Zoning ordinances. These ordinances regulate, by district, the uses of land and buildings for trade, industry, residence, and other purposes. The purpose of zoning is to protect the public's health, safety, morals, and general welfare. State and local governments, by making zoning ordinances, limit the size, height, density, and types of buildings that can be erected; regulate areas of open spaces, yards, and courts; and regulate and restrict the location of trade, industries, and buildings. (See "Are You Violating Zoning Laws?" in this chapter.)

Mortgage commitment. This is a written notice from a bank informing a loan applicant that it will grant the mortgage loan for the purchase of specified real estate under certain terms and conditions.

ANATOMY OF A PURCHASE CONTRACT

Whether you are buying or selling real estate, your first contact with the legalities of the closing will most likely be the purchase agreement. This is a legally binding contract that spells out all of the buyer's and seller's legal rights and obligations concerning the sale of the real estate. Ten basic legal requirements a purchase agreement must satisfy if it is to be valid include the following:

1. *Competent adults.* The buyer and seller each must be over the age of consent (18 in most states) and mentally competent.

2. *Warning.* According to the New York court case of *Duncan & Hill Realty v. Department of State,* the contract must contain a warning in boldface type: **This is a legally binding contract: If not fully understood, seek competent advice.**

3. *Names.* The names and addresses of the parties should be stated. If a corporation is a party to the contract, the type of corporation, the state of the incorporation, and the corporation's principal office or place of business should be stated.

    If a party is signing under a power of attorney, there must be a properly executed power of attorney document currently in existence. In most instances, real estate salespeople cannot sign as agents for their clients. The real estate agent's authority usually is limited to bringing the buyer and seller together. Salespeople can sign as agent only if they have specifically been granted the power to do so.

4. *Agreement.* The contract must contain an express agreement by one party to sell and by the other party to buy.

5. *Property description.* The purchase contract must contain a legal description of the real estate, which usually is obtained from the deed or title search. Street or lot numbers alone are insufficient.

6. *Price and terms of payment.* The contract should state the method of financing— whether there is going to be a mortgage assumption or a new bank mortgage, or whether the seller will hold the mortgage. In some states it is improper and constitutes illegal practice of law for a real estate broker to insert detailed legal terms of a seller-financed mortgage. Even in states where the services of an attorney are not required, prudent sellers and buyers will seek out the advice of an experienced real estate lawyer.

    If the contract is contingent upon the buyer's obtaining a mortgage commitment, the terms of the mortgage and the period of time the buyer has to obtain the mortgage commitment should be stated.

7. *Deed.* The seller must agree to transfer title to the buyer by deed. The type of deed should be specified, the warranty deed being the most desirable from the buyer's point of view.

8. *Closing.* The place, date, and hour of the closing must be specified. If there is a special reason for it to be held on the exact closing date specified in the contract, the contract should state that "time is of the essence."

   The closing will not necessarily take place on the exact date specified in the contract. Closing delays may arise because of a simultaneous purchase of another property by the seller, health department approval problems, title problems, delays in obtaining mortgage financing, or necessary repairs.

9. *Signatures.* The contract must be signed by both the buyer and the seller.

10. *Personal property.* The contract should also list any personal property included in the sale.

These are merely the basics of the purchase agreement and are by no means an exhaustive listing of everything that should be contained in the agreement.

INSPECTION CONTINGENCY

Make sure that the building you buy is structurally sound. The contract of sale should contain a contingency clause or rider providing that the contract is contingent on an inspection by a professional inspector, engineer, or construction expert at the buyer's expense. There are basically two types of such clauses:

1. If dissatisfied with the inspection report, the buyer may cancel the contract within a reasonable amount of time.

2. The buyer must give the seller an opportunity to repair any deficiencies set forth in the inspection report or agree to reduce the purchase price by the cost of repairing the deficiencies. If the seller decides not to make the repairs or reduce the purchase price and so notifies the buyer, the buyer may either remove the contingency and accept the house "as is" or cancel the contract and recover the down payment.

When using a contingency clause, keep the following four points in mind:

1. The first type of contingency is more advantageous for the buyer because it makes it easier for the buyer to cancel the contract and requires less communication with the seller.

2. The buyer should find a reputable inspector well in advance of signing the contract.

3. There is no such thing as a standard contract. Real estate contracts are negotiable. Variations can be made to previous contingencies depending on the circumstances.

4. Always consult with your attorney before signing the contract.

Real Estate Closing Documents

Are you bewildered by the mountain of paperwork at the real estate closing? This mountain is growing every year with more and more laws and regulations. To help you better understand these documents, below is a brief summary of most of the documents involved in a residential closing:

- A *deed,* which transfers ownership of real estate, contains the names of the buyer and seller and a legal description of the property sold. The most common, as well as the most advantageous, type of deed is the *warranty deed,* which promises that the seller has the right to sell the property and that the property is free of encumbrances.

- A *mortgage* creates a lien upon real estate as security for the payment of a debt. A separate *Note* is also signed by the borrowers in which they give a personal guarantee to repay the loan.

- *County/Town tax receipts* usually cover the period of January through December.

- *School tax receipts* usually cover the period of July 1 through June 30.

- *City or village tax receipts*

- A *certificate of occupancy* is a statement by a building inspector that the building complies with all building codes and zoning regulations. It is required for new construction or a building containing three or more units.

- A *village tax certificate or search* states that all taxes and water charges have been paid.

- An *occupancy tax receipt* states that the city occupancy tax has been paid.

- A *closing statement* contains adjustments for such items as the purchase price, down payment, assumed and seller-held mortgages, taxes, heating oil, rents, deposits, and flat water charges.

- A *judgment affidavit* states that the buyer or seller has no judgments, warrants, bankruptcies, or incompetency proceedings against him or her.

- An *amortization schedule* is prepared when there is a seller-held mortgage. It states the interest, principal, and balance owing on a monthly basis.

- *Water, refuse, and sewer receipts*

- An *assumption statement* and *escrow assignments* are used if the mortgage is being assumed. The statement sets forth the balance of the mortgage principal and escrow account. The assignment transfers the insurance and tax escrow from the seller to the buyer.

- HUD Form 1: *Disclosure/Settlement Statement,* which is required by the Real Estate Settlement and Procedures Act, contains all of the actual settlement costs and amounts.

- *Homeowners' insurance binder and receipt* must name the lender as a loss payee.

- A *mortgage discharge/satisfaction* is filed with the county clerk and removes the lien of the seller's mortgage.

- A *search,* also known as the *Abstract of Title,* is a historical digest of every document that has been recorded concerning a particular piece of property, including deeds, easements, mortgages, rights-of-way, oil and gas leases, bankruptcies, estate proceedings, tax liens, and judgments. Excerpts from each legal document are arranged chronologically with the names of the parties involved, the type of document, and the date the document was signed and recorded.

- The *survey* is a blueprint drawn by a surveyor showing the measurements, boundaries, and area of the property. It also shows fences, driveways, streams, and all buildings located on the property. Most real estate contracts require that a new survey be prepared.

- *Fee title insurance* is issued if the buyer objects to the seller's title. A mortgagee policy is usually required by the lending bank.

- A *release of lien of state estate tax* is necessary if a prior owner has died.

- A *mortgage commitment* is a written notice from a bank informing a loan applicant that it will grant the mortgage loan under certain terms and conditions.

- *Health department approval* of the septic system and well water

- A *smoke alarm affidavit* states that there is a smoke alarm on the property.

- A *transfer tax/credit line affidavit,* which is filed with all deeds and easements, is used to compute the state transfer and capital gains taxes.

- An *early occupancy agreement* is drafted if the purchaser is moving in before the closing and requires the purchaser to pay rent, utilities, and maintenance costs.

- A *real property transfer report* is a state board of equalization and assessment form containing the details of the sale and is forwarded to the village, city/town, county, and state property tax authorities.

- *IRS Form W-9* and *Seller's Information* are used to verify the seller's Social Security number and details of the sale according to income tax regulations (see forms in this chapter and Chapter 7).

- A *sump pump certificate* is required in some municipalities.

ENVIRONMENTAL CONSIDERATIONS

Environmental hazards can not only make real estate worthless, but they can subject buyers, sellers, and lenders to millions of dollars in clean-up costs, fines, and lawsuits. Under the Comprehensive Environmental Response, Compensation and Liability Act (Superfund) and numerous state laws, present and former owners and operators of real estate may be held liable for the consequences of environmental contamination caused by activities on their property.

Civil liability for environmental hazards is strict, joint, and several. Thus, for example, the banks, developers, construction companies, and real estate agents involved in a project to build a housing development on the former site of a wood-creosoting operation were all held to be potentially liable for damages.

The Superfund Amendments and Reauthorization Act of 1986 (SARA) created an exception under which an "innocent landowner" can escape the disastrous consequences of purchasing contaminated property. To be free from liability, the buyer must undertake all appropriate inquiries into the previous ownership and uses of the property consistent with good commercial or customary practice. It is necessary to establish that the buyer had no reason to know that any hazardous substance had been released or was disposed of at the facility at the time of acquisition.

Sellers of property do not escape their obligations by selling the property. The Superfund laws impose continual responsibility for waste disposal on past owners of property. Some states, such as New Jersey, require some type of environmental audit before closing.

Banks have been held liable for the cost of cleaning up hazardous dump sites merely because they took title to the site through foreclosure or became involved in a borrower's day-to-day operations (e.g., by serving on the board of directors). Therefore, banks require purchasers of commercial properties to provide an environmental assessment of the property.

Environmental Assessment

An initial environmental investigation or *assessment* identifies the presence of potential environmental problems associated with past activity on the property. The environmental company performing the investigation does the following:

- Examines the title search and county clerk's records for previous uses and owners of the property.
- Personally interviews the borrower, present owner, former owners, and neighbors.
- Visually inspects neighboring land and aerial photographs if available.
- Contacts federal and local government agencies regarding prior uses of the property and possible violations. This review includes (1) geological surveys from the U.S. Department of the Interior; (2) national priority lists of hazardous substances from the U.S. Environmental Protection Agency (EPA); (3) lists of active and inactive hazardous waste sites from a state department of environmental conservation; (4) environmental reviews from a county department of environment; (5) groundwater information from the U.S. Department of the Interior; (6) geological information from the appropriate state agency; (7) soil surveys from the U.S. Department of Agriculture; (8) zoning information and underground utilities from

a town zoning department; and (9) information regarding underground storage tanks and heating-oil tanks from a town assessor.

- Inspects the site for discolored ground; pipes protruding from the ground; oily puddles of water; absence of vegetation; discolored or odorous liquids; odors; waste containers; sources of drainage; roads; railroad tracks; paths; structures (standing or demolished); unpaved parking areas where PCPs may have been used for dust control; fuel storage and transfer lines; receiving or storage areas; pollution control equipment; sanitary, process-waste, and storm sewers and pump stations; asbestos; and urea formaldehyde wall insulation.

The buyer uses the environmental audit to help with the following:

- Decides whether to buy the property.
- Negotiates the final purchase price.
- Drafts contract provisions to protect the buyer from liability for the seller's past activities. (It is advisable to have indemnification clauses in the contract, but the seller may want to have an "as is" clause or a disclaimer referring to hazardous substances.)
- Determines which permits are needed. (The contract should also contain representations and warranties by the seller regarding existing and threatened litigation and proceedings, as well as compliance with environmental laws and site conditions.)
- Establishes a basis for the innocent-landowner defense.
- Determines what special insurance is necessary.
- Identifies potential future risks posed by site conditions other than past disposal areas. (An old PCB transformer, for example, may result in huge clean-up costs and liability for exposure to employees.)

Radon

Another environmental concern is *radon,* an invisible, odorless, radioactive gas emitted by certain rock formations that tends to accumulate in basements. Prolonged exposure to radon can cause lung cancer; however, inexpensive ventilation measures will usually reduce it to safe levels. To obtain information on radon testing, call either the federal hot line (800-SOS-RADON) or contact your state radon office.

Groundwater Contamination

Groundwater contamination occurs when (1) hazardous chemical wastes, pesticides, or other agricultural chemicals (e.g., fertilizer) seep down through the soil into underground water supplies; (2) faulty private septic systems, improperly maintained municipal sewer systems, or leaking industrial injection wells contaminate water supplies; and (3) underground storage tanks discharge gasoline, petroleum products, and other hazardous liquids into the soil and groundwater sources. For information on the EPA's drinking-water regulations and programs, call its hot line at 800-426-4791.

Sick Buildings

Buildings can pose health hazards from materials used for construction, utilities, and insulation (including asbestos, water pipes containing lead, lead paint, and urea formaldehyde insulation). Improper application of termite pesticides can contaminate the air for years.

Formaldehyde is a colorless, gaseous chemical compound that is generally present at low, variable concentrations in both indoor and outdoor air. It is emitted by many construction materials and consumer products that contain formaldehyde-based glues, resins, preservatives, and bonding agents. Formaldehyde also is an ingredient in foam that was used for building insulation until the early 1980s.

Whether the task of reducing formaldehyde levels is a simple or complex one depends on the source of the gas. Initial procedures often include steps to increase ventilation and improve the circulation of outside air through the building. If new furniture, drapery, or other sources are contributing to higher-than-normal levels of formaldehyde, removal of these items or limiting the number of new items introduced into the building may be all that is needed.

In some instances, subflooring or walls may be the source of formaldehyde, or foam insulation between inner and outer walls may be emitting the gas. If increased ventilation does not produce acceptable results in these instances, you may be required to remove the formaldehyde-bearing material. Such procedures are costly, time-consuming, and will temporarily disrupt your business operations.

Extreme care should be exercised in handling, cleaning, or working with material suspected of containing asbestos. Asbestos-containing material should be left in place if it is in good condition and is in an area where it is not likely to be disturbed. If the material is likely to be banged, rubbed, handled, or taken apart—especially during remodeling—hire a trained contractor and reduce your exposure as much as possible. Common construction and remodeling operations can release varying amounts of asbestos fibers. These operations include hammering, drilling, sawing, sanding, cutting, and otherwise shaping or molding the material. Routine cleaning operations (such as brushing, dusting, vacuum cleaning, scraping, and scrubbing) also can release hazardous fibers from asbestos-containing materials. Vinyl flooring products that contain asbestos can be cleaned in a conventional manner, but these products can release some asbestos fibers if they are vigorously sanded, ground, drilled, filed, or scraped.

The repair or removal of asbestos-containing products generally is a complicated process. It depends on the amount of these products present, the percentage of asbestos they contain, and the manner in which asbestos is incorporated into the product. Total removal of even small amounts of asbestos-containing material is usually the last alternative. You should contact local, state, or federal health or consumer product agencies before deciding on a course of action. To ensure safety and elimination of health hazards, asbestos repair or removal should be performed only by properly trained contractors.

Many remodeling contractors do not yet have the requisite tools, training, experience, or equipment to work safely with asbestos or to remove it from a home. Furthermore, asbestos removal workers are protected under federal regulations that specify special training, protective clothing, and special respirators.

The Toxic Substances Control Act (TSCA) Assistance Information Service Hot Line (202-554-1404) provides both general and technical information and publications about toxic substances (including asbestos) and offers services to help businesses comply with TSCA laws (including regulatory advice and aid, publications, and audiovisual materials).

Warning: It is extremely important for both the seller and buyer of property to discover existing and potential environmental problems before the closing. No matter how the purchase agreement is drafted to provide protection to the buyer and the seller, the government can still proceed against both the buyer and the seller while litigation is pending between them. If you have questions on the Resource Conservation and Recovery Act and the Comprehensive Environmental Response, Compensation and Liability Act (Superfund), call the hot line at 800-424-9346.

LEAD POISONING: THE SILENT DISEASE

Lead affects virtually every system of the body. Although it is harmful to individuals of all ages, lead exposure can be especially damaging to children, fetuses, and women of childbearing age. As recent studies have identified previously unrecognized effects, there has been increasing concern about lead levels in the blood once thought to be safe. Since 1978, the Centers for Disease Control and Prevention (CDC) has lowered the blood lead level of concern from 60 ug/dL (micrograms per deciliter) to 10 ug/dL.

Lead poisoning has been called "the silent disease" because its effects may occur gradually and imperceptibly, often showing no obvious symptoms. Blood lead levels as low as 10 ug/dL have been associated with learning disabilities, growth impairments, permanent hearing and visual impairment, and other damage to the brain and nervous systems. In large doses, lead exposure can cause brain damage, convulsions, and even death. Lead exposure before or during pregnancy can also alter fetal development and cause miscarriages.

In 1991, the Secretary of the Department of Health and Human Services (HHS) characterized lead poisoning as the "number one environmental threat to the health of children in the United States." Although the percentage of children with elevated blood lead levels has declined over the past 20 years, millions of U.S. children still have blood lead levels high enough to threaten their health. The Third National Health and Nutrition Examination Survey (NHANES III) indicates that over the past two decades, the average child's blood lead level has decreased from 12.8 ug/dL to 2.8 ug/dL. NHANES III also indicates, however, that in 1991 approximately 1.7 million U.S. children under the age of six still had blood lead levels that exceeded the CDC 10 ug/dL level of concern.

Efforts to reduce exposure to lead from sources like gasoline and food cans have played a large role in past reductions of blood lead levels in the United States. Despite these successes, a significant human health hazard remains from improperly managed lead-based paint. From the turn of the century through the 1940s, paint manufacturers used lead as a primary ingredient in many oil-based interior and exterior house paints. Usage gradually decreased through the 1950s and 1960s as largely lead-free latex paints became more popular. Although the Consumer Products Safety Commission (CPSC) banned lead-based paints from residential use in 1978 (currently, paints may not have more than .06 percent of lead by weight), EPA and HUD estimate that 83 percent of the privately owned housing units built in the United States before 1980 contain some lead-based paint. By these estimations, approximately 64 million homes may contain lead-based paint that may pose a hazard to the occupants if not managed properly.

Lead from exterior house paint can flake off or leach into the soil around the outside of a home, contaminating children's playing areas. Dust caused during normal lead-based paint wear (especially around windows and doors) can create a hard-to-see film over surfaces in a house. In some cases, cleaning and renovation activities can increase the threat of lead-based paint exposure by dispersing fine lead dust particles in the air and over accessible household surfaces. If managed improperly, both adults and children can receive hazardous exposure by inhaling the fine dust or by ingesting paint dust during hand-to-mouth activities. Children under age six are especially susceptible to lead poisoning. See the forms at the end of this chapter and Chapter 15 for the lead disclosure forms that are required in the sale or rental of properties built before 1978.

LEASE WITH OPTION TO PURCHASE

A lease with option to purchase can be advantageous to both buyers and sellers of real estate. Sellers have more security than they would if they held a mortgage because they retain ownership of the property. In addition, they continue to receive rental income and enjoy income tax deductions. Another function of the option is that it gives potential buyers more time to qualify for mortgage financing.

Under the lease with an option to buy, a tenant rents the property until he or she moves out or exercises the option. The renter's right to purchase the property depends on the terms of the particular lease involved.

The option may be either absolute or conditional upon the landlord's desire to sell. Under a lease provision giving the tenant the first option to buy the property in the event the landlord decides to sell, the landlord, on receiving an offer from a third party, must then offer the property to the tenant on the same terms. This *right of first refusal* comes into play only when the owner offers the property for sale to others.

Legal Title

An option to purchase does not give the tenant legal title to the real estate. The tenant becomes a purchaser only upon exercise of the option, at which time the landlord-tenant relationship ceases and the option becomes an absolute and binding contract of sale.

Purchase Price

The lease option may contain a provision giving the tenant the first option to buy at a certain price if the landlord decides to sell or the right to purchase the property at the price offered to the landlord by another prospective buyer. The lease may provide for the tenant to receive credit toward the purchase price for rent paid or the value of the unexpired period of the lease.

The Due-on-Sale Clause

A *due-on-sale clause* in a mortgage permits the bank to call the mortgage due when the property is sold, thus preventing the buyer from assuming the mortgage. Whether the due-on-sale clause will be triggered by the lease with an option to buy depends on the terms of the seller's mortgage and the particular lease involved. The lease with an option to buy may be a way of avoiding the due-on-sale clause, at least until the tenant exercises the option to purchase. However, you should have an attorney review your mortgage to determine whether it has a due-on-sale clause, what type of clause it is, and whether the particular lease option

will trigger it. The mortgage also may have a provision forbidding leasing of the property.

The option should be recorded with the county clerk to put others on notice of the tenant's rights, thus preventing the seller from selling to another buyer. However, a seller that has financial problems during the lease term may not be able to give the tenant good title when the option is exercised.

To make the best use of the lease with an option to buy, consult an attorney.

THE UPS AND DOWNS OF OFFICE CONDOS

You can enjoy the convenience of renting an office while you obtain the tax deductions and special capital gains treatment available to an owner. You can have all of these conveniences and benefits if you buy an office condominium. The condominium method of ownership is becoming increasingly popular for office, home, and vacation use, especially as the result of increased building and land costs.

What Is a Condominium?

In a condominium, or a condo, you own a separate unit in a multiunit project. You have your own deed, mortgage, and property tax bill. You also have an undivided interest or share in the common areas and facilities that serve the project, including land, roofs, basements, floors, stairways, lobbies, elevators, halls, parking lots, heating plants, and recreational and community rooms.

Your ownership interest in the common areas are determined by the ratio of the value of your unit to the total value of all units. This ratio determines (1) your voting power in the condominium owners' association, (2) your share of the maintenance costs of the common areas, (3) your property taxes, and (4) the amount a bank will be willing to lend you for a mortgage. Maintenance costs are collected either in the form of rent or as a monthly assessment.

Condo owners must obey the rules and regulations governing the use and occupancy of both their own unit and the common areas. They cannot be evicted for violating the rules, but they may be subject to court action resulting in the filing of liens or ordering compliance with the declaration.

The Declaration

The condominium is formed by recording the *declaration,* which includes a legal description of the land, the building, the units and the common areas; a statement of each owner's rights and duties regarding the common areas; a statement of the use for which the buildings are intended; the method by which the declaration may be amended; and the measures to be taken against delinquent owners. It gives authority and power, through the bylaws, to the condo association's board of directors.

The declaration and a copy of the floor plans of the building showing the layout, locations, and dimensions of each office unit must be recorded before any units are sold.

Check the Bylaws

The bylaws spell out the internal administration and operation of the condominium development, including building maintenance, budgeting, assessment, elections, capital improvements, and occupant control. A copy of the bylaws must be attached to the declaration. The bylaws cannot be modified or amended unless so stated in a recorded amendment to the declaration.

Shopping for a Condo

When shopping for a condominium, you should not sign a subscription or purchase agreement or any other sales contract until you have done at least the following:

- Reviewed all of the basic condominium documents and informational material disclosing the terms of sale: the offering statement, declaration, bylaws, management agreement, and regulatory agreement. Obtain legal advice if you do not understand these documents because they spell out your legal rights and obligations as a condominium owner.
- Inspected the operating budget to determine the amount of monthly assessments for maintenance and related expenses of the common areas, and determined whether these expenses were underestimated. The extent of your obligation in buying a condo is not limited to the cost of your individual unit. The monthly assessments are in addi-tion to your mortgage, tax, and insurance payments.
- Made sure that there is sufficient liability and fire insurance and workers' compensation covering the entire condo development. The insurance policy should name as insured the board of directors and each unit owner individually as co-owner.
- Seen whether there were any restrictions on your right to resell the condo.

If you are buying a used condo,

- ask whether there are any amendments or proposed amendments to the declaration or bylaws;
- study a recently audited financial statement;
- ask whether there are any pending lawsuits involving the association or any special assessments;
- ask for a copy of the rules and regulations and proof that the present owner's dues are paid in full; and
- find out how the condo is managed; the builder's and manager's reputations; the quality and condition of plumbing, electrical, and heating systems; and whether the budget has an adequate reserve fund for major expenses, such as a leaking roof or replacement of the furnace.

Condo versus Co-op

Unlike a condo owner, the occupant of a cooperative does not actually own his or her unit but is instead a corporate shareholder and tenant. The tenant pays his or her share of the cost of operation, maintenance, repairs, taxes, mortgage, insurance, and other expenses for the whole project and also maintains his or her own unit.

Each tenant is personally liable for the entire blanket mortgage debt as well as the purchase of the required number of shares of stock. There is only one mortgage and tax bill for the entire project. Each tenant has one vote and elects a board of directors.

The main advantage of the condo over the co-op is the fact that the condo unit, being separately owned, can be separately mortgaged. The condo owner has only his or her own mortgage payments to keep up. The co-op building is usually covered by a blanket mortgage. If one or more tenants default in paying their share of the monthly carrying charges, the other tenants may have to make up the deficit to prevent foreclosure of the mortgage. The condo owner, unlike the co-op tenant, has a choice of whether to have a mortgage. Because co-op tenants are tied down with a co-op mortgage, a co-op is harder to sell than a condo.

In both co-ops and condos, the bylaws may require consent to transfer any unit. The purpose of the restrictions must be lawful and not discriminatory.

WHEN IS TITLE INSURANCE NECESSARY?

Do you have title insurance coverage on your real estate? Title insurance is quite different from other forms of insurance. The function of most other forms of insurance is risk assumption under which the insurance company pays for losses arising out of an unforeseen future event such as death or accident. The primary purpose of title insurance, however, is to eliminate risks and prevent losses caused by defects in the real estate title arising from past events. There are two types of title insurance policies: (1) the mortgagee policy, and (2) the fee policy (owner's policy).

If you are financing a real estate purchase with a mortgage, most banks require that you obtain mortgagee title insurance. The mortgagee policy is issued only to the bank holding the mortgage and does not protect you even though the bank requires you to pay for it. Only your own fee policy will protect you if you try to sell or refinance your real estate and discover that your title is defective. The mortgagee policy ensures for the bank that the mortgage is a valid lien on the property.

If you have a fee policy, the title company will reimburse you for any financial losses resulting from title defects that were not discovered by a search of the public records. The title company will also pay for all legal expenses in defense of your title. The title defect could be a prior invalid deed, a deed by someone of unsound mind, or a mistake in the recording of legal documents. The deed may have been forged, or the seller may have received the deed from an estate in which an heir was deliberately left out of the estate proceedings and may later claim rights to your property. The title insurance company would reimburse you for your losses from the heir's claim and/or pay your expenses of defending

the heir's lawsuit. A title insurance policy the seller had when purchasing the property will not protect you.

Special Condominium Problems

Condominiums pose unique title problems, thus creating special needs for title insurance. Strict compliance with state laws is necessary to create a valid condominium. If the documents that created the condominium were improperly drawn up, serious title problems may result. Condominium owners without title insurance protection may be unable to sell or refinance their units. They may face problems when the builder doesn't construct the condominium unit according to the original specifications and the condominium declaration or master deed doesn't provide or allow for these deviations. Condominium owners are also adversely affected by restrictive covenants in the use and occupation of the unit and by nonconformance with state condominium laws.

The Title Insurance Policy

Title insurance will not provide total protection for you or the bank. The title insurance policy guarantees that at the time you receive the deed from the seller, the title is marketable except as specified in the certificate of title. The title company issues a certificate of title stating the policy terms, exceptions, condition of the property, and all title objections, such as encumbrances and title defects on public record. Excepted from coverage are documents that are on public record, such as mortgages and tax liens; defects and encumbrances that occur after the policy date; zoning and building ordinance violations; unpaid water bills; and any problems that a survey would reveal.

A one-time premium, based on the purchase price of the real estate, is charged for the fee policy. The mortgagee policy premium is based on the amount of the mortgage. A mortgagee policy is cheaper if it is purchased simultaneously with the fee policy.

Title insurance is not a substitute for an attorney's advice. When you enter into a contract to buy real estate, consult an attorney to determine whether you will need title insurance.

CAN THE BANK FORECLOSE YOUR MORTGAGE?

Do you realize that even if you make your mortgage payments, your bank may have the right to foreclose its mortgage if you fail to pay taxes or keep your property in repair? Do you know whether you can prepay your mortgage?

The following discussion outlines your rights and obligations under your mortgage. Basically, a *mortgage* is a written instrument that creates a lien upon real estate as security for the payment of a debt. A mortgage gives the bank (or any other person holding the mortgage) security for the loan by creating a lien on the land, just as a docketed judgment or mechanic's lien does.

The bank records the mortgage with the county clerk so that people subsequently dealing with the real estate are on notice of the existence of the lien. The mortgage continues to be a lien on the property until the mortgage debt is paid in full. If the mortgage is not paid, the bank can enforce its lien by foreclosure.

Is the Bank Entitled to Possession or Title?

A mortgage does not give the bank title to the real estate. The owner has legal title to the real estate and the right to keep possession until foreclosure. The owner, even if in default, is entitled to possession of the real estate and can be deprived of possession only if the real estate is foreclosed.

Prepayment Penalties

Generally, the owner has no right to prepay the mortgage if there is no agreement permitting it. Without prepayment privileges, the owner cannot pay off the mortgage even though the property is destroyed or the owner wishes to refinance when interest rates decline.

Acceleration Clause

The acceleration clause is one of the most important clauses of the mortgage. It enables the bank to declare the whole debt due and sue for foreclosure, not only for the payments in default, but for the entire amount of the mortgage balance.

The owner's default in the performance of any agreement contained in the mortgage does not operate to accelerate the debt unless there is a clear and specific clause permitting it. If there is such a provision, there may be acceleration of the debt upon the owner's failure to pay a principal or interest installment; pay taxes, water rates, and assessments; assign or deliver fire insurance policies to the bank; reimburse the bank for fire insurance premiums; furnish a statement of the amount due on the mortgage and whether there are any offsets or defenses against the mortgage debt; keep the property in repair; obtain the bank's consent for alterations; make payment on a prior mortgage; or complete construction without delay.

A provision authorizing acceleration must be strictly followed before the bank may exercise its right to accelerate. The conditions for acceleration usually are the borrower's (mortgagor's) default for a specific length of time and a notice of default supplied by the lender (mortgagee).

However, no particular conditions to acceleration are required, and the parties are free to specify any they wish. Thus, if there are no provisions for notice and demand, they are not prerequisites to acceleration.

Foreclosure

A *mortgage foreclosure* is a lawsuit by which the bank uses the acceleration clause to enforce its lien on the real estate. The most common method of mortgage foreclosure is a court action seeking a judgment, which fixes the balance due on the mortgage (principal and interest), orders a judicially controlled sale of the property, and applies the sale proceeds to payment of the mortgage debt. The court appoints an attorney as a referee to compute the total amount due and to supervise the foreclosure sale.

Regardless of what the mortgage says, the owner has an absolute right to save the real estate from foreclosure by paying the mortgage off before the foreclosure sale. The owner must pay the court the amount due for principal and interest and the costs and expenses of the foreclosure action. The bank may purchase the property at the foreclosure sale.

If a balance is still owing after the foreclosure auction, the bank may obtain a deficiency judgment that can be enforced against any of the owner's assets.

This is only a basic overview of mortgage law. You should read your own mortgage to determine your particular rights and obligations.

IS YOUR BUSINESS A "NUISANCE"?

No one has the absolute freedom to use real estate as he or she wishes. A property owner cannot unreasonably use property to the injury and detriment of a neighbor's legal rights.

There are two categories of nuisances: (1) private nuisances, and (2) public nuisances. A *private nuisance* is interference with the use and enjoyment of land. The law of private nuisances is a law of degree and involves the question of fact as to whether the use is reasonable under all of the particular circumstances.

The nuisance need not drive neighbors from their property. It is enough that neighbors' enjoyment of their property is rendered uncomfortable; however, the injury must be material and actual, not just causing discomfort. That which is merely disagreeable, which simply displeases the eye, offends the taste, or shocks an oversensitive nature is not a nuisance, no matter how irritating or unpleasant. Although the conduct need not be habitual or periodical, a nuisance must generally be of a continuous or recurring nature.

What Is Reasonable Use?

Whether the use of property is reasonable regarding the comfortable enjoyment of property generally depends on such factors as (1) the location, nature of the use, extent and frequency of the injury, and effect on health and the enjoyment of property; (2) the character of the surrounding neighborhood and such activities as are naturally incident to the character of the vicinity and the nature of the adjacent property; and (3) the economic benefits to others and the relative economic status of the parties.

Examples of nuisances are open burning by a city in a landfill, discharge by a cement company of large quantities of dust on neighboring properties, excessive vibration from blasting, fences over ten feet tall that deprive neighbors of light and air, the stench from a stable that forces a homeowner to keep the windows closed, and a pile of sand blowing onto and damaging a neighbor's property.

Remedies

There are two remedies available to a person damaged by a nuisance: (1) a money damage award, or (2 a court order restraining the nuisance or directing the removal of it. A suit for negligence and trespass may also be involved.

Parties to the Lawsuit

When a nuisance diminishes the property value of rental property, only the owner, even if not in actual possession of the property, can sue. Where both rental and property values are affected, both the landlord and tenant may sue.

An owner's liability for a nuisance continues even after the property is sold and until the new owner has had reasonable opportunity to discover the condition and to make necessary repairs. A tenant is not responsible for a nuisance unless it is shown that the tenant had notice of the existence of the nuisance or had enough time to obtain knowledge of it.

Public Nuisances

A *public nuisance* is a crime involving injury to the public. A criminal or public nuisance occurs when a person either (1) by unlawful or unreasonable conduct knowingly or recklessly creates or maintains a condition endangering the safety or health of a considerable number of persons, or (2) knowingly conducts or maintains a premise where persons gather to engage in unlawful conduct, such as prostitution or drug dealing. A person who suffers a private and particular injury from a public nuisance may sue to stop the nuisance and recover special damages.

DON'T LOSE YOUR PROPERTY TO A SQUATTER

You can actually lose ownership of your land through a law known as *adverse possession* that is a remnant of ancient times, when title to property was determined by possession rather than by deed.

You should always investigate for potential squatter's rights if you are considering purchasing real property that is occupied by someone other than the seller. If the seller claims the occupant is a tenant, demand to see a lease and interview the tenant. If the property in question is unimproved but is maintained in some form (whether fenced, mowed, or cultivated), then determine who has been paying for the maintenance.

Through adverse possession, those who remain on property for ten or more continuous years (depending on the state) acquire legal title to that property if the possession is as follows:

- *Hostile to the owner's rights.* Possessors must not have had a relationship of trust and confidence with the owner (e.g., husband-wife, father-son, employer-employee) and must possess the land without the owner's consent.

- *Under a claim of right or title.* Possessors, by their acts or conduct, claim to be the owner of the land.

- *Open and notorious.* The possession must be noticeable to the owner.

- *Exclusive.* Possessors must hold the land for themselves as their own and not for another.

- *Actual.* The property is either cultivated or improved (including mowing) or protected by a substantial enclosure (such as a fence). Possessors need not actually live or reside on the land.

Similar rules also apply to an *easement* (the right to use land, usually as a driveway or a path). The main difference between acquiring land by adverse possession and acquiring an "easement by prescription" is that the property does not have to be actually possessed but merely used.

These are only the basic requirements for adverse possession. The advice of an attorney, who has examined all of the surrounding facts, would be necessary to determine whether the adverse possession law applies to a particular situation.

HISTORICAL
PRESERVATION DISTRICTS

An increased interest in historical preservation districts recently is a result of the rapid rise in city property values, the back-to-the-city movement, nostalgic appreciation, and the high cost of new construction. Property values in some preservation districts are accelerating at a greater rate than certain suburban areas.

Although many people believe historical preservation laws apply only to residential buildings, that perception is incorrect. Many lengthy and worthy lawsuits have centered on the renovations of former factories, office buildings, and other commercial properties. Preservation ordinances protect buildings from any alteration or demolition that is not in keeping with the historical character of a district.

The purpose of local, state, and federal historical preservation laws is to

- protect, enhance, and perpetuate buildings of special character or the special historic or aesthetic interest of districts that represent a city's cultural, social, economic, political, and architectural history;

- stabilize and improve property values in historical preservation districts;

- foster civic pride in the beauty and noble accomplishments of the past;

- protect and enhance a city's attractions to tourists and visitors, and support and stimulate business and industry; and

- strengthen a city's economy and broaden its tax base by encouraging the use of historic and aesthetic buildings that have architectural value.

Before making exterior structural changes to a building in a preservation district in New York state, a *certificate of appropriateness* must be obtained from a landmark and preservation board. The certificate is not a substitute for requirements of zoning board regulations. The purpose of a preservation board is not a zoning purpose to protect public health, safety, and welfare generally but rather to determine whether a proposed improvement is consistent with a preservation ordinance's purpose to preserve the integrity of the areas and structures that have been determined to merit special protection. The board's main consideration is not whether the improvement is beautiful or tasteful, or even whether it promotes noise or quiet, but rather whether it interferes with the preservation of the character and values of the district.

If a preservation board has denied an application for a certificate of appropriateness or an application for a notice to proceed, an applicant may appeal to the Committee on Legislation of the Common Council.

A *notice to proceed* may be issued by a preservation commission or a legislation committee if the applicant has established that a strict application of the provisions of the law will create an extreme hardship. A notice to proceed is an authorization for work that requires a certificate of appropriateness but does not meet the standards for issuance of a certificate.

A notice to proceed may not be granted unless the applicant proves that the land or building cannot yield a reasonable financial return if the proposed construction or demolition is not permitted; that the proposed alteration, construction, removal, or demolition will not alter the essential character of any preservation site; and that the hardship has not resulted from an omission by the landowner.

In addition to city ordinances, state laws require state governments to exert leadership, accelerate their historic preservation programs and activities, give maximum encouragement and assistance to agencies and individuals undertaking preservation by private means, encourage and assist local governments and local preservation programs, and cooperate with the federal government in such programs.

Check with your tax adviser concerning the tax benefits for rehabilitating historical buildings.

HOW TO REDUCE YOUR PROPERTY TAXES

Property taxes are a cost of doing business and owning real estate that can be reduced. The tax assessor does not have the final word concerning your property taxes. Many property owners have successfully reduced their property tax bills.

Definitions

To understand how to reduce your property taxes, you should understand the following "words of art" used in the New York state tax procedure:

- *Appraisal*—the judgment of your property's market value by an assessor or appraisal firm

- *Fair market value*—the sale price that you could get for your property in an ordinary real estate transaction

- *Assessment*—the assessor's determination of the value of your property for real property tax purposes expressed as either the full amount of the appraised value or a fraction of the appraised value

- *Assessment roll*—the assessor's list that gives an approximate assessment of every piece of property in the tax district

- *Tax rate*—the rate applied to the assessed valuation to determine your real property tax bill that is usually stated as the number of dollars per thousand of assessed value

Determine Your Property's Market Value

To know whether your assessment is unfair, you must first determine your property's present fair market value. A real estate broker can provide you with an estimate of your property's market value. Three grounds on which an assessment may be reduced are overvaluation, inequality, and illegality.

Overvaluation. Overvaluation occurs when property is assessed higher than its fair market value. The property is usually assessed too high because a mistake was made about the size or character of the building and lot.

Inequality. Inequality occurs when your property is appraised at a higher proportion of its value than other properties in the area. To reduce your assessment, you must prove that your property is assessed at a higher percentage of its fair market value than the average of all property on the assessment roll. To prove inequality, you must compare numerous properties. If you took a sample of a few properties in your town, each with a market value of $60,000 and an assessed value of $20,000, the ratio of market value to assessed value would be 3:1. If the market value of your property is $50,000 and the assessed value is $25,000, an inequality of assessment has occurred. The ratio of market value to the assessed value of your property is 2:1 as compared to the ratio of 3:1 for other properties.

Illegality. An illegal assessment is one placed on a piece of real estate that is legally exempt from property taxation, such as a church.

The Local Hearing

You have the right to challenge your property assessment at a local hearing before .the appropriate administrative body after a board of assessment review. If your assessment has been increased, a notice will be mailed to you. If you feel that your assessment is unfair, you must file a written complaint requesting the board to review your case at the hearing. A board of assessment review will hear your complaint and determine if the final assessment is correct.

To prepare your assessment reduction case, first examine the assessor's report for errors, such as an incorrect description of the property, incorrect room dimensions, or any other details of the property.

Inspect the assessment rolls at the assessor's office. Compare the actual cost of your property with the assessed valuation. If your purchase price is substantially lower than the assessed valuation and you purchased the property recently, this information will be helpful to your case.

If you have income property, see if there are any errors, such as an incorrect statement of rental income or expenses. Study your records of rental income and expenses for the past few years. The earning capacity of income property is the most important factor in determining its market value for reducing your tax assessment.

Compare the market value and assessed valuations of comparable property in your area. Comparable properties are those of the same size and floor space on similar lots in similar neighborhoods.

The testimony of expert witnesses is usually the most important part of your case. Building experts and real estate experts, such as appraisers, should be used; a real estate expert, for example, can testify about the market value of your property.

If a board of assessment review fails to correct your assessment after a hearing, you have the right to challenge its decision in court. If you do, you must serve a petition and notice on the assessor. You will have the burden of proving that the assessment is erroneous or illegal.

You and the municipality may hire appraisers to appraise sample properties in the area and give their opinions of the market value of your property. They will testify as to what they believe the assessed valuation should be.

If the court determines that the assessment is illegal, it will order the assessment to be stricken from the rolls. If the court determines that the assessment is erroneous or unequal, it will order a reassessment to correct the assessment roll.

ARE YOU VIOLATING ZONING LAWS?

You are not free to do as you wish with your property. You may be in violation of zoning ordinances and building codes even if you make what you believe is a modest change to existing real property.

If you sign a purchase agreement to buy real estate that is in violation of zoning ordinances or not zoned for the needs to which you wish to put it, you cannot get out of the contract.

The following discussion examines the basic aspects of zoning and how you can challenge zoning ordinances.

What Is Zoning?

Zoning ordinances regulate, by districts, the uses of land and buildings for trade, industry, residence, and other purposes. The purpose of zoning is to protect the public's health, safety, morals, and general welfare. By enacting zoning ordinances, state and local governments limit the size, height, density, and types of buildings to be erected; regulate areas of open spaces, yards, and courts; and regulate and restrict the location of trades, industries, and buildings.

Zoning ordinances define what cannot be put on land, such as junkyards and factories.

Zoning Districts

Boundaries are established for each zoning district. A municipality is divided into various types of districts that permit agricultural use, one-family residential use, two-family residential use, industrial use, business use, trailer camp and park use, or open-space use. Each municipality has its own system of classifying zoning districts. A residential use, for example, in one municipality may permit professionals or certain business offices to operate out of a home.

Retroactivity

Zoning laws are not retroactive. A building in existence at the time a zoning law is adopted cannot be declared illegal. But if the illegal structure is destroyed, the owner may rebuild only in accordance with present zoning laws without substantially enlarging the building.

Variances

A variance authorizes a landowner to use property in a manner forbidden by the zoning ordinance if the zoning creates particular difficulties or unnecessary hardships. The two categories are area variances and use variances.

An *area variance* affects the size of the property, such as a one-acre variance sought by a landowner who owns 1.9 acres and sells one lot, leaving him with 0.9 of an acre.

A *use variance* affects how land can be used in a particular neighborhood, such as the use of property for a gasoline station in a residential neighborhood. An application for a use variance must show that the zoning law imposes an undue hardship.

For a change of use, the owner may be required to show a special hardship—that is, proof in the form of dollars and cents that the property does not yield a reasonable return. The owner-applicant is required to show that the land cannot yield a reasonable return if used only for the purpose allowed in that zone, the owner's plight is due to unique circumstances and not to the general conditions in the neighborhood, and the use to be authorized by the variance will not alter the locality's essential character.

If your application for a variance is rejected, you may appeal to the courts.

Unconstitutional Zoning

Zoning regulations must be reasonable, uniform, and not unduly oppressive to landowners. If a zoning ordinance unreasonably restricts the uses of a district, it can be attacked as being unconstitutional. There must be specific damage, however, to bring such a lawsuit. Although a landowner does not have to own property actually situated within the zoned area, the land must be adversely affected by the zoning law.

Zoning is constitutional if reasonable consideration has been given to the character of

the district, its suitability for a particular use, the conservation of property values, and well-planned building development.

If you plan to alter property you are buying or use it for a business, check with an attorney before signing the purchase contract to determine whether you will be walking into a zoning law problem.

ARE YOU GUILTY OF HOUSING DISCRIMINATION?

Even if you aren't a landlord or property owner, you may be sued for housing discrimination. Discrimination laws apply to real estate brokers, building contractors, mortgage lenders, appraisers, real estate salespeople, and property managers as well as landlords and property owners. It is an unlawful, discriminatory practice to

- refuse to sell, rent, or lease based on a prospective buyer's or tenant's race, creed, age, color, national origin, religion, sex, marital status, physical or mental handicap, or having children;

- discriminate in the terms of the sale, rental, or lease of housing or services in connection with housing; or

- print or circulate any statement, advertisement, or publication for the purchase, rental, or lease of housing that discriminates.

Racial Discrimination

The following are examples of racial discrimination:

- *Racial steering*—showing houses or apartments in certain locations only to whites while showing other locations to minorities

- *Blockbusting*—representing that a neighborhood is deteriorating (because its racial or ethnic composition is changing) in order to cause panic selling of houses

- *A refusal to rent or sell*—refusing to rent or sell an available apartment or house on the basis of race, such as falsely telling a black person that a house or apartment has been sold and then showing it to a white person

- *Redlining*—the refusal of banks and insurance companies to grant mortgages or insurance in predominantly minority areas

- *Price variations*—quoting one price or rent to whites and another to minorities

Housing discrimination plaintiffs must prove

1. they are a member of a racial minority;
2. they applied for and were qualified to rent or purchase a certain property or housing;
3. that the plaintiff was rejected; and
4. the housing or rental opportunity remained available thereafter.

Once a plaintiff has established these four facts, the burden shifts to the defendant to rebut the presumption of discrimination by showing a legitimate nondiscriminatory reason for rejecting the plaintiff.

Other Types of Discrimination

Discrimination based on a person's disability is prohibited under state and federal law. It is illegal to discriminate against blind or deaf persons by refusing to allow seeing-eye dogs or dogs assisting the deaf under a "no pets" policy. In some states it is a criminal misdemeanor to refuse to rent to a tenant who has children or to evict tenants who subsequently have children.

Who Is Covered?

Federal laws apply to sellers, landlords, real estate brokers, real estate salespeople, building contractors, and those who sublet. However, there are exemptions for senior citizen housing and where local, state, or federal laws restrict the maximum number of occupants permitted to occupy a dwelling. The law does not apply to single-family houses sold or rented by an owner who does not use a real estate broker or publish an advertisement.

Complaints

Discrimination complaints may be filed with either a state attorney general, a state division of human rights, the U.S. Department of Housing and Urban Development (HUD), or a U.S. district court. Complaints on the federal level in district court must be made within two years, and those to HUD must be made within one year after the discriminatory housing practice.

If discrimination charges are issued, the case will go either to an administrative law judge who can award compensatory damages, issue injunctions, and assess civil penalties or to a U.S. district court for trial. The penalties are $10,000 for the first offense, $25,000 for the second offense within the past five years, $50,000 for the third violation, and $100,000 for any subsequent violation.

Complaints against real estate brokers and salespeople are made to a state's licensing department for appropriate action. The exhaustion of administrative remedies is not required as it is in other types of discrimination cases. You may bring an action concurrently with the administrative body and the courts. A plaintiff can sue for attorney fees, punitive damages, and actual damages. A tester who is sent by a housing agency to investigate discrimination can also sue for discrimination.

HUD may issue discrimination charges within 100 days after a complaint is filed if it determines that (1) reasonable cause exists to believe a discriminatory housing practice has occurred or is about to occur, and (2) conciliation cannot be reached. Conciliation is the attempted resolution of issues raised by a complaint, or by the investigation of such complaint, through informal negotiations involving the aggrieved person, the person accused of an unfair housing practice, and HUD.

Handicap-Accessible Apartments

Landlords must allow handicapped tenants, at the tenant's expense, to make reasonable and necessary modifications to an apartment. The tenant must restore the premises to its original condition on vacating the apartment. Newly constructed four-unit multifamily apartments must be designed to accommodate the physically handicapped, including doors, light switches, electrical outlets, thermostats, bathroom grab bars, and kitchens.

THE LANDLORD'S DUTY TO MITIGATE

Whether landlords have a duty to mitigate their damages when a tenant moves out by renting the property depends on the particular state and sometimes on the particular county involved. Some jurisdictions impose a duty on landlords to mitigate damages after a tenant wrongfully abandons the premises before the end of the lease. On a tenant's wrongful abandonment in the "no mitigation" jurisdictions, landlords may follow any of these four options:

1. Accept a substitute tenant offered by the defaulting tenant. (The original tenant, however, remains liable to the landlord in the event the substitute tenant defaults.)

2. Accept the abandonment of the property as a surrender by the tenant, thereby terminating the tenancy, and enter into possession and recover the rent owed up to the date of the landlord's entry.

3. Refuse to treat the abandonment as a surrender but reenter and sublet the premises, holding the defaulting tenant liable for any difference between the rent reserved under the lease and the amount actually received from the sublessee.

4. Allow the premises to lie idle and sue the tenant for the rent as it becomes due, or wait until the term has expired and sue for any unpaid rent. (For example, a tenant who abandons the premises after two months of a three-year lease may be held liable for the rent due for the remainder of the lease term, and the landlord would be under no obligation to relet the property.)

HOW AND WHEN TO USE THE FORMS IN THIS CHAPTER

Cotenancy Agreement. This is used when two or more people buy real estate together. It contains provisions regarding repairs, maintenance, occupancy, and sale of the premises.

Real Estate Listing Service Contract. This form enables you to provide the basic information concerning the features of the real estate. It includes an agreement by the property owner hiring the real estate broker as agent.

Real Estate Listing Information Sheet. This is used to set out key information about the property in order to list it with a real estate broker.

Mobile Home Park Rules and Regulations. This form sets out the mobile home park owner's legal rights and provides for better communication with the tenants. Copies should be posted at the main office of the park and mailed to all tenants.

Seller's Information. This form and IRS form W-9 (see Chapter 7) must be completed by the settlement agent when real estate is sold.

Disclosure of Lead-Based Paint and/or Hazards (Sales). Sellers of residential real property built before 1978 are required to provide the buyer with any information on lead-based paint hazards and notify the buyer of any known lead-based paint hazards. The buyer must be given a ten-day opportunity to conduct a risk assessment or inspection.

COTENANCY AGREEMENT

IN CONSIDERATION of the mutual covenants had herein, this   day of   199   ,

            and   , his wife, their executors, administrators, heirs, and assigns, and

            and   , his wife, their

executors, administrators, heirs, and assigns hereinafter referred to as

"PARTIES" regarding premises commonly known as   , City of   , County of

      , State of   , being a two-family dwelling agree as follows:

I. Use and Occupancy

The   and their children shall have the right to possess and occupy the lower

apartment. The   and their children shall have the right to possess and occupy the upper

apartment. Said apartments must be used only as private apartments to live in and for no other reason.

II. Sale of the Premises

A) The premises shall not be sold within five (5) years from the date of the transfer of title to the parties except on written consent of all parties. Upon the expiration of five (5) years, if a party decides to sell the property, they shall notify the other party in writing of said intention and the property shall be sold, at the fair market value as determined below. Provided, however, the other party shall have thirty (30) days, from the date of the said notice to sell, to exercise an exclusive first option to purchase the other party's interest in the premises at the current fair market value.

B) The fair market value referred to in (A) above will be determined by an appraisal, with the appraiser to be mutually agreed upon by the parties. If the parties are unable to agree on an appraiser, each party will obtain their own appraisal and the fair market value shall be determined to be the average of the two (2) appraisals.

C) The purchasing party will also be required to obtain Releases of the first and second mortgages for the benefit of the selling party.

III. Arrears

If either party is three (3) months or more in arrears of their share of the mortgage payments, taxes, and insurance, or in violation of this agreement, the other party, upon fifteen (15) days written notice may require a sale or buy the defaulting parties' interest in the premises at the current fair market value, which value shall be determined as set forth in paragraph II.

IV. Repairs and Maintenance

A) The parties will share equally all costs of major improvements to the dwelling, including: the exterior of the residence (with the exception of noncommon windows), all electric wiring, common plumbing and plumbing repairs (except above the floor level), furnace and hot water tank, roof, outside walls, foundation, sidewalks, drainage, painting of the exterior at least every four years of a color and quality paint approved by all parties, removal of all ice and snow from the sidewalks in front of the premises, maintenance of the grounds (including trees, bushes, and shrubs), and maintenance of all pavements, fences, gutters, sewers and pipes. The improvements shall be performed by contractors approved by both parties.

B) Each party shall maintain the interior of their respective apartment, including interior walls, floors, and ceilings which become necessary through structural defects, through normal wear and tear, or through circumstances beyond their control. Each party shall keep the drains, waste and sewer pipes, and connections free from obstruction; provide for the prevention and extermination of rodents, rats, mice, or other pests; prevent the accumulation of waste or refuse material; properly dispose of all garbage and refuse; and keep the interior and exterior surfaces of the windows clean.

C) All necessary repairs, restorations, and replacements shall be of a first quality and done in a good and workmanlike manner. If the party charged with making such repairs, restorations, and replacements shall fail within fifteen (15) days after written request from the other party to commence the making of such repairs, restorations, and replacements and complete the work with reasonable diligence, they may be made and completed by the requesting party but at the expense of the defaulting party.

D) The parties agree not to do or suffer any waste or nuisance upon said premises, or injure, place any objects therein in excess of the floor load per square foot area, or deface the same, or any part thereof, or suffer or permit the same to be injured, overloaded, or defaced.

V. Services

Each party will supply and pay for their own heat, water, electric, gas, telephone, and other utility services.

VI. Fire, Accidents, Defects, Damage

Each party must give the other party prompt notice of any fire, accident, damage, or dangerous or defective condition regarding the premises.

VII. Liability

Neither party shall be liable for loss, expense, or damage to any person or property, unless due to their negligence. Each party must pay for damages suffered and money spent by the other party relating to any claim arising from any act or neglect of the other party.

VIII. Entry

Each party may at reasonable times, enter the other party's apartment to examine, make repairs or alterations, and to show it to possible buyers or lenders.

IX. Insurance

Neither party may do anything that will increase insurance premiums. They shall equally share property taxes, special improvements, and insurance premiums for liability and fire.

X. Marketability of Title

Neither party shall cause the marketability of the premises to be encumbered with any lien, easement, judgment, or other encumbrance except for the mortgages existing on the above date.

XI.

and   shall equally share all credits, deductions, gains, and income for federal and state income tax purposes.

XII.

Upon the death of both   and   , or   and   the other party shall have the exclusive first option to purchase the other parties' interest in the premises from their estate at the current fair market value which shall be determined as set forth in paragraph II.

XIII.

In the event that   vacate the lower apartment,   shall have the first option to occupy said apartment and   shall have the right to rent out the upper apartment. Approval of any and all tenants must be by mutual consent of all parties. If both   and   vacate the premises, all income and expenses shall be shared equally.

XIV. This Agreement may be modified only in writing.

_____

_____

REAL ESTATE LISTING SERVICE CONTRACT

To   (REALTOR)   (DATE LISTED)

In consideration of your agreement to promptly list through the Multiple Listing Service of
the within described property at

I hereby grant to you, a member of the Multiple Listing Service, for the term of   months from
the date hereof, the exclusive right and privilege to sell, exchange, and /or rent or lease said property for
the sum of $ or at such lesser price or terms to which I may consent. I agree to pay you a
commission of   of the sale price, providing said property is sold, exchanged, and/or rented or
leased before the expiration of this authority, whether such sale is made by you, by me, by any member of
the Multiple Listing Service of   or anyone else.

Should I contract to sell, exchange, and/or rent or lease the property within   after the
above expiration date to a purchaser who inspected the property during the term of this listing, I further
agree to pay you at the same rate of commission. In the event of sale I agree to furnish a fully guaranteed
tax and title search and a new survey and tender to the purchaser a good and marketable title. I hereby
agree to pay the prevailing sellers' loan fee, if any, and to furnish all information necessary for mortgage
processing.

Signed _____   Signed _____
                    REALTOR   OWNER

By _____   Signed _____
                    REALTOR   OWNER

OWNER MUST RECEIVE COPY OF CONTRACT AT TIME OF SIGNATURE

REAL ESTATE LISTING INFORMATION SHEET

BUS.—COMM.—INDUS.—APT.

DIST.	ADDR:		
BROKER			
PHONE #	TYPE	BRMS	BTH
MORTGAGE	TAXES		
LOT SIZE			

Price _____ Listing Date _____ / _____ / _____ Expiration Date _____ / _____ / _____

Addr:		Dist			
Near		N E S W		Twp.	
Owner				Ph.	

Addr:			Legal		
Check One:	Lot Size:		sq. ft.	Taxes	
[ ] Bus. only	Zoning		Cond. F G E		
[ ] Bus. & Prop.	Stories		Const.	Assess Val.	
[ ] Comm. Propr.	Heat		Fuel		
[ ] Apts. only	Age		Roof	Mfg.	
Sale or Lease	Sprklr		bsm't	Type	
[ ] [ ]	Parking		Docks	Int.	
Owner Financing: [ ] yes [ ] no TERMS:				Matures	
Remarks:				Mo. pmt.	
				Inc. [ ] Tax [ ]	
				[ ] Asmbl [ ] Cr. ck	
				Held by	
				Inc. $	
				Exp. $	
				Net $	

C. Slmn.		Ph.
Realtor	No.	Ph.

MOBILE HOME PARK RULES AND REGULATIONS

1. Use

All tenants must register with the landlord and complete an application form prior to moving into the park. The tenant's mobile home must be used only as a private home to live in and for no other reason. A one-year lease is available by contacting the landlord

2. Rent

The rental payment for each month must be paid on the first day of that month at landlord's address. Rent must be paid in full and no amount subtracted from it. Tenant may be required to pay other charges to the landlord. They are to be called "added rent." This added rent is payable as rent, together with the next monthly rent due. If tenant fails to pay the added rent on time, landlord shall have the same rights against tenant as if tenant failed to pay rent. A late charge of $20.00 plus $1.00 per day will be due as added rent for rent payments received after the fifth of the month. There is a service charge of $10.00 for dishonored checks.

3. Security Deposit

If tenant fully complies with all rules and regulations and terms of any lease, landlord will return the security after the term ends. If tenant does not fully comply, landlord may use the security to pay amounts owed by tenant, including damages.

4. Tenant's Duty to Obey Laws and Regulations

Tenant must, at tenant's expense, promptly comply with all laws, orders, rules, requests, and directions, of all governmental authorities, landlord's insurers, Board of Fire Underwriters, or similar groups. Tenant may not do anything which may increase landlord's insurance premiums. If tenant does, tenant must pay the increase as added rent.

5. Eviction

A tenant may be evicted for the following reasons:

a) The tenant defaults in payment of rent or added rent and demand for rent has been made, or at least three days notice in writing has been served upon him.

b) The home is used for prostitution or any illegal trade or business.

c) The tenant violates a federal, state, or local law or ordinance, resulting in a situation detrimental to the safety and welfare of the other tenants.

d) The tenant or anyone occupying the home is in violation of any park rule or regulation for more than ten days after being given written notice.

e) The tenant defaults under the terms of the written lease.

f) The tenant stays in the park after the expiration of his lease term without permission.

If the lease or term is ended or landlord takes back the lot, rent and added rent for the unexpired term becomes due and payable. Tenant shall be responsible for the landlord's cost of re-renting, the cost of repairs, attorney's fees, and moving the home. Tenant shall continue to be responsible for rent, expenses, damages, and losses.

6. Interior Improvements

Interior improvements must be in compliance with building codes and other laws and adequate utilities must be available. Prior written consent of next door neighbors and the landlord is necessary to install window air conditioners.

7. Amendments

Fees, charges, assessments and rental fees may be increased on ninety (90) days written notice. These rules and regulations may be changed on thirty (30) days notice to the tenant.

8. Sale of the Home

In order to sell the mobile home, the tenant must give the landlord twenty (20) days prior written notice of his intention to sell. Landlord reserves the right to approve the purchaser as a tenant for the remainder of the seller's lease term. Tenant must obtain the prior written approval of the landlord in order to sell the mobile home.

9. Liability

Landlord is not liable for loss, expense, or damage to any person or property, unless due to landlord's negligence. Tenant must pay for damages suffered and money spent by landlord relating to any claim arising from any act or neglect of tenant. Tenant is responsible for all acts of tenant's family, employees, guests, or invitees.

10. Prohibitions

The following is prohibited, without exception: babysitting on the premises by tenants for remuneration; any type of business or commercial activity; pets; washing or repairing of cars; use of air rifles, guns, and archery sets; swimming or wading pools; buildings and wooden structures; honking of car horns; business signs; excessive noise; and subletting or assignment of lease.

11. Lawns

Lawns and grounds are to be cut on a regular basis and properly maintained. Otherwise, they will be cut and maintained by the landlord at the tenant's expense. The lot must be kept free of debris and weeds. All garbage must be wrapped and placed in the proper receptacles.

12. Fences

No storage under the mobile home is allowed unless attractively enclosed with an approved fence or skirting. Decorative fences may be no higher than one (1) foot from the ground.

13. Automobiles

Each tenant may keep only two licensed cars on the lot. Travel trailers, motor homes, boats, snowmobiles, and unlicensed vehicles of any type are not permitted on the lot. Automobiles are to be parked according to accepted parking patterns and not on the patio. The maximum speed limit is five (5) mph at all times.

14. Electric Lines

The electric line from the home to the meter is the tenant's responsibility. Each home must be grounded to the water line.

15. Snow Plowing

Snow plowing and maintenance may be performed only by authorized equipment.

16. Skirting

Skirting must be made of aluminum, vinyl, or other approved materials.

17. Lot Number

Tenant's name and lot number must be readable from the road.

18. Alternate Locations

Landlord reserves the right to move the mobile home to another location on the park grounds.

19. Cleaning Sewers

Tenant is responsible for the cost of cleaning sewers if caused by tenant's misuse of the mobile home plumbing system.

20. No Waiver

Landlord's acceptance of rent or failure to enforce any term in these rules and regulations or in any lease is not a waiver of any of the landlord's rights. If a term of these rules and regulations or of any lease is illegal, the rest of these rules and regulations and any lease remain in full force and effect.

21. Bankruptcy

If 1) tenant assigns property for the benefit of creditors, 2) tenant files a voluntary petition or any involuntary petition is filed against tenant under any bankruptcy or insolvency law, or 3) a trustee or receiver of tenant or tenant's property is appointed, landlord may give tenant 30 days notice of cancellation of the tenancy. If any of the above is not fully dismissed within the 30 days, the term shall end as of the date stated in the notice. Tenant must continue to pay rent, damages, losses, and expenses without offset.

Dated:

SELLER(S) INFORMATION FORM

ADDRESS OF PROPERTY: _____

GROSS SALE PROCEEDS (CONTRACT SALES PRICE): $ _____

REIMBURSED PREPAID TAXES: $ _____

CLOSING DATE: _____

SELLER 1: _____

CURRENT ADDRESS: _____

_____

FORWARDING ADDRESS: _____

_____

SELLER 2: _____

_____

CURRENT ADDRESS: _____

_____

FORWARDING ADDRESS: _____

_____

TRANSACTION INVOLVES: ❏ PRIMARY RESIDENCE ❏ OTHER PROPERTY

ALLOCATION OF PROCEEDS AMONG SELLERS:

SELLER 1: _____

SELLER 2: _____

NAME OF ATTORNEY(S) FOR SELLERS:

_____

_____

_____   _____
SOCIAL SECURITY NUMBER/EIN   SELLER 1

_____   _____
SOCIAL SECURITY NUMBER/EIN   SELLER 2

DISCLOSURE OF LEAD-BASED PAINT AND/OR HAZARDS
(Sample Disclosure Format for Target Housing Sales)

Lead Warning Statement

Every purchaser of any interest in residential real property on which a residential dwelling was built prior to 1978 is notified that such property may present exposure to lead from lead-based paint that may place young children at risk of developing lead poisoning. Lead poisoning in young children may produce permanent neurological damage, including learning disabilities, reduced intelligence quotient, behavioral problems, and impaired memory. Lead poisoning also poses a particular risk to pregnant women. The seller of any interest in residential real property is required to provide the buyer with any information on lead-based paint hazards from risk assessments or inspections in the seller's possession and notify the buyer of any known lead-based paint hazards. A risk assessment or inspection for possible lead-based paint hazards is recommended prior to purchase.

Seller's Disclosure

(a) Presence of lead-based paint and/or lead-based paint hazards (check (i) or (ii) below):

    (i)——Known lead-based paint and/or lead-based paint hazards are present in the housing (explain).

    (ii)——Seller has no knowledge of lead-based paint and/or lead-based paint hazards in the housing.

(b) Records and reports available to the seller (check (i) or (ii) below):

    (i)——Seller has provided the purchaser with all available records and reports pertaining to lead-based paint and/or lead-based paint hazards in the housing (list documents below).

    (ii)——Seller has no reports or records pertaining to lead-based paint and/or lead-based paint hazards in the housing.

Purchaser's Acknowledgment (initial)

(c)——Purchaser has received copies of all information listed above.

(d)——Purchaser has received the pamphlet *Protect Your Family from Lead in Your Home.*

(e)——Purchaser has (check (i) or (ii) below):

    (i)——received a 10-day opportunity (or mutually agreed upon period) to conduct a risk assessment or inspection for the presence of lead-based paint and/or lead-based paint hazards; or

    (ii)——waived the opportunity to conduct a risk assessment or inspection for the presence of lead-based paint and/or lead-based paint hazards.

Agent's Acknowledgment (initial)

(f)——Agent has informed the seller of the seller's obligations under 42 U.S.C. 4852d and is aware of his/her responsibility to ensure compliance.

Certification of Accuracy

The following parties have reviewed the information above and certify, to the best of their knowledge, that the information they have provided is true and accurate.

_____	_____	_____	_____
Seller	Date	Seller	Date
_____	_____	_____	_____
Purchaser	Date	Purchaser	Date
_____	_____	_____	_____
Agent	Date	Agent	Date

15

Leasing Strategies: Real Estate and Equipment

Leasing real estate or equipment for your business may prove to be more advantageous than buying it. Knowing how to negotiate the lease can enhance these advantages.

HOT SITE

Landlord Legal Survival

(http://www.friran.com/landlord.html)

LEASE IT AND SAVE!

Does your business lack the capital necessary to acquire an automobile, building, computer, machinery, or office furniture? The answer may be to lease, rather than buy, these items. A *lease* is an agreement to rent equipment, land, buildings, or any asset where the lessee makes periodic payments to the lessor.

Types of Leases

The four types of leases are the following:

1. The *financial lease* is written for a term not to exceed the economic life of the equipment. It usually provides for (1) periodic payments; (2) ownership of the equipment to revert back to the lessor at the end of the lease term; (3) a noncancellable relationship requiring the lessee to continue payments until the end of the term; and (4) the lessee to maintain the equipment. Financial leases are usually known as *net leases* because the lessee is responsible for expenses, such as maintenance, taxes, and insurance.

2. The *operating lease,* also known as the *maintenance lease,* can usually be canceled under conditions spelled out in the lease agreement. Maintenance of the asset is usually the lessor's responsibility. Operating leases are often used for computer equipment.

3. The *sale and lease-back,* which is often used for the lease of buildings, is similar to the financial lease. The owner of the asset sells it to another party and at the same time leases it back for a specified term.

4. With a *full pay-out lease,* the lessor recovers the original cost of the asset during the term of the lease.

Advantages of Leasing

Leasing offers the following advantages over purchasing:

- No down payment is required, whereas a loan often requires 25 percent down.
- There are no restrictions on a company's financial operations, as loans often impose.
- Payments are spread out for a longer period than loans permit, thus involving lower monthly payments.

- Protection against the risk of equipment obsolescence is automatic because the lessee disposes of the equipment at the end of the lease.
- There are income tax benefits. Lease payments are fully deductible as operating expenses if the agreement is a true lease.
- Accounting is easier. The lessor handles most of the accounting and paperwork, relieving the lessee of the administrative details of recordkeeping. The lessor also has responsibility for complying with state regulations and completing and filing required forms.
- There are sales tax benefits. Thirty-two states permit sales tax to be paid as part of each rental payment instead of in one initial lump-sum payment. That can be a beneficial tax break when the leased property is traded in before it is fully depreciated, because the lessee will have paid only a portion of the total sales tax.
- The lessor will usually have experience with the equipment and can provide expert technical advice.
- In the event of bankruptcy, claims of the lessor against the assets of the lessee are more restrictive than those of general creditors.
- The lessee can upgrade to more sophisticated equipment as needs change.

Disadvantages of Leasing

Some disadvantages of leasing when compared with purchasing are as follows:

- Leasing usually costs more because the lessee loses certain tax advantages available to owners of an asset, such as depreciation deductions. However, leasing will not cost any more if the lessee cannot take advantage of these benefits because of low tax liability.
- The lessee loses the economic value of the asset at the end of the lease term because the lessee does not own it.
- A lease is a long-term legal obligation that the lessee usually cannot cancel.
- Leasing requires a large deposit.

Precautions

Investigate the following before signing a lease: check out the lessor's financial condition and reputation; compare the lease arrangements with other lessors; be sure that the equipment is really what you need; and be sure that the lease is for a term that you need.

The major features of the lease agreement are

- the specific nature of the financing,
- the payment amount,
- the term of the agreement,
- the disposition of the asset at the end of the term, and
- the schedule of the value of the equipment for insurance and settlement purposes in case of damage or destruction.

Review the lease agreement with your attorney and tax consultant before signing it.

HOW TO NEGOTIATE COMMERCIAL LEASES

A commercial real estate lease, like any other contract, *can be* negotiated. Do not accept the form lease submitted to you by the other party (see the lease form at the end of this chapter). The lease should be slanted so that you obtain the maximum legal, economic, and tax advantages.

Keep in mind that any ambiguities in the lease are usually construed by the courts against the person who drew it—usually the landlord. Before signing a lease, you should understand not only the terms contained in it but also the legal and tax effects of those terms. To fully and adequately protect your legal rights, see an attorney before you sign the lease.

A *lease* is a contract transferring control and possession of real estate from the landlord to the tenant for a specified period of time in exchange for rent. A lease must usually be in writing and signed by the landlord and tenant if it covers a term of more than one year. The following states require a written lease only if the term is in excess of three years: Indiana, New Jersey, New Mexico, North Carolina, Ohio, and Pennsylvania. Maine requires written leases in excess of two years. Even when an oral lease is to be legally binding, prudent parties will put it in writing so that the landlord's and tenant's legal rights and obligations are specifically spelled out.

The landlord and all tenants should sign the lease. Some states require witnesses, seals, or acknowledgments. If you record the lease, it must be acknowledged like a deed. To ensure secrecy regarding the rental amount, some states (such as New York, Pennsylvania, and Ohio) permit recording a brief memorandum of the lease instead of the lease itself.

There are no particular words necessary to constitute a lease, but the following checklist should be used:

Parties

- An accurate description of the parties with their full legal names, states of incorporation, and principal business addresses and assurances that every party is of legal age (usually 18) and competent to sign a contract

Premises

- A full and accurate description of the premises, including the suite number, street address, municipality, state, and zip code
- The square footage as measured by either rentable square feet (including a portion of common areas), by usable square feet (limited to space within four walls of the premises), by referring to various points within the building (such as from the outer walls to the center of some point), or by referring to the Building Owners and Managers Association International (BOMA) standards

Term and Possession

- The number of months or years of the lease
- If the building is under construction and the commencement date is not specified, the tenant is to receive adequate advance written notice when the premises will be ready
- The tenant to move in and start paying rent when there is substantial completion; issuance of a certificate of occupancy; when the premises are ready per specifications and plans; or when only minor details of construction, decoration, or mechanical adjustments remain to be completed.
- The tenant's remedies if possession is delayed through no fault of the tenant: rent abatement, money damages, or cancellation or reimbursement of prepaid money

Rent

- Rent stated as flat rent, step-up rent (gradual increase in rent), percentage of gross sales with a guaranteed minimum, base rent plus percentage of gross sales, base rent plus percentage of net sales, or expense—participating lease (fixed rent plus share of real estate taxes, insurance, and certain repairs)

- Grace period of a specified number of days before a penalty is charged for late rent
- Periodic rent increases according to operating expenses (pro-rata share) by the consumer price index or by a fixed percentage with a maximum cap on the increase

Security Deposit

Limitations on the Use of the Premises

Compliance with Laws

- Warranty by the landlord that the premises are in compliance with all applicable laws.

Services and Utilities

- Whether the landlord or tenant to provide and pay for heating, ventilating, and air-conditioning; electric lighting; water; janitorial service; and snow removal
- During what days and hours these services are provided

Repairs and Maintenance

- Landlord's and tenant's responsibilities for repairs or maintenance

Alterations

- Landlord's consent for improvements, additions, installations, and decorations
- Tenant's right to remove trade fixtures; all alterations; alterations owned or paid for by the tenant, such as improvements made at the commencement of the lease and paid for by the tenant

Insurance Coverage by Tenant and Landlord

Environmental Warranty and Indemnification

- Warranty by the landlord that any use, storage, treatment, or transportation of hazardous substances on the premises has been in compliance with all applicable federal, state, and local laws, regulations, and ordinances
- Landlord's warranty that no release, leak, discharge, spill, disposal, or emission of hazardous substances has occurred on the premises
- Landlord's agreement to indemnify and hold harmless the tenant from any claims, damages, fines, judgments, penalties, liabilities, and costs incurred because of any investigation of the site or any cleanup, removal, or restoration mandated by federal, state, or local agencies arising from the presence of hazardous substances on the premises placed there before the tenant took occupancy or by

the landlord as part of a renovation of the premises

Casualty

- Landlord's obligation to repair and restore the premises damaged by casualty as soon as reasonably possible
- Abatement of the tenant's rent obligation in proportion to the nature and extent of damages, impairment of the use (diminution of value), or in proportion to the amount of unusable square feet

Condemnation

- Abatement of the rent from the date of taking
- The right of the tenant to terminate the lease if a substantial part or a specified percentage of the premises is taken or if the premises are no longer suited for their intended use
- If the lease is terminated because of condemnation, the tenant's right to reimbursement for prepaid rent, and other prepaid expenses

Prohibition of Assignment and Subletting Default

- Ten days' written notice from the landlord advising the tenant that it is in default
- Automatic default in the event of the tenant's bankruptcy, receivership, seizure of assets, or assignment for the benefit of creditors

Renewal of Lease Term

- The parties' wish for an automatic renewal unless either party gives notice of termination
- Whether the tenant has an option to extend the term for one or more years on the same terms and conditions with the exception of rent
- The way rent be determined for the option term: By a fixed percentage? In proportion to the consumer price index? By a fixed dollar amount? By a current market rate?

Improvements

- Itemization of all proposed improvements on the blueprints, and specifications attached as exhibits to the lease

Attorney Fees

- Each party entitled to have its attorney fees paid if it is the prevailing party in any litigation to enforce the lease

Right to Enter

- Assurance that the landlord will give the tenant reasonable advance notice when it will exercise its right of entry except in emergencies

Compliance with the Americans with Disabilities Act (see Chapter 17)

SHOPPING CENTER LEASES THAT VIOLATE ANTITRUST LAWS

A shopping center landlord may be violating antitrust laws by using clauses requested by other tenants if those clauses restrict the use of the property and give certain tenants a competitive advantage. The following clauses are illegal:

- The exclusion by department stores of discount stores—a vertical group boycott between the landlord and the department store
- Requirements that all new tenants be approved by the department stores in a mall—a *horizontal group boycott*
- Requirements as to the quality, price range, or types or brands of merchandise that retail stores may carry, which may be interpreted as price fixing

The following types of restrictions are permissible:

- Requiring the landlord to maintain a balanced and diversified group of retail stores, merchandise, and services in a shopping center
- Retaining the right to prohibit nonretail facilities
- Retaining the right to prevent the developer from allowing objectionable tenants, such as pornography shops, massage parlors, and body and fender shops
- Retaining the right to approve the initial layout of the shopping center

Courts consider the following seven factors when determining the validity of a restrictive covenant:

1. Intent of the parties
2. Importance of the covenant to the consideration exchanged
3. Clear and express language
4. Notice to later parties

5. Reasonableness of area and duration

6. Interference with public interest

7. Changed circumstances

CHECKLIST FOR NEGOTIATING A SHOPPING CENTER LEASE

This checklist should be carefully reviewed because shopping center leases are much more complex than other types of commercial leases. Provisions regarding remodeling and construction of the leased property are included. (An asterisk following an entry means that the action in question is subject to the landlord's written consent.)

Premises
- ❏ Drawing
- ❏ Number of square feet
- ❏ Use of parking areas and other common areas

Term
- ❏ Number of years
- ❏ Date lease commences
- ❏ Date lease ends

Permitted Uses
- ❏ Products that may be sold
- ❏ Hours of operation
- ❏ Vending machines*
- ❏ Displays of merchandise and show windows

Tenant's Trade Name
- ❏ On signs
- ❏ Advertising
- ❏ Change of name*

Annual Minimum Rent
- ❏ Amount
- ❏ Monthly installments

Percentage Rent

Landlord's Address
- ❏ For sending rental payments
- ❏ For sending notices by registered or certified mail

Landlord's Warranties
- ❏ Peaceful and quiet use and possession of the premises by tenant without hindrance from landlord

Lease Subordination
- ❏ Tenant's rights subordinate to any mortgages

Gross Sales Defined

Records and Reports
- ❏ Tenant to keep a permanent and accurate set of books and records on the premises
- ❏ Tenant to provide landlord with monthly informal statements

Taxes
- ❏ Tenant to pay its share of all taxes, assessments, and other governmental charges
- ❏ How share of taxes is computed

Tenant's Share of Common Expenses
- ❏ Maintenance and operation of common areas
- ❏ Repairing foundations, exterior walls, roof, downspouts, and gutters
- ❏ How share is computed
- ❏ Definition of *common area*

Utility Services
- ❏ Electricity, water, and sewer
- ❏ Heating, air-conditioning, and ventilating
- ❏ Landlord's right to discontinue trash and rubbish removal, water, electricity, air-conditioning, heating, ventilating, or antenna service upon ten days' written notice to tenant
- ❏ Landlord not liable for interruption of service
- ❏ Tenant to reduce energy consumption in the event of energy shortages

Merchants Association
- ❏ Tenant membership and participation
- ❏ Dues and annual assessments payable to the association

Care of the Premises
- ❏ Window and door glass
- ❏ Exterior surfaces
- ❏ Replacement of glass
- ❏ Storage of garbage
- ❏ Compliance with all laws, ordinances, rules, and regulations
- ❏ Lighting of show windows and exterior signs
- ❏ Landlord to keep in good repair foundations, exterior walls, downspouts and gutters, and utility systems

- ❏ Tenant parking, decorating, or displaying of signs*
- ❏ Landlord's right to use roof of the premises

Insurance

- ❏ Tenant's insurance: public liability, boiler, workers' compensation, and fire with extended coverage

Tenant Indemnity of Landlord

Mechanic's Liens

- ❏ Tenant to promptly pay all money owed for labor, services, materials, supplies, and equipment
- ❏ Tenant to notify landlord of liens and discharge them within ten days

Assignment or Subletting*

Damage to Premises by Fire

- ❏ Landlord to repair
- ❏ Landlord's option to terminate the lease
- ❏ Rent adjustments

Bankruptcy or Insolvency of Tenant

- ❏ Landlord may reenter the premises and declare the lease terminated.

Default of Tenant

- ❏ Failure to pay rent, failure to perform lease terms, and vacating or abandonment of premises
- ❏ Landlord's right to make alterations and repairs upon reentering the premises in order to rerent
- ❏ Attorney fees on default

Rent Adjustment for Expansion of Tenant's Premises

Interest on Past Due Rent

Inspection by Landlord

Nonwaiver

- ❏ Landlord's failure to insist upon a strict performance

Applicable State Law

Authority to Act

- ❏ Tenant's execution of lease pursuant to board of director's resolution

Preparation of Drawings for Construction

- ❏ Tenant to provide design drawings, working drawings, shop drawings, and specifications*

Preparation for Construction

- ❏ Use of first-class materials and work and equipment to be warranted for a minimum of one year from installation
- ❏ Tenant's contractors*—bondable and licensed
- ❏ Permits and licenses to be obtained by tenant

Commencement of Tenant Construction

- ❏ On-site meeting between tenant and landlord to be held a specified number of days before the commencement of tenant construction at which time tenant must provide landlord with a copy of tenant's building permit; certificate setting forth main address of tenant's general mechanical, electrical, and sprinkler contracts; certificates setting forth proposed commencement date of construction and estimated completion dates; certificate of insurance regarding tenant's general contractor and subcontractors, required minimum coverage, and limits of liability (workers' compensation, comprehensive general liability insurance, comprehensive automobile liability insurance, tenant's protective liability insurance, and tenant's builders risk insurance)

Tenant Construction

- ❏ Temporary services provided by tenant's contractors during construction: temporary power, heat, trash, removal, barricades
- ❏ Field drawings
- ❏ Landlord inspection
- ❏ Punch list
- ❏ Occupancy permit obtained by tenant

General Requirements

- ❏ Proof of payment by tenant of all costs of construction

Drawing Criteria

Architectural Criteria

Heating, Ventilating, and Air-Conditioning Criteria

Electrical Criteria

Plumbing Criteria

Telephone

Fire Sprinkler Criteria

Tenant's Reimbursable Items

HOW AND WHEN TO USE THE FORMS IN THIS CHAPTER

Equipment Lease and **Lease of a Computer.** These forms should be used when renting equipment. Included is a specific example based on leasing a computer.

Option Agreement. This should be used in conjunction with a commercial lease if you would like to reserve the rental property but are not sure whether you will need it in the future.

Commercial Lease. This lease is advantageous for both the landlord and tenant because it provides for unforeseen difficulties and documents the agreement between the parties.

Agreement Releasing Tenant. This agreement provides that in return for retaining the tenant's security deposit, the landlord agrees to release the tenant from further liability under the lease. This form should be used only after the landlord has inspected the property and is reasonably confident that the cost of repairs to correct any damage caused by the tenant will not be greater than the dollar amount of the security deposit.

Sublease Agreement. This may require a consent. The consent form attached to the agreement assumes the consent must be given by a bank.

Lease Assumption Agreement. This is used in the sale of a franchise.

Disclosure of Lead-Based Paint and/or Hazards (Leases). Before renting pre-1978 residential housing, landlords must disclose the presence of known lead-based paint and/or hazards.

EQUIPMENT LEASE

This agreement is made   between   , of   ,
hereinafter referred to as "lessor," and   corporation having its principal place of
business at   hereinafter referred to as "lessee."

1. Equipment. For and in consideration of the covenants and agreements hereinafter contained, lessor has leased to lessee the personal property known and described as follows: (hereinafter referred to as "equipment") for the period of   months commencing from the   day of   and upon the conditions and agreements hereinafter stipulated.

2. Repossession. Retaking possession of the equipment, pursuant to the provisions of this contract, shall not prejudice lessors' right or claim for rents and payments due hereunder.

3. Return of equipment. At the end of the term, lessee shall return the equipment freight prepaid to lessor at the place from which equipment was shipped in as good condition as it existed at the commencement of the term, reasonable wear and tear excepted.

4. Rent. Lessee shall pay as rent for the leasing the sum of   Dollars ($) per month for   months due the   day of each month, commencing on   .

5. Default. If lessee shall default in paying any rent due; or if any execution or other writ or process shall be issued in any action or proceeding against lessee, whereby the equipment may be seized or taken or detained; or if a proceeding in bankruptcy, receivership, or insolvency shall be instituted by or against lessee or his property; of if lessee shall enter into any arrangement or composition with its creditors; or if lessee should breach any other term, covenant, or condition of this lease, lessor shall have the right to retake immediate possession of the equipment and for such purpose lessor may enter upon any premises where the equipment may be located, and with or without notice of its intention to retake the same, and without being liable to any suit or action or proceeding by lessee. If any step is taken by legal action or otherwise by lessor to recover possession of equipment or otherwise enforce this agreement or to collect monies due hereunder, lessee shall pay lessor the equivalent of the monies expended or charges incurred by lessor in such behalf, including reasonable attorney's fees.

6. Location. The equipment shall be used only at: , and lessee shall not remove it from said location without the written consent of lessor.

7. Indemnification of lessor. Lessee agrees to protect and hold lessor harmless against any and all losses or damage to equipment by fire, flood, explosion, tornado, or theft. Lessee hereby assumes all liability to any person arising from the location, condition, or use of equipment, and shall indemnify and does indemnify lessor of and from all liability, claim, and demand whatsoever arising from the location, condition, or use of equipment whether in imperfect or defective equipment, and from every other liability, claim, and demand whatsoever during the term of this lease or arising while equipment is in the possession of lessee. Lessee also agrees to promptly reimburse lessor, in cash, for any and all personal property taxes levied against equipment and paid by lessor.

8. No assignment. Neither this lease nor any right or interest thereunder shall be assigned by lessee in any respect whatsoever.

9. Choice of law. This lease and agreement shall be deemed to have been executed and entered into in the State of _____ and shall be construed, enforced, and performed in accordance with the laws thereof.

10. Exclusion of oral statements. This instrument contains the entire agreement of the parties. No oral or other statements, proposals, or agreements shall be binding on either of the parties.

11. Insurance. Lessee shall at all times during the term of this lease at its expense keep equipment insured to the amount of at least _____ Dollars ($ _____) for such risks as lessor shall require, with carriers acceptable to lessor, for lessor's benefit. Lessee will deliver the policies of insurance to lessor. Lessor shall be entitled to receive all insurance proceeds collected under the policies.

12. Inspection by lessor. For the purpose of examining and inspecting the condition of the machinery, lessor may from time to time enter any premises where the machinery may be located.

13. Purchase Option. Lessee has the option to purchase the equipment during the term of the lease upon payment of $ _____ % of rental payments shall be credited toward the purchase price and the balance of such purchase price shall be paid in cash.

(Lessor's Name)   (Lessee's Name)

BY: _____   BY: _____
           (Name, Title)   (Name, Title)

LEASE OF A COMPUTER

, hereinafter called lessor, whose address is

, City of   , State of   , does hereby lease,

and   Consultants, hereinafter called lessee, whose address is   ,

City of   , State of   , does hereby lease from lessor, for use at lessor's place of

business (premises) subject to the following terms, provisions, conditions, and covenants:

(Complete description of computers):

1. Rental

The total rental fee shall be $ for the term of   weeks dating from

, 199   .

2. Title to Computers

Title to the computers that are the subject matter of this lease shall be and remain with lessor at all times during the term hereof.

3. Maintenance of Machines

Lessor guarantees, at its own cost and expense, to keep the computers in good working condition during the term of this lease.

4. Liability

Lessee shall not be liable in any way, or to any extent at all for or on account of any injury to any property at any time in said premises or on account of the theft, or destruction of any property at any time on said premises. Lessee shall not be responsible for the locking-up and securing of premises.

5. Maintenance

Lessor shall at all times keep the premises in a clean, safe, and sanitary condition in accordance with the laws, rules, and regulations of the government agencies having jurisdiction at the sole cost and expense of lessor.

6. Location

The above-mentioned computers shall be used at the lessor's place of business and the lessor grants to the lessee adequate space to enable it and its agents, employees, and others acting with its permission to operate the computers. Lessee will be granted free access to the premises between the hours of

A.M. and   P.M. on each day of the week in order to operate and use the computers.

7. Applicable Law

This lease shall be governed by and construed under the laws of the State of   .

8. Lease as Entire Agreement; Severability

This lease embodies the entire agreement between the parties. It may not be modified or terminated except as provided herein or by other written agreement between the parties. If any provision herein is invalid, it shall be considered deleted from this lease, and shall not invalidate the remaining provisions of this lease.

9. Manner of Giving Notice

Any notice to be given under this lease shall be mailed to the party to be notified at the address set forth herein, by registered or certified mail with postage prepaid, and shall be deemed given when so mailed.

Dated: _____

_____

_____

OPTION AGREEMENT

Re: _____

THIS AGREEMENT, made this   day of   , 199   between

(landlord) doing business at   and   (tenant) doing business at

, WITNESSETH:

IN CONSIDERATION OF the sum of   Dollars ($) paid by the tenant to the

landlord, the receipt whereof is hereby acknowledged, the landlord hereby grants to the tenant, its

successors, and assigns, the exclusive option to lease the above mentioned property as per the attached

Lease, upon the following terms and conditions:

1. *TERM OF OPTION:* This option and all rights and privileges hereunder shall expire the   day of

, 199   .

2. N*OTICE OF EXERCISE OF OPTION:* This option is to be exercised by the tenant by written notice

delivered personally or forwarded by registered or certified mail, return receipt requested, within the time

limited in paragraph 1 to the landlord at the address first above recited.

3. *APPLICATION OF OPTION PAYMENT:* In the event that the tenant does not exercise his option as herein

provided, all sums paid on account thereon shall be retained by the landlord as consideration for this option

free of all claims of the tenant, and neither party shall have any further rights or claims against the other.

4. *EFFECT OF EXERCISE OF OPTION:* In the event that the tenant does exercise its option as herein

provided, the sum paid on account of the option shall be applied to the first month's rent, and the terms,

covenants, and conditions in the attached Lease Agreement shall become the contract of the parties.

IN WITNESS WHEREOF, the parties hereto have caused this instrument to be duly executed the day

and year first above written.

_____ , INC.   _____ , INC.

BY: _____   BY: _____
                              , President   , President

COMMERCIAL LEASE

DATE: _____

(Landlord) doing business at   agrees to

rent to   (Tenant) doing business at   the

following premises:

for a term of   years beginning on   and ending on   at the annual

rent of $ to be paid monthly at $ with a security deposit of $ deposited in

bank.

1. Tenant shall use the premises for only the following purposes:

2. Landlord may not unreasonably withhold its consent to Tenant subleasing or assigning this lease.

3. Tenant shall pay rent on the first day of each month at Landlord's mailing address. The first month's rent is to be paid when the Tenant signs this lease.

4. Tenant agrees to allow the Landlord, in person or by agent, to: enter the premises at all reasonable times of the day and place on or about premises, notices indicating that the premises are for sale or rent; and to enter upon and pass through premises for the purpose of showing it to persons wishing to purchase or lease it.

5. Tenant agrees: to obey all Federal, State, County, and Municipal laws, regulations, rules, and ordinances in regards to the premises, all walks adjacent thereto; to keep said walks free of ice and snow; to take such care of premises as may be required by any and all Federal, State, County, and Municipal authorities and departments; and to obey all lawful requirements of the State Fire Insurance Rating Organization, or any similar body, with reference to the premises. In the event that the insurance premium rate upon the building shall be increased, by reason of any act of omission or commission on the part of the tenant or by reason of the nature of the occupancy of the premises, the tenant agrees to pay the amount of any such increase. Tenant shall save the Landlord and hold it harmless from any expense, loss, or damage by reason of the violation of such laws, regulations, rules, ordinances, and requirements, or by reason of any damage that might be sustained by reason of the Tenant's negligence.

6. Tenant agrees to maintain the lawn and shrubbery in a presentable condition, and to care for, erect, and store screens, storm windows, doors, and awnings, which may be on the premises.

7. Tenant shall take special care that no damage occurs to the building or any fixtures therein, in the use of electricity, water, or gas and be liable for all damages occasioned by the Tenants, their agents or servants, in the commission or omission of any acts causing such damage; and to observe all the rules and regulations of the utility companies and the sewer authority supplying such premises with electricity, gas, water, and use of sewer, and promptly pay bills for same.

8. The Tenant must return the premises broom-clean at the expiration of the lease to the Landlord and in the same condition as when taken, reasonable wear and tear excepted.

9. In the event of the violation of the tenant of any Clause, agreement, or condition contained in this lease, Landlord shall have the following rights:

    A. Landlord may give Tenant 3 days written notice to correct any violation of a Lease condition or move.

    B. If the Tenant fails to correct the violation, the Tenant must leave and surrender to Landlord the keys to the premises.

    C. Tenant continues to be responsible for rent, expenses, damages, and leases.

    D. Landlord may enter the premises to remove any Tenant or property and/or use disposess, eviction, or other legal methods to take back premises.

10. If the Lease is ended, all rent for unexpired term is due and payable. Landlord may re-rent the premises. Tenant shall be responsible for Landlord's cost of repairs, brokers' fees, legal fees, advertising, and any other costs for preparing the premises for re-renting. Any rental the Landlord receives, after deducting Landlord's costs, shall be applied by the Landlord in reducing the amount owed by the Tenant. Tenant agrees not to return to the premises after legal removal.

11. In case the premises herein leased shall be partially damaged by fire, the same shall be repaired as speedily as possible by the Landlord. In case the premises shall be totally destroyed by fire, or so much damaged as to render them untenantable, either party hereto may serve personally, or by registered mail, upon the other party within ten days after such fire, a thirty-day written notice of the intention of such party to terminate this lease and the term therein provided for and at the end of such thirty days the Tenant shall pay all rent to the date of said fire and surrender up to the owner said premises discharged of this lease.

12. Notice of Rules will be posted or given to Tenant. Landlord need not enforce Rules against other tenants. Landlord is not liable to Tenant if another tenant violates the Rules. Tenant receives no rights under the Rules.

13. All promises made by the Landlord are contained in this Lease.

14. All improvements made by the Tenant to or upon the demised premises shall remain the property of the Landlord.

15. Landlord shall furnish the following utilities:

16. Late charges of $ per day will be added to the rent for rental payments made after the fifth of the month.

17. For the duration of the lease, Tenant, at his/her expense, shall insure Landlord, Landlord's agent, and him/herself against liability for injury to persons in connection with the entire premises with a comprehensive general public liability insurance with limits of at least one million dollars with respect to injury or death of any one (1) person and two million dollars with respect to any one accident, disaster, or occurrence, and one hundred thousand dollars with respect to property damage. Tenant shall deposit

the original policy with evidence of premium payment with Landlord prior to the commencement date of the term of this lease. Proof of renewal or replacement shall be given by Tenant to Landlord at least thirty (30) days prior to expiration of any policy. Landlord may, at his option, procure the said insurance and charge the expense thereof to the tenant as additional rent to become due and payable on demand.

In Presence of,

_____ ls   _____

_____ ls   _____ ls

State of   _On the   day of_

County of   **ss.:**   _before me, the subscriber, personally appeared_

to me personally known and known to me to be the same person(s) described in and who executed the within instrument, and he (she) (they) acknowledged to me that he (she) (they) executed the same.

_____

State of

County of   **ss.,**

On this   day of   , 19   , before me personally came

that he (she) is the   of

the corporation described in, and which executed, the within instrument; that he (she) knows the seal of said corporation; that the seal affixed to said instrument is such corporate seal; that it was so affixed by order of the Board of Directors of said corporation; and that he (she) signed his (her) name thereto by like order.

_____

Notary Public   , Commissioner of Deeds

_My Commission expires _____

AGREEMENT RELEASING TENANT

THIS AGREEMENT made this   day of   , 199   , between
                    , having its principal office at   Street,
(hereinafter referred to as "D"; and   (hereinafter referred to as "L" residing at
                    .

WITNESSETH

WHEREAS, L has entered into a lease agreement for premises known as   at
                    Street,   ;

WHEREAS, L in conjunction with the above mentioned lease, paid the sum of $ as a
security deposit; and

WHEREAS, L has vacated the above mentioned premises and wishes to be released from said lease.

NOW, THEREFORE, in consideration of mutual covenants and promises herein contained, the parties
agree as follows:

1. Upon payment of   dollars ($) by L to D and execution of this agreement
by all parties, D hereby releases L from any and all liability for payment of rent for the above mentioned
lease.

2. In further consideration of being released by D, L assigns and transfers all right, title, and interest to
its above mentioned security deposits plus any and all accrued interest to D.

In witness whereof the parties have executed this agreement.

By: _____

_____

_____

SUBLEASE AGREEMENT

This Sublease made the   day of   , 199   , between a(n)
corporation organized and existing under and by virtue of the laws of the State of   with its
principal office at   ,   (hereinafter referred to "T") and a corporation
organized and existing under and by virtue of the laws of the State   of and authorized to
do business in the State of   , with its principal office at   (hereinafter
referred to a "E").

WITNESSETH

1. That T hereby leases to E,   square feet of the building known as   , Town of
                    , for a term to commence on the   day of 199   and to end on the
day of 199   .

2. The said premises are the same premises, referred to in a lease between
(hereinafter referred to as C) dated   , and a sublease between   , as
sublessor, and T, as subleasee, dated   , 199   .

3. The terms, covenants, provisions, and conditions of said sublease are hereby incorporated herein and
shall be binding upon both parties hereto, those applying to the sublessee therein shall apply to E herein
with the following exceptions:

   a. Paragraph   shall not apply to the sublease.
   b. This sublease is subject to written consents executed by the   BANK, and

IN WITNESS WHEREOF, the parties have executed this sublease in duplicate the day and year first above
written.

By_____   By_____

CONSENT

Pursuant to Paragraph   of the SUBLEASE AGREEMENT dated   between
                    and   , the BANK hereby consents to the attached Sublease
Agreement.

BANK

By _____   Date: _____ ,199   .

LEASE ASSUMPTION AGREEMENT

It is hereby Agreed by and between _____ under a certain Franchise Agreement with _____ as Licensee under said Franchise Agreement, that _____ hereby assumes and undertakes all of the terms and conditions of a certain lease between _____ , as Landlord and _____ , as Tenant for premises prescribed therein located _____ as its own obligations. A copy of said lease is attached hereto and made a part of thereof and marked Exhibit A:

It is further Agreed that _____ as Licensee under the aforesaid Franchise Agreement shall make all payments of rent and other obligations for the premises under the aforesaid lease between _____ as Landlord directly to _____ at the address designated by _____ for such purposes on or before the 25th day of the month preceding the due date of such payments. Licensee will be responsible for rent beginning on the date that it opens for business.

It is further Agreed that _____ as Licensee, shall have the right to use and occupy the said premises described under the aforesaid lease between _____ as Landlord and _____ as Tenant during the term of the lease only so long as Licensee is in full compliance with all of the terms and conditions of the aforesaid Franchise Agreement and the terms and conditions of the lease for said premises.

GRANTOR

By _____

LICENSEE

By _____

Dated: _____   _____

DISCLOSURE OF LEAD-BASED PAINT AND/OR HAZARDS
(Sample Disclosure Format for Target Housing Rentals & Leases)

Lead Warning Statement

Housing built before 1978 may contain lead-based paint. Lead from paint, paint chips, and dust can pose health hazards if not managed properly. Lead exposure is especially harmful to young children and pregnant women. Before renting pre-1978 housing, lessors must disclose the presence of known lead-based paint and/or lead-based paint hazards in the dwelling. Lessees must also receive a federally approved pamphlet on lead poisoning prevention.

Lessor's Disclosure

(a) Presence of lead-based paint and/or lead-based paint hazards (check (i) or (ii) below):

(i)——Known lead-based paint and/or lead-based paint hazards are present in the housing (explain).

(ii)——Lessor has no knowledge of lead-based paint and/or lead-based paint hazards in the housing.

(b) Records and reports available to the lessor (check (i) or (ii) below):

(i)——Lessor has provided the lessee with all available records and reports pertaining to lead-based paint and/or lead-based paint hazards in the housing (list documents below).

(ii)——Lessor has no reports or records pertaining to lead-based paint and/or lead-based paint hazards in the housing.

Lessee's Acknowledgment (initial)

(c)——Lessee has received copies of all information listed above.

(d)——Lessee has received the pamphlet *Protect Your Family from Lead in Your Home.*

(e)——Lessee has (check (i) or (ii) below):

(i)——received a 10-day opportunity (or mutually agreed upon period) to conduct a risk assessment or inspection for the presence of lead-based paint and/or lead-based paint hazards; or

(ii)——waived the opportunity to conduct a risk assessment or inspection for the presence of lead-based paint and/or lead-based paint hazards.

Agent's Acknowledgment (initial)

(f)——Agent has informed the lessor of the lessor's obligations under 42 U.S.C. 4852d and is aware of his/her responsibility to ensure compliance.

Certification of Accuracy

The following parties have reviewed the information above and certify, to the best of their knowledge, that the information they have provided is true and accurate.

Lessor	Date	Lessor	Date
Lessee	Date	Lessee	Date
Agent	Date	Agent	Date

16

Protecting Your Small Business

Without proper planning, a divorce or liability lawsuit could severely disrupt or bankrupt your business.

You have a duty to maintain your store, office building, or other place of business that is open to the public in a reasonably safe condition. This duty requires you to take the following steps:

- Regularly inspect your premises to ensure that there are no hazards to the safety of your customers or clients. This is especially important if slippery conditions are created by customers coming in from rainy or snowy weather or your floors have recently been washed or waxed.

- Post warning signs if any unusual conditions exist.

- Doors, floors, aisles, steps, lighting, and displays of merchandise should be properly maintained.

- Entrances and exits should be properly lighted.

If you fail to meet your duties, a customer who suffers an injury on your business premises may have a right to sue your business if it can be proven that

- an unsafe condition existed on your premises;

- the customer's injury was caused by the unsafe condition; or

- you knew of the unsafe condition, or the condition had existed for so long that you

should have discovered it during the course of regular inspections.

The applicable law will depend on the particular state and the particular facts involved. For example, a woman who was shopping in a New Jersey produce market slipped and fell on a vegetable leaf on the floor. The court determined that the leaf was a hazard to customers and that the fall was caused by the vegetable leaf. However, the market was not liable because there was no proof that the management knew the leaf was there or that the leaf had been on the floor so long that the management should have discovered it. However, a Pennsylvania storekeeper was found liable when a customer slipped on an oily substance on a staircase because the substance had been on the staircase for two hours before the accident.

HOT SITE

Personal Injury Legal Survival

(http://www.friran.com/personal_html)

PURPOSE OF INSURANCE

The basic purpose of insurance is to anticipate catastrophic losses that could financially impair your future. Insurance should not be purchased for small exposures as the cost of premiums is prohibitive and may waste dollars you'll need to cover your major exposures.

Three basic procedures for determining your insurance needs are to

1. eliminate or reduce your risk by properly managing maintenance, repair, training, and safety programs;
2. assume the risk yourself by paying small losses and buying high deductibles; and
3. transfer the risk by buying the proper amounts of insurance tailored to your specific needs.

A small business cannot operate without insurance. It allows owners to minimize risk of loss from circumstances beyond their control. The first step is to identify the risks of the business that need to be covered and determine the largest amount of possible loss.

Cause of Loss

The cause-of-loss form insures your property against all risk of direct physical loss, including the following: fire; volcanic action; smoke; sprinkler leakage; sinkhole collapse; explosion; vandalism; riot or civil commotion; lightning; windstorm or hail; aircraft or vehicles; glass breakage; damage from falling objects on the building exterior; damage to building walls or roof from the weight of snow, ice, or sleet; water damage caused by accidental discharge or leakage from a plumbing, heating, or air-conditioning system or domestic appliance; and the collapse of building walls or roof.

The following losses are excluded from the cause-of-loss form: mysterious disappearance of property; damage done to property being worked upon; artificially generated electrical currents; wear, tear, marring, or scratching; insects or vermin; dampness or dryness of the atmosphere; changes in temperature; rust or corrosion; theft from an unattended or unlocked auto; fidelity of an employee or officer of the bank; damage done by rain, snow, or sleet to property in the open; earthquake; flood (surface waters or water that backs up through sewers or drains); water below the surface of the ground, including that which exerts pressure or flows, seeps, or leaks through sidewalks, driveways, foundations, walls, basement floors, or any opening; and the explosion of steam boilers and steam pipes.

Coverage is provided on the basis of full replacement costs without deduction for depreciation on any loss, subject to the terms of the coinsurance clause. Since replacement costs fluctuate, you should constantly check your insurable values to make sure that you have adequate coverage.

Under the terms of the 90 percent coinsurance clause, you should insure your property to the stipulated percentage of value. If you fail to do so, you will not be fully reimbursed for any loss that may occur. How a coinsurance clause would work in the event of a partial loss is illustrated as follows:

Insurable Value	$100,000
Insurance Carried	60,000
Insurance Required—90%	90,000
Amount of Loss	10,000
Policy Pays	6,667
Insured Pays	3,333

The insured carried $60,000 worth of insurance but should have carried $90,000. Because the amount carried was only two-thirds of what should have been carried, the insured will receive payment for only two-thirds of the $10,000 partial loss despite the fact that the face amount of the policy was $60,000. If the value of your building or its contents substantially increases, notify your insurance agent immediately to increase your coverage and thus avoid any coinsurance penalties.

Business Income

The purpose of business income insurance is to replace the operating income of your business when damage to your premises or other property prevents you from earning income. If your business suffers a business interruption and has to close for several months or operate at a reduced pace because of fire or other perils covered by this form of insurance, operating income will not be reduced.

Business income insurance covers the actual loss sustained by the insured resulting directly from the necessary interruption of business caused by damage or destruction of real or personal property.

For insurance purposes, business monthly income is defined as follows:

Total net profit	$ _____
Payroll expense	− _____
Taxes	− _____
Interest	− _____
Rents	− _____
All other operating expenses	− _____
Monthly income	+ _____
Monthly amount $___ × ___ months =	$ _____

Rental Insurance

Rental insurance provides coverage for actual loss of rental income resulting from untenantability of all or a portion of the insured's building from damage or destruction of real or personal property by an insured peril. Insurance may be written subject to a 50 percent, 60 percent, 80 percent, 90 percent, or 100 percent contribution clause.

Boiler and Machinery Insurance

The boiler and machinery policy pays for a loss or damage to or by an insured object resulting from an accident. Your property, as well as the property of others in your care, custody, or control for which you are held legally liable, are covered. An "accident" is a sudden and accidental breakdown of an object (pressure and refrigeration, mechanical, electrical, or turbine), or a part of it, that manifests itself at the time of its occurrence by physical damage to the object that necessitates repair or replacement of the object or part. The company may do periodic inspections in accordance with the terms of the policy.

Workers' Compensation

Workers' compensation coverage pays benefits required under the workers' compensation laws and employers' liability to employees not covered by workers' compensation laws. If you subcontract certain operations, workers' compensation laws provide that the principal contractor is responsible for compensation to the employees of uninsured subcontractors. In determining compensation premiums, you will be charged a premium for coverage in connection with employees of subcontractors unless the subcontractors have insured this obligation and have furnished satisfactory evidence of such insurance. You should always obtain certificates of insurance from all subcontractors working for you.

If a minor employed by you is injured, you may be assessed additional punitive damages equal to or greater than the basic award. These punitive damages are not covered by your compensation policy.

Coverage can be provided for employees who occasionally work in other states by adding an all-states endorsement.

The policy is written subject to audit, and payroll records should be kept so that they show any overtime you have paid.

Comprehensive General Liability

Comprehensive general liability is a single contract policy that provides insurance needed to cover liability for injuries or property damage sustained by the public. It covers accidents occurring on your premises or away from your premises as a result of business operations. It automatically covers certain hazards that do not now exist but that may develop during the life of the policy, and it contains fewer exclusions than individual policies.

The two basic forms of comprehensive general liability insurance are (1) owners', landlords', and tenants' (OL&T), and (2) manufacturers' and contractors' (M&C). OL&T is intended for those risks whose primary exposure is confined to a specific location. Coverage is provided for any occurrence arising from the ownership, maintenance, or use of the specified premises and any operations that are necessary or incidental to these premises.

Coverage is also automatically afforded for some types of incidental written agreements. However, it is best that any agreement containing a hold-harmless clause be submitted to the company for review in order to avoid any misunderstanding as to coverage.

Coverage is provided for the payment of all sums that the insured may become legally obligated to pay as damages because of bodily injury or property damage caused by an occurrence that arises out of the ownership and maintenance or use of the business's premises and the operations or business activities of the insured.

The M&C form is used for risks primarily associated with manufacturing or contracting operations and is rated primarily on payroll.

Personal Injury Liability

Personal injury liability extends general liability to cover alleged injury resulting from

- false arrest, detention, or imprisonment or malicious prosecution;
- libel, slander, or defamation of character; and
- wrongful entry or eviction or other invasion of the right of private occupancy.

Completed Operations

Completed operations insurance coverage is needed by all firms that do construction or installation and servicing work. This type of coverage is necessary because basic liability coverage provides protection only while the work is in progress and not after the work is completed or abandoned. The completed operations coverage applies only after the operations have been completed or abandoned and the occurrence happens away from the premises owned by or rented to the insured.

Contractual Liability (Assumed)

All forms of liability insurance exclude liability assumed by the insured under any contract. Coverage for a warranty of the fitness or quality of the insured's products is available, as is insurance to back up a warranty that work will be performed in a workmanlike manner.

Products Liability

All manufacturers, wholesalers, retailers, restaurants, bottlers, and packaging firms, or any firm that has anything to do with a product that reaches the public, should have products liability insurance. This coverage is provided by the comprehensive general liability policy unless excluded. Products coverage provides protection for bodily injury and property damage claims arising out of the insured's products or reliance upon a representation of warranty made by the insured. The bodily injury or property damage must occur away from the premises owned by or rented to the named insured and after physical possession of the product has been relinquished.

Excluded from coverage are

- loss of use of property not physically damaged when the product fails to perform the function or serve the purpose intended by the insured; and
- claims that arise when the insured is forced to recall or replace all identical products on the market. Claims for damages could occur for loss of use of the product, for damage to reputation, or for actual costs of withdrawal.

In most states, a local store is liable for products claims merely because it sells the article even if it is impossible for the store's owner to determine whether the article is defective or contains foreign matter. Many store

classifications (e.g., drugstores, bakeries, cigar stores, confectioneries, ice cream shops) in the *OL&T Manual* are not protected by products liability coverage either *on or away* from the premises.

Business Auto Coverage

Business auto policies cover the following:

- *Owned automobiles*—covers liability arising out of the ownership, maintenance, or use of owned automobiles
- *Personal injury*—coverage for vehicle passengers under no-fault law provisions
- *Uninsured motorists*—protects insureds who are not contributorily negligent against bodily injury caused by negligent uninsured and hit-and-run motorists
- *Hired automobiles*—covers liability for the use of hired automobiles in your business
- *Nonowned automobiles*—covers the liability for the use of nonowned automobiles in your business (e.g., employees using their own car on an errand for you)
- *broad form drive-other-car coverage*—provides coverage for individuals named on endorsement and for a spouse using a nonowned car, sometimes referred to as *borrowed car coverage*
- *Comprehensive*—pays for loss of or damage to automobiles from perils other than collision or upset
- *Specified perils*—pays for loss caused by fire, theft, windstorm, hail, earthquake, explosion, flood, malicious mischief, or vandalism and the sinking, burning, collision, or derailment of any conveyance transporting the covered auto
- *Collision*—pays for loss of, or damage to, automobiles from collision with another object or upset

Umbrella Excess Liability

Umbrella excess liability insurance provides

- excess coverage over other liability insurance carried by you, which is called the *underlying insurance;*
- coverage of all but a few specifically excluded liability exposures subject to a large deductible; and

- automatic replacement coverage for underlying liability policies that are reduced or exhausted by loss.

Umbrella liability insurance can also be provided as personal protection for executive officers of a corporation and partners of a partnership.

Employment Practices Coverage

Employment practices liability insurance provides defense and indemnity protection against claims arising from the employer-employee relationship. It covers damages arising from a wrongful employment act, including actual or alleged action, error, or omission triggered by wrongful termination, sexual harassment, or discrimination. Coverage is provided for the business entity, directors, officers, employees, and former employees. Liability limits can be several million dollars and deductibles range from $2,500 to $25,000.

Commercial Crime

Commercial crime policies provide coverage for the following:

- *Employee dishonesty*—pays for loss sustained by insured employer, up to a specified amount, caused by a dishonest act of an employee or employees covered under the policy
- *Premises theft and outside robbery*—covers actual or attempted theft of property other than money and securities inside the premises or actual or attempted robbery outside the premises in the care and custody of a messenger
- *Theft, disappearance, and destruction*—covers money and securities inside the premises, at banking premises, or outside the premises in the care and custody of a messenger for theft, disappearance, or destruction
- *Robbery and safe burglary*—covers loss caused by actual or attempted robbery inside the premises of property other than money and securities that is in the care and custody of a custodian and while outside the premises in the care and custody of a messenger; covers actual or attempted safe burglary inside the premises of property other than money and securities inside a safe or vault

- *Premises burglary*—covers property other than money and securities inside the premises for loss caused by actual or attempted robbery of a watch person or actual or attempted burglary
- *Computer fraud*—covers loss of money, securities, and property other than money and securities loss caused by computer fraud

Fidelity Bonds

Fidelity bonds fall into two categories:

1. *Commercial blanket bonds*—cover all officers and employees of a firm collectively. The amount of the bond is available for losses caused by employee dishonesty or for any dishonesty in which an employee is implicated.
2. *Blanket position bonds*—cover money, securities, or property belonging to the insured or for which the insured is legally liable. The burden of proof rests with the insured. The policy does not cover inventory losses based on an inventory computation or a profit and loss computation unless the insured can prove, through evidence wholly apart from the computation, that the loss was sustained through dishonest acts of employees. Each employee is bonded in the same amount.

DIVORCE PLANNING

At the time of marriage, most people usually don't plan their business affairs in anticipation of some day being divorced. However, if you wish to avoid being "taken to the cleaners" in the event of divorce, early divorce planning is an absolute necessity.

To understand divorce planning, you must understand the basics of the equitable distribution law (EDL), which most states have. The EDL, which recognizes marriage as an economic partnership, has the following requirements:

- Upon divorce, separation, or annulment, property accumulated during the marriage must be distributed in a manner reflecting the individual needs and circumstances of the husband and wife regardless of ownership.

- Maintenance (formerly known as alimony) should be awarded to meet the reasonable needs of either spouse. Maintenance is a temporary or permanent payment provided for under a written agreement or awarded by the court.

In addition to a maintenance award by the court, there is also an equitable distribution award and distributive award. The old divorce laws did not permit division of property acquired during the marriage unless title was held jointly by both husband and wife. Under the EDL, a court distributes marital property equitably between the husband and wife, giving consideration to the particular circumstances of the case. Equitable distribution does not mean *equal* distribution. Equitable, but not equal, division may be made even of jointly owned property, such as a home or bank account.

HOT SITE

Divorce Legal Survival

(http://www.friran.com/divorce.html)

Marital Property

Marital property is all property acquired by either or both spouses during the marriage regardless of who has ownership. It must be acquired before a separation agreement is signed or a matrimonial action is started. It does not include separate property or property provided for in a written agreement. Goodwill in an exclusively owned professional corporation is subject to equitable distribution. Goodwill is transferable and marketable and should be treated like any other property for distribution purposes. Goodwill, however, is differentiated from earning capacity, licenses, and educational degrees.

Separate Property

Separate property includes (1) property acquired before the marriage, (2) a gift from a third party, (3) an inheritance, and (4) personal compensation. If separate property is transferred into joint names, it becomes subject to equitable distribution as marital property.

Some of the factors that courts consider in determining the amount of the equitable distribution award are (1) the income and property of each spouse at the time of marriage and the start of the lawsuit, (2) duration of the marriage and the age and health of the spouses, (3) the need of the parent having custody of the children to occupy the marital residence and own or use the household contents, (4) lost pension or inheritance rights, (5) the amount of the maintenance award, and (6) the future economic circumstances of each spouse.

If equitable distribution is not feasible, a fixed-sum distributive award is granted. A *distributive award* is a property settlement provided by a written agreement or court order in place of, or in addition to, the equitable distribution of assets.

Dos and Don'ts

Set forth below are six dos and don'ts of divorce planning for small business owners:

1. *Do* enter into a prenuptial or postnuptial agreement. Under the EDL, before or during their marriage, a couple may provide in writing for the ownership, division, or distribution of separate and marital property, including business interests.

2. *Do not* make your spouse a corporate officer or director.

3. *Do not* pay your spouse a salary.

4. *Do* be careful as to how stock is valued when buy-sell agreements, employee stock options, and net worth statements are prepared. (See "How to Restrict the Transfer of Stock" in Chapter 13.)

5. *Do* have an employment agreement prepared if your spouse participates in the corporation. The agreement should provide that shares issued to the spouse are in consideration for his or her services to the corporation, and you should have your spouse sign a buy-sell agreement that goes into effect if the marriage ends.

6. *Do* seek the advice of a competent attorney.

Warning: All divorce planning should be done only with the advice and guidance of a lawyer proficient in the areas of divorce law, tax law, and corporate law. A complete explanation of the purposes behind this discussion of divorce planning is beyond the scope of this book and can be best explained by consulting an attorney.

17

The Americans with Disabilities Act

The Americans with Disabilities Act of 1990 (ADA) covers employment, public accommodations, transportation, and telecommunications; and it affects the employment, training, promotion, compensation, and termination policies of every employer having 15 or more employees. It also affects businesses that provide goods and services to the public.

The ADA borrows the definition of *disability* from the Rehabilitation Act of 1973, by defining it as (1) "a physical or mental impairment that substantially limits one or more of the major life activities," (2) "a record of such impairment," or (3) "being regarded as having such an impairment."

The ADA excludes

- homosexuality, bisexuality, transvestism, transsexualism, pedophilia, exhibitionism, voyeurism, gender identity disorders not resulting from physical impairments, and other sexual disorders;

- compulsive gambling, kleptomania, and pyromania; and

- individuals using illegal drugs when their employer treats them adversely on the basis of that drug use. Persons suffering from psychoactive substance use disorders also are not protected by the ADA. However, an individual who is engaged in, or has completed, drug rehabilitation and is no longer using drugs is protected under the act.

The ADA protects an employee or job applicant who is able to perform the essential functions of the job, whether the employer makes a "reasonable accommodation" for any disability that the individual may have. The ADA further provides that an employer's determination of what constitutes the "essential functions" of a job will be given consideration. A written job description prepared before the employer advertises or otherwise seeks applicants for a job will also be considered evidence of the essential functions of a job.

The ADA requires employers to make reasonable accommodations for an employee's disability. Examples of such accommodations include making existing facilities used by employees readily accessible to and usable by individuals with disabilities as well as job restructuring, part-time or modified work schedules; reassignment to a vacant position; acquisition or modification of equipment or devices; appropriate adjustment or modification of examinations, training materials, or policies; the provision of qualified readers or interpreters; and other similar accommodations for disabled employees.

The ADA was intended to help thousands of disabled persons achieve respect and dignity. However, most claimants are workers with back problems, mental disorders, and neurological illnesses. Under the Americans with Disabilities Act, mental disabilities and physical disabilities are governed by identical legal standards, although the issues surrounding mental disabilities are far more complex and elusive. Whereas a physical disability, such as blindness, may be obvious, a mental disability such as depression, may be exhibited in a vague manner or perhaps not at all.

The ADA, the Federal Rehabilitation Act, and state disability statutes cover people who are "regarded" as having a disability as well as people who actually have one.

Many lawsuits have involved employers who claimed that they fired their employees because of poor work or interpersonal skills and employees who claimed that their problems were due to psychological disabilities. These employees claimed that their employer had to either counsel them or otherwise obtain help for them rather than fire them.

A postal worker won $865,000 for being terminated because he had a "volatile personality" and "generally went out of control"; and his employer was afraid he would become violent. A newspaper editor received a settlement under the ADA for being fired because she threw temper tantrums and locked coworkers in their offices.

A government investigator received a settlement under the ADA because he was fired for not doing any work. He claimed he stopped working because he was depressed and his employer should have accommodated him. A salesman obtained a settlement under the ADA for being fired because he could not follow verbal directions; he claimed he suffered from an "attention deficit disorder."

An in-house legal counsel won $1.1 million after his company refused to "accommodate" his depression by giving him shorter hours, a more supportive boss, and a positive job evaluation. A jury awarded $912,000 to a saleswoman who was fired because her manic-depressive illness caused her to be rude to customers and disrupt sales meetings.

UNDUE HARDSHIP

The ADA provides employers with the defense of *undue hardship*, which is defined as "requiring significant difficulty or expense." The following criteria are used to establish this defense:

- The size of the business
- The size of its budget
- The nature of its operation
- The number of its employees
- The composition and structure of its workforce
- The nature and cost of the accommodation

A large or wealthy employer would be required to spend more money or to undertake a greater effort to accommodate an individual's disability than would a smaller company. The ADA prohibits discrimination on account of disability in the following areas of employment:

- Hiring
- Promotions and transfers
- Training
- Compensation
- Fringe benefits
- Layoffs
- Terminations

The following actions constitute unlawful discrimination:

- Classifying or segregating disabled employees or job applicants in such a way that their employment or promotional opportunities are different from those of able-bodied employees
- Requesting or permitting an employment agency, executive recruiter, union, or provider of insurance or other fringe benefits to discriminate against its applicants or employees
- Using job placement tests or standards that may not have the purpose or effect of discriminating against an employee or applicant who is disabled but in fact do discriminate
- Refusing to hire someone who lives with a disabled relative or whose spouse or child is disabled
- Refusing to make reasonable accommodations to assist a disabled employee or an applicant unless it would cause an undue hardship
- Using employment tests or criteria that tend to screen out disabled applicants unless the test is job related and there is a business necessity for it

DRUGS AND ALCOHOL IN THE WORKPLACE

The ADA permits an employer to

- fire or refuse to hire an individual who is a current user of illegal drugs;
- ban all employees from using alcohol or illegal drugs in the workplace;
- require employees not to be under the influence of alcohol or illegal drugs in the workplace;

- require employees to conform to the requirements of the Drug-Free Workplace Act;
- hold alcoholic or drug-addicted employees to the same standards as all other employees even if their unsatisfactory job performance is caused by their drug addiction or alcoholism;
- test employees for drug use (a drug test is not considered a medical examination—see Chapter 11); and
- require employees to comply with Department of Defense, Nuclear Regulatory Commission, and Department of Transportation drug policy and testing regulations.

However, an employee is protected as "an individual with a disability" when he or she has completed a drug rehabilitation program and is not a current user of drugs; is currently undergoing a drug rehabilitation program and is not a current user of drugs; is erroneously perceived as a drug user but in fact is not engaging in drug use; or is an alcoholic, unless posing a direct threat.

MISCELLANEOUS PROVISIONS

The ADA requires the posting of notices, according to The Civil Rights Act of 1964, that are provided by the Equal Employment Opportunity Commission. The ADA does not preempt other federal, state, or local laws providing equal or greater protection to the disabled. The ADA does not prohibit employers from implementing policies that limit or prohibit smoking in the workplace.

The ADA prohibits an employer from retaliating against an individual who opposes any unlawful practices or who participates in a proceeding brought under the ADA. Attorney fees may be awarded to prevailing parties.

HOW TO COMPLY WITH THE ADA

Following are ten actions employers should take to comply with the ADA:

1. *Develop job descriptions.* Employers should identify job prerequisites (appropriate educational background, employment experience, skills, licenses, or other job-related requirements for the position) and essential functions to determine whether an individual is qualified to perform an essential job function, with or without a reasonable accommodation. The job description should be prepared *before* advertising a job or interviewing candidates. Identify the essential and nonessential job functions and prepare descriptions that may serve as evidence of your nondiscriminatory intent.

2. *Review employment applications.* Employment applications should be examined to ensure that they comply with federal and state laws. Insert questions about the company's prerequisites (e.g., education and certifications required). Questions should be deleted if they address an applicant's disability status, health, past medical problems, and workers' compensation claims. Specific job-related questions should be used to help determine whether applicants can perform the essential functions of the job. A statement should be added to the employment application informing job applicants that the employer encourages applications from qualified individuals with disabilities.

3. *Review employment tests and other selection criteria.* Employers may not use an employment test that tends to screen out individuals with disabilities unless the test is shown to be job related for the position and consistent with business necessity. The company must also select and administer employment tests in a manner that ensures they accurately reflect the skills, aptitudes, or other factors that the test is designed to measure rather than impaired sensory, manual, or speaking skills of the applicant.

4. *Review preemployment drug-testing procedures.* Applicants may be required to take a drug test before a job offer is made. The sole purpose of the test must be to detect the use of illegal drugs and it must comply with federal, state, or local laws regarding quality control, confidentiality, and rehabilitation.

5. *Review medical examination procedures.* The use of preemployment medical examinations before a job offer is made is prohibited. Employers may require physical examinations of an applicant after the offer of a job has been made if (1) all applicants are examined regardless of any disability; (2) the results of those examinations are collected and maintained on separate forms and are kept in separate, confidential files;

(3) examination results are not used for any purpose prohibited by the ADA; (4) supervisors, managers, and safety/first-aid personnel are advised of the disability and of any required restrictions or accommodations that must be made; (5) an employer demonstrates that the medical examination was job related and that there was a business necessity for it; and (6) an employer inquires whether an employee or applicant is able to perform a job-related function (e.g., lifting heavy objects or operating complex machinery).

6. *Train employees.* Employees of all levels should be sensitized to working with disabled people. Special orientation and training programs should be designed for new employees with disabilities.

7. *Safety programs.* Review safety procedures and practices, especially for employees with disabilities. Design emergency drills with disabled employees in mind.

8. *Revise the personnel policies manual.* A neutral policy should be drafted concerning attendance and lateness. Make certain these policies are communicated to the employees and uniformly enforced. Develop part-time or modified work schedules to help accommodate all employees. Draft objective interview and discipline forms indicating why an individual was hired, disciplined, or demoted.

9. *Disability compliance procedures.* A written policy should be distributed to all employees. The policy statement should explain the company's commitment to adhere to and enforce its obligations under the ADA and other nondiscrimination laws. Emphasize that all employees are expected to help implement the goals of the company. Establish a procedure whereby job applicants and employees can file complaints if they feel there has been discrimination on the basis of disability.

After an employee discloses his or her disability, discuss possible accommodations with the employee. Identify the barriers to job performance resulting from a particular disability. Assess the reasonableness of each accommodation in terms of effectiveness, equal employment demands, and employer hardship. Implement the accommodation that is most appropriate and causes the least hardship to the company.

10. *Review contracts.* All contracts with employment agencies, organizations providing fringe benefits and training, and insurance companies should be reviewed to ensure nondiscriminatory terms and language.

HOW THE ADA AFFECTS WORKERS' COMPENSATION

If a worker is eligible for workers' compensation, does this mean he or she automatically has a disability for purposes of the Americans with Disabilities Act?

No. Many injuries that qualify for workers' compensation are not serious enough to make someone disabled for purposes of filing an ADA claim. Injured workers are disabled under the ADA only if their injury makes them "substantially limited in a major life activity" such as working, walking, or breathing.

However, the ADA also covers workers whose company perceives them as disabled. Therefore, even if workers aren't injured seriously enough to be disabled, they might still be covered if their employer discriminates against them because of the impairment, such as by refusing to let them come back to work.

Can job applicants be asked if they have filed workers' compensation claims in the past?

No. However, after a company has made a job offer, it can ask for limited information about past on-the-job injuries so long as it has a legitimate need for the information and asks the same questions of all new employees in similar jobs.

Can workers sue under the ADA if they are fired for taking a leave after filing a compensation claim?

Maybe. Workers would have to show they are disabled and that being given a short-term leave would be a reasonable accommodation.

Can a company give a medical exam to workers who file a comp compensation claim?

Yes. A company can require a medical exam or ask questions about an on-the-job injury to find out what benefits workers should get or determine if they are healthy enough to return to work.

However, if a company asks for more information than it needs to process a claim or forces a worker to have many exams or repeatedly answer the same questions, this may be "disability-based harassment" under the ADA.

Can a company refuse to hire because an applicant has filed compensation claims in the past or because hiring this applicant will result in higher compensation costs?

No. However, a company can refuse to hire people who are so likely to injure themselves that they pose a direct threat to the workplace.

If a company provides light-duty jobs for workers who are injured on the job, must it also offer them to workers who are disabled for other reasons?

If a company creates these jobs on a case-by-case basis, it doesn't have to offer them to workers whose disabilities are not work related. However, if a company holds open a certain number of light-duty jobs to give to workers who are injured on the job, it must also offer them to other disabled workers.

If injured workers take workers' compensation leave, can the company refuse to let them return to work until they are ready for a full-duty job?

No. If workers are disabled under the ADA, the company must allow them to return to work as soon as they can perform the essential functions of the job with reasonable accommodation.

Even though workers are permanently disabled according to a workers' compensation board, must the company give them their job back?

Yes, so long as they can do the job with reasonable accommodation. For example, workers who have become blind or lost the use of their legs may be permanently disabled for purposes of receiving compensation benefits but can still sue under the ADA if they can perform the essential functions of the job with reasonable accommodation.

PUBLIC ACCOMMODATIONS AND COMMERCIAL FACILITIES

The ADA requires developers, management companies, landlords, and tenants to provide disabled individuals with physical accessibility to commercial facilities (e.g., office buildings, factories, and warehouses) and places of public accommodation (e.g., restaurants, theaters, and retail establishments).

Existing public accommodations must be retrofitted to remove barriers to disabled accessibility and must provide auxiliary aids (e.g., braille print) if it is readily achievable or can be easily accommodated or carried out without much difficulty or expense. Commercial facilities are subject to the ADA's accessibility requirements only when the facility is a new construction or when an existing building undergoes alterations, renovations, remodeling, historic preservation, or structural changes that affect the usability of the building.

Readily achievable barrier removal in public accommodations may include the following:

- Installing ramps and making curb cuts in sidewalks and entrances
- Repositioning shelves and telephones
- Rearranging tables, chairs, display racks, vending machines, and other furniture
- Adding raised markings on elevator control buttons
- Installing flashing alarm lights
- Widening doors or installing offset hinges to widen doorways
- Eliminating a turnstile or providing an alternative accessible path
- Installing accessible door hardware
- Installing grab bars in toilet stalls
- Rearranging toilet partitions to increase maneuvering space
- Insulating lavatory pipes under sinks to prevent burns
- Installing a full-length bathroom mirror
- Repositioning the paper-towel dispenser in a bathroom
- Creating designated accessible parking spaces
- Installing an accessible paper-cup dispenser at an otherwise inaccessible water fountain
- Removing high-pile, low-density carpeting
- Installing vehicle hand controls

Because both landlords and tenants are equally responsible for compliance with the ADA's accessibility requirements, landlords should protect themselves from being fined for noncompliance and having to pay for alterations by using lease clauses that provide the following:

- The tenant is responsible for any alterations that may trigger compliance requirements and for complying with the Americans with Disabilities Act and all federal, state, and local laws.
- The landlord is permitted to enter the leased space to make any alterations that

the tenant has neglected to make in order to comply with the ADA.

- The tenant will hold the landlord harmless and indemnify him or her for loss, damage, or attorney fees for the tenant's failure to comply with federal, state, and local laws.

When purchasing commercial property, buyers should protect themselves by (1) using contract clauses that provide for a feasibility study by an architect or engineer to determine whether barriers to accessibility have been removed and whether such removal is readily achievable; (2) examining current leases to determine whether they allocate responsibility for compliance with the ADA between the landlord and tenant; and (3) obtaining a warranty by the seller that the building complies with the Americans with Disabilities Act and all federal, state, and local laws.

Private individuals may bring lawsuits to stop discrimination. Individuals may also file complaints with the U.S. attorney general, who is authorized to bring lawsuits in cases of general public importance or where a "pattern or practice" of discrimination is alleged. In these cases, the attorney general may seek monetary damages and civil penalties. Civil penalties may not exceed $50,000 for a first violation or $100,000 for any subsequent violation.

The Internal Revenue Code allows a deduction of up to $15,000 per year for expenses associated with the removal of qualified architectural and transportation barriers. Small businesses may receive a tax credit for certain costs of compliance with the ADA. An eligible small business is one whose gross receipts do not exceed $1 million or whose workforce does not consist of more than 30 full-time workers. Qualifying businesses may claim a credit of up to 50 percent of eligible access expenditures that exceed $250 but do not exceed $10,250. Examples of eligible access expenditures include the necessary and reasonable costs of removing architectural, physical, communications, and transportation barriers; providing readers, interpreters, and other auxiliary aids; and acquiring or modifying equipment or devices.

HOW AND WHEN TO USE THE FORM IN THIS CHAPTER

IRS Form 8826-Disabled Access Credit. Eligible small businesses use this form to claim the disabled access credit, which is part of the general business credit.

Form **8826**

Department of the Treasury
Internal Revenue Service

Disabled Access Credit

▶ **Attach to your return.**

OMB No. 1545-1205

19**96**

Attachment
Sequence No. **86**

Name(s) shown on return

Identifying number

Part I **Current Year Credit**

1	Total eligible access expenditures	1		
2	Minimum amount	2	$ 250	00
3	Subtract line 2 from line 1 (if less than zero, enter -0-)	3		
4	Maximum amount	4	$10,000	00
5	Enter smaller of line 3 or line 4	5		
6	Current year credit. Multiply line 5 by 50% (.50)	6		

7 Disabled access credits from flow-through entities:

If you are a—	Then enter total of current year disabled access credit(s) from—
a Shareholder	Schedule K-1 (Form 1120S), lines 12d, 12e, or 13
b Partner	Schedule K-1 (Form 1065), lines 13c, 13d, or 14

7		

8 **Total current year disabled access credit.** Add lines 6 and 7, but do not enter more than $5,000 . | 8 | | |

Part II **Tax Liability Limit** (See **Who Must File Form 3800** to find out if you complete Part II or file Form 3800.)

9 Regular tax before credits:

- Individuals. Enter amount from Form 1040, line 38 . . . .
- Corporations. Enter amount from Form 1120, Schedule J, line 3 (or Form 1120-A, Part I, line 1) } . .
- Other filers. Enter regular tax before credits from your return . . . .

9	

10a	Credit for child and dependent care expenses (Form 2441, line 10) .	10a	
b	Credit for the elderly or the disabled (Schedule R (Form 1040), line 20)	10b	
c	Mortgage interest credit (Form 8396, line 11)	10c	
d	Foreign tax credit (Form 1116, line 32, or Form 1118, Sch. B, line 12)	10d	
e	Possessions tax credit (Form 5735)	10e	
f	Credit for fuel from a nonconventional source	10f	
g	Qualified electric vehicle credit (Form 8834, line 19)	10g	
h	Add lines 10a through 10g	10h	
11	Net regular tax. Subtract line 10h from line 9	11	

12 Alternative minimum tax:

- Individuals. Enter amount from Form 6251, line 28 . . . .
- Corporations. Enter amount from Form 4626, line 15 . . . . }
- Estates and trusts. Enter amount from Form 1041, Schedule I, line 41 . .

12	

13	Net income tax. Add lines 11 and 12	13

14 Tentative minimum tax (see instructions):

- Individuals. Enter amount from Form 6251, line 26 . . . . .
- Corporations. Enter amount from Form 4626, line 13 . . . . . }
- Estates and trusts. Enter amount from Form 1041, Schedule I, line 37 . . . .

14	

15 If line 11 is more than $25,000, enter 25% (.25) of the excess (see instructions) . . . .

15	

16	Enter the greater of line 14 or line 15	16
17	Subtract line 16 from line 13. If zero or less, enter -0-	17

18 **Disabled access credit allowed for current year.** Enter the **smaller** of line 8 or line 17 here and on Form 1040, line 42; Form 1120, Schedule J, line 4d; Form 1120-A, line 2a; Form 1041, Schedule G, line 2c; or the applicable line of your return . . . . . . | 18 | | |

Section references are to the Internal Revenue Code.

Paperwork Reduction Act Notice

We ask for the information on this form to carry out the Internal Revenue laws of the United States. You are required to give us the information. We need it to ensure that you are complying with these laws and to allow us to figure and collect the right amount of tax.

You are not required to provide the information requested on a form that is subject to the Paperwork Reduction Act unless the form displays a valid OMB control number. Books or records relating to a form or its instructions must be retained as long as their contents may become material in the administration of any Internal Revenue law. Generally, tax returns and return information are confidential, as required by section 6103.

Cat. No. 12774N

Form **8826** (1996)

The time needed to complete and file this form will vary depending on individual circumstances. The estimated average time is:

Recordkeeping . . . . 4 hr., 47 min.

Learning about the law or the form . . . . . . 47 min.

Preparing and sending the form to the IRS . . . . 55 min.

If you have comments concerning the accuracy of these time estimates or suggestions for making this form simpler, we would be happy to hear from you. You can write to the IRS at the address listed in the instructions of the tax return with which this form is filed.

General Instructions

Purpose of Form

Eligible small businesses use Form 8826 to claim the disabled access credit. This credit is part of the general business credit.

A partnership or S corporation that is an eligible small business completes Part I of the form to figure the credit to pass through to its partners or shareholders.

Definitions

Eligible small business.—For purposes of the credit, an eligible small business is any business or person that **(a)** had gross receipts for the preceding tax year that did not exceed $1 million or had no more than 30 full-time employees during the preceding tax year and **(b)** elects (by filing Form 8826) to claim the disabled access credit for the tax year.

For purposes of the definition:

1. Gross receipts are reduced by returns and allowances made during the tax year.

2. An employee is considered full time if that employee is employed at least 30 hours per week for 20 or more calendar weeks in the tax year.

3. Generally, all members of the same controlled group and all persons under common control are considered to be one person. See section 44(d)(2).

Eligible access expenditures.—For purposes of the credit, these expenditures are amounts paid or incurred by the eligible small business **to comply with applicable requirements** under the Americans With Disabilities Act of 1990 (Public Law 101–336) as in effect on November 5, 1990.

Eligible access expenditures include amounts paid or incurred:

1. To remove barriers that prevent a business from being accessible to or usable by individuals with disabilities;

2. To provide qualified interpreters or other methods of making audio materials available to hearing-impaired individuals;

3. To provide qualified readers, taped texts, and other methods of making visual materials available to individuals with visual impairments; or

4. To acquire or modify equipment or devices for individuals with disabilities.

The expenditures must be reasonable and necessary to accomplish the above purposes.

Eligible expenditures do not include expenditures in **1** above that are paid or incurred in connection with any facility first placed in service after November 5, 1990.

Eligible access expenditures must meet those standards issued by the Secretary of the Treasury as agreed to by the Architectural and Transportation Barriers Compliance Board and set forth in regulations. See section 44(c) for other details.

Disability.—For an individual, this means:

1. A physical or mental impairment that substantially limits one or more of the major life activities of that individual;

2. A record of such an impairment; or

3. Being regarded as having such an impairment.

Specific Instructions

Part I

Line 1.—Enter total eligible access expenditures paid or incurred during the tax year. See **Eligible access expenditures** above for a definition and other details.

Controlled groups.—All members of a controlled group of corporations (within the meaning of section 52(a)) and all persons under common control (within the meaning of section 52(b)) are treated as one person for purposes of the credit. The group member with the most eligible access expenditures should figure the group credit in Part I and skip Part II.

On separate Forms 8826, each member of the group skips lines 1 through 5 and enters its share of the group credit on line 6. Each member then completes the remaining applicable lines (or Form 3800, if required) on its separate form. Each member must also attach to its Form 8826 a schedule showing how the group credit was divided among all members. The members share the credit in the same proportion that they contributed eligible access expenditures.

Denial of double benefit.—To the extent of the credit shown on line 6, the eligible access expenditures may not be claimed as a deduction in figuring taxable income, capitalized, or used in figuring any other credit.

Who Must File Form 3800

If for this year you have more than one of the credits included in the general business credit listed below, or have a carryback or carryforward of any of the credits, or have a disabled access credit from a passive activity, you must complete **Form 3800,** General Business Credit, instead of completing Part II of Form 8826 to figure the tax liability limitation.

The general business credit consists of the following credits:

- Investment (Form 3468),
- Work opportunity (Form 5884),
- Alcohol used as fuel (Form 6478),
- Research (Form 6765),
- Low-income housing (Form 8586),
- Enhanced oil recovery (Form 8830),
- Disabled access (Form 8826),
- Renewable electricity production (Form 8835),
- Indian employment (Form 8845),
- Employer social security and Medicare taxes paid on certain employee tips (Form 8846),
- Orphan drug (Form 8820),
- Contributions to selected community development corporations (Form 8847), and
- Trans-Alaska pipeline liability fund.

The empowerment zone employment credit (Form 8844), while a component of the general business credit, is figured separately and is never carried to Form 3800.

Part II

Complete Part II if you do not have to file Form 3800.

Line 14.—Enter the tentative minimum tax (TMT) that was figured on the appropriate alternative minimum tax (AMT) form or schedule. Although you may not owe AMT, you must still compute the TMT to figure your credit.

Line 15.—See section 38(c)(3) for special rules that apply to married couples filing separate returns, controlled corporate groups, regulated investment companies, and real estate investment trusts.

Line 18.—If you cannot use part of the credit because of the tax liability limit (line 17 is smaller than line 8), carry it back 3 years, then forward 15 years. See the separate Instructions for Form 3800 for details.

 Printed on recycled paper   *U.S. Government Printing Office: 1996 — 417-677/40227*

18

Credit, Collections, and Bankruptcy

Bad checks, bad debts, and bankruptcies are on the rise. Collecting debts may be almost impossible if you don't take the necessary precautions. On the other side of the coin, knowing your credit rights, where to obtain financing, and what collateral to use will increase your chances of obtaining a loan. Because many small business people often use their personal credit to get their operation off the ground, this chapter also will discuss consumer credit concerns.

THE TOP TEN DANGER AREAS

The top ten danger areas leading to statutory damages, actual damages, attorney fees, and punitive damages for violating consumers' rights are the following:

1. Requiring a spouse to cosign a loan in violation of the Equal Credit Opportunity Law

1. Pursuing collection efforts, lawsuits, garnishments, or repossessions in violation of a bankruptcy stay or discharge

1. Failure of a credit bureau to prevent the same error from recurring in a consumer's file in violation of the Fair Credit Reporting Act

1. Attorneys allowing debt collectors to use their names in collection letters without first adequately reviewing the debtor's file in violation of the Fair Debt Collection Practices Act

1. New loans and second mortgages for debt consolidation or home repairs with outrageous terms

2. Sellers raising the cash price and implementing hidden finance charges for high-risk debtors in violation of the Truth in Lending Act and state credit statutes

3. Car lessors withholding interest on security deposits or improperly disclosing early termination penalties, purchase options, trade-ins, taxes, or warranties in violation of the Consumer Leasing Act

4. Faulty notice of or commercially unreasonable auto repossession sales

5. Used car sales involving reset odometers, salvaged vehicles or "lemon" laundering

6. Consumer contracts providing that a lease, future service contract, or other transaction can't be canceled or that a dealer is not subject to the oral promises of its employees

THE FAIR CREDIT REPORTING ACT

State and federal fair credit reporting acts impose mandatory disclosure requirements on those who use credit reports.

Consumer Report

A consumer report may contain information regarding a customer's credit history (how credit was used and whether credit payments were made on time), character, personal characteristics, mode of living, or reputation. It is used to determine eligibility for credit, insurance, or employment.

HOT SITE

Consumer Legal Survival

(http://www.friran.com/consumer.html)

Obsolete Information

If a credit bureau reports adverse information from public records, it must make sure that the information is both up-to-date and complete. A credit bureau may not report the following information: bankruptcies more than 14 years old, unpaid judgments, paid tax liens, accounts placed for collection, records of conviction, information regarding drug or alcohol addiction and mental institution confinement, or any other information more than seven years old.

These time limitations do not apply to credit transactions of at least $50,000, underwriting of life insurance of at least $50,000, or employment involving an annual salary of at least $25,000. There are also other exceptions to these time limitations.

Consumers' Rights if Rejected

If a consumer is rejected for credit, insurance, or employment based on a credit report, he or she must be given the name and address of the credit bureau so that any misinformation in the file can be corrected.

The consumer has the right of access to the files of the bureau even if adverse action isn't taken. You, as the consumer, have the right to know the nature, substance, and source of the information in the file except for medical information. You also have the right to know who received your credit report for employment purposes during the previous two years and for other purposes during the previous six months.

The consumer reporting agency must promptly advise consumers of the agency's obligation to (1) disclose its files either in person, by mail, or by telephone; and (2) provide a decoded written version of files or a written copy of files with an explanation of any code used if a consumer so requests. All consumers

must be specifically advised that if they have been denied credit in the past 30 days, they are entitled to receive a written copy of their complete file on request at no charge whatsoever.

Inaccuracies

Credit bureaus are required to reinvestigate disputed items of information and correct those found to be inaccurate. Unverified or inaccurate information must be deleted from the report. If a dispute is not resolved, the existence of the dispute must be noted in the file as well as a statement of the consumer's version of the dispute.

If any disputed item is reinvestigated and found to be in error or can no longer be verified, the bureau must promptly mail the consumer a corrected written copy of the file at no charge.

Enforcement of the Law

It is a crime to obtain information from a credit bureau under false pretenses. A bureau may be liable for providing information to someone unauthorized to receive it. Consumers may sue a credit bureau for failure to comply with the Fair Credit Reporting Act.

Suppliers and users of information and credit bureaus can be sued for libel, slander, or invasion of privacy if the information is false, is furnished with malice or willful intent to injure the consumer, or if there is negligent noncompliance with the act.

WOMEN AND CREDIT

Both men and women are protected from credit discrimination based on sex or marital status. You may not be denied credit just because you are a woman or just because you are married, single, widowed, divorced, or separated. State laws and the federal Equal Credit Opportunity Act provide the following protection from discrimination in credit lending.

Sex, marital status, and child-bearing plans. Creditors may not ask your sex on an application form except for loans to buy or build a home. You do not have to use Miss, Mrs., or Ms. with your name on a credit application, but in certain cases a creditor may ask whether you are married, unmarried, or separated. "Unmarried" covers single, divorced, and widowed persons.

Creditors may not ask about birth control practices or whether a woman plans to have children, and they may not assume anything about a woman's intentions to have a child.

Income and alimony. Creditors must consider all of your income, even income from part-time employment. You do not have to disclose child support or alimony and maintenance payments as income. But if you do, creditors must consider them as income.

Telephones. Creditors may not consider whether you have a telephone listed in your name because this discriminates against married women. But creditors may ask if there is a telephone in your home.

Your own accounts. You have a right to your own credit account based on your own records and earnings. Your own credit means a separate account or loan in your own name, not a joint account with your husband or a duplicate card for his account. Creditors may not refuse to open an account solely because of your sex or marital status. You may choose to use your first name and maiden name (Mary Jones), your first name and husband's last name (Mary Smith), or a combined last name (Mary Jones-Smith).

If you are creditworthy, a creditor may not require your spouse to cosign your account except when property rights are involved. Creditors may not ask for information about your spouse or former spouse when you apply for your own credit based on your own income unless that income is alimony, child support, or separate maintenance payments from your spouse. This last rule does not apply if your spouse is going to use your account or is responsible for paying your debts.

Change in marital status. Creditors may not require you to reapply for credit because you marry, become widowed, or are divorced, nor may they close your account or change the terms of your account on these grounds: some indication that your creditworthiness has changed is required. For example, creditors may ask you to reapply if you relied on your spouse's income to get credit and subsequently seek additional credit based solely on your own earnings. Setting up your own account protects you by giving you your own history of debt management to rely on if circumstances change as a result of widowhood or divorce.

A creditor may consider whether income is steady and reliable, so be prepared to show that you can count on a steady income, particularly if the source of income is alimony payments or part-time wages.

State laws specifically prohibit discrimination on the basis of sex or marital status in an application of credit for the acquisition, construction, rehabilitation, repair, and maintenance of housing. The Federal Housing Act specifically prohibits discrimination in granting federally related home mortgage loans.

If credit is denied. You must be notified within 30 days after your application has been completed whether your loan has been approved. If credit is denied, this notice must be in writing, and it must explain the specific reasons for denying credit or tell you of your rights to request an explanation. You have the same rights if your account is closed. You may have to ask the creditor for an explanation if your credit has been denied. You are entitled to your credit file from the credit bureau. If you feel that you have been discriminated against, consult an attorney.

Under state laws, if you have been discriminated against, you can go to either the state division of human rights, the superintendent of banking, or you can file a suit in state court. Under federal law, you can go either to the appropriate federal agency or to a U.S. district court.

Keep in mind that creditors are permitted to consider your willingness and ability to repay the loan by looking at your assets, income, expenses, and credit history.

THIRTEEN SOURCES OF CASH FOR YOUR BUSINESS

1. Friends and relatives
2. Liquidating or borrowing from retirement funds, such as an IRA, KEOGH, or 401(k) account, although income tax is imposed on all funds that you withdraw as well as a 10 percent penalty if you are under 59½ years old
3. A home equity line of credit, second home mortgage, or refinancing your original home mortgage

4. Asking your customers to pay in advance for products or services

5. Asking your suppliers to give you 60 to 90 days to pay for materials

6. Obtaining an SBA Microloan for up to $25,000

7. Using credit cards even though the interest rates may be higher than on other types of loans

8. Obtaining an SBA-guaranteed bank loan for $150,000 to $750,000

9. Seeking a private investor

HOT SITE

The Angel Capital Electronic Network (ACE-NET) was designed by the U.S. Small Business Administration Office of Advocacy to provide a link between private investors and small companies looking for $250,000 to $5 million in investment capital. ACE-NET acts solely as a listing service for small corporate stock offerings. It is not a matching service and does not act as an adviser, broker, or securities dealer. The network produces videos and educational materials aimed at helping small businesses become more investment-savvy. Information can be found at http://www.sbaonline.sba.gov or http://www.ace/net.unh.net.

---

10. Obtaining a business loan or line of credit from a bank

11. Factors, who typically purchase your uncollected receivables for about 96 cents on a dollar

12. Venture capital firms that buy a piece of your company to help it grow

13. Taking your company public by issuing stock in an initial public offering

HOW TO COME UP WITH COLLATERAL FOR A BANK LOAN

Your signature alone may not be sufficient as security to obtain a bank loan. Banks require assurance that a loan will be repaid. The kind and amount of such security depends on the particular bank and borrower. If the loan you require can't be justified by your financial statements alone, a pledge of any of the following as security may satisfy the bank:

Endorsers. To bolster your own credit, you could get someone to sign a note as an endorser—someone who is contingently liable for the note. If you fail to pay the bank, the endorser is expected to pay the note and may also be asked to pledge assets or securities.

Comaker. A comaker creates an obligation jointly with the borrower. The bank can collect directly from either the maker or the comaker.

Guarantor. A guarantor guarantees the payment of a note by signing a guaranty commitment. Both private and government lenders often require guarantees from officers of corporations to ensure continuity of effective management. A manufacturer, for example, may act as a guarantor for its customers.

Assignment of leases. The assigned lease is used in franchise situations. The bank lends money on a building and takes back a mortgage. The lease between the franchisee and the franchisor is assigned to the bank so that it automatically receives the rent payments.

Warehouse receipts. Banks take commodities as security by lending money on warehouse receipts delivered directly to the bank. The receipts show that the merchandise used as security has either been placed in a public warehouse or been left on your premises under the control of one of your employees who is bonded (as in field warehousing). These loans are generally made on stable or standard merchandise that can be readily marketed. The typical warehouse receipt loan is for a percentage of the estimated value of the goods used as security.

Trust receipts and floor planning. Merchandise such as automobiles, appliances, and boats usually have to be displayed in order to be sold. The only way that many retailers can afford such displays is by borrowing money secured by a note and trust receipt.

The trust receipt is used for serial-numbered merchandise. On signing, you (1) acknowledge receipt of the merchandise, (2) agree to keep the merchandise in trust for the bank, and (3) promise to pay the bank as you sell the goods.

Chattel mortgages. Chattel mortgages are used for equipment (such as a cash register or a delivery truck) in which you give the bank a lien on the equipment. The bank will (1) evaluate the present and future market value of the equipment being used to secure the loan; (2) look at how rapidly it will depreciate; and (3) see whether the borrower has the necessary fire, theft, property damage, and public liability insurance on the equipment.

Real estate. Real estate is used for long-term loans. A bank determines the location of the real estate, its physical condition, its foreclosure value, and the amount of insurance carried on the property.

Accounts receivable. This form of collateral may be taken by a bank on a notification or a nonnotification basis. Under the notification plan, purchasers of goods are informed by the bank that their account has been assigned to it, and the purchasers are told to pay the bank. Under the nonnotification plan, purchasers continue to pay the sellers the sums due on their account, and the sellers pay the bank.

Savings accounts. Savings accounts may be assigned to a bank. The bank obtains an assignment from you and holds your passbook. If an account in another bank is assigned as collateral, the lending bank asks the bank that has your account to mark its records to show that the account is held as collateral.

Life insurance. Banks lend up to the cash value of an insurance policy if you assign the policy to the bank. If the policy is on the life of an executive of a small corporation, corporate resolutions must be made authorizing the assignment.

Most insurance companies are willing to use the cash value of a life insurance policy as collateral for a loan to their insureds.

Stocks and bonds. Marketable stocks and bonds can be used as collateral. As a protection against market declines and possible liquidation expenses, banks usually lend no more than 75 percent of the market value of high-grade stock. On U.S. or municipal bonds, they may be willing to lend 90 percent or more of the bonds' market value.

A bank may ask the borrower for additional security or payment whenever the market value of the stocks or bonds drops below the bank's required margin.

EQUAL CREDIT OPPORTUNITY ACT

The Equal Credit Opportunity Act requires that commercial lenders

- notify small business applicants in writing of any adverse action taken, and notify small business applicants of their right to a statement of the reasons for the adverse action;

- act on a small business's application within 30 days; and

- retain records of small business applicants and any adverse action taken for 12 months.

Commercial lenders can inquire about a business applicant's marital status only if the applicant resides in a community property state (Arizona, California, Idaho, Louisiana, Nevada, New Mexico, Texas, Washington, and Wisconsin) or relies on property located in a community property state to secure the debt.

To exercise their rights to a statement of reasons for adverse action, small business applicants must request the statement within 60 days of notification of an adverse action. On receipt of such a request, the lender must provide a written answer within 30 days. The Equal Credit Opportunity Act covers only small businesses that are defined as start-up businesses and borrowers with gross revenues of $1 million or less in the preceding fiscal year. Trade credit and credit incident to factoring arrangements are not covered by the law even when a small business applies for this type of credit.

ARE DEBTORS GETTING AWAY WITH MURDER?

How would you like it if you went through all of the expense and trouble of going to court and getting a judgment against a customer who owed you $4,000 and you still couldn't collect a cent?

You may very well suffer this frustrating experience because our laws favor the debtor. This favoritism is evident in three areas of the law: (1) judgments, (2) bankruptcy, and (3) landlord-tenant relations.

Judgments

The judgment that you obtain against a debtor may be worthless and uncollectible if the debtor is not employed and has no property. Even if the debtor owns property or has income, in order to seize the debtor's nonexempt property or garnish the debtor's nonexempt wages, you must first ascertain the debtor's place of employment and an exact description of the debtor's property, including serial numbers. Even if the debtor is employed, federal law exempts from garnishment 75 percent of all disposable earnings per workweek or an amount equal to 30 times the federal minimum hourly wage, whichever is greater. If the debtor files for bankruptcy, you cannot garnish the debtor's wages, seize the debtor's property, or sue the debtor; and even worse, the debt may be wiped out.

HOT SITE

Creditor Legal Survival

(http://www.friran.com/creditor.html)

Bankruptcy

The bankruptcy law is invitingly named a "fresh start" law. A debtor can erase most debts and judgments and still keep most of his or her property, even a mortgaged home. If the debt is not secured, it is wiped out.

A person can file for bankruptcy even if he or she has a good job. An example is a surgeon who was guaranteed $10,000 per month from a hospital. During a leave of absence, he wiped out $45,000 worth of debts by filing for bankruptcy after which he returned to work at another hospital at the same salary.

Landlord-Tenant Relations

If a tenant does not vacate leased premises at the end of the lease period or after 30 days notice, the landlord cannot lock out or throw the tenant out without a court order. Even after the landlord obtains a court order and warrant of eviction, the sheriff or another court-appointed officer is required to give the tenant 72 hours notice to move out. If the tenant still has not moved out by this time, the landlord must store the tenant's property. Although the landlord may get a judgment against the tenant for rent, damages, and court costs, the judgment is worthless if the tenant is unemployed and has no assets.

The High Cost of Favoritism

Some of the results of the favorable treatment accorded debtors are that (1) business and landlords are passing their losses on to consumers; (2) credit is being tightened; (3) it is becoming more difficult for certain groups to obtain apartments, especially the young and those on welfare; and (4) worst of all, it is destroying the work ethic: People are finding out that they are better off not working and thereby avoiding their financial obligations.

Correcting the Problem

If you are wondering what can be done to correct this problem, here are some suggestions:

- Urge your federal and state legislators to pass laws making it easier to collect judgments and harder to go bankrupt.

- Business owners should (1) make sure their loans and sales are secured, giving them the right to repossess the property; (2) obtain complete information about a debtor's background, property, and places of employment (see the "Consumer Credit Application" form at the end of this chapter); (3) have contracts provide for payment of attorney fees, late charges, and interest in the event of default; and (4) have customers sign a promissory note as added security for repayment of debts (see the "Promissory Note" form at the end of this chapter).

- Landlords should obtain substantial security deposits, conduct careful and thorough reference checks, and protect their rights through well-drafted leases.

- Almost everyone can use small claims court for collections. (See *How to Survive Legally as a Landlord,* published by Victoria Square Publishing Co., Inc., Akron, NY 14001-0031, for further information regarding small claims court and landlord-tenant laws.) The court costs are less in small claims court and you don't need an attorney, but if you hire one, his or her fee is usually less than it would be for a regular lawsuit. You can recover triple damages plus attorney fees from a defendant against whom you have at least three unpaid small claims judgments.

- Don't wait too long to start a suit against someone who owes you money. The longer you wait, the worse your chances are of collecting.

The best way to protect your rights as a creditor is to consult an attorney before it is too late. Preventive law is always the best policy.

SUCCESSFUL DEBT COLLECTION

Are you losing money because of any of the debt collection problems and concerns listed below?

- You lack office procedures for handling credit and collections.
- You lack information about debtors to help you collect debts.
- You are unable to recover expensive attorney fees, late charges, and interest.
- Your business is hit with too many bad checks.
- You are unable to locate debtors.
- You fear being sued for harassing debtors.
- You have waited too long to sue.
- Your debtors turn out to be judgment-proof.

Many businesses are losing thousands of dollars by not taking some very simple precautions. Collecting debts may be almost impossible if you do not take these steps:

Step #1	Prepare a policy and procedure manual.
Step #2	Use a credit application form.
Step #3	Use a credit agreement.
Step #4	Prevent bad checks.
Step #5	Learn how to skip trace.
Step #6	Know what collection practices are prohibited.
Step #7	Don't procrastinate.
Step #8	Pursue all responsible parties.
Step #9	Find a good collection attorney.

Step #1: Prepare a Policy and Procedure Manual

Developing a credit/collection policy and procedure manual, which contains procedural guidelines and legal references, is the first step toward improving debt collection practices. The manual should be specifically tailored to the needs of your business and should include information on the following:

- *Credit procedures*—credit applications (see step #2), credit ratings, credit line evalua-

tions, credit reporting agencies, and financial ratio analysis
- *Collections*—delinquency collection techniques, bankruptcy, deductions, and debit memos
- *Credit/Collection duties and responsibilities*—cash flow projections, cash flow statements, gross profit reviews, letters of credit, surety bonds, promissory notes, personal guaranties, bank guaranties, adjustments, criminal prosecution for bad checks, and payment terms

The manual should also include information on final settlement checks. If you receive a check containing the words "final settlement" or similar wording, you must return the check to the debtor within a reasonable time if you do not agree to receive it in full discharge of the indebtedness. However, there are two exceptions to this rule. If you mistakenly deposit the check, you can promptly and effectively repudiate this by having the check returned from the bank and causing adjustments in the bank accounts of both your customer and you so that you do not have any beneficial use of the debtor's funds. If the payee strikes the "full payment" notation and substitutes its own statement that the check is "accepted in partial payment under protest and without prejudice," that is sufficient if the check is for the sale of goods but not for services rendered.

Step #2: Use a Credit Application Form

It is absolutely essential that you obtain the client's or customer's Social Security or employer identification number, date of birth, place of employment, names of closest relatives, and bank account and motor-vehicle information. This information is very useful in collecting a judgment and identifying potential problem customers. Be cautious about customers who have frequent address changes or frequent employment changes. The "New Account Transmittal Form" at the end of this chapter includes the type of information that you will have to provide to your attorney or collection agency to make collection of a judgment possible.

Adequate credit information is necessary to reduce the risk with new customers. It is also important to update the information periodically so that you can accurately reevaluate current customers. It is important to obtain and update the following information:

- The correct name, location, management, principals, ownership, and legal structure of a company
- Background information concerning a company's current and past business activities and relationships (line of business, how long in that business, any name changes, any ownership changes, any past or pending litigation)
- Personal financial statements from guarantors
- Name and reputation of the company's accountant(s)
- Date and state of incorporation

(See the sample application for credit form at the end of this chapter.)

A number of sources from which you can get pertinent information include the following:

- Specialized directories, such as the Dun and Bradstreet Reference Book and *Polk's World Bank Directory* and directories published by many chambers of commerce.
- Financial and trade periodicals, such as the *Wall Street Journal* and local newspapers
- Specialized databases and online credit reference services
- City, county, and state public records. You can research public records on your own or use a reputable search firm that can retrieve information from public filings at minimal cost. Public records provide essential information concerning lawsuits, bankruptcies, liens, UCC filings, and the like. But be sure to pursue any such information that you find. For instance, if a lien has been filed, you will want to find out if it has since been released. If your loan will be collateralized, check with the state and county to see whether the company's collateral is already encumbered.
- Local libraries whose business sources include encyclopedias, journals, and information on public records
- Local telephone directories to help verify some of the information supplied by businesses or individuals

Step #3: Use a Credit Agreement

Attorney fees, late charges, or interest are not recoverable unless debtors agree to pay for them in writing. Your credit agreements should be signed by the customer and his or her spouse and should provide for

- 33.33 percent attorney fees,
- interest and late charges, and
- personal guarantees by the shareholders if the customer is a small corporation (see step #8).

Step #4: Prevent Bad Checks

The use of bad checks is on the rise but they can be avoided. Your policy and procedure manual should have specific guidelines on accepting checks. There are basically seven types of checks:

1. A *personal check* is written and signed by the customer who makes it out to you or your firm.

2. A *two-party check* is issued by one person (the maker) to a second person who endorses it so that it may be cashed by a third person. This type of check is susceptible to fraud because the maker can stop payment at the bank.

3. A *payroll check* is issued to an employee for wages or salary earned. It usually contains the name of the employer, a check number, and the word *payroll.* The employee's name is printed by a check-writing machine or typed. Unless you know the company officials and the employee personally, you should never accept a payroll check that is hand-printed, rubber-stamped, or typewritten even if it appears to be issued by a local business and drawn on a local bank.

4. *Government checks* are issued by the federal, state, county, and local government. Such checks cover salaries, tax refunds, pensions, welfare allotments, and veterans benefits. Be particularly cautious with government checks; often they are stolen and the endorsement forged. In some areas, theft of government checks is so great that banks refuse to cash Social

Security, welfare, relief, or income tax checks unless the customer has an account with the bank. You should follow this procedure also. In short, know your endorser.

5. A *blank check,* also known as a *universal check,* is no longer accepted by many banks because Federal Reserve regulations prohibit standard processing without encoded characters. The universal check may be used, but it requires the bank to go through a special collection process and incur an additional cost.

6. *Counter checks* are still used by a few banks. They are issued to depositors who withdraw funds from their accounts and are not good at other banks. Some stores have their own counter checks for the convenience of their customers. A counter check is not negotiable and is so marked.

7. A *traveler's check* is sold with a preprinted amount in round figures. The traveler signs the checks at the time of purchase and should countersign them only in the presence of the person who cashes them.

In addition, a money order can be used in place of a check. However, money orders are usually mailed. Most businesses should not accept money orders in face-to-face transactions.

Close examination of the key items of a check may tip you off to a worthless check. Before accepting a check, closely examine it for the following:

- *Nonlocal banks.* Use extra care in examining a check that is drawn on a nonlocal bank. Ask for positive identification. List the customer's local and out-of-town address and phone number on the back of the check.

- *Date.* Examine the date for accuracy of day, month, and year. Do not accept the check if it's not dated, if it's postdated, or it's more than 30 days old.

- *Location.* Be sure that the check shows the name, branch, town, and state where the bank is located.

- *Amount.* The numerical amount must agree with the written amount.

- *Legibility.* Do not accept a check that is not written legibly. It should be written and signed in ink and must not have any erasures or written-over amounts.

- *Payee.* When you take a personal check on your selling floor, have the customer make it payable to your business. Unless you know your customer well, it's not wise to accept a two-party check.

- *Amount of purchase.* Personal checks should be drawn for the exact amount of the purchase. Do not give the customer change.

- *Checks over your limit.* Set a limit on the amount that you will accept on a check. If a customer desires to go beyond that limit, have the sales clerk refer the customer directly to you.

- *Low sequence numbers.* Be more cautious with low sequence numbers. A higher proportion of these checks are returned. Most banks issue personalized checks beginning with the number 101.

- *Amount of check.* Most bad-check passers issue checks in the $25 to $35 range on the assumption that the retailer will be less cautious when presented with a check for a small amount of money.

- *Types of merchandise purchased.* Be vigilant about the types of merchandise purchased. Random sizes or selections or lack of concern about prices indicate that caution should be exercised when accepting a check.

After you have ascertained that a check is valid, determine if the person holding the check is the right person. Requiring identification can help you in this determination, but no identification is foolproof. Obtain enough identification so that the customer can be identified and located if the check turns out to be worthless. The following types of identification are useful:

- *Current automobile operators license*

- *Automobile registration card.* The name of the state should coincide with the bank location. Compare the signature on the registration to that on the check.

- *Store charges.* Use store charges or other credit cards as identification for the signature or photograph. Retail merchants organizations in some areas issue lists of stolen shopping plates to which you can refer when identifying the check passer.

- *Government passes.* These carry the name of the employing department and the employee's serial number. Building passes should also carry a signature.

- *Identification cards.* Those issued by the armed services, police departments, and companies should carry a photo, description, and signature. Police cards should also carry a badge number.

The following types of cards and documents are *not* good identification because they can be easily forged: Social Security cards, business cards, club or organization cards, bankbooks, work permits, insurance cards, learner's permits, letters, birth certificates, library cards, initialed jewelry, unsigned credit cards, and voter's registration cards.

You may also wish to take these precautions: Photograph customers and their identification, and verify their address and telephone number in the local telephone directory or with the information operator.

Regardless of the type of identification you require, it is essential that you compare the signature on the check with the one on the identification. You should also compare the customer with the photograph and/or the description on the identification.

To recover double or special damages for bad checks, in most states you must post a sign warning customers of the law and send two written notices to customers that their check has been dishonored. If a customer's check is returned for insufficient funds, you can recover damages. If a customer writes a check on a closed account, you can recover up to double damages. Make photocopies of all checks for your records.

Step #5: Know How to Skip Trace

If customers stop paying, their phone has been disconnected, and you cannot find them, use these resources to locate these debtors and their assets:

- City directories
- Post office (for a forwarding address)
- A customer's employer
- Department of motor vehicle license and registration records
- "In case of emergency" name and address or closest relatives listed on a credit application
- Credit reports
- Law journals
- Old files
- The Internet
- Skip-tracing services
- Tax accessor
- Credit bureau reports
- Neighbors
- Directory assistance
- Undirectories

Step #6: Know What Collection Practices Are Prohibited

Although credit grantors are excluded from the provisions of the Fair Debt Collection Practices Act, the District of Columbia and the following states include creditors in their debt collection laws: Arkansas, California, Colorado, Connecticut, Florida, Iowa, Kansas, Louisiana, Maine, Maryland, Massachusetts, Michigan, New Hampshire, New York, North Carolina, Oregon, Pennsylvania, South Carolina, Texas, Vermont, West Virginia, and Wisconsin.

You are prohibited by law from doing any of the following:

- Simulating a law enforcement officer or a representative of any government agency
- Knowingly collecting, attempting to collect, or asserting a right to any collection fee, attorney fee, court cost, or expense unless such charges are justly due and legally chargeable against the debtor (see step #3)
- Disclosing or threatening to disclose information affecting the debtor's reputation for creditworthiness with knowledge or reason to know that the information is false
- Communicating or threatening to communicate the nature of a consumer claim to the debtor's employer before obtaining final judgment against the debtor. (However, you may communicate with the debtor's employer to execute a wage assignment agreement if the debtor has consented to such an agreement.)
- Disclosing or threatening to disclose information concerning the existence of a debt known to be disputed by the debtor without disclosing that fact
- Communicating with the debtor or any member of his or her family or household with such frequency or at such unusual hours or in such a manner as can reasonably be expected to abuse or harass

- Threatening any action that you, in the usual course of your business, do not in fact take

- Claiming to enforce a right with knowledge or reason to know that the right does not exist

- Falsely using a communication that simulates in any manner legal or judicial process or that gives the appearance of being authorized, issued, or approved by a government agency or attorney-at-law

Step #7: Don't Procrastinate

The longer you wait to sue, the less your chances of successfully recovering the debt. Accounts that are 90 to 120 days in arrears should be turned over for collection. Although there is a four-year statute of limitations (the time during which a suit can be started) for contracts for the sale of goods, these time periods can be renewed or stopped.

The statute of limitations starts all over again when

- the debtor signs an acknowledgement of the debt, or

- the debtor makes a partial payment.

The statute of limitations stops running when

- the debtor is outside the state,

- the debtor is using an alias,

- the debtor is adjudged insane (maximum ten years),

- the debtor is in the military, or

- the debtor has filed a workers' compensation claim.

Step #8: Pursue All Responsible Parties

There may be more than one individual who is responsible for the debt. Do not overlook the following possibilities:

- *Partners.* Each partner is responsible for debts of the partnership. Check the business certificates in the county clerk's office for the names and addresses of the individual partners.

- *Guarantors of payment.* They are responsible if the guarantee is in writing.

- *Deceased debtors.* File a proof of claim with the surrogate or probate court. If there is no will, those who have inherited property from the decedent are responsible for his or her debts.

- *Spouses.* They are responsible if the creditor relied on their credit.

- *Parents.* They are usually responsible for their children's necessities until they reach age 21.

Step #9: Find a Good Collection Attorney

A good collection attorney can help you collect your delinquent accounts faster and with greater success. Ask the attorney if he or she provides

- "same-day service" for installment loan collections, credit card delinquencies, bankruptcy motions, and foreclosures;

- instant answers to your legal questions by telephone or e-mail at no charge;

- educational services and publications to keep you up-to-date on the latest developments in collection and bankruptcy law;

- every possible effort, including contempt proceedings, to locate debtors and their assets;

- prelegal dunning by collectors;

- national coverage by electronic referrals;

- instant status reports to keep you informed of the progress of your cases;

- computerized skip-tracing services;

- free training of your employees; and

- strict compliance with the Fair Debt Collection Practices Act.

Attorneys in many instances can give you just as good service as a collection agency with fees that are no higher. Some firms contact debtors both by telephone and in writing. Valuable time is saved by turning your accounts directly over to an attorney. Payment negotiation can be accomplished while suit is in progress.

MECHANIC'S LIENS

If you do remodeling work for a property owner who refuses to pay your bill, you can put a lien on his or her home without first having to sue. To obtain a mechanic's lien, a laborer or materialman must improve real estate with the owner's consent and file a notice of lien.

A mechanic's lien diminishes the value of real estate but does not make it unsalable. It merely makes a sale more difficult by rendering the title unmarketable. A mechanic's lien grants a builder or materialman the right to have the debt paid by a foreclosure sale of the property.

Laborers/Material Suppliers

The following persons who perform labor or furnish material for the improvement of real estate are entitled to a mechanic's lien: contractors; subcontractors; laborers; material suppliers; landscape gardeners; nurserymen; or sellers of fruit or ornamental trees, roses, shrubbery, or vines.

A *material supplier* is one who furnishes building materials; supplies machinery, tools, or equipment; compresses gases for welding or cutting; or supplies fuel or lubricants for machinery and motor vehicles.

Improvements

Real estate improvements include demolition, erection, alteration, or repair; work done and materials furnished for permanent improvements; drawings by an architect, engineer, or surveyor; the reasonable rental value for the use of machinery, tools, and equipment; and the value of fuel and lubricants used.

Consent

The work or materials must be with the consent of the owner or the owner's agent, contractor, or subcontractor. Consent may be implied from the owner's conduct.

Where a building contract is made with a husband or wife and the property belongs to either or both of them, the spouse who signs the contract is presumed to be the agent of the other. However, the other spouse may, within ten days after learning of the contract, give the contractor written notice of his or her refusal to consent to the improvement.

Notice of Lien

The lien is created by filing a notice of lien with the county clerk. The notice of lien must be properly filed in order to be legally effective.

Notice to the property owner is required so the owner can ascertain whether the material was actually furnished or the work was actually performed and its value. The amount of the lien is the value, or the agreed price, of the labor performed or materials furnished plus interest. This includes materials manufactured but not delivered.

If you are entitled to a mechanic's lien, see an attorney so that all technical requirements are strictly followed.

HOW TO COLLECT A MONEY JUDGMENT

Even if you win a money judgment against a customer for an unpaid bill, you may not always be able to collect the judgment. It is your responsibility to take the necessary action to collect your judgment.

If you have not received your money from the defendant within 30 days after he or she has received notice of the judgment, you should contact the defendant. If the defendant refuses to pay you or if you are unable to reach the defendant after several attempts, it will be necessary to use the services of an enforcement officer, such as a sheriff, marshall, constable, or police officer (whoever is empowered to enforce judgments of the court where you sued) to help collect your judgment.

Your chances of collecting the judgment depend on the resources of the defendant and the type of information you provide about the nature and location of the defendant's resources or assets. The likelihood of having your judgment satisfied is remote if the defendant has no known property or income, has prior judgments, and has a very low salary or other income. If the defendant has other judgments against him or her, you may have to wait your turn to collect.

Your chances of collecting greatly increase when you can supply the enforcement officer with such specific information as the license number and description of the defendant's car and where it is usually parked, bank account numbers, and employment information. If you can supply the name and location of the bank where the defendant has savings or checking accounts, the enforcement officer can seize money in the defendant's accounts and use the funds to satisfy your claim.

To ascertain the location of the defendant's bank, look at the back of a canceled check that you may have given to the defendant, or check your records to locate checks you may have received from the debtor in the past. If you are unsure where the defendant maintains an account, you may use an information subpoena to inquire of any bank whether the defendant has an account there. You must provide the enforcement officer with a notice to garnishee. After the defendant's account has been seized, the judgment and interest that has accrued on it will be paid to you along with reimbursement for the expenses that you incurred enforcing the judgment.

If the defendant is employed, you may be able to collect your judgment from the defendant's salary. To do so, you must use an income execution. If the defendant fails to pay the judgment after the income execution has been served, the enforcement officer will serve a copy of the income execution on the defendant's employer, who must make deductions from the defendant's wages.

If the employer fails to honor the income execution, it will be liable for the amount of the judgment. If the defendant changes jobs, you will need to locate the new employer and start the process all over again.

When giving the enforcement officer the employer's name and address, you must pay a fee in advance for the income execution. You are entitled to recover this fee (in addition to your judgment plus interest) from the wages turned over by the defendant's employer.

If the defendant owns real estate, you may be able to collect your judgment from its sale or have a lien placed against it.

A judgment can also be satisfied from the sale of personal property, such as an automobile, stocks, and bonds. However, certain property, such as clothing and basic household goods, is exempt. You must provide the enforcement officer with the model, year, and license plate number of the vehicle and a property execution. You can determine if the defendant owns an automobile by filling out a registration information request at the department of motor vehicles. The execution against a motor vehicle is not always practical, especially if there is an unpaid auto loan or if the automobile is old and not in very good condition. The expense of seizure, towing, and storing of the vehicle and of advertising and conducting an auction sale may not justify the effort.

If you are unable to locate any of the defendant's assets, you may conduct a discovery proceeding that requires the defendant to appear before a court to answer questions about any property he or she owns. You must prepare a subpoena to take the deposition of the judgment debtor.

You may have the court order a self-employed defendant to make periodic payments out of earnings by making a motion for an installment payment order for which you will need an attorney's assistance.

CONSUMER'S RIGHT TO ATTORNEY FEES

Whenever a consumer contract entitles the creditor or seller to recover attorney fees and expenses from the debtor or buyer for a breach of contract, it is implied that the creditor will be obligated to pay the attorney fees and expenses of the debtor or buyer if the creditor breaches the contract or the consumer successfully defends the suit brought by the creditor or seller. This right cannot be waived by the consumer.

BANKRUPTCY

If your company is experiencing serious difficulty in meeting its debt obligations, contact an attorney before your business suffers disruption. An attorney can assist your company in either (1) reaching an agreement with all of your creditors to extend repayment of your debts and avoid the necessity of bankruptcy, or (2) obtaining the protection of the U.S. Bankruptcy Court's automatic stay if all of your creditors will not agree to a voluntary repayment plan and are threatening to proceed with collection efforts such as judgments, liens, and property seizures.

An attorney can determine whether bankruptcy is appropriate for your company after reviewing your debts, assets, mortgages, sources of income, contractual obligations, leases, pending and future lawsuits by or against you, judgments, liens, and recent asset transfers.

As soon as a bankruptcy petition is filed, your business receives the protection of an automatic stay, which prevents all listed creditors from any further collection activities against it. The court sends notices to all creditors listed in the petition, ordering them to cease any collection efforts. The court also sets a date for the first meeting of creditors at which they may question you about the business's property, debts, and other relevant facts.

The following debts are not dischargeable in bankruptcy: (1) maintenance and support ordered in a decree of dissolution of marriage; (2) certain unpaid tax debts; (3) certain student loans; and (4) fines and restitution ordered in criminal cases.

The bankruptcy court may recover fraudulent conveyances made within a year before the filing of the petition. A *fraudulent conveyance* is a transfer made without the receipt of equivalent value in return, or a transfer made with the intent to deceive or defraud creditors.

A *preference* is a payment on account of debt that is made within a limited period (usually 90 days prior to filing for bankruptcy), which gives a creditor more than it would expect to receive if your property were liquidated. The bankruptcy court may recover these transferred assets.

Individuals may file for either liquidation under Chapter 7 or for a repayment plan under Chapter 13. Farmers may use a repayment plan under Chapter 12 or liquidate. Chapter 12 is more liberal than Chapter 13 in that there is an allowance for income that is seasonal in nature and a much higher total debt limitation than Chapter 13. Corporations and partnerships may use a repayment plan under Chapter 11 or liquidate.

HOT SITE

Internet Bankruptcy Library Worldwide Trouble Company Resources (http://bankrupt.com) offers hot news in the bankruptcy world, Internet discussion groups and mailing lists, conferences and meetings, publications, distressed securities data, bankruptcy and insolvency resource materials, a worldwide directory of bankruptcy and insolvency professionals, an online directory of bankruptcy court clerks, consumer Chapter 7 and 13 bankruptcy issues, and miscellaneous Internet resources.

Chapter 7—Liquidation

Most types of debts will be discharged under Chapter 7, which allows the debtor to make a "fresh start." However, some assets are likely to be liquidated, and the bankruptcy will appear on the debtor's credit record for up to ten years. The debtor turns over all nonexempt property to a bankruptcy trustee. The trustee sells that property and uses the proceeds to pay the creditors. Property that is exempt under state or federal laws may be retained by the debtor. Exempt property includes the following:

- A certain amount of equity in a personal residence (However, a bank holding a mortgage retains most of its rights under the mortgage; if payments are in arrears and a debtor cannot cure or correct the default, the mortgagor may be able to foreclose on the residence.)

- A certain amount of equity in an automobile

- Personal and household items within limits

- Tools of your trade

After exemptions are taken into account and administration expenses are paid, unsecured creditors will receive the remaining proceeds proportionately. The portion of unsecured debts not fully paid will be discharged under an order from the bankruptcy court except for nondischargeable debts such as

- alimony and child support,
- certain taxes,
- certain student loans,
- certain consumer credit debts incurred shortly before the bankruptcy proceeding,
- debts incurred through fraud or larceny, and
- liability for damages caused by willful and malicious acts.

Chapter 13—Repayment Plan

If you have stable income and debts not higher than certain limits, you may be able to use a Chapter 13 repayment plan. This may involve repaying all of your debts over a three- or five-year period.

The court also may reduce the size of the debt to be paid. The unpaid amount may be discharged except for secured debts (e.g., mortgage loans to the extent of the value of the property) and nondischargeable debts (e.g., alimony and child support obligations and certain taxes).

Your proposed repayment plan will be presented to a bankruptcy trustee. If the plan is approved by the court, unsecured creditors must generally accept it as long as they will receive as much of the principal due to them as they would if the debtor's property were liquidated.

After the bankruptcy court approves your repayment plan, you must make monthly payments as required by the plan. If you cannot make the scheduled payments called for by an approved Chapter 13 plan, then your bankruptcy will be converted to a Chapter 7 liquidation.

The advantages of Chapter 13 are as follows:

- Debtors can keep their property while the repayment plan is in effect. Liquidation of assets may not be necessary. The owner of an unincorporated business may continue to own and operate the business under a Chapter 13 repayment plan. In a Chapter 7 liquidation, the business or its assets will be sold.

- The automatic stay protects codebtors, cosigners, or guarantors of consumer debt while the plan is in effect.

- The bankruptcy court may approve the reduced payments on secured debts.

- Chapter 13 allows you to discharge debts that are not dischargeable under Chapter 7, such as debts resulting from fraud, embezzlement, and larceny and debts resulting from injury caused by willful and malicious acts and certain educational loans. However, Chapter 13 will not allow a discharge for certain long-term debts where the last payment under the note is due after the Chapter 13 repayment period.

- Debtors who receive a Chapter 13 discharge do not lose the right to file for Chapter 7 bankruptcy in the future.

Chapter 11—Repayment Plan

The bankruptcy code protects financially troubled corporations or partnerships by allowing them to continue in business as they satisfy their debts. The business may be allowed to reduce its debts and pay its remaining debts over three to five years and can continue operating under the control of the current owner. However, if the creditors demonstrate that there is unfit management or fraud, a trustee will be appointed to run the company.

Under Chapter 11, the business must propose a good-faith business plan that shows that projected income over the repayment period will be adequate to cover its restructured debts. The plan must also show that the creditors will receive more from the debt restructuring and extended payout than they would from the liquidation of the company. Creditors are allowed to vote on the approval of the plan.

Businesses with debts under $2 million can opt for the "streamlined" Chapter 11 process in which only one court appearance (instead of two or more) is required, creditors must file repayment plans within 100 days of filing (rather than 120 days), and the plan's confirmation deadline is 160 days (instead of 180 days). This can result in saving attorney and trustee fees.

Bankruptcy as a Creditor

Secured creditors are usually more likely than unsecured creditors to recover at least part of their claim in bankruptcy. Creditors' rights depend on whether their claim is secured, the nature of the security interest, and whether the debtor has filed under Chapter 7, 11, or 13.

If the debtor does not reaffirm the debt, secured creditors generally seek to recover their collateral. Creditors may ask the bankruptcy court to lift the automatic stay for cause such as where its interest in the property is not adequately protected or the debtor does not have enough equity in the property and the property is not necessary to the debtor's reorganization.

The automatic stay does not apply to codebtors, guarantors, or partners of the bankrupt.

HOW AND WHEN TO USE THE FORMS IN THIS CHAPTER

Consumer Credit Application. This form should be used when you grant credit to a customer. It will enable you to determine whether the customer is a good risk.

Business Application for Credit and **Guarantee of Account.** These forms should be used when you grant credit to a partnership or corporation. They contain a personal guarantee to be signed by a partner or corporate officer.

General Release. This form should be exchanged whenever a lawsuit or claim is settled. It provides that each party releases the other from any further liability.

New Account Transmittal Form. This form should be used when placing accounts for collection with your lawyer or collection agency.

Bankruptcy Proof of Claim. This form should be filed with the bankruptcy court when you receive notice that the debtor has filed for bankruptcy. Documentation, such as security agreements, should be attached to this form.

Promissory Note. This form sets out the soundest way to get a promise to pay in writing. It is easier to sue on a debt that is based on a promissory note.

CONSUMER CREDIT APPLICATION

Is this a joint application? ☐ Yes ☐ No. if "Yes," applicant 1 should fill in the spaces on the lines numbered 1, and applicant 2 the spaces on the lines numbered 2. If any information is the same for both applicants, applicant 2 may write in "same."

Name		Date of Birth	# Dependents	Phone Number	Social Security Number
1		/ /			
2		/ /			

Address # Street City State Zip		How Long?	Previous Address # Street City State Zip		How Long?
1			1		
2			2		

Employer (name/address) (If retired, list "retired")		Business Phone	Position	How Long?	Dept./Badge No.	Gross Mo. Salary
1						
2						

Previous Employer	How Long?	Other income (income from alimony, child support, or separate maintenance payments need not be revealed if you do not choose to rely on such income in applying for credit.	Source (name, address, description)	Mo. Amt.
1				
2				

1 ☐ Own 2 ☐ Rent	Mo. Payt.	Includes Taxes? ☐ Yes ☐ No Then list annual amt. $ _____	Mtg. Balance	Mtg. Holder or Landlord	Checking Acct. at	Savings Acct. at
1 ☐ Own 2 ☐ Rent	Mo. Payt.	Includes Taxes? ☐ Yes ☐ No Then list annual amt. $ _____				

List all finance companies at which you have had credit (paid loans only)	Appl 1 previous bankruptcy? ☐ Judgment ☐ Garnishment? ☐
1	Appl 1 previous bankruptcy? ☐ Judgment ☐ Garnishment? ☐
	Either applicant list name & address of nearest relative at different address

List all debts to banks, stores, finance companies, credit unions and others. Include alimony, child support or separate maintenance.

Applicant's Creditors	Balance	Mo. Payt.	Applicant's Creditors	Balance	Mo. Payt.
Auto loan at Year _____ Make _____			Auto loan at Year _____ Make _____		

Signature (all applicants)

INFORMATION: All information given in this application is true, correct, and complete, and is given for the purpose of obtaining credit from you. I authorize you to verify any information given in the application. In addition, I authorize you to obtain any information you feel is necessary in connection with this application or in connection with any review, update, extension, renewal, or connection with any review, update, extension, renewal, or collection of any credit you extend as a result of this application. Finally, I authorize you to give information about me and your credit experience with me to others such as banks, stores, and credit reporting agencies.

KEEPING APPLICATION: I agree that you may keep this application whether or not you approve it.

ACKNOWLEDGMENT: I acknowledge receipt of a Notice Regarding Credit Reports.

Applicant 1 Signature _____ Date _____

Applicant 2 Signature _____ Date _____

- -

NOTICE REGARDING CREDIT REPORTS (Detach and retain for your records)

In connection with your application or any review, update, extension, renewal, or collection of any credit we extend you as a result of the application, a credit report may be requested from a credit reporting agency. Upon request, we will tell you if a credit report was requested and, if so, the name and address of the credit reporting agency furnishing the credit report. To request the information, call _____ or write

APPLICATION FOR CREDIT   CONFIDENTIAL

Please complete the following in detail

BILLING & BUSINESS INFORMATION   DATE _____

BUSINESS/CORPORATE NAME _____ d/b/a or (trade style) _____

_____   MAILING ADDRESS _____

_____   _____
Street   Street

_____   _____
City   State   Zip   City   State   Zip

TELEPHONE NUMBER _____

PARENT COMPANY _____
                        Name   Address

COMPANY PROFILE

Corporation _____ Partnership _____ Limited Partnership _____ Franchise _____

Date you started business or assumed control _____ Nature/Type of Business _____

(If under 1 year, personal guarantee required. See reverse side.)

_____   _____
No. of Employees   Name and address of Previous: Business   Employer

Officers or Principals: _____

_____
Name   Title   Residence   SS#

_____
Name   Title   Residence   SS#

_____
Name   Title   Residence   SS#

Has Corporation been registered with the Secretary of State? _____

What State _____   Date of Filing _____

CREDIT REFERENCES: Media/Trade References:

_____
Name   Street   City   State   Zip   Ph.   Acct.#

_____
Name   Street   City   State   Zip   Ph.   Acct.#

_____
Name   Street   City   State   Zip   Ph.   Acct.#

BANK REFERENCES: C—Checking   S—Savings   M—Mortgage/Loan   CPD—Charge

_____
Name   Street   City   State   Zip   Ph.   Acct.#

_____
Name   Street   City   State   Zip   Ph.   Acct.#

I certify that the information provided in the application is true and correct. I hereby authorize the release of credit information requested relevant to the above account.

_____   _____
Signature of Officer   Title   Date

328

GUARANTEE OF ACCOUNT

Date _____ 199 ____

To:

Gentlemen:

For value received and in consideration of the credit that you may hereafter extend, the undersigned hereby jointly, severally, and unconditionally guarantee payment when due, at your office in   , of any and all present or future indebtedness owed to you by the applicant named on the reverse hereof, hereinafter called the debtor, and hereby agree punctually to pay such indebtedness if default in payment thereof be made by the debtor, plus attorney fees of 25% of said amounts if placed for collection.

The undersigned expressly waives notice of acceptance of guarantee demand, and notice of nonpayment, and consents to any extension of time of payment of any and all of the indebtedness hereby guaranteed.

This guarantee shall continue to apply to all sales made, services rendered, and advances made by you to the debtor, and to all such present and future indebtedness however arising.

This is intended to be a personal guarantee and not a corporate guarantee, and will personally bind the signer notwithstanding any title or designation made by me.

Witnessed this _____ day of _____ 199 ____

Witness _____

Witness _____

Signature _____

Address _____

Signature _____

Address _____

GENERAL RELEASE

Know Ye, That

for and in consideration of the sum of

Dollars ($),

lawful money of the United States of America to   in hand paid by

the receipt whereof is hereby acknowledged, have remised, released, and forever discharged and by these

presents do   for   heirs, executors, and administrators,

remise, release, and forever discharge the said

successors and assigns, heirs, executors, and administrators, of and from all, and all manner of action and

actions, cause and causes of action, suits, debts, dues, sums of money, accounts, reckonings, bonds, bills,

specialties, covenants, contracts, controversies, agreements, promises, variances, trespasses, damages,

judgments, extents, executions, claims, and demands whatsoever, in law or in equity, which against the said

ever had, now have   or which

heirs, executors, or administrators, hereafter

can, shall or may have for upon or by reason of any matter, cause or thing whatsoever from the beginning

of the world to the day of the date of these presents. Rights against parties not named herein are reserved.

For Individual

In Witness Whereof,   *have hereunto set   hand   and seal*

the   day of

IN PRESENCE OF

_____ *LS*

_____ *LS*

Individual Acknowledgment

STATE OF

SS: COUNTY OF

OF

On this   day of   , before me personally appeared to me known, and known to me to be the

same person described in and who executed the within Instrument and   acknowledged to me that

executed the same.

_____

Notary Public, State of   County of _____

My Commission expires _____

In Witness Whereof, *the undersigned has caused its corporate seal to be hereunto affixed and these presents to be signed by its duly authorized officer the*

day of

_____ *LS*

(Seal)   By_____

                                                              Title _____

STATE OF   *Corporate Acknowledgment*

COUNTY OF   SS:

OF

On this   day of   , before me came to me known, who, being by me duly sworn,

did depose and say that   resides in   that   is the

of   the corporation described in, and which executed, the

foregoing instrument; that knows the seal of said corporation; that the seal affixed to said Instrument is such corporate seal; that it was affixed by order of the Board of Directors of said corporation; and that signed name thereto by like order.

_____

Notary Public, State of   County of _____

My Commission expires _____   General Release

NEW ACCOUNT TRANSMITTAL FORM

Date: _____

DEBTOR INFORMATION

1. Name _____
2. AKA/FKA_____
3. Marital Status _____
4. SS#_____
5. Date of Birth _____
6. Physical Description _____
7. Spouse's Name _____
8. St. Address & Apt. # _____
9. City, State, Zip_____
10. County_____
11. Res. Tel. #_____
12. Employer_____
13. Employer's Address_____
14. Employer's Tel. #_____
15. Position/Dept./Badge #_____
16. Date Emp. Verified _____
17. Hrs./Wages _____
18. Auto Make, Model, Year _____
19. Bank Acct. Info._____
20. Dependents _____
21. Assets _____

CREDITOR INFORMATION

1. Name _____
2. Date of Service _____
3. Street Address _____
4. City, State, Zip _____
5. County_____
6. State of Inc._____
7. Services Rendered to_____
8. Principal Bal. Due _____
9. Credits_____
10. Interest _____
11. Add. Fees _____
12. Total Amt. Owing_____
13. Attachments: _____
❏ Promissory Note _____
❏ Security Agreement_____
❏ Invoice_____
❏ Credit Application _____
❏ Correspondence _____
❏ Returned Check _____
❏ Leases _____
❏ Ledgers _____
❏ Contracts _____
❏ Truth-in-Lending Forms _____

BANKRUPTCY PROOF OF CLAIM

United States Bankruptcy Court

District of

In re (Name of Debtor)

Proof of Claim

Case Number

NOTE: This form should not be used to make a claim for an administrative expense arising after the commencement of the case. A "request" of payment of an administrative expense may be filed pursuant to 11 USC §503.

Name of Creditor
(The person or entity to whom the debtor owes money or property)
Name and Address Where
Notices Should Be Sent

❏ Check box if you are aware that anyone else has filed a proof of claim relating to your claim. Attach copy of statement giving particulars.
❏ Check box if you have never received any notices from the bankruptcy court in the case.
❏ Check box if the address differs from the address on the envelope sent to you by the court.

Telephone No.

THIS SPACE
IS FOR COURT
USE ONLY

ACCOUNT OR OTHER NUMBER
BY WHICH CREDITOR IDENTIFIES
DEBTOR:

Check if this claim ❏ replaces}
❏ amends}
a previously filed claim, dated:

1. BASIS FOR CLAIM
   ❏ Goods sold
   ❏ Services performed
   ❏ Money loaned
   ❏ Personal injury/wrongful death
   ❏ Taxes
   ❏ Other
      (Describe briefly)

❏ Retiree benefits as defined in 11 USC §1114
❏ Wages, salaries, and compensation
   (Fill out below)
   Your Social Security number: _____
   Unpaid compensations for services performed
   from _____ to _____
          (date)   (date)

2. DATE DEBT WAS INCURRED:

3. IF COURT JUDGMENT, DATE OBTAINED:

4. CLASSIFICATION OF CLAIM. Under the Bankruptcy Code all claims are classified as one or more of the following: (1) Unsecured Nonpriority, (2) Unsecured Priority, (3) Secured. It is possible for part of a claim to be in one category and part in another. CHECK THE APPROPRIATE BOX OR BOXES that best describe your claim and STATE THE AMOUNT OF THE CLAIM.

BANKRUPTCY PROOF OF CLAIM
(continued)

❑ SECURED CLAIM $ _____

Attach evidence of perfection of security interest. Brief description of Collateral:

❑ Real Estate
❑ Motor Vehicles
❑ Other (Describe briefly)

Amount of arrearage and other charges included in secured claim above, if any
$ _____

❑ UNSECURED NONPRIORITY CLAIM
$ _____ .

A claim is unsecured if there is no collateral or lien on property of the debtor securing the claim or to the extent that the value of such property is less than the amount of the claim.

❑ UNSECURED PRIORITY CLAIM $ _____

Specify the priority of the claim

❑ Wages, salaries or commissions (up to $2,000), earned not more than 90 days before filing of the bankruptcy petition or cessation of the debtor's business, whichever is earlier—11 USC §507(a) (3)
❑ Contributions to an employee benefit plan—11 USC §507 (a) (4)
❑ Up to $900 of deposits toward purchase, lease, or rental of property or services for personal, family, or household use—11 USC §507 (a) (6)
❑ Taxes or penalties of governmental units—11 USC §507 (a) (7)
❑ Other—11 USC §§507 (a) (2), (a) (5)— (Describe briefly)

5. TOTAL AMOUNT OF CLAIM AT TIME CASE FILED:

$ _____ $ _____ $ _____ $ _____
(Unsecured)   (Unsecured)   (Priority)   (Total)

❑ Check this box if claim includes prepetition charges in addition to the principal amount of the claim. Attach itemized statement of all additional charges.

6. CREDITS AND SETOFFS: The amount of all payments on this claim has been credited and deducted for the purpose of making this proof of claim. In filing this claim, claimant has deducted all amounts that claimant owes to debtor.

THIS SPACE IS FOR COURT USE ONLY

7. SUPPORT DOCUMENTS. *Attach copies of supporting documents,* such as promissory notes, purchase orders, invoices, itemized statements of running accounts, contracts, court judgments, or evidence of security interests. If the documents are not available, explain. If the documents are voluminous, attach a summary.

8. TIME-STAMPED COPY: To receive an acknowledgment of the filing of your claim, enclose a stamped, self-addressed envelope and copy of this proof of claim.

Date   Sign and print the name and title, if any, of the creditor or other person authorized to file this claim (attach copy of power of attorney, if any)

Penalty for presenting fraudulent claim: Fine of up to $500,000 or imprisonment for up to 5 years, or both. 18 USC §§152 and 3571.

PROMISSORY NOTE

8—PROMISSORY NOTE

Sanders Legal Publishers
Buffalo, NY 14202

Amount $ _____   _____ 19 _____

FOR VALUE RECEIVED the undersigned promises to pay, without notice or demand, to the order of

the sum of   Dollars

at

in installments as follows:

$ on the   day of   19   , $ on

the   day of   19   and a like sum of $ on

of each and every week/month until the amount stipulated herein shall have been paid in full.

If any installment of this note is not paid on date due, the entire amount unpaid hereon shall become due and payable forthwith, plus 35% for attorney's fees and collection charges.

I hereby authorize any attorney to appear for me in any court of record in the State of

after this obligation becomes due and waive the issuance and service of process and confess a judgement against me in favor of the holder of this note for the amount of this note plus interest together with the cost of suit thereon including the aforesaid 35% of the amount due thereon for attorney's fees. Stay of execution is hereby waived and the exemption of personal property from levy and sale on any execution is also expressly waived.

It is agreed that the acceptance of a payment after default shall not be deemed a waiver of any action or right which the holder of this note may have by reason of such default.

VALUE RECEIVED with interest from

date _____

_____ Seal
Maker's Signature

_____
Address

_____
Co-Maker

_____ Seal
Address

Source: Sanders Legal Publishers, Inc. Used with permission.

How to Prevent Workplace Violence

How safe is your company? Workplace violence has escalated into a national occupational health and safety hazard of epidemic proportions. Homicide is the leading cause of occupational death for women and the third leading cause of death for all workers. Employers are facing increasing pressure to prevent workplace violence. However, they face liability both for ignoring potential violence and for taking aggressive action to prevent it. The screening of job applicants to prevent workplace violence often conflicts with applicants' rights under the Americans with Disabilities Act (ADA), the Civil Rights Acts, and the corrections statutes.

Preventing workplace violence should be of concern to businesses of all sizes. According to the National Institute for Occupational Safety and Health, the following workplaces have the highest risk of work-related homicide: taxicab establishments, liquor stores, gas stations, detective/protective services, grocery stores, jewelry stores, hotels/motels, and eating/drinking establishments.

More than 70 percent of companies have reported at least one incident of workplace violence—assaults, threats, or homicide—at their companies during the past year. Almost one-third have reported nonfatal batteries such as pushing, hitting, and other forms of intentional physical injury. Thirty-seven percent have reported one or more verbal threats but no physical violence at their companies.

A ten-step prevention plan for reducing the risk of violence is analyzed under these topics: employers' legal obligations and liabilities; how to fire and screen employees; physical security;

> **HOT SITE**
>
> The National Institute for Occupational Safety and Health (http://www.cdc.gov/niosh/homepage.html) is a federal agency established by the Occupational Safety and Health Act of 1970. It is responsible for conducting research and making recommendations for the prevention of work-related illness and injuries.

warning signs; personnel policy manuals; reporting systems; employee assistance programs; incidence response teams; delivering bad news; and when to call the police.

Human resource managers, security officers, corporate counsel, hospital administrators, supervisors, managers, and chief executive officers should learn how to immediately develop violence prevention strategies; identify high-risk occupations and workplaces, evaluate factors or situations that might put workers at risk; implement necessary intervention efforts; and safely hire, discipline, and terminate employees.

A TEN-STEP PREVENTION PLAN

Possible causes of increased work violence are corporate downsizing and restructuring, worker alienation, violence as an accepted part of everyday life, drug usage and dealing, the nontraditional family, the O.J. Simpson verdict, the media creating news for entertainment, the "world owes me" attitude, employers as role models, and protection of the mentally disabled.

Step #1. Know your legal obligations and liabilities. Under the Americans with Disabilities Act, mental disabilities and physical disabilities are governed by identical legal standards, although the issues surrounding mental disabilities are far more complex and elusive. Whereas a physical disability such as blindness may be obvious, a mental disability such as depression may be exhibited in a vague manner or perhaps not at all.

Employers are responsible for knowing their legal obligations under the ADA, the Rehabilitation Act of 1973, workers' compensation laws, OSHA, the National Labor Relations Act, corrections statutes, the Civil Rights Acts, security guard statutes, criminal laws, California hospital emergency room legislation, human rights laws, and labor laws.

Employers face liability for negligent hiring and retention, defamation, wrongful discharge, invasion of privacy, interference with economic advantage, discrimination, breach of contract, sexual harassment, and retaliatory discharge.

Step #2. Know how to hire and screen employees through demographic and psychological profiles; identifying high-risk jobs and workplaces; applications/interviews; background/reference checks; and drug and alcohol testing (see Chapter 11).

Step #3. Implement physical security with alarms, cameras, bullet-proof barriers, landscaping, lighting, metal detectors, security personnel, and access control.

Step #4. Know the warning signs. Train supervisors, managers, and employees about the warning signs and stages of violence.

Step #5. Draft a personnel policy manual defining how employees are expected to behave with coworkers and customers, procedures for responding to problem situations, and grounds for discipline and termination (see Chapter 11).

Step #6. A reporting system provides early identification and intervention by requiring that all employees report every action of a coworker or customer that is threatening or intimidating or that might lead to violence.

Step #7. Employee assistance programs provide counseling for employees or their families for problems caused by drugs, alcohol, family discord, or mental disorders.

Step #8. Incident response teams consist of security, human resources, employee assistance program, legal, and psychological assistance personnel. They ensure confidentiality, interview those involved, alert security or the police, and report their findings.

Step #9. Know how to deliver bad news. Address the problem early; ensure a support network; practice what you will say; do not do it alone; plan the physical setting; speak with confidence; address the problem; listen to the employee; follow up; and have security personnel ready (see Chapter 11).

Step #10. Know when to call the police for bomb threats, stalking, orders of protection/restraining orders, strikes, and trespassing (see the "Bomb Threat Guide" at the end of this chapter).

NEGLIGENT HIRING AND RETENTION OF A DANGEROUS EMPLOYEE

Many employers are faced with the following dilemma: They are forbidden by law from asking a prospective employee certain questions, yet they can be sued for the negligent hiring or retention of a dangerous employee. A Minnesota landlord, for example, was held to have been negligent in hiring a resident manager who raped a tenant. Although the manager had a criminal record, he was furnished with passkeys to tenants' apartments. In its ruling in this case, the Minnesota Supreme Court defined the following aspects of the law:

- *Negligent hiring.* Negligent hiring is an independent cause of action; in other words, it constitutes the basis for a legal claim by an injured party.

- *Duty of care.* Employers have a duty to exercise reasonable care in hiring individuals who, because of the type of employment and amount of contact with the public, may pose a threat of injury to members of the public.

- *Foreseeability.* The employer need not have foreseen the plaintiff's particular injury (i.e., rape), but the landlord had reason to anticipate that its employee, with a history of violent crime, might well commit another violent crime, even if this crime wasn't identical to the employee's previous offenses. Therefore, the employee's rape of the tenant was foreseeable.

- *Reasonable investigation.* Although employers have no independent affirmative duty to investigate an applicant's criminal record, such an investigation is a reasonable precaution if other factors validate it. Because the employee's application contained only a three-month work history and listed only two relatives as work references, an inquiry into these facts would have alerted a careful employer into making a reasonable investigation of a possible criminal record. Employers breach their duty of care when, despite suspicious facts on an employee's application, they fail to make a proper investigation.

- *Cause.* The landlord's negligent hiring was the proximate cause of the plaintiff's injuries. This conclusion was based on the fact that the manager, who had a criminal record for assault and night prowling and two and a half months of psychiatric care in a hospital, was furnished with a passkey to tenants' apartments.

Employers have been found liable for negligent hiring or retention of dangerous or incompetent employees in most states, including Alaska, California, Florida, Georgia, Illinois, Kansas, Maryland, New Mexico, and New York.

Negligent retention is the breach of an employer's duty to be aware of an employee's unfitness and to take corrective action through retraining, reassignment, or discharge. The employer must be careful when the responsibilities of an employee are changed over a period of time. Consider, for example, an employer who hires an employee to work on the grounds of a town house development. Because the employee will have little contact with the residents, the employer is not required to investigate the employee's past. However, if the employee later is transferred to inside maintenance work and is given access to apartment passkeys, the employer now has a duty to investigate the employee's past record.

Negligent hiring and retention actions are often brought where traditional theories of vicarious liability are unavailable. *Vicarious liability* is a theory under which an employer is liable for an employee's acts outside the scope of employment if the employer knew or should have known that the employee posed an unreasonable risk of harm.

The following examples will provide an overview of the situations in which liability has been imposed on employers:

- A camp counselor playfully pointed a gun at a camp ranger's son and shot him in the neck.

- A realty company was held liable for a real estate agent who duped someone into paying off a $158,000 loan even though the company knew nothing of the misrepresentations that the agent had made to the person. The company knew that the agent had forged documents for a former employer, had been convicted of passing bad checks, and had lied about obtaining a realty license. Nevertheless, the company still vouched for the agent's character. Knowledge of the risk the agent posed made the company liable for the agent's subsequent misconduct.

- A taxicab company was liable for a person beaten by a taxicab driver after paying his fare and leaving the cab.

- The U.S. District Court for the Southern District of New York awarded $1.5 million to a woman and her son who suffered physical and psychological injuries following a sexual assault on the woman by the maintenance man employed at the defendant's apartment complex.

- A taxicab company was held liable for negligence in hiring a criminally violent driver who raped and robbed a woman in the presence of her two young children.

- An employer was held liable for the negligent hiring and retention of a sexually aggressive employee with a criminal record who subsequently raped a female coemployee.

- A security company was liable for the negligent hiring, training, supervision, and assignment of a security guard who aided outside confederates in the theft of $200,000 worth of gold certificates.

HOW AND WHEN TO USE THE FORMS IN THIS CHAPTER

Bomb Threat Guide. This information should be reviewed by all appropriate personnel and kept at all telephones.

NIOSH Alert: Preventing Homicide in the Workplace. Post this alert and distribute copies to workers.

BOMB THREAT GUIDE

WHAT DOES A BOMB LOOK LIKE? No one can say for sure, for it is up to the imagination of the builder of the bomb. It is possible that the bomb could be disguised as a pack of cigarettes, a small radio, a lunch box, a book, or a cigarette lighter.

This pamphlet was created because the information contained within may at times help to save lives. NO CALL OR THREAT SHOULD EVER BE DISREGARDED.

THE BOMB THREAT BY PHONE

1. Training of switchboard operators or others likely to receive such calls to keep calm, and to elicit specific information as to the location of the device.
2. Make a note of the exact words used by the caller.
3. Make note of any background noise such as traffic, music, airplanes, etc.
4. Note voice characteristics such as age, sex, accent, pitch, etc.

EVACUATION PLANNING

1. The decision to evacuate is a managerial decision.
2. Prearrange your evacuation plan. Be aware that it is a mistake to move large numbers of people unless complete control is maintained. The evacuation should be done in an immediate but orderly fashion.
3. Avoid panic.
4. Prior training and planning, as well as calm leadership, at the scene of the evacuation will minimize the danger of undesirable behavior.
5. If the police have not been previously called in, this should be done immediately.

THE EVACUATION

1. Avoid panic.
2. Windows and doors should be open to relieve pressure should there be an explosion.
3. Leave all electric switches as they are.
4. Employees should remove, at the time of the evacuation, all of their personal property that is in the immediate vicinity (briefcases, lunch boxes, shopping bags, etc.).
5. Upon evacuation of the building, the employees should be moved to an area at least 300 feet away from the building.

THE SEARCH

1. The primary search of a building is the function of the police department. It is their responsibility to locate destructive devices and take appropriate action. However, the best people suited to search any given area are those who work in that area, for they will have the least difficulty spotting any new or foreign objects. This search should be made on the employees' way out of the building and should not keep the searching employees beyond a reasonable evacuation time. Avoid a prolonged search.
2. Each area should have one or more persons who are assigned the task of searching their own area, and they should act as a team.
3. The use of common sense or logic in searching is necessary. Do not rely on random or spot checking.
4. It is of the utmost importance not to touch or move a suspected device.
5. Remember that a device may not be in the building but may have been placed on the outside of the building or somewhere on the grounds (in high grass, shrubbery, on window sills, etc.).

EXAMPLE: BOMB THREAT REPORT

COMPLAINANT (PERSON TAKING CALL): _____

HOME ADDRESS: _____

HOME PHONE NUMBER: _____ THREAT PHONE NUMBER: _____

BUSINESS OR BUILDING NAME: _____

ADDRESS OF BUILDING: _____

DATE: _____ TIME: _____ AM/PM PLACE: _____

ORIGIN: LOCAL _____ LONG DISTANCE _____ BOOTH _____

LOCATION OF BOMB: _____

TIME SET FOR DETONATION: _____

WHAT DOES IT LOOK LIKE: _____

_____

WHAT KIND OF EXPLOSIVE: _____

_____

WHY WAS IT PLACED: _____

_____

EXACT WORDS USED: _____

_____

IDENTITY OF CALLER

VOICE

LOUD _____   SOFT _____

PITCH _____   DEEP _____

RASPY _____   PLEASANT _____

INTOX. _____   OTHER _____

SPEECH

FAST _____   DISTORTED _____

DISTINCT _____   NASAL _____

STUTTER _____   SLOW _____

OTHER _____

LANGUAGE

GOOD _____   POOR _____

FOUL_____   OTHER _____

ACCENT

LOCAL _____   FOREIGN _____

REGIONAL _____   RACIAL _____

MANNER

CALM _____   ANGRY _____

RATIONAL _____   IRRATIONAL _____

COHERENT _____   INCOHERENT _____

DELIBERATE _____   EMOTIONAL _____

RIGHTEOUS _____   NERVOUS _____

SEX: MALE _____ FEMALE _____ ADULT _____ CHILD _____

ESTIMATED AGE: _____

BACKGROUND

OFFICE _____   TRAFFIC _____

FACTORY _____   TRAIN _____

ANIMAL _____   MUSIC _____

PLANE _____   QUIET _____

VOICES _____   OTHER _____

OBTAIN AS MUCH DETAIL AS POSSIBLE ABOUT THE BOMB AND ITS LOCATION. LEGITIMATE CALLERS USUALLY WISH TO AVOID INJURY OR DEATH. REQUEST *MORE* DATA BY EXPRESSING A DESIRE TO SAVE LIVES.

BOMB DISPOSAL UNIT AVAILABLE IN THE AREA:

1. _____ COUNTY SHERIFF'S DEPARTMENT

   CALL: _____

NIOSH
ALERT

Preventing Homicide in the Workplace

WARNING!

Workers in certain industries and occupations are at increased risk of homicide.

Homicide is the third leading cause of death from occupational injury for all workers. Guns are the most commonly used weapon. Employers and workers should take the following steps to protect themselves from homicide in the workplace:

1. **Be aware of which workplaces and occupations have the highest risk of work-related homicides:**

    Workplaces

    - Taxicab establishments
    - Liquor stores
    - Gas stations
    - Detective/protective services
    - Justice/public order establishments
    - Grocery stores
    - Jewelry stores
    - Hotels/motels
    - Eating/drinking places

    Occupations

    - Taxicab drivers/chauffeurs
    - Law enforcement officers
        (police officers/sheriffs)
    - Hotel clerks
    - Gas station workers
    - Security guards
    - Stock handlers/baggers
    - Store owners/managers
    - Bartenders

2. **Learn the factors that may increase the risk of homicide:**

    - Exchange of money with the public
    - Working alone or in small numbers
    - Working late night or early morning hours
    - Working in high-crime areas
    - Guarding valuable property or possessions
    - Working in community settings

3. **Evaluate your workplace and take steps that may prevent homicides. Preventive measures may include the following:**

    - Make high-risk areas visible to more people.
    - Install good external lighting.
    - Use drop safes to minimize cash on hand.
    - Carry small amounts of cash.
    - Post signs stating that limited cash is on hand.
    - Install silent alarms.
    - Install surveillance cameras.
    - Increase the number of staff on duty.
    - Provide training in conflict resolution and nonviolent response.
    - Avoid resistance during robbery.
    - Provide bullet-proof barriers or enclosures.
    - Have police check on workers routinely.
    - Close establishments during high-risk hours (late at night and early in the morning).

Homicide is a leading cause of death from injury in the workplace.

   See back of sheet to order complete Alert.

For additional information, see *NIOSH Alert: Request for Assistance in Preventing Homicide in the Workplace* [DHHS (NIOSH) 93–109], or call 1–800–35–NIOSH. Single copies of the Alert are available free from the following:

Publications Dissemination, DSDTT
National Institute for Occupational Safety and Health
4676 Columbia Parkway
Cincinnati, OH 45226

Fax number: (513) 533–8573

U.S. Department of Health and Human Services
Public Health Service
Centers for Disease Control and Prevention
National Institute for Occupational Safety and Health

20

Your Small Business Dot Com

The Internet provides a speedy, cost-effective way for businesses and professionals to compete internationally. Whether you are operating from your basement or Madison Avenue, your business can look like a million dollars.

The Internet has leveled the playing field between big and small businesses. A small business can reach as many potential customers as a large business. The Web gives a whole new meaning to the phrase "home-based business."

The Internet is

- a marketing tool to publicize your product or service, to obtain feedback and statistics on visitors, and to process orders—a combination of direct marketing and mass media;
- a communications tool through e-mail and newsgroups; and
- a resource tool to access government and business information and directories.

With a Web site your business is always open. Customers can instantaneously obtain information or request information without telephoning or writing to you.

A Web site can be obtained for little or no money. However, for you to use it effectively for marketing, customers must find your site easily through links, search engines, and press releases. You must provide an incentive for customers to visit by providing updated content.

This chapter is not a primer on the Internet (there is enough printed material available) but a collection of practical tips on how to make money with it, assess its costs and benefits, and avoid common pitfalls.

STEPS FOR ESTABLISHING YOUR WEB SITE

The seven steps in setting up and maintaining a Web site are selecting an ISP, registering a URL, selecting a design, registering with search engines, initiating publicity, attracting visitors, and adding monthly updates.

Step #1. Select an Internet service provider (ISP) that will provide you with an Internet account consisting of e-mail access, the ability to access other computers (telnet), the ability to transfer files from and to different networks (FTP, or file transfer protocol), and server space for a Web site. Some ISPs also provide design services. Monthly charges are $20 to $100. Avoid ISPs that charge by the "hit" or limit the amount of bandwidth (information) that visitors are allowed to download.

Step #2. Register a domain name or universal resource locator (URL). For a small fee, your ISP may assist you on obtaining a URL. Choose a name that best represents your product or service. A domain name cannot be reserved like a trademark. It should be easily remembered and identify your company; the simpler the better. The two levels of domain names are (1) a top-level name, dedicated domain name, shell account, or commercial account (e.g., www.yourbusiness.com), and (2) a subdomain name (e.g., www.your business.hostcompanyname.com or www.hostcompany.com/yourbusiness).

Domain names are administered by Inter-NIC Registration Services through Network Solutions, Inc. (703-742-4777). The registration fee is $100, which covers the first two years, and $50 per year thereafter. InterNIC conducts a conflict check on a proposed domain name and if a name is already in use, an alternate must be selected (http://rs.internic.net).

Even though InterNIC clears domain names, a full trademark search should be done. This will save you from being forced to stop using a name after having invested a considerable amount of time and effort.

HOT SITE

Synaptic Communications, Inc. (http://www.synaptic.net/domain.html) allows you to check current domain name availability.

Step #3. Design your Web site. Decide what you want your site to accomplish: (1) a brochure highlighting your products or services; (2) video clips of your products; (3) a catalog of your products; and/or (4) online ordering and payment. Obtain ideas for your site by browsing through your competitors' Web sites.

Web sites can be designed either by using HTML (Hypertext Markup Language), which is the universally recognized code for programming Web site content, or you can hire a Web design service or Internet consultant to design the site and input text and images. Consultant and designer service fees will range from a few hundred dollars to thousands of dollars plus monthly update charges of a few hundred dollars. Ask designers or consultants whether they design as well as give marketing and hosting advice; they have a background in your particular industry; they will register your site with search engines; they will get you linked; they will publicize your site (and how they plan to do this); whether they will send out press releases to the media and your customers; and whether they have references from other similar sites that they have designed.

Content is very important. Visitors are interested in seeing more than a billboard or ad. They want current useful information. It is also important that the site loads quickly so that visitors do not leave the site before all images appear. Encourage visitors to bookmark your site so that they can find it again quickly.

Step #4. Register your site with search engines such as Yahoo, Lycos, Infoseek, Webcrawler, and the like. If you use a registration service, make sure that they reregister your site each time you add a new focus and have a continuous registration service for new search engines, directories, and list services. The search registration forms will ask for a category identifying your business, the title of your site, a brief description of the site, and key words.

HOT SITES

Submit-it! (http://www.submit-it.com) will register your site in several different search engines. However, search engines that have their own unique form will reject your application. Free Links (www.freelinks.com) lists the location and registration forms for hundreds of search sites. Postmaster (www.netcreations.com/postmaster) and Godhwanis Register It! (www.register-it.com) provide do-it-yourself registration through customized forms for individual search and directory sites.

Step #5. Publicize your site. You can do this best by sending out press releases announcing its benefits, purchasing banner ads, and having cross-links to other sites. Use your URL on all promotional material such as letterheads, business cards, Yellow Page ads, newspaper ads, radio ads, and television ads. Include your URL on every e-mail message using a signature (or sig) file. Newsgroup and forum readers will be prompted to visit your site if you indicate your URL.

HOT SITES

Send press releases to Web site reviewers CNET (www.cnet.com) and NetGUIDE (www.netguide.com). The Internet Link Exchange (www.linkexchange.com) provides a free exchange of links and banners.

Step #6. Keep track of who is visiting your site by offering free samples or brochures and a free monthly e-mail newsletter subscription. Access logs provided by some ISPs and log data software record the number of hits or visitors to the site by time, date, country source, and so on. Ask visitors to complete questionnaires and provide comments in your "guestbook."

Step #7. Update your site monthly. Visitors are turned off by out-of-date information. A free e-mail subscription is the best way to keep in touch with potential customers. You can write your own newsletter or use a newsletter with a "private label." There are so many sites on the Internet that visitors are unlikely to visit your site a second time. Therefore, rather than having them come to you, you can go to them every month by sending an e-mail newsletter promoting your product or service.

HOT SITES

Leebow's Letter (home.navisoft.com/vip/norman.htm) and the *Legal Survival Newsletter* (www.friran.com) provide private label newsletters.

LEGAL PITFALLS

The seven legal pitfalls to having your own web site are as follows:

Pitfall #1. You become subject to trademark and copyright infringement lawsuits for using audio and video content that you do not own or have the right to use in the design of your site.

Pitfall #2. You don't have contracts providing that you retain ownership of graphic, development, editorial, and computer-programming material created by your employees and freelancers.

Pitfall #3. You become subject to lawsuits for defamation and for copyright and trademark infringement on the basis of statements made and actions taken by bulletin board users. Site owners that have policies of not editing, monitoring, or controlling the content of their bulletin board services are held less liable than those who monitor the content of their services.

Pitfall #4. You permit others to sell products from your site without agreements setting forth responsibilities, warranties, and indemnification provisions that protect you from product liability, tax liabilities, and third-party claims. Verify that your product liability insurance policy covers online sales.

Pitfall #5. You use e-mail addresses in violation of consumer privacy rights.

Pitfall #6. You have no agreements with purchasers, advertisers, and users specifying the law and jurisdiction that will apply to actions involving the site.

Pitfall #7. You become the target of lawsuits by your employees for invasion of privacy for reading their e-mail. The e-mail policy should be part of the company personnel manual (see the form at the end of this chapter). It should state that the company reserves the right to access and disclose all messages sent over its electronic mail system for any purpose. A message should also be displayed on the e-mail home screen reminding employees each time they use the system that it is not intended for personal messages. The key factor is to establish that the employee does not have an expectation of privacy.

HOW AND WHEN TO USE THE FORM IN THIS CHAPTER

Electronic Media Policy. This policy should be incorporated into your company's personnel manual.

ELECTRONIC MEDIA POLICY

1. Employees have access to various forms of electronic media and services (computers, e-mail, telephones, voicemail, fax machines, external electronic bulletin boards, wire services, online services, and the Internet (hereinafter referred to as "media").

2. The company encourages the use of media. However, media provided by the company are company property and its purpose is to facilitate company business.

3. The following procedures apply to all media which are:

    A. accessed on or from company premises;

    B. accessed using company computer equipment or via company-paid access methods;

    C. communications that make reference to the company in any manner; and/or

    D. used in a manner that identifies the employee with the company.

4. Media may not be used for transmitting, retrieving, or storing any communications that are of a discriminatory or harassing nature; derogatory to any individual or group; obscene; of a defamatory or threatening nature; for "chain letters"; for personal use; illegal or against company policy; or contrary to the company's interest.

5. Electronic information created and/or communicated by an employee using media will not generally be monitored by the company. However, the company routinely monitors usage patterns for both voice and data communications (e.g., number called or site accessed; call length; times of day called) for cost analysis/allocation and the management of the Internet server. The company also reserves the right, in its discretion, to review any employee's electronic files and messages and usage to the extent necessary to ensure that media are being used in compliance with the law and with company policy. Therefore, employees should not assume electronic communications are private and confidential.

6. Employees must respect other people's electronic communications. Employees may not attempt to read or "hack" into other systems or logins; "crack" passwords; breach computer or network security measures; or monitor electronic filings or communications of other employees or third parties except by explicit direction of company management.

7. Every employee who uses any security measures on a company-supplied computer must provide the company with a sealed hard copy record of all passwords and encryption keys (if any) for company use if required.

8. No e-mail or other electronic communications may be sent that attempt to hide the identity of the sender or represent the sender as someone else or someone from another company.

9. Media may not be used in a manner that is likely to cause network congestion or significantly hamper the ability of other people to access and use the system.

10. Employees may not copy, retrieve, modify, or forward copyrighted materials except as permitted by the copyright owner or except for a single copy for reference use only.

11. Any information or messages sent by an employee via an electronic network are statements identifiable and attributable to the company. All communications sent by employees via a network must comply with company policy, and may not disclose any confidential or proprietary company information.

12. Network services and World Wide Web sites monitor access and usage and can identify at least which company—and often which specific individual—is accessing their services. Accessing a particular bulletin board or Web site leaves company-identifiable electronic "tracks" even if the employee merely reviews or downloads the material and does not post any message.

13. Any employee violating this policy will be subject to corrective action and/or risk losing the privilege of using media for him/herself and possibly other employees.

Index

Income taxes, 86
Incorporation
    choosing state of, 7
    legal consultation and, 1
Independent contractor agreement,
        180, 184–88
Independent contractors, 162–64
    common law rules, 162–63
    employers' precautions, 163–64
    safe harbor, 163
    statutory employees, 163
Informer's Act, 174
Inheritance tax, 216
Inspection contingency, 247
Insurance, 3, 9, 46, 295–99
    accident and health, 117
    boiler and machinery, 297
    business auto coverage, 298
    business income, 296
    cause of loss, 296
    commercial crime, 299
    completed operations, 298
    comprehensive general liability,
        297
    contractual liability (assumed),
        298
    employment practices coverage,
        299
    fidelity bonds, 299
    group, 115
    life, 118
    personal injury liability, 297
    products liability, 298
    purpose of, 295–96
    rental, 297
    supplementary, 115
    title, 254
    umbrella excess liability, 298–99
    workers' compensation, 177, 297
Intangible assets, 44
Intellectual property protection,
        175–76
Intent-to-use applications, 148,
        149
Inter vivos trusts, 217–18
Internal Revenue Code,
        partnerships and, 18
Internal Revenue Service. See also
        IRS Forms
    avoiding penalties, 91
    excessive compensation
        challenge, 33
International investors, 20
Internet Bankruptcy Library
        Worldwide Trouble Company
        Resources, 324
Internet Link Exchange, 347
Interns, 164
Invention(s)
    marketing, 152
    protection of. See Patent

Inventory, 46, 89
    tax treatment of, 45
Investment brokers, 12
Investment capital, raising, 112
Irrevocable life insurance trust,
        218
Irrevocable trusts, 217
IRS Forms
    ATF forms, 87
    IRS Form 1099, 87
    IRS Form 11-C, 87
    IRS Form 2290, 87
    IRS Form 2553, 37, 39–42
    IRS Form 4562, 111–12
    IRS Form 4797, 71–76
    IRS Form 5305 (SIMPLE), 121,
        127–32
    IRS Form 730, 87
    IRS Form 8300, 87, 92, 106–9
    IRS Form 8826 (disabled access
        credit), 307–10
    IRS Form 911, 92, 102–3
    IRS Form SS-4, 85, 92, 94–97
    IRS Form W-4, 85
    IRS Form W-9, 85, 92, 98–101,
        248

Job descriptions, 8, 303
Joint ownership, 222
Joint venture, 18
Judgment affidavit, 248

Labor/management relations, 2, 4
Land, tax treatment of, 45
Landlord-tenant relations, 316
Landmark status, 257
Laws affecting small businesses,
        210–14
    commercial arbitration clauses,
        213
    corporate minutes review, 212
    drug testing of drivers, 212
    duty to report product hazards,
        210
    environmental reporting
        requirements, 212–13
    Freedom of Information Act,
        210–11
    immigration law, 213–14
Lead poisoning, 251
Lease, 2, 276. See also Leasing
        strategies
Lease assumption agreement, 281,
        293
Lease with option to purchase,
        251–52
Leaseholds, 46
Leasing strategies, 275–94
    advantages of leasing, 275–76
    agreement releasing tenant, 281,
        291
    antitrust violations, 278–79

commercial lease, 281, 288–90
computer lease, 281, 285–86
disadvantages of leasing, 276
disclosure of lead-based paint
        and/or hazards, 94, 281, 294
equipment lease, 281, 283–84
lease assumption agreement,
        281, 293
negotiating commercial leases,
        276–78
option agreement, 281, 287
shopping center leases, 279–80
sublease agreement, 281, 292
types of leases, 275
Leebow's Letter Web site, 348
Legal, 1–6. See also Laws affecting
        small businesses
    attorney's fees, 6
    client's rights, 1
    consulting an attorney, 1–3
    ethical considerations, 6
    finding an attorney, 5
    prepaid legal plans, 5–6
    preventive legal audits, 3–4
Letters of intent, 137
Liabilities, sale of business and,
        47
Liability insurance policies, 173
Licenses, sale of business and, 46
Licensing, 3
Licensing agreements, 4
Lien(s), 45, 321–22
    defined, 245
    on equipment, 9
    mechanic's liens, 321–22
Life insurance, 118
    as collateral, 315
    sale of business and, 46
Limited disclosure agreement, 155,
        156
Limited liability companies, 2,
        20–22
    advantages of, 21–22
    articles of organization, 20, 25,
        32
    disability benefits and, 118
    disadvantages of, 22
    health insurance and, 118
    limited life of, 22
    members and managers of, 21
    mortgage financing and, 22
    operating agreement, 20–21
    taxation in, 21, 24
    withdrawal of member from, 20
Limited partnerships, 19, 24
Limited warranty, 138
Lincoln Law, 174
Liquidated damages, 135
Litigation, 2
Litigation, sale of business and, 46
Living trust, 8, 218–19
Loans, 8

About the Author

Robert Friedman is an attorney with Friedman & Ranzenhofer, P.C., which maintains offices in Akron, Batavia, Clarence, Buffalo, and West Seneca, New York. The law firm's *Legal Survival* Web site (http://www.friran.com) contains a free electronic monthly newsletter, informational pamphlets, an online bookstore, checklists, answers to frequently asked questions, links, forms, seminar listings, prepaid legal plans, and an attorney referral network. Mr. Friedman is prosecutor for two municipalities. He is a frequent lecturer, author of *How to Survive Legally as a Landlord,* and a columnist for the *Buffalo News.* He received a B.A. in 1975 from SUNY at Buffalo and a Juris Doctor in 1977 from Hamline University School of Law.

How to Install and Use the Software

TO INSTALL THE APPLICATION FOR WINDOWS

- Insert the disk in drive A:.
- From Program Manager or the Start menu select **Run.**
- Enter A:\Setup.exe.
- Follow prompts on screen.

HOW TO USE THIS APPLICATION

The forms processing application provides a minimized word processor to allow you to customize, revise, and change the forms contained on this disk. We've provided it to allow you to be productive immediately with the forms contained in this guide. To open the application from Program Manager or the Start menu, select the Dearborn program group and click on the icon. The basic commands and features of the application are described below.

To Select a Form to Edit

Select the **File** and **Open Form** command to access the forms available with this application. The Open Form command presents the forms dialog box where you can select a form to customize. To select a form, click on a form number in the list on the left side of the dialog box. The form and any notes about it appear on the right side of the dialog box. If this is the form you want to edit, select **Open.**

Editing the Form

To edit the form and customize it for your use, select the **Find** button in the toolbar at the top of the form window to automatically locate fields in the form where you need to enter information. These fields are noted with a ">". Of course, you may change or revise any of the text in the form at will.

The menu at the top of the form provides you with several controls. These are as follows:

- **Edit**: You can cut, copy, and paste segments of text.
- **Style**: You can bold, italicize, and underline text, as well as select a font and type size for selected text.

Many of the functions available as menu selections are also available as button commands in the toolbar. These are:

- **Font:** Select from the fonts available on your system by pressing the down arrow and clicking on the font name.
- **Size:** Select the font size by clicking the down arrow and highlighting the font size.
- **Bold (B), Italic (I), Underline (U):** Select the text you want to change and press the button to change the format.
- **Justification:** You may change the text to flush right, left, centered, or justified by selecting the text and pressing the appropriate button.

Note: Save any edited forms under a different or new file name.

Favorites

If you are like most people, you'll likely use a few forms repeatedly. This application allows you to save forms as "favorites" to provide quick access to those forms frequently used. **To add a form to Favorites:**

- Open a form as you normally would.
- Choose **Favorites** from the File menu and select **Add to Favorites.**
- Enter the name for the file and choose Save.
- To reselect the form, select Favorites from the menu, and select Open Favorite Files. Select the file and press Open.

Help

To learn more about the forms application and the commands available to you, select **Help** from the menu.

IF YOU ALREADY HAVE A WORD PROCESSOR . . .

If you have and are already familiar with one or more of the word processing applications available to you, you can use the functionality available in those programs to work with these forms. Select and edit any one of the forms directly from the forms subdirectory created on your hard drive during installation. The files are unformatted ASCII text files that work with all current applications. Text that you need to enter in order to complete a form is preceded by a ">" character. Using your word processor's search function to locate these areas will allow you to quickly customize the forms to suit your needs.

Another way to use the forms in this application with other word processors is to save the file as either a text file (txt) or rich text file (rtf). To do this, select **File** and **Open** from the menu. Open the file you wish to edit and choose **Save As.** Select or enter the name of the file and choose the location where you want it to go. Select **OK.** Open the file in your word processor as you would any other file and edit. (Keep in mind that once you work on a file in another word processor and save it, it probably won't work in the forms processor application without conversion back to a standard text or ASCII file.)

TECHNICAL SUPPORT IS NOT AVAILABLE ON THE ENCLOSED COMPUTER DISK. Please read the installation and operating instructions carefully before attempting to use the disk.

LICENSE AGREEMENT

OPENING ENVELOPE VOIDS RETURNABILITY OR MONEY-BACK GUARANTEES
PLEASE READ THIS DOCUMENT CAREFULLY BEFORE BREAKING THIS SEAL

By breaking this sealed envelope, you agree to become bound by the terms of this license. If you do not agree to the terms of this license do not use the software and promptly return the unopened package within thirty (30) days to the place where you obtained it for a refund.

This Software is licensed, not sold to you by DEARBORN FINANCIAL PUBLISHING, INC. owner of the product for use only under the terms of this License, and DEARBORN FINANCIAL PUBLISHING, INC. reserves any rights not expressly granted to you.

1. **LICENSE**: This License allows you to:

(a) Use the Software only on a single microcomputer at a time, except the Software may be executed from a common disk shared by multiple CPU's provided that one authorized copy of the Software has been licensed from DEARBORN FINANCIAL PUBLISHING, INC. for each CPU executing the Software. DEARBORN FINANCIAL PUBLISHING, INC. does not, however, guarantee that the Software will function properly in your multiple CPU, multi-user environment. The Software may not be used with any gateways, bridges, modems, and/or network extenders that allow the software to be used on multiple CPU's unless one authorized copy of the Software has been licensed from DEARBORN FINANCIAL PUBLISHING, INC. for each CPU executing the Software.

(b) The Software can be loaded to the harddrive and the disk kept solely for backup purposes. The Software is protected by United States copyright law. You must reproduce on each copy the copyright notice and any other proprietary legends that were on the original copy supplied by DEARBORN FINANCIAL PUBLISHING, INC.

(c) Configure the Software for your own use by adding or removing fonts, desk accessories, and/or device drivers.

2. **RESTRICTION:** You may not distribute copies of the Software to others or electronically transfer the Software from one computer to another over a network and/or zone. The Software contains trade secrets and to protect them you may not de-compile, reverse engineer, disassemble, cross assemble or otherwise change and/or reduce the Software to any other form. You may not modify, adapt, translate, rent, lease, loan, resell for profit, distribute, network, or create derivative works based upon the Software or any part thereof.

3. **TERMINATION:** This License is effective unless terminated. This License will terminate immediately without notice from DEARBORN FINANCIAL PUBLISHING, INC. if you fail to comply with any provision of this License. Upon termination you must destroy the Software and all copies thereof. You may terminate the License at any time by destroying the Software and all copies thereof.

4. **EXPORT LAW ASSURANCES:** You agree that the Software will not be shipped, transferred or exported into any country prohibited by the United States Export Administration Act and the regulations thereunder nor will be used for any purpose prohibited by the Act.

5. **LIMITED WARRANTY, DISCLAIMER, LIMITATION OF REMEDIES AND DAMAGES:** The information in this software (Materials) is sold with the understanding that the author, publisher, developer and distributor are not engaged in rendering legal, accounting, banking, security or other professional advice. If legal advice, accounting advice, security investment advice, bank or tax advice or other expert professional assistance is required, the services of a competent professional with expertise in that field should be sought. These materials have been developed using ideas from experience and survey information from various research, lectures and publications. The information contained in these materials is believed to be reliable only at the time of publication and it cannot be guaranteed as it is applied to any particular individual or situation. The author, publisher, developer and distributor specifically disclaim any liability, or risk, personal or otherwise, incurred directly or indirectly as a consequence of the use an application of the information contained in these materials or the live lectures that could accompany their distribution. In no event will the author, publisher, developer or distributor be liable to the purchaser for any amount greater that the purchase price of these materials.

DEARBORN FINANCIAL PUBLISHING, INC.'S warranty on the media, including any implied warranty of merchant ability or fitness for a particular purpose, is limited in duration to thirty (30) days from the date of the original retail. If a disk fails to work or if a disk becomes damaged, you may obtain a replacement disk by returning the original disk and a check or money order for $5.00, for each replacement disk, together with a brief explanation note and a dated sales receipt to:

DEARBORN FINANCIAL PUBLISHING, INC.
155 NORTH WACKER DRIVE
CHICAGO, IL 60606-1719

The replacement warranty set forth above is the sole and exclusive remedy against DEARBORN FINANCIAL PUBLISHING, INC. for breach of warrant, express or implied or for any default whatsoever relating to condition of the software. DEARBORN FINANCIAL PUBLISHING, INC. makes no other warranties or representation, either expressed or implied, with respect to this software or documentation, quality, merchantability performance or fitness for a particular purpose as a result. This software is sold with only the limited warranty with respect to diskette replacement as provided above, and you, the Licensee, are assuming all other risks as to its quality and performance. In no event will DEARBORN FINANCIAL PUBLISHING, INC. or its developers, directors, officers, employees, or affiliates be liable for direct , incidental, indirect, special or consequential damages (including damages for loss of business profits, business interruption, loss of business information and the like) resulting from any defect in this software or its documentation or arising out of the use of or inability to use the software or accompanying documentation even if DEARBORN FINANCIAL PUBLISHING, INC. an authorized DEARBORN FINANCIAL PUBLISHING, INC. representative, or a DEARBORN FINANCIAL PUBLISHING, INC. affiliate has been advised of the possibility of such damage.

DEARBORN FINANCIAL PUBLISHING, INC. MAKES NO REPRESENTATION OR WARRANTY REGARDING THE RESULTS OBTAINABLE THROUGH USE OF THE SOFTWARE.

No oral or written information or advice given by DEARBORN FINANCIAL PUBLISHING, INC. its dealers, distributors, agents, affiliates, developers, officers, directors, or employees shall create a warranty or in any way increase the scope of this warranty.

Some states do not allow the exclusion or limitation of implied warranties or liabilities for incidental or consequential, damages, so the above limitation or exclusion may not apply to you. This warranty gives you specific legal rights, and you may also have other rights which vary from state to state.

COPYRIGHT NOTICE: This software and accompanying manual are copyrighted with all rights reserved by DEARBORN FINANCIAL PUBLISHING, INC. Under United States copyright laws, the software and its accompanying documentation may not be copied in whole or in part except in normal use of the software or the reproduction of a backup copy for archival purpose only. Any other copying, selling or otherwise distributing this software or manual is hereby expressly forbidden.

SIGNATURE_____

SIGN IF BEING RETURNED UNOPENED FOR REFUND